THE SEARCH FOR ENVIRONMENT *The Garden City: Before and After*

THE SEARCH FOR ENVIRONMENT

The Garden City: Before and After

Walter L. Creese

NEW HAVEN AND LONDON YALE UNIVERSITY PRESS 1966

TO G. C.

PREFACE

There is always risk of intrusion when one ventures out of his own country into another's in quest of modern history. The lifelong accumulation of experience, the shades of mood and voice, the dictates of unconscious feeling that guide a native in relation to his associates and surroundings are, of course, difficult for the stranger to master, no matter how many written records or people he may consult. Architecture and planning are so wholly arts of place that any slight failure in comprehension could distort the total picture which the foreigner, as a historian, would most wish to present. Hence it must first be made plain that this book is not intended to reach fixed conclusions, even if they were attainable, but only to indicate patterns of history which may have slipped too far below the level of international consciousness.

As a new idea, the English garden city of the 1900s was much like the American skyscraper of the 1880s. Everyone saw it, hailed it as a great discovery accessible to all, and readily employed it. Yet too few seem to have considered its cultural implications over an extended period. The larger problem in time comes to be: What does a society in transition do with its more conspicuous innovations after the first shock wave of public novelty and the second of direct utility have worn off? Does it react with apathy and torpor against their initial sudden stimulus or come forward with additional suggestions for their further and more gradual evolution?

In Britain during the nineteenth and twentieth centuries there appears to have developed a condition that both encouraged and sustained novelties. The sympathy between generations and individuals never allowed circumstances to stretch the natural differences in outlook to the breaking point. This produced innovations which could be kept in better temporal alignment than in other nations. The British profited steadily from their own utopian planning over a century and a half because they were able to keep it running through the motions, at least, of customary attitudes, even after earlier habits and skills were superseded. Howard wrote of a "peaceful path to real reform." Recent British architects, with their understandable enthu-

siasm and zeal for leading their country back into the mainstream of contemporary architectural design, have consistently underrated this achievement in planning. To put the distinction another way through analogy, the
Englishman in his search for a better town life was looking for a fruit both
fresh and ripe, whereas the creative American or German or Frenchman,
especially after the crisis of World War I, was more apt to take it green if
only he could be assured that it was the first of the season.

Another important question asked about the modern pattern by the British was whether beauty and emotional satisfaction do still deserve a priority
among the most basic considerations in urban and country life. There was
something arresting in the fact that the thirst for environmental beauty
should reach its peak in Britain in the 1890s, just when the garden city was
being invented, as it did in America with the City Beautiful movement, and
in Austria, Germany, and Finland through the theories of Camillo Sitte, first
put forth in 1889. But the recognition of this, along with the further coincidence that the diagrams of the garden city, the concentric city, the radial city,
the linear city, and the satellite city all appeared at approximately the same
time, should lead us to suspect that too many coincidences make a trend. The
twentieth-century citizen, harassed and constrained by cataclysmic wars and
depressions, finds it difficult to conceive that any previous decade, so near his
own, could afford such an all-inclusive, temperate, and constructive atmosphere. He knows the decade of the 1890s well, but he has never experienced
a stable enough period himself in which to assess it properly. Meanwhile
planning goes on, unconsciously employing many of the conventions of the
1890s and the succeeding years up to World War I, just as architecture depends heavily on the 1920s, which were followed by the astringent conditions
of the 1930s. The present working tradition appears to be an informal and
largely unacknowledged one.

Even this tentative essay toward bridging a gap in understanding between
several countries and two centuries would not have been possible without
the opportunity that came to me through a postdoctoral Fulbright grant to
the University of Liverpool in 1955–56, followed in 1960 by a Rehmann fellowship from the American Institute of Architects. The courtesies of the
staff at Liverpool, particularly in the Department of Civic Design, which in-

cluded Professor Myles Wright, Josephine Reynolds, Paul Brenikov, D. H. Crompton, and R. E. McCaughan, went far beyond what a transient scholar ought to expect. This group, and later my colleagues at the University of Illinois, especially Professors Alan K. Laing, Ernest Conally, and Herman Pundt, suffered all varieties of distraction because of the preparation of the book.

Checking facts and impressions would likewise have been difficult without the outstanding resources of the University of Illinois Library and its planning and architecture branches under the direction of Mrs. Mary Vance and Miss Cerilla Saylor. At the Avery Library of Columbia University I was able to locate fragmentary documents from the end of Sir Raymond Unwin's career. For knowledge of them I am indebted to Professors Adolph Placzek, George R. Collins, and J. Marshall Miller. At Harvard University during the summer of 1961 I had an opportunity to go further in reading with the aid of a bibliography prepared by Miss Katherine McNamara on garden cities and new towns, which I had originally encountered in the Royal Institute of British Architects Library in London. I, like everyone who has ever worked in the literature of planning, hold a permanent debt to Miss McNamara, for so many years Librarian at Robinson Hall at Harvard. I also owe much for last-minute checking to the librarians of the University of Oregon and especially to Mrs. Frances S. Newsom and Mrs. Jane Hascall of the art library. Doctors Lucile Golson and Julio San José of the faculty of the School of Architecture and Allied Arts have assisted me with distant addresses. The redrafting of several of the plans was undertaken by Hadi Saraidarpour, then a graduate student.

The help and extraordinary patience of my wife and the ever confident attitude of my son have done much to get the job done.

My understanding of Parker and Unwin as personalities would have been impossible were it not for the exemplary preservation of the papers and photographs of her husband's work by Mrs. Barry Parker. Her collection at Letchworth was of a scope authors sometimes dream of. She allowed me to examine all of it. She also put me in touch with Mrs. Edward Unwin and Mrs. Curtice Hitchcock, the daughter-in-law and daughter of Sir Raymond Unwin, as well as with Mrs. William Sully Unwin, his sister-in-law. Mrs. Edward Unwin had personal papers which I was authorized to examine. Mr. Malcolm Bruce Glazier, whose father and mother were early friends of Unwin, was of great assistance in enabling me to understand his early life.

Upon some librarians in Britain I am sure I descended too abruptly and on others too often. In the latter category belong most of all Mr. James C. Palmes and Mr. R. H. Williams of the Royal Institute of British Architects. The books and pictures in their charge were an unending source of information. Miss Wood and Mr. Peeler of the Town Planning Institute also assisted me to obtain specific data, as did the librarians of the Victoria and Albert and British Museums in regard to more general material. Miss W. M. Heard and Florence M. Green of the Borough of Brentford and Chiswick Public Libraries, through their unusually careful reference work, were able to furnish a quantity of unpublished sources and illustrations. Mr. Bryan Robertson, Director of the Whitechapel Art Gallery, advised on the gallery's relation to its founders, the Barnetts.

In the North of England the information was more scattered, but I was often able to work more directly from original documents. For the history of Manchester and its surroundings I am grateful to Mr. Sidney Horrocks, Mr. H. Horton, and Miss E. M. Jones of the Public Library; to Mr. A. Mackenzie, Director of Housing for Manchester; and to Mr. R. Nicholas, City Surveyor. In the City Art Gallery, Director Emeritus S. D. Cleveland and the present Director G. L. Conran were of great service in obtaining illustrations. At the University of Manchester, Dr. Frank Jenkins, Mr. John Archer, and the late Professor R. A. Cordingley granted me ready access to their remarkable research materials and also lent personal encouragement when the task seemed overly long. So too did the late Mr. Cecil Stewart of the Regional College of Art.

In Liverpool, Mr. Keith Andrews of the Public Library found a number of rare items on Port Sunlight and Aintree. For the Leeds area, Mr. H. Nichols and Mr. T. K. Greenwood enabled me to gain an awareness of the history of the town in a necessarily short time. This was added to afterward by the Chief Public Health Inspector for Leeds, Mr. James Goodfellow.

For the Halifax District, Mr. Douglas Taylor, Chief Assistant Librarian, went to considerable lengths to dig out obscure material, an exercise which was made particularly pleasurable for the author because the Halifax Library is in Belle Vue, the former mansion of Sir Francis Crossley, across from the People's Park planned by Joseph Paxton. Mr. L. A. Hoyle informed me about the early history of Copley nearby. Mr. Ivor Burton, Borough Librarian and Museum Curator of Buxton, Mr. G. R. Micklewright, Chesterfield Librarian, Mr. Ronald J. Webb, Derbyshire County Librarian at Staveley, Mr. Geoffrey Hayhurst and Miss Jean Burwell of the Bradford Library, Miss Joan Knott of the Public Library and Institute of Shipley, and Mr. Brook and Mr. J. P. Lamb of the Sheffield libraries also came early and graciously to my aid. Professor W. H. G. Armytage and Professor Emeritus Stephen Welsh of the University of Sheffield, although I began to correspond with them quite late, sent the most prompt and full replies to my queries. Professor Armytage directed me to Dr. Roger Gill of the Royal West of England Academy School of Architecture in Bristol, who kindly microfilmed and sent parts of his unpublished thesis from the University of Sheffield, "Till We Have Built Jerusalem," shortly before the completion of my own manuscript. It is to be hoped that at least some of its sections will be published.

At Bournville, Mr. F. N. Barlow, Secretary and Manager of the Bournville Village Trust, generously opened the library and his recollections to me. Mr. Ralph Fastnedge, Curator of the Lady Lever Art Gallery, provided a similar service for Port Sunlight, which was supplemented by letters from Mr. J. Lomax-Simpson and Mr. F. A. Lawman. At Hampstead, Mr. Cowles Voysey, and in Letchworth (besides Mrs. Barry Parker), Mr. Courtenay M. Crickmer, Mr. Horace Plinston the retired Clerk of the Council, and Mr. M. Kelly the present Clerk, acquainted me with aspects of local history I should otherwise not have known.

The editors of the *Journal of the Society of Architectural Historians* and the *Journal of the American Institute of Planners* have generously given permission to use information from two of my slightly earlier articles commemorating the centennial birth date of Sir Raymond Unwin, Many other individuals have contributed smaller but equally vital amounts of information, and I can only hope that I may be pardoned for omitting their names here although I remember them with gratitude.

One cannot finish a book covering so many places and a considerable spread of time without recalling also the body of information and understanding offered by the writings of such distinguished authors as Nikolaus Pevsner, Sir John Summerson, John Brandon-Jones, Henry-Russell Hitchcock, Christopher Tunnard, Turpin Bannister, Sir Frederic Osborn, Clarence Stein, Carl Feiss and, always without saying, Lewis Mumford. They have established a frame of reference without which it would have been impossible for me or anyone else to proceed. All of them have most kindly given me, either through correspondence or personal word, their advice on the whole subject treated here. The beginnings of curiosity I gained from them, but the errors, the oddities, and the pronounced opinions are my own.

Eugene, Oregon   W. L. C.
1965

CONTENTS

CONTENTS

LIST OF ILLUSTRATIONS

* Photos by author.

1. WHERE DOES THE CITY STAND?

 Are the outlines of great concepts likely to lose their clarity when they become generally accepted? The garden city ideal, which was so immediately applicable, has been especially plagued by the constant semantic confusion in the literature describing the model villages, garden villages, garden suburbs, garden cities, and new towns as they appeared. Even now the phenomenon occurs in connection with the ordinary suburb.

If a person has been accustomed to regard the garden city as a reaction against the highly industrialized and urbanized environment of the Western nations, it comes as a further surprise to discover the terms "garden city" and "new town" turning up frequently in the housing pamphlets of the so-called underdeveloped countries to signify the increasing prestige of their industrial advance.

When we move out of the realm of practical application toward the germ of the idea itself, the likelihood of distortion is nearly as great. An exercise can be prepared to show that the United States, with its rapid growth in the nineteenth century and its receptivity to novel schemes, contributed substantially to the impetus of the garden city movement. It would require only a little chauvinism to persuade us that most of the basic premises of the garden city originated here. Holyoake declares in 1873 that it was not until Harriet Martineau described the American cooperative villages in her writings that the English public became aware of the issues involved.[1] Robert Baker urged in 1851 that the English reformers look to the American industrial village of Lowell in Massachusetts for their model.[2] Edward Bellamy's utopian picture of Boston in A.D. 2000, *Looking Backward,* touched off Ebenezer Howard's desire to hasten his garden city into being, as Howard has

1. George Holyoake, *John Stuart Mill As Some of the Working Classes Knew Him* (London, Trubner, 1873), p. 3.
2. Robert Baker, *The Present Condition of the Working Classes* (London, Longman, Brown, 1851), p. 54. Actually the first attempt at model industrial housing appears to have been David Dale's at his cotton mill at New Lanark in Scotland in 1793. See W. R. Croft, *The History of the Factory Movement* (Huddersfield, Whitehead, 1888), p. 10.

acknowledged.[3] Sir Frederic Osborn has observed too that the very term, garden city, was current in the United States well before Howard adopted it.[4] The layouts of the American landscape architect Frederick Law Olmsted, and the attention focused on land values by American economic critics like Henry George, seem to have played a role in Howard's education which was to be supplemented by his early years of residence in the United States.[5] The American "neighborhood unit" and "Radburn plan" appear often in the later garden city literature.

However, these methods of analysis, the operative and the ideological, omit something basic in terms of the history of the garden city as it relates to its setting. We must take era and geographic location into account if for no other reason than that the garden city did not remain an idea bound within a book as did many earlier utopian schemes. It sprang as an inspiration out of its own age and returned to the actual fabric of the society as a practical experiment almost as quickly.

A more comprehensive approach might be derived from the assumption that the course of events in England from the late eighteenth-century utopian schemes to the twentieth-century new towns can be best explained against the somber background of a chronic visual insufficiency, a shortage of the ambient qualities of beauty in the whole environment. No great originality can be claimed for this, because the Hammonds have already developed a similar viewpoint in their social history of Great Britain during the early nineteenth century, *The Age of the Chartists, 1832–54;* remarking it is simply to endorse its validity and to suggest that its ramifications can be extended on through the nineteenth and twentieth centuries. It offers an opportunity to reconcile evidence which may, at first sight, appear completely contradictory.

The Hammonds point to a baffling crosscurrent of thought in a brief summary of the observations of three educated visitors to English industrial towns during the 1830s and 40s—an Englishman, a Frenchman, and a German. They report: "All three observers agreed that the poor man in England had certain advantages over the poor man on the Continent, and that he had a share in the benefits brought by the agrarian and industrial revolutions," especially in respect to food, drink, and clothing. "But they were struck by the social incoherence of these towns, their cold unhappiness, the class divi-

---

3. Dugald Macfadyen, *Sir Ebenezer Howard and the Town Planning Movement* (Manchester University Press, 1933), pp. 20–21.

4. Frederic Osborn, *Greenbelt Cities* (London, Faber and Faber, 1946), p. 181. Also F. J.

Osborn, "A Note on Terminology," in Ebenezer Howard, *Garden Cities of To-morrow* (London, Faber and Faber, 1946), Preface, p. 26.

5. Ibid., pp. 20, 136.

sion of interests and pleasures, the concentration on a limited and limiting purpose." Little heed was paid, said one of their visitors, to " 'any comprehensive plan, any attention to general convenience, or to beauty and architectonic art. Capital is employed solely in the creation of new capital. What is not calculated to promote this end is regarded as useless and superfluous.' "[6] This utilitarian viewpoint promoted elaboration and specialization in technology but left little place in the visible culture for expressive or visually emotive elements which in earlier centuries had been considered indispensable. "Men were so engrossed in building mills that towns were left to build themselves."[7] Because the ultimate test of building activities now depended upon specific, short-term, and tangible returns, the arts were largely dismissed as irrelevant. It became a question not of whether the mill or town was built, but of how little could be invested in the town to get by. Therefore, to take the conventional position that the architectural and planning history of industrial England can be interpreted only through mill construction, greenhouses, railroad terminals, viaducts, and bridges, because those were the only praiseworthy accomplishments, would not be entirely inaccurate but it would be incomplete.

This paradox comes out clearly again in the journals of Karl Friedrich Schinkel, the German neoclassic architect. He visited England in the mid-1820s to absorb technical knowledge at the behest of the Prussian government. While there he could not refrain from commenting that the factories he saw in Birmingham and Manchester (Fig. 1), for all their promise of a new age, appeared to be huge misshapen piles of soot-covered brick. They were deprived of the beneficial touch of the architect's hand.[8] His use of the adjectives "gloomy" or "uncanny" in describing his overall impression of the factories in 1826 shows the depth of his perception, because the English industrial towns, like the factories, often do convey a silent and empty, almost surrealistic, mood—too real to be believable. He writes of Birmingham as a "sad" industrial community, and it becomes obvious that he was reacting in romantic shock from the sheltered isolation of his previous environment in Prussia. Schinkel learned just enough to return to Germany to create buildings of iron, glass, and terra cotta, economical by necessity of the pov-

6. J. L. Hammond and Barbara Hammond, *The Age of the Chartists, 1832–1854* (London, Longmans, Green, 1930), pp. 335–36. See also *The Bleak Age* by the same authors.

7. J. L. Hammond and Barbara Hammond, *The Town Labourer 1760–1832* (London, Long-mans, Green, 1920), p. 44.

8. Alfred von Wolzogen, ed., *Aus Schinkel's Nachlass, 3* (Berlin, 1863), 113–14. See also L. Ettlinger, "A German Architect's Visit to England in 1826," *Architectural Review* (May 1945), pp. 131–34, for an excellent summary.

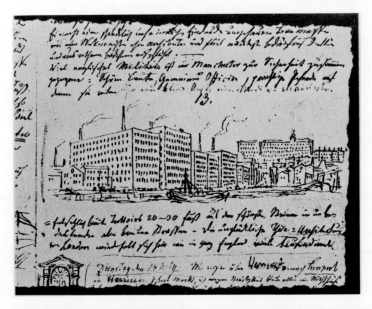

Fig. 1. New factories in Manchester, from Schinkel's "Notebook," mid-1820s. The official Prussian architect admired their novelty but deplored their "grim utilitarianism."

erty of his state, but exhibiting an architectonic imagination that would prove of lasting value in the affirmation of the dignity of Berlin which, as official Prussian architect, it was his duty to foster. He said he wished to take advantage of the "new mechanical conditions," but not to lose himself in dead formalism and "grim utilitarianism."

The insight into the history of industrialism provided by the Hammonds thus eliminates the perennial question, already being asked in the early nineteenth century, of how the industrial revolution could possibly be considered in any way unfortunate when it was obvious, as the three educated visitors from different countries had agreed, that it would eventuate in a higher level of income for all. Even the poorest were destined to share its bounty, once sufficient risk capital had accumulated. Still the Hammonds questioned the sense of life for the town. It was the arbitrary arrangement of the customs and uses of wealth they disparaged rather than its imperfect distribution. "Beauty was allowed no place in industry, in religion or in city life," they said.[9] So it came about that "the new age offered the prizes of wealth and rank to those who excelled in that toil, but it treated delights, that had once made the hardships of common life less rigid and monotonous, as the rewards of rare success. The arts, instead of helping the complaining

9. Hammond and Hammond, *Age of Chartists*, p. 358.

and miserable to forget themselves and their wrongs, were employed to give a new lustre to good fortune, to declare the glory of sudden wealth."[10] So, too, Romanticism in the arts, by anticipating beauty from the unusual object or the distant place, merely strengthened the conviction that it was not to be required in the everyday world nor from any previous tradition. The Hammonds, unlike many of the earlier town critics such as Pugin in his *Contrasts,* drew invidious comparison between cities of the industrial revolution and classical Greek and Roman urbanism, rather than the more usual contrast with a medieval English village or town. Thus, it was not the "universal" or "eternal" city this type of social critic doubted, as is so often implied today, but a peculiar brand of city produced within the single, short, and brutish nineteenth century.

It would be frivolous then to overemphasize the American influence on garden city thought. Enormous distances, migration, and regional differences in the United States have tempered many wounds on the landscape. It is only in the smaller and relatively concentrated New England states with their quaint Colonial villages placed cheek by jowl with huge nineteenth-century mill and factory towns that one is keenly aware of a similar unfavorable contrast with a better visual past. The Englishman's cultural history was more vulnerable than an American's. It was recorded deeply everywhere on the land and among the buildings in which he lived. As the Englishman of intellect and good conscience saw the city and countryside of his ancestors assailed, scarified, and erased forever by the urban and industrial revolution, the responsibility for the creation of new communal beauty was more and more manifest. The garden city movement can never be properly assessed if it is regarded, and it sometimes is by Americans and others, as an effort directed solely toward the future or offered only as an alternative to modern metropolitanism. It included these aims, but its deeper harmony and greater success would depend upon how well it *reconciled* the past with the present, town with country, and agriculture with industry.

Finally, the method of visual analysis may furnish some inkling of why the garden city is so persistently suspect as the root of suburban scatteration and sprawl in Great Britain and the United States. As Osborn, Mumford, Stein, and others have pointed out (with apparently inexhaustible patience), anyone who will take the trouble to investigate the systems of financing, industrial and agricultural planning, organized amenity, and population distribution advocated by Ebenezer Howard and his architects, Parker and Unwin,

10. Ibid., p. 362.

can hardly avoid the realization that the underlying principles of the garden city and the suburb are absolutely different.[11] Osborn felt that one explanation for the basic misunderstanding could be found in the abrupt introduction of electric traction and the motor car, which debilitated the garden city principle of self-containment before it had an adequate chance to stand and be understood by the general populace. Even the steady rise in real income for the lower economic levels became a disrupting factor, he thought. All too true, but a visual explanation might be even simpler. The suburb with its winding and tree-lined streets, its low and separate houses, and its green lawns does *look like* a garden city at first glance. The instinct of hunters of suburban sprawl seems to be always to seek visual analogies. The crucial evidence in planning for them lies ultimately in how a community looks, feels, smells, and sounds and not in literary theories. For the needs of our age this attitude also has some significance.

No matter how mistaken their conclusions in regard to the derivation of the conventional suburb from the garden city, the direct dependence of their criticism on pictorial criteria is in the older modern tradition of creative urban reform and follows the same basic impulse as the garden city. For the modern mind, particularly in Britain, to take part in the act of seeing must be to believe. Or, as the older modern poet Browning had put it:

> For, don't you mark? We're made so that we love
> First when we see them painted, things we have passed
> Perhaps a hundred times nor cared to see . . .

Thus in the more casual context, the garden city was for them a kind of painting, an idealization, of a conventional suburb. To effectively perceive the latter, the former apparently had to be invoked, even though the two have little authentic relation to each other in the history of ideas.

 Fairfield

That communities purposefully designed to qualify the life within them did exist in England outside utopian essays and before the onset of industrialism is conveniently demonstrated by two little-known but neighboring examples near Manchester, the capital of early industrialism. They are the Moravian settlement at Fairfield of 1783–85 (Fig. 2) and the project for Hanover Square

11. See F. J. Osborn, "The Garden City Movement," *Britain Today* (Dec. 12, 1941), p. 6, and Lewis Mumford, "The Garden City Idea and Modern Planning," pp. 34–35, in Howard, *Garden Cities of To-morrow*.

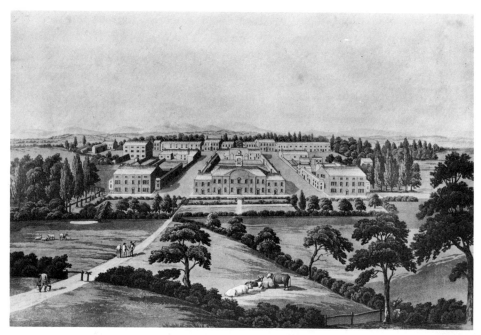

Fig. 2. Fairfield; Moravian settlement near Manchester, 1783–85. Protestant utopian villages were built in England before the onset of the industrial revolution.

Fig. 3. Hanover Square and Zoological Gardens, Broughton, near Manchester; Haley and Brown, 1836–38. Romanticism was carried so far as to require the presence of wild animals in the ornamental kiosks.

and Zoological Gardens in Salford of 1836–38 (Fig. 3). Their aspects were also highly expressive of their sequence in time. The first is mostly a manifestation of Protestant conscience, the second of Protestant enterprise. Fairfield was the last of five Moravian settlements in England, the original being Fulneck near Bradford in Yorkshire. Fulneck was begun in 1744 and provided the early environment of one of the first of America's architect-engineers, Benjamin Latrobe. That Fairfield was forty years later than Fulneck is signified by its more systematic layout and its execution in a restrained Georgian style which recalls the early nineteenth-century Shaker settlements in the United States. But the entire Moravian architectural influence in England reposes comfortably within the eighteenth century. It was a pretechnical and antiurban community, basing its aspirations upon a peaceful reform of the habits of the spirit. The location of Fairfield, isolated in the countryside four miles from Manchester and two fields back from the Ashton turnpike road, reflected the founders' desire for self-sufficiency. There was to be a permanent balance of labor between agriculture and hand manufacture, with none of the ever-increasing specialization of jobs which so bedeviled the progress of the later textile towns and villages. The only indication of the proximity of Fairfield to the bustling cotton center of Manchester lies in the three-story houses. The top floors were used as cotton mills for spinning and weaving, the separate rooms being connected by doors.[12]

The central chapel with its cupola dominated the arrangement, as in other Moravian communities. To the east and west in perfect Palladian balance were the workshop-houses of the single brethren and sisters. In addition there were sixty dwellings for families. Across the back on the north ran a street containing the shops and an inn. Facing the door of the chapel was the large burial ground, making it impractical for the approaching lane to come in at the middle and thus providing the exception to the prevailing symmetry. Religiosity was conveyed through a calm, restrained, orderly rationale. The architectural vocabulary was modest and disciplined, in keeping with the tenor of its community life.

Fulneck was built on two terraces an eighth of a mile long on the side of a steep Yorkshire valley. "The Fairfield Square Settlement" rested on a platform in the midst of gently rolling land. It was a pedestrian village, as the flag paths running along and across the cobbles of the streets still testify. More worthy of note, however, was the absence of trees, until hawthorn and ash

12. Arthur J. Dobb, "The History of Moravian Architecture in England," unpublished thesis, Regional College of Art (Manchester, 1951), p. 34.

were planted in 1848,[13] and the lack of any provision within the settlement for open or recreational spaces. The surrounding countryside was depended upon for both. Such omissions would have been regarded as most serious in the nineteenth-century model villages and in the garden cities as well, despite their greenbelts, but this community did share with the later examples the assumption that moral or spiritual uplift could be assisted by the careful composition of the physical environment. That the influences from such settlements continuously impinged upon one another, because of their geographic proximity, is evident. Fulneck was only a short distance off the Leeds-to-Bradford road along which Sir Titus Salt traveled from his home at Methley to his factory settlement twenty miles away at Saltaire; and Sellers and Wood built an exemplary little garden suburb in 1912–13 on the edge of the Fairfield land which in the disposition of its volumes, scale, and detailing bore more than a superficial resemblance to the earlier architecture.[14]

 Hanover Square

With Hanover Square and Zoological Gardens (1836) the quiet restraint of the eighteenth century—even in the throes of social reform—drops away. There is no longer a separation posited between man and nature. Symmetrical organization is abandoned and informal nature is brought in among the dwellings for the edification of the inhabitants. The mood has changed as well as the manners. The techniques of the two prints (Figs. 2 and 3) suggest the difference. The rich black crayon of the Hanover Square lithograph exhibits a theatricality which is entirely lacking in the dry and nearly shadowless aquatint of Fairfield. The composition of Fairfield is intended to pacify with its logic and communal simplicity; Hanover Square must excite and titillate with its novelty. The earlier colony signified a withdrawal from the city, nature, and the contaminating world in general, while the later one, just on the other side of Manchester in manufacturing Salford, is so stuffed with these elements that their redistribution was necessary to try to bring them into a more effective adjustment. The assurance of the eighteenth-century order had vanished at Hanover Square and in its place appeared a nervous, self-assertive individualism resulting in a wide and irregular placement of villas for commuting merchants. Only the architecture clung to the earlier classic symmetry. The independence of the dwelling units reflected

13. Ibid., p. 31.
14. I owe the recognition of this similarity to Mr. John Archer of the University of Manchester, the expert on Sellers and Wood.

a still heavier dependence on the nearby metropolis of Manchester and its sources of commercial and industrial wealth.

The botanical gardens and zoo were designed to provide a focal point for the newly aroused curiosity of the 1830s which one writer, in attempting to explain the sudden proliferation of such collections, attributed to the expanding trade of England and a more serious interest in the natural sciences.[15] It was also the counterpart of the Romanticism of the artists Delacroix (Fig. 4), Géricault, and Barye in France, transformed on the instant

Fig. 4. Tiger Resting; Eugene Delacroix, c. 1830. The tranquil beast (animals were actually exhibited at Hanover Square and Zoological Gardens) was symbolic of the Romantic energy potential of the 1830s everywhere.

into villas which were to be surrounded by wild animals. What is notable about the total picture is that the houses of the merchants retained the older provincial Regency style while the landscape spurted ahead into the sphere of exoticism. Thus Romanticism was not so much manifest in a single style or a single art here, as by a compromise among them all.

Only a few houses were built, and Hanover Square and the Zoological Gardens somehow became separated in the process. The animal displays in-

15. George Jennison, in "An Ambitious Enterprise That Failed, Manchester Zoo at Higher Broughton," *Manchester Guardian* (July 17, 1925), says there were "zoological gardens in London at this period, and also at Bristol, Cheltenham, Dublin and Edinburgh, as well as a small one on a commercial basis at Liverpool." The layout was by Richard Forrest, who also arranged the Bristol and Cheltenham gardens. There was another at Leeds which opened in 1840 and was likewise sold at auction in 1848. John Mayhall, *Annals of Yorkshire* (Leeds, Johnson, 1862), p. 467.

cluded a leopard, lions, an elephant, a rhino, a dromedary, kangaroos, buffa-
loes, monkeys, and polar bears. There are mentions of as many as twenty
kiosks for housing the beasts, scattered over fifteen acres, but it is doubtful
the animals ever inhabited antiquarian delights like the temples, towers, and
pagodas represented in the early promotional lithograph. The double pond
to the left in the picture was dug, however. It was stocked with gold and silver
fish, ducks, swans, and otters, and was 220 yards long. It also had a pelican
island in the center, reached by rustic bridges.[16] This pond in Broughton
Park, along with a few crumbling old stucco houses in Hanover Park some
distance away, appear to be the sole remnants today.

The Zoological Gardens lasted only a brief while, from 1838 until 1842,
but if one is to judge from the literary reminiscences appearing years later,
its passing was deeply regretted, by the younger generation at least. Miss
C. C. Armstrong in her lively recollections of 1875 states: "For a few years
they were very attractive and would have proved a success had not the evan-
gelical clergy raised such an outcry when some of the shareholders were wish-
ful to have them open on the Sunday for the benefit of the working classes."[17]
The earlier Protestant attitude was clashing with the later. This was also the
time of the Chartist agitations, beginning with the Peterloo massacre in Manchester in 1819, and the zoo was to have some connection with them. An
adverse demonstration scheduled for the day of Queen Victoria's marriage
on February 10, 1840, was cleverly forestalled by throwing open the museum,
botanical gardens, and Broughton Zoo to the workers, with no admission
charged.[18]

Besides the animals, the preserve had an archery range, museums, a camera
obscura, and a maze. The last feature must have pushed the complexities of
Romantic planning as revealed in the lithograph to their ultimate confusion,
for Miss Armstrong tells us that one of her favorite pastimes as a child was
guiding lost parties out of the maze. In an effort to revive a failing enterprise
the directors originated a panorama with fireworks in 1841, representing the
Siege of Acre and, in 1842, the Eruption of Vesuvius with the Destruction of
Pompeii and Herculaneum.[19] The mountain alone stood sixty feet high on

16. Ibid.
17. "Manchester As It Was," *Manchester Review* (Spring 1960), p. 23.
18. P. G., letter to the editor, *City News* (undated; Manchester Local History Library Collections). Also *Inquiry Into the Sanitary Condition of the Labouring Population of Great Britain*, Report of the Poor Law Commissioners (London, Clowes, 1842), p. 267.
19. Jennison, "Ambitious Enterprise That Failed."

the canvas. On the last night a tightrope walker performed and in his "concluding march across the rope, fireworks were thrown up and coloured lights thrown upon the scene."[20] All that remained after this brave farewell and the subsequent auction was a ditty:

> Manchester Zoological Gardens now have fled, sir,
> For Fletcher with his hammer has knocked them on
>   the head, sir.
> The O, dear O,
> Manchester could not support a wild beast show.[21]

20. W. Parsons, *City News* (Jan. 5, 1916).   21. P. G., op. cit.

2. THE BRADFORD–HALIFAX SCHOOL
OF MODEL VILLAGE BUILDERS

The first model villages at the advent of the industrial revolution were clustered in the wool and worsted manufacturing centers in the West Riding of Yorkshire. A triangle drawn on a map with Halifax and the larger city of Leeds at the base and Bradford at the apex would contain the area well. There is a wide choice of reasons for this concentration. Often heard in the district itself is the explanation that the medieval tradition of responsibility was unusually strong there. The records of earlier philanthropy seem to bear this out, particularly as represented by such figures as Nathaniel Waterhouse (mid-seventeenth century), who built numerous workhouses, almshouses, and orphans' schools around Halifax. The ancient, if humble, lineage of the first industrialists, their frequent interest in armorial bearings, and the poems written to celebrate their accomplishments make it plain that both they and their workers were thoroughly conscious of the ancient feudal responsibilities. As the funeral orator put it in summing up the career of Sir Titus Salt:

> He was a pioneer; a creator of the new era. He showed how the graces of the old feudalism that was being supplanted, could be grafted on and exemplified by the men who brought forth and moulded the better age. No feudal lord could have set open his doors and offered his resources to the retainers of generations, in the way he provided for those that laboured under his directions.[1]

A natural accompaniment was the paradigm of the self-sufficient village life of the region. The villages to the east and the hillside cottages to the west were being rapidly supplanted by the manufacturing towns. Psychologically

---

1. Rev. Robert Balgarnie, *Sir Titus Salt, Baronet: His Life and Its Lessons* (London, Hodder and Stoughton, 1878), p. 313.

they both came to be invested with the powerful symbolism of the soon-to-be-lost cause of the cottage industry. James Graham, Esq., in giving testimony before a Parliamentary Committee on the "State of the Woollen Manufacture" in 1806 felt that the apprehension brought on by the appearance of four or five factories in the Leeds area was premature. They were still outnumbered by the "domestic clothiers" who could not help but benefit by the competition. However, he did admit that "improvements" in machinery would no doubt be possible only for the capitalist, with his surplus funds for research and his factory to exploit the discoveries on a large scale.[2]

Graham's account of his effort to foster the domestic clothier is the most arresting part of the testimony. He relates that in 1795 he divided several farms in the neighborhood of Leeds into small holdings for such men. His uncle by marriage, Edmund Lodge, undertook the same plan at Eccleshill. Graham studied the cloth-makers' houses already in existence and built twelve or fourteen units according to the "best plan" for this purpose. The clothiers, "instead of living shut up in narrow streets, in towns" would henceforth dwell in the open countryside adjoining the smaller villages.[3] He thought the behavior of the people had measurably improved in the last decade except in the bigger towns where "they have encreased in idleness and wretchedness."[4] His good intentions were to be matched by the builders of the later model villages of the factory system.[5] The motivation for establishing these tiny communities came, in part at least, from a similar impulse to find some middle ground between the cottage of the hand weaver and the town of the manufacturer. Nevertheless, at the beginning of the nineteenth century the Luddite Riots of 1811–12 against the new machines and steam power, followed by the Chartist demonstrations of the 1840s for political reform, rapidly forced such discussions out of the realm of polite inquiry. By 1837 when Charles Wing published his *Evils of the Factory System Demonstrated by Parliamentary Evidence,* the lines of the argument had considerably hardened. Wing realized that with the French Revolution at the end of the eighteenth century "pity and terror had been too much exhausted to be easily excited" by local conditions. But now the time had come to consider seriously the altered status of the English cottage worker.

2. *Report and Minutes of Evidence on the State of the Woollen Manufacture of England* (London, Committee on the Woollen Trade, 1806), pp. 444–47.

3. Ibid., p. 444.

4. Ibid., p. 447.

5. The Chartist advocacy of small holdings, particularly O'Connor's Land Scheme of 1845–48, had much in common with Graham's idea. See G. R. Dalby, "The Chartist Movement in the District of Halifax," unpublished B.A. thesis, Halifax Public Library (1948).

They were taken from their cottages, where they worked at their pleasure, with more or less intensity, and at a time when, in consequence of the demand for labour being greater than the supply, their wages were amply sufficient to maintain them, and placed in mills, where their labour was regulated by the machinery, and where sordid masters dictated what wages they chose, and what hours they chose.[6]

It was reformers like Wing, who was Surgeon to the Royal Metropolitan Hospital for Children in London and so aimed his attacks mainly at the hardships of child labor, as well as Lord Shaftesbury the aristocratic amateur, and Sir Edwin Chadwick the busy governmental administrator, who brought to the attention of the public the circumstances of the unfortunate millworkers. Many of the early entrepreneurs, however, were equally aware of these conditions and had the wealth and power to correct them through model villages.

The villages particularly deserve scrutiny because there was no delay or need for persuasion in building them. Their distinguishing feature is that they were conceived and executed largely by one man's mind, that of the factory owner. Sir Titus Salt of Saltaire near Bradford; Colonel Edward Akroyd with his Copley and Akroydon; and John, Joseph, and Sir Francis Crossley with the development of their West Hill Park area (all the latter in or near Halifax) exemplify this more than adequately. The last of these great northern manufacturers was Lord Leverhulme, who built Port Sunlight near Liverpool at the end of the nineteenth century and was notable for his proclivity in employing architects' plans as if they were merely aids with which to improve and implement his own cogitations.

It is not easy to ascribe the direct action of the capitalists to influences from the literature of reform. Titus Salt, when asked a leading question, replied that it was impossible for a man responsible for the daily bread of several thousand people to do much reading.[7] It has nevertheless been observed by J. M. Richards, Dewhirst, and others that Salt admired Disraeli and that the resemblance between Saltaire and Mr. Trafford's model factory and village in Disraeli's novel *Sibyl*, published in 1845, is a close one.[8]

Such numbers of workers as Sir Titus Salt employed had never before been assembled. The mother of the Crossleys, the matriarch who was not above giving Sir Titus himself a bit of advice and comment when he called on

6. (London, Saunders and Otley), p. vi.
7. Balgarnie, p. 214.
8. J. M. Richards, "Sir Titus Salt," *Architec*-

tural Review (Nov. 1936), pp. 213–18. Robert K. Dewhirst, "Saltaire," *Town Planning Review* (July 1960), pp. 136–37, 139.

her, would not consent in her prosperity to move from the site of her late husband's mill. In her old age she had a mirror placed in her room at a convenient angle so that she might examine the countenances of the thousands of workers as they walked past her window going to and coming from the huge aggregation of Crossley factories and sheds at Dean Clough.[9] It had been her vow that if the enterprise succeeded, the poor should "taste of it."[10]

The change was primarily a qualitative one insofar as it related to the breakdown of family life in the cottage with its balance between agriculture and hand manufacture. It was significantly quantitative in that it brought these same families to settle around the coal-burning factories in the valleys of the enlarging towns. In 1837, on the death of the original John Crossley, the employees of his firm numbered some 300.[11] It has been estimated that by the 1870s between 5,000 and 6,000 people worked for the Crossleys.[12] As Wing had inferred, one of the greatest hardships and disruptions had been in terms of time, with the cottage laborer suddenly transfixed on a pin of specialization to a long day within a rigid factory schedule. But the loss of spatial locus and personal identity must have been equally damaging to his sense of security and self-respect.

Only in the case of Colonel Akroyd can the link with social science and reform be easily documented. During one of his Halifax speeches in his second campaign for a seat in Parliament, he declared that in domestic legislation he attached more importance to social improvements than to the political questions of the day, which seemed to absorb everyone else's attention.[13] In another address of 1862 to a social science group, he observed that the good example of model housing in the West Riding of Yorkshire was not being followed in the cotton districts of Lancashire because the American Civil War was having such a depressing effect upon the cotton industry that little could be hoped for until the arrival of a more settled period.[14] Wars appear to have largely determined the prosperity and hard times of both textile regions. Thomas Baines, the chronicler of the Yorkshire region, believed that the improved trade following on the American Revolution led to the application of machine methods to the woollen industry, permitting it to

9. R. Bretton, "Crossleys of Dean Clough," Part I, *Trans. Halifax Antiquarian Society* (1950), p. 7.

10. *Sir Francis Crossley, Bart.* (London, Religious Tract Society, Bio. Series 1028, undated), pp. 4, 12.

11. Bretton, "Crossleys of Dean Clough," Part II (1951), p. 78.

12. *Sir Francis Crossley, Bart.*, p. 5.

13. "Mr. Akroyd and the Representation of Halifax," Leeds and Yorkshire Biographical Clippings, Leeds Library, Vol. I, A–F (undated).

14. Edward Akroyd, *On Improved Dwellings for the Working Classes* (London, Shaw, 1862), p. 14.

catch up with the earlier mechanization of cotton manufacture. He likewise felt that the conflict with France had given Bradford an edge over Halifax after 1800.[15] Others thought that these same events had stimulated the "energy of political inquiry which has ever since distinguished the inhabitants of this department of Yorkshire."[16]

Regardless of the rivalry of the two communities or the influence of outside upheavals, the close connection between the industrial revolution and the remnants of the medieval cloth trade is evident from a series of events beginning in 1825, three years after Titus Salt had become a permanent resident of Bradford. One of his biographers, the Reverend Robert Balgarnie, judged that the impetus was given with the traditional Septennial Festival of Bishop Blaize, the patron saint of the wool combers. "In 1825 the festival was celebrated with greater pomp than ever, and the streets had never before presented such a scene of dissipation and frivolity."[17] To get rid of what the Reverend Balgarnie termed a "semi-barbarous celebration," despite its religious overtones, was the goal of efforts begun by Salt and others. Public meetings were held to discuss methods for the moral and intellectual improvement of the populace. As in several other cities at the time, a mechanics' institute had also been established at the beginning of the year; this was to have a school of design attached to it in 1848, foreshadowing similar institutions at Saltaire.

These reforms were evidently too late or ineffectual, for other difficulties intervened. On June 14 a strike of 20,000 operatives began which lasted for twenty-three weeks. In December a number of banks throughout the kingdom went bankrupt, including the firm of Wentworth, Chaloner, and Rishworth which had branches in London, York, Wakefield, and Bradford. Payment was suspended and public panic ensued.[18] Balgarnie reports that on the first and third of May, 1826 the crisis came when the "operatives, thinking that the introduction of weaving machinery was the cause of all three disasters, and inflamed by popular demagogues, proceeded to attack Horsfall's Mill."[19] Salt first tried to reason with the mob. When this proved futile, he had himself sworn in as a special constable. Ultimately the dreaded Riot Act was read by Colonel Plumbe Tempest; gunfire followed, and two persons were killed and several more wounded. Neither the long strike nor the brief

15. T. Baines, *Yorkshire Past and Present, 1* (London, Mackenzie, 1871–77), Part 2, 678.

16. Edward Parsons, *The Civil, Ecclesiastical, Literary, Commercial and Miscellaneous* *History of Leeds, Halifax, Huddersfield, Bradford, Etc., 1* (Leeds, Hobson, 1834), 226.

17. Balgarnie, p. 52.

18. Parsons, op. cit., p. 231.

19. Ibid., pp. 42–43.

attack on Horsfall's mill was successful, and two of the rioters were sent to prison at York Castle.[20]

The disturbances at Halifax came later, during 1842, at the height of Chartist excitement everywhere. Heavy unemployment and the high cost of bread, plus a cut in wages, brought on a condition that was considered alarming and "largely favored the agitation which had been commenced for the repeal of the corn laws."[21] On August 15th and 16th, mobs invaded the town. On the first day they stopped several mills, including Akroyd's. On the next they formed in the neighborhood of his mills on Haley Hill. They were turned aside by an uphill charge of hussars, police, and infantry and they then headed toward Akroyd's mansion, Bankfield, but musket fire drove them off from that also. There were wounded on both sides from these three clashes.[22]

During the week before, Akroyd, apparently with the same naive confidence in his persuasive powers that had led Salt to try to reason with the mob in Bradford in 1826, had written two letters to the *Halifax Guardian*, trying to demonstrate that machinery would become a blessing, not a curse.[23] These letters came out of an exchange between him and the paper, relating to the primary cause for the current distress. An editorial of July 30th had declared that overproduction was the chief cause and criticized Akroyd for emphasizing the Corn Laws as the basic difficulty. Evidently the editor believed what has been also remarked by later historians, that the call for the repeal of the Corn Laws often provided a convenient distraction from other deeper grievances, such as those leading to Chartism. According to the paper, Akroyd had carried his conviction so far as to appear with a local deputation before Sir Robert Peel and the principal cabinet ministers in London to testify against the Corn Laws, But the *Guardian* thought the whole lamentable procedure had begun when the domestic home weavers had been displaced:

> There was so much of a home character in their little half farmstead, half clothing-shop; the master and his men and domestic apprentices were so much associated in friendly, almost family, intercourse, that the destruction of such a system cannot but be productive of evil, succeeded as it has been by the gloomy factory system.

20. Ibid., pp. 231–33. Also John Mayhall, *Annals of Yorkshire* (Leeds, Johnson, 1862), pp. 318–19, 324–25.

21. R. Bretton, "Colonel Edward Akroyd,"

Trans. Halifax Antiquarian Society (June 5, 1948), p. 69.

22. *Halifax Guardian* (Aug. 20, 1842).

23. Ibid. (Aug. 6, 13, 1842).

Akroyd replied that the specialization of labor had already begun when one domestic manufacturer had hired other weavers to stay at their looms while he attended to collecting and marketing their individual productions in the towns. If the paper wished to return to the "good old times" it would have to destroy both the spinning machines and the power looms. It was as reasonable to ask that a good harvest be abandoned or that the newspaper call for the destruction of the printing press in favor of a revival of domestic scribes.

His factory now turned out two thousand pieces a week against the four or five pieces of the cottage manufacturer.[24] When the newspaper asserted that overabundance of production reduced the wages of the workmen, Akroyd countered that this also had reduced the unit cost of clothing and that the laborer had now to work fewer hours to make the same cloth for a garment. The individual of his grandfather's day was compelled to wear a coat for eight to ten years, whereas the present middle-class man often wore his no longer than twelve months and could afford two at a time. A reduced price was sure to increase the demand for cloth and the benefit would filter down. His major conclusion was, however, that neither he nor the publisher would have been able to prevent the present difficulties. His company had adopted the power.loom only when it had become necessary to do so or face a decline in business. No matter what the cause of the crisis was—overproduction or underdistribution—he wished to protest the editor's incitement of the operatives when they were faced with the sight of starving wives and children and were already close to desperation. "Are you, Sir, whilst we are treading on a volcano of smothered popular excitement, to point at large concerns as if they were another cause of the people's misery?" he asked.

Two days later his mills and home were under actual attack. By the end of the week a notice appeared in the *Guardian* saying that "the Magistrates earnestly exhort those Mill Owners who have not already set their Mills to work, to do so immediately, and to furnish their Workmen with Arms;" in case of a further attack by those "mistaken and deluded creatures," the Chartists.[25]

Despite these calamities and the obscurity of their causes, Akroyd persisted in his agitation to have the Corn Laws abolished. He became well acquainted with the leading political figures of the region. On the 29th of November he addressed an Anti–Corn Law meeting at Halifax, his speech

24. See also Bretton, "Colonel Edward Akroyd," p. 69.
25. (Aug. 20, 1842).

following that of the chairman, the Rt. Hon. Charles Wood, later Viscount Halifax. Richard Cobden also spoke.[26] In 1857 he defeated Cobden as the candidate to Parliament from nearby Huddersfield.[27] In 1867 Akroyd presented a bust of Cobden to the Halifax Chamber of Commerce.[28] It was Cobden who suggested Frank Crossley as the Liberal candidate to Parliament from Halifax in 1852.[29] John Crossley was to succeed Edward Akroyd in the same office at the general election of 1874. According to Robert Balgarnie, Titus Salt also "was a liberal subscriber to the Corn Law League, and an ardent admirer of Cobden, Bright and General [Perronet] Thompson."[30] The latter was the author of the "Corn Law Catechism," a free trade advocate, and the editor of Bentham's Utilitarian *Westminster Review,* beginning in 1832. He was elected M.P. from Bradford in 1848 as a consequence of his "sound" views.

The three families—the Salts, the Akroyds, and the Crossleys—had then industrial, political, and religious aspirations in common. They were also friends and relations. Catherine, daughter of Joseph Crossley and niece of Frank Crossley, married Titus Salt, son of Sir Titus, in 1866.[31] One of the last friends allowed to see Sir Francis Crossley before his death in 1872 was Colonel Edward Akroyd.[32] The rapidly acquired wealth of these families also derived from the type of invention against which the workmen had demonstrated. The Salt fortune was founded upon a method of weaving Russian Donskoi wool, mohair from Turkey and, especially, alpaca from Peru. About 1852 Salt entered an agreement with James Akroyd & Son to purchase from Samuel Lister[33] the French "Heilmann's Patent" for combing wool. The Jacquard loom engine, also from France, had first been used in worsted manufacture by the Akroyd firm in 1827.[34] The Crossleys' rise to affluence was similarly forwarded by the invention by George Collier of a power loom for weaving tapestry and Brussels carpets, of which they became the world's leading manufacturers.[35] It is this community of experience and disposition, as well as its actual physical results, that suggests the term, "The Bradford–Halifax School" of model village builders.

Unless one actually visits the West Riding, two additional features of the

26. Bretton, "Colonel Edward Akroyd," p. 70.
27. Ibid., p. 84.
28. Ibid., p. 92.
29. Bretton, "Crossleys of Dean Clough," Part VI, *Trans. Halifax Antiquarian Society* (1954), p. 14.
30. Balgarnie, p. 95.
31. Abraham Holroyd, *Saltaire and Its Founder* (Bradford, Brear, 1873), p. 83.

32. Bretton, "Crossleys of Dean Clough," Part VI, p. 26.
33. Balgarnie, p. 154.
34. Baines, *Yorkshire Past and Present,* 2, Part 2, 407.
35. Bretton, "Crossleys of Dean Clough," Part II (1951), p. 72.

surroundings are apt to remain concealed, even from the camera. The Reverend John Watson, in describing the Halifax of 1775, predicted that brick would supplant the local gritstone as a basic building material, but probable as this still sounds, it never happened.[36] The towns and model villages alike were built of local stone so uniform in texture and color, and then overlaid with decades of soot, that it is today difficult to distinguish among them. Form and reform are apt to blend into one amorphous mass. The rain and mist of the valleys and the hanging smoke of the mills carry this effect of fusion even further.[37]

The landscape, by way of contrast to the buildings, conveys a definite drama. The Wharf, the Aire, the Calder, and the Colne flow down the dales between the moors and uplands that rise from five hundred to a thousand feet. This scenery is not rugged, but it is sufficiently picturesque to be constantly remarked as one moves about the valley floors. These unusual pictorial possibilities were early recognized by one author, T. J. Maslen, who was the son of an architect and had been a civil servant in India. He considers, in his *Suggestions for the Improvement of Our Towns and Houses* (1843), the remarkable hill overlooking Halifax in terms of what the natives of India would have done with it. Such a hill (which in its projected ornaments resembles Hanover Square and Zoological Gardens of a few years earlier) would have been made "subservient to their romantic habits, their delightful religious festivals, and their numerous holidays." He felt that

> even the hill of Halifax might be adorned and decorated with appropriate little cottages, pavilions, kiosks, summer-houses, temples, tea and coffee canteens, sycamore groves, and long alleys, suitable to the miserable climate. It would be well if the English would throw off the phlegmatic, cold, calculating, money-saving habits they seem so fond of, and join together with a little more generous public spirit in local enterprises, uniting *pleasure* with schemes for improvement.[38]

It would have been difficult for the model village builders to respond to this admonition even if they had known or cared about it. But they were soon to invest "a more generous spirit in local enterprises," and this was done with a considerable degree of awareness of the surrounding natural beauty.

36. T. W. Hanson, *Story of Old Halifax* (Halifax, King, 1920), pp. 209–10.

37. F. W. Ledgar, in "The Pattern, Structure and Character of Building Settlement in Rural England 1550–1850" (unpublished Ph.D. thesis, University of Manchester, 1956, p. 85),

says, "Some of the mill stone grits, when freshly quarried, range in colour from a warm light brown to a pinkish gray which fosters the belief that, in the absence of air pollution, at least some of the harshness would disappear."

38. (London, Smith, Elder), pp. 124–26.

By the first quarter of the eighteenth century it was already a hard-working, pragmatic landscape. Daniel Defoe in his *Tour* of 1724–27 described the land around Halifax as follows:

> Then it was I began to perceive the Reason and Nature of the Thing, and found the Division of the Land into small Pieces, and scattering of the Dwellings was occasioned by, and done for the Convenience of the Business which the People were generally employ'd in . . . We could see that almost at every House there was a *Tenter* and almost on every Tenter a Piece of *Cloth,* or Kersie, or Shalloon . . . so every Manufacturer generally keeps a Cow or two, or more, for his Family, and This employs the two, or three, or four Pieces of enclosed Land about his House, for they scarce sow Corn enough for Their Cocks and Hens; . . . Among the Manufacturers Houses are likewise scattered an infinite number of Cottages or Small Dwellings, in which the Workmen which are employed, the Women and Children of whom, are always busy Carding, Spinning, &c. so that no Hands being unemploy'd, even from the youngest to the antient . . . hardly anything above four years old, but its Hands are sufficient to its self.[39]

In this description lies the explanation of many facets of the present scene, particularly the small fields and the little houses high up on the hillside terraces. It required only the "putter-out," mentioned by Akroyd as beginning the factory system—the "factor" who gathered the production of the cottages —and the intermediate construction and abandonment of the water mills for wool manufacture in the moorland cloughs, before the population could be induced to move from the heights to cluster in the valley bottoms around the coal-burning factories. And it suggests the origin of child and female labor in the nineteenth-century factories, why working hours were so long, and why cheap corn from outside the country would someday be so favored.

 Copley

The first of the model villages of the Bradford–Halifax School was Copley, two miles out of Halifax (Fig. 5). Twenty acres were purchased as a mill estate by the Akroyd firm in 1844. In 1846 a second mill was built, equal in size to

39. Vol. III (London, Strahan, 1727), pp. 98–101.

Fig. 5. Copley Model Village near Halifax; George Gilbert Scott and W. H. Crossland(?), 1844–53. The Akroyd factory lies on a bend of the River Calder. The railroad viaduct runs across the foreground.

the older one completed about 1837.[1] The model houses went up during the years 1849–53 "to be secure against the sudden withdrawal of workpeople."[2] They were contained in three long rows, together with four shops. There still exists an older row of seven cottages near the mill (Fig. 6). These are said to have served as drying houses for a yet earlier woollen mill.[3] They have no style beyond a certain chunky, diminutive effect that places them around 1800–20,[4] and represents an earlier type of workers' domicile.

The older cottages are built along the easy curve of the river; the Akroyd units are backed against the railroad embankment. The tracks were com-

1. "Copley," Part 1, Turner Clippings of the Halifax Public Library, *4* (June 19, 1880), 222.

2. Ibid., Part 2, says, "It became evident [in 1846] that if the undertaking was to be secure against the sudden withdrawal of workpeople, some provision of dwellings must be made other than those which then existed." With the success of Copley the Boy Mill at Luddenden Foot was closed and most of the workers transferred

to Copley. Col. Akroyd gives the date for the cottages of 1849–53 in his *On Improved Dwellings,* p. 4.

3. Ibid.

4. Ibid., p. 5. I owe these dates and whatever other understanding I have of these seven cottages to the late Professor R. A. Cordingley at the University of Manchester.

Fig. 6. Earlier cottages at Copley, 1800–20; probably once used as drying houses for the mill.

pleted in 1842, two years before the land at Copley was bought by the firm.[5] In an old print of Copley the embankment lies just above the roofs of the houses (Fig. 7). The householders looked up over the low walls of the conveniences and piggeries to the rails along which the trains ran rapidly and inexorably through the countryside, across the viaducts, through the tunnels and cuts, beside the canals, on a direct line that brooked no interference. The railroad embankment was there first and the row houses followed its cue. Still the question remains why they were built so close to it. An article of 1880 states that Colonel Akroyd had originally wished to place them upon the hill in back, farther from the factory and near the present site of the forking railroad branch into Halifax.[6] A look at the ground persuades one, however, that he may have been thinking of the final location of the road leading by the dwellings to the mill. The garden allotments, kept tidy at company

5. Geoffrey Capener, "A Study of Copley Vale, Halifax," unpublished thesis, Borough Road Training College, Isleworth, Middlesex (1955), p. 5. Mr. Capener states that the larger viaduct was completed in 1840 and the smaller one in July 1844. The date given in the Turner Clippings for opening the main line of the railroad is also 1842. The important point is, of course, to discover which came first at Copley, the railroad or the row house.

6. Turner Clippings, "Copley," Part 2.

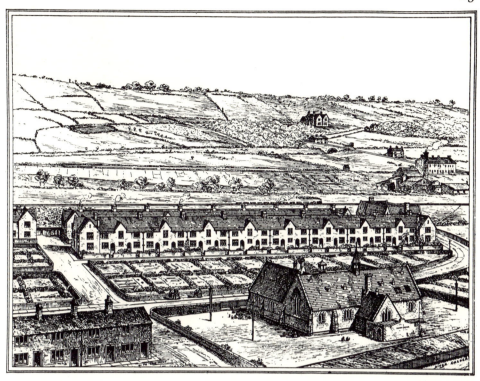

Fig. 7. Bird's-eye view of Copley. The back-to-back houses were Gothicized and prefaced with allotments. The earlier "folk" cottages are at the lower left. At the lower right is the village school.

expense, would thus be made especially conspicuous in front of the houses. The flower and vegetable show was the occasion of the annual visit of Colonel Akroyd and his friends to the village. Another possible reason for the layout was the frequent flooding of the Calder, although the plain was so flat here that building back from the river was a negligible advantage. On November 16 of 1866 the water spilled over its banks in the early morning hours and had covered the streets to the height of two or three feet by daylight. The pigs had to be rescued and removed to the weaving shed of the factory and the stable of The Volunteers' Arms and by afternoon the workers were isolated from their homes.[7] The sanitary commission, having had to cope with previous inundations, finally caused a strong wall to be constructed along the river, which improved the drainage to such an extent that this was the last flood. The same commission, seldom at rest, also changed the name of Pig Street to Railway Terrace, to the resentment of those model villagers who were already settling into their mental habits.

7. Ibid.

The older row of houses had seven units in it, whereas the model blocks of Akroyd had eighteen to each front, thirty-six in all.[8] The first block built was that facing the allotments. When the second block was put up behind it, Pig Street was created against the railway embankment, and the beginnings of an urban "corridor" or interminable street appeared between. This effect in the intervening St. Stephen's Street was due to the extraordinary regularity and length of the blocks (Fig. 8). The double row of houses in the open setting at this early date is interesting for its incongruity.

Fig. 8. St. Stephen's Street, Copley; a corridor street, but with open country beyond. The houses are of one and, less frequently, two bedrooms.

There was no longer any thought of weaving in the houses. The company provided a special shed for the older hand combers and weavers, much as John Foster did at his Black Dyke Mill between Halifax and Bradford, where he kept the hand workers going until they died out.[9]

The new age was typified in the neo-Gothic blocks by a tall, flat, thin, dry,

8. Except that the third and last row had forty units in it which cost only £90 apiece.

9. Bretton, "Colonel Edward Akroyd," p. 74, and J. S. Fletcher, *The Making of Modern Yorkshire 1750–1914* (London, Allen and Unwin, 1918), p. 142. Mr. T. A. Hoyle, the present owner of Copley, writes in a letter of July 18, 1960, that he never heard that hand weaving took place in the older cottages near the river, although he had been told that there was some hand weaving in the village.

pen-and-ink kind of facade which sought to relieve the monotony of extension by assigning one gable and chimney cluster to each two houses in the
earliest block and concluding the rows with larger gables and projecting
bays. The roofs, in true neo-Gothic style, are steeper than those of the seven
older cottages which were equipped with the traditional low Pennine slope,
usually of thirty-five degrees, dictated by the strong local winds and heavy
roofing flags into which the millstone grit naturally split.[10]

Self-conscious architect's architecture, or, as it might be called for its book-
ish flavor, black and white building, had now come into vogue. This new
fashion deserves some emphasis, for it is obvious that the village builders had
a specific objective in mind when they went to the trouble and expense of
academic styling for domiciles intended for the lowest economic level.[11]
Colonel Akroyd states in his essay, *On Improved Dwellings for the Working
Classes,* that the Gothic was a thoroughly conscious choice:

> A picturesque outline was adopted in a modified old English style,
> approximating to the character of many old dwellings in the neigh-
> bourhood, and also in harmony with the beautiful site, which lies
> on a bend of the river Calder. In front of the cottages facing the
> river are allotment gardens, flanked by a recreation ground; and
> on the bank is seated the village school with its separate play yards.
> On the opposite side it is proposed to erect a church, of which the
> foundations are laid; meanwhile a weekly service is held in the
> school room. A classroom serves for the village library and news-
> room.[12]

The purpose of the houses was not only to gather a "sufficient number of
operatives" but also to improve "their social condition." An attractive community harmonizing with tradition and providing all the institutional needs
was sought, even though the village, as distinguished from the architecture,
was still rudimentary in plan, amounting to little more than rows of houses
and a mill at the end.

There was one great flaw in the housing, according to contemporary and
later accounts. The Akroyd units were of the much-condemned back-to-back

10. F. W. Ledgar (n. 37 above), p. 84.

11. Professor Nikolaus Pevsner in his guide
to the West Riding, *The Buildings of England*
(London, Penguin, 1959, p. 170), observes that
the architect of the church at Copley, St.
Stephen's, was W. H. Crossland, who also appears to have taken Akroydon over from Scott.

Professor Henry-Russell Hitchcock (*Early Victorian Architecture in Britain,* New Haven,
Yale University Press, 1954, p. 462) suggests
that Crossland was probably the architect of
Copley. Despite a further search, I have not
been able to improve on these conjectures.

12. Pp. 4–5.

or half-house type, having only a living room downstairs and, in Blocks Two
and Three, merely one bedroom upstairs. Akroyd defended this arrangement
by describing it as also "in the common style of the country." He says that
the single bedroom was required by a class of tenant unwilling to pay for the
two bedrooms of the earlier Block One.[13] The downstairs living room was to
be used nocturnally by the parents in its "shut-up" bedstead. As for the back-
to-back feature, he remarked, "notwithstanding the well-founded objections
raised against this mode of structure on account of deficient ventilation, practically no inconvenience has been found in this respect. The windows are
well provided with lattice openings, and the staircase also conveys ventilation."[14]

The Builder, in commenting upon Copley in the next year, 1863, does not
let him off so easily. "There can be no apology for back-to-back houses," this
journal says, "and though it is one of the common features of the country in
this neighbourhood, we believe strong efforts are now being made to put a
stop to the practice."[15] Parliamentary action to outlaw back-to-back houses
had indeed begun in the 1840s, but it was not until 1909 that they were made
illegal everywhere. The article goes on to soften its criticism by noting that
the Copley types are undoubtedly the best examples of the half-house that
can be found in Yorkshire and that in the open country the type is not so
pernicious as in the city. With a final burst of Victorian eloquence, which in
its abundance and clarity of detail resembles the architectural styles of the
era, it concludes:

> The fair test of the system is to be found in the lowest parts of a
> manufacturing town, where every foot of ground is valuable, and
> where the factory smoke pollutes the air, and the dye houses poison
> the streams; where streets cannot well be described than as canals in
> wet weather, and the tracks of simoons in dry weather; where it is
> difficult to get air at all, and impossible to get it untainted by the
> chimneys and the sewers; where the refuse of a thickly populated
> district lies rotting on the open streets, and the gutters do duty for
> more than surface drainage. In such a place—and there are many—
> what must it be *never* to have a draught of air through the house?
> . . . At Leeds, for instance, where this system of half-houses is the
> most common, the people have been said to succeed in everything
> but in making health; and it has been asserted that the rates of mor-

13. P. 5.
14. Ibid.

15. (Feb. 14), p. 109.

tality are higher than can be accounted for, except by the explanation that the people are cannibals, and live upon each other as surely as if they eat one another.[16]

A somewhat crabbed description it is, but it grasps implicitly what was just beginning to be recognized through such discussions, namely, that building types, no matter how standardized or "universal," still conveyed little meaning if judged outside their particular environment. James Hole of Leeds, another authority of the period, in writing about Copley approached the same view:

> It is commonly supposed that the objection to back to back houses is the defective ventilation. Ventilation is quite practicable in back to back houses, though it is seldom attended to. The objection to back to back houses exists more specially in towns, where, on account of the limited space, each house cannot have its own conveniences, without either obtruding a nuisance on the public street, or using water-closets, a wasteful way of disposing of valuable material.[17]

It is difficult today to avoid evaluating a model village as a fixed quantity in time. It ostensibly lacks the potential for change and informal growth. In planner's terms, it is not "organic." Yet a brief review of the history of the Copley site itself shows that while Akroyd was alive it supported a higher level of existence than before or since. During the period of 1837–44 just before his advent: "the locality had obtained a somewhat unenviable notoriety. Gamblers made the mill a constant resort, rows and disturbances occurred, and not infrequently persons met with serious ill-treatment from roughs of this character."[18] By 1880, after Akroyd's day, "Some of the older inhabitants are becoming ashamed of many of those who now live here— 'foreigners' they choose to call them, inasmuch as they are neither Halifax nor Yorkshire born, but hail from the south." They were unworthy of a village formerly so "select" and "charming."[19] The "foreigners" were apt to be prodigal, intemperate and, worst of all, untidy. The lesson follows from all the villages. The model without the man to give it purpose and cohesion could, and often did, deteriorate seriously.

---

16. Ibid.
17. *The Homes of the Working Classes* (London, Longmans, Green, 1866), p. 70.
18. Turner Clippings, "Copley," Part 1.
19. Ibid., Part 2.

Fig. 9. Saltaire factory and village from Saltaire Park; Lockwood and Mawson, 1850–63. Unlike the other model villages, Saltaire was rational and antiromantic. The Congregational Chapel and wool factory face across Victoria Road. Both buildings and the name of the road are highly expressive of the moral and commercial commitment behind the origin.

 Saltaire

Saltaire (Fig. 9) represents the next step beyond Copley. Titus Salt, the son, said in 1876 that he was almost weary of hearing of its promised completion.[1] But unlike the other model villages, it was intended to be entirely self-sufficient from the outset.

Saltaire was considerably larger than Copley. It originally contained 792 houses, contrasted with 112 in Copley. When Salt engaged his architects Lockwood and Mawson in November 1850, he instructed them to build the factory first, the cottages second.[2] Employment was available from only the one company, but it was there when the workers moved into the houses, an advantage arising from amassed capital and single control which was never to be equaled in later history. Before the houses were constructed (1853–63) the laborers commuted the three or four miles from Bradford, just as special

1. Balgarnie, *Sir Titus Salt,* p. 287.   2. Ibid., p. 117.

trains were run the day of the opening of the factory. The other unique outcome was that Saltaire, far from acting as a decentralizing influence on the
affairs of the company, led to consolidating the operations of Salt's six mills
in Bradford, which brought the labor supply into such proximity that any
kind of transport became unnecessary.[3] Everyone was provided with housing
at Saltaire except Sir Titus, who never got around to building a mansion,
although he had selected a site above the works.[4]

Those who regard the planning of the garden city and new town as too
loose and undisciplined, too low in density, and lacking in urbanity, find
comfort in Saltaire. Robert Dewhirst has described the gross density of Saltaire as several times greater than that of the new towns (Fig. 10), pointing
out that despite this it has continued to function satisfactorily as a model village for over a century, compensating for its density with the balance of its
institutions and services.[5] Such green spaces as exist are conservatively handled; they face Victoria Road, like the forty- and sixty-foot setbacks in front
of the Institute and the school and the Alexandra Quadrangle (Fig. 11)
around which the forty-five almshouses for the aged and retired are grouped.[6]
However, in true mid-nineteenth-century style, the major open area is concentrated in the fourteen-acre park across the Aire from the houses and factory.[7] The density of the buildings reinforces the Italianate mode which the
architects affected and results in a blend of *quattrocento* (Fig. 12), with the
brooding, introspective character of the Brontë sisters' village of Haworth up
in the moors not far away (Fig. 13). The soot depresses every color, and the
fact that the community and factory are no longer in symbiotic relationship
no doubt intensifies this austere and solitary effect today.

The pavilion units of the housing, projecting in some locations and standing free in others, varied between two and three stories according to the
number of bedrooms and hence the size of the family that went with each
house, but suggested no essential social distinction (Fig. 14). The overlookers'
and managers' houses were grouped by themselves along Albert Road on the
western edge of the town. Each of these had a small garden in front. The

3. *Leeds Mercury* (Dec. 30, 1876) says his
first mill in Bradford was Thompson's, followed
shortly by the acquisition of Hollings', Brick-
lane, Beecroft, and Union Mills. William Cud-
worth in *Saltaire: A Sketch*, published by the
Salt Co. in 1895, mentions that there were six
but does not list them (p. 18).

4. Balgarnie, p. 184.

5. Dewhirst, *Town Planning Review* (July
1960), pp. 141–42.

6. The growth of Shipley as a suburb of
Bradford was in part explained by the excellent
schools at Saltaire. *Shipley (and District)
Through the Camera* (Leeds, Hanson and Oak,
1902), p. 10.

7. The *London Times* (Sept. 22, 1853) mentions "spacious squares, with gardens attached"
but whether this was an exaggeration of existing conditions or something vaguely planned is
not clear.

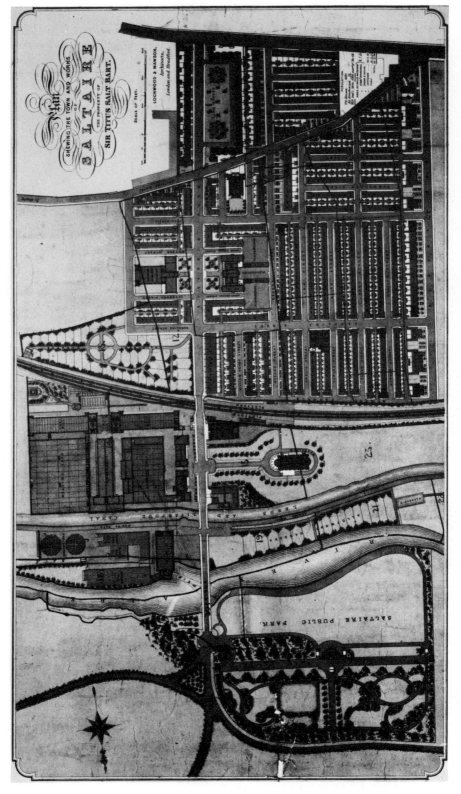

Fig. 10. Plan of Saltaire by Lockwood and Mawson. The population was to be 4,356. Although the ancient roads and river had some effect, the borders of the fields were not permitted to distort the regularity of the scheme. This could have happened only in the 1850s.

Fig. 11. Almshouses facing Victoria Road, Saltaire. The quad arrangement of the cottages follows the medieval tradition of the district. Across the street was the hospital and the institute and club and farther down the great factory itself. Above are the moors, the ancient recreation ground. The tenants of these almshouses presented Salt with a gold-headed cane and spectacles when he reached an appropriate age.

Fig. 12. Boarding houses on Caroline Street, Saltaire. The neo-Renaissance buildings lent the atmosphere of an ideal fifteenth-century Italian town, but with some of the austerity of Yorkshire and the regimentation and anonymity of developing industrialism.

Fig. 13. Black Bull Hotel, Haworth. The quiet and brooding atmosphere of Saltaire, the square arrangement of its forms, and the hip roofs were in some respects anticipated by the villages on the moors like Haworth, where the Brontë sisters lived.

Fig. 14. Looking down George Street, Saltaire. The tower of the Congregational Chapel and the Salt mausoleum appear at the end. It can be noticed here how well the blocks and the arcuated rhythm of the ground floors go with a grid plan for the town.

Renaissance style established a uniform three-dimensionality rather than the linearism and flat silhouette of Akroyd's neo-Gothic, through which Akroyd hoped to arouse in the working man an appreciation for the beauty of out-lines and an interest in a native tradition. The neo-Renaissance adapts well to the regularity of the nineteenth-century row-in-block plan, and one notices this particularly at the corners. The arcuated rhythm of the ground-story windows and doors also conducts the eye easily along the street.

There were no back-to-back houses at Saltaire. Small backyards were pro-vided on rear service lanes, each with privy, ashpit, and coal storage. The rooms have much the same interior dimensions as those of Copley, but there are more of them. In the workingmen's cottages there is a living room in front (14 x 13 feet) and a good-sized scullery in back (14 x 9 feet) with two, three, or four bedrooms above. At Copley and Saltaire the stairwells had to be closed to avoid draughts. These were then put to another use as well, be-coming a scullery at Copley and, more suitably, a vestibule and closet at Saltaire. The overlookers' cottages were distinguished only by the introduc-tion of a through stairhall and slightly larger rooms.

The absence of street incidents is still striking upon entering Saltaire. It has a tidy, fixed, and diagrammatic quality that somehow recalls James Silk Buckingham's Victoria city project of 1849. We learn from old accounts that Sir Titus did not appreciate clutter in his town.[8] On one occasion he in-structed a photographer to remove a platform in the street immediately, de-laying his usual work until this was accomplished. He did not want to see clothing lines or other paraphernalia, either.[9] This was a chronic problem for districts without back yards. The Leeds Corporation *Statistical Report* of 1839 stated that in Leeds with its back-to-back housing nearly half the streets were "weekly so full of lines and linen as to be impassable for horses and carriages, and almost for foot passengers."[10] In 1893 a Leeds newspaper was still complaining about this result of overcrowding (Fig. 15). To take care of the problem in his town, Salt set up a steam laundry with a remarkable sched-ule: clothes washed, dried, mangled, and folded within the hour.[11]

Although Salt's gratitude to his architects, Lockwood and Mawson, prompted him to name two streets after them, it is evident that he was a man with a reputation for taste and little hesitation in applying it. His occupa-tion must have conditioned him in that direction. His obituary in the *Leeds*

8. Balgarnie, p. 144.
9. J. Horsfall Turner, *Historical Notices of Shipley, Saltaire, Idle, Windhill, Etc.* (Idle, Ship-ley Express Offices, 1901), pp. 40–41.

10. A reprint with a foreword by Mr. Coun-cillor Hawkyard, M.D. (Leeds, 1932), p. 12.
11. Balgarnie, pp. 144–45.

Fig. 15. Nineteenth-century street in the Hunslet District of Leeds. The custom of hanging laundry in the public thoroughfare, to which Titus Salt so vehemently objected, still survives.

Mercury states that he took great pride in furnishing his large estate, Crow Nest, "for he had an almost faultless eye for beauty of form and colour as well as for excellence of texture or quality, and though simple in his personal attire and careful in all his expenditure, he could not tolerate any mean surroundings."[12]

Admiration for his discriminatory powers was not unanimous, however. J. S. Fletcher in his *Picturesque History of Yorkshire* toward the end of the century saw little to praise in Saltaire. His only excuse for a careful inspection of it would be "for the sake of proving how very uninteresting and featureless a model village may be made."[13] It gladdened him to think that the utopian age was still far distant, when he left Saltaire for the ancient weaving village of Baildon on the hillside just above (Fig. 16). This village was a traditional center for hostility toward machinery.[14] The sympathy of the author for the antique and picturesque prejudiced him against the orderly coding of Saltaire. He considered it regimented and unrelated to its natural

12. (Dec. 30, 1876).
13. (London, Dent, 1899), *1*, 397.
14. Parsons, *Civil . . . History of Leeds . . . Etc.* (*1*, 230) tells of a power loom being seized there by weavers from constables in 1822, smashed, and then having its roller and warp dragged through the streets to be derided by the populace.

Fig. 16. Baildon Village, just above Saltaire. Again the two- and three-story buildings with low roofs are seen. Baildon was a center of hostility to mechanization and in 1822 a power loom was dragged through the streets to the hoots and jeers of the mob, much as the aristocrats in tumbrels were treated during the French Revolution.

surroundings. And, indeed, even now its foursquare shapes, brackets, string courses, deep reveals, and arcading do appear heavy-handed and arbitrary when compared with the folk architecture of the surrounding region. Nevertheless, for all his visual acuity, Fletcher did miss important aspects of Saltaire. In praising nearby Bradford as an up-and-coming town where new buildings around the two railroad stations demonstrated its wealth and made it "pleasing to the eye," and where industry and commerce were not allowed to "obtrude themselves in disagreeable or unpleasant fashion,"[15] he failed to recognize that Saltaire was its working-class equivalent, made more complete, even though smaller. A local source reveals that "Lockwood and Mawson were virtually the architectural dictators of Bradford" between 1850 and 1880 when most of the buildings in the center were rebuilt.[16] "The city," it adds, "owes its essential character to them." Mercantile pride in the appear-

15. Ibid., p. 409; Baines in his *Yorkshire Past and Present* (2, Part 1, 335) also notes the imposing appearance of Bradford. Pride in appearance, which is also evident in the urban and model village undertakings of the Crossleys, was a factor much to be reckoned with in the employment of architects in this region.

16. Undated newspaper clipping in the Bradford Public Library.

ance of buildings, which shows up both in the urban centers and the model villages, can be substantiated, since capable architects were employed to design them.

Professor Hitchcock has noticed the excellence of the ashlar stereometry and the dignity of the detailing at Saltaire.[17] The neo-Renaissance mode was typical of the industrial and commercial rebirth of Bradford, along with the more usual "French Gothic." Lockwood and Mawson, with the other leading architectural firms of Bradford, Andrews and Pepper, and Milnes and French, employed it regularly as an alternative style. If the architecture of Saltaire be further compared with earlier villages like Haworth or Baildon, other similarities emerge. The variation between two- and three-story buildings was entirely traditional as was the low slope of the Saltaire roofs. At Haworth the Black Bull Hotel (Fig. 13), where the brother of the Brontë sisters spent a good deal of his time, is capped with a low hipped roof and has exactly the same feeling of foursquare solidity as the three-story corner pavilions of Saltaire. There can be no denial of the pedantry of Saltaire, but it may not be so artificial and foreign to the district as it has been described. It was the product of an era, and this, rather than its lack of reference to the region, is probably what annoyed Fletcher. The decade of the fifties was one of simple initiative and direct thought, moving temporarily away from the attitudes of Romanticism. Earlier accounts had described Bradford as one of the smokiest and dirtiest towns in the kingdom, and it is with this in mind, rather than the supposed need for picturesqueness, that we must judge Saltaire. Contemporary eyewitnesses like James Hole observed: "We find none of the squalor and filth which seem so prevalent among the dwellings of the operatives elsewhere. The streets and pavements are moderately wide, and they are clean and tidy."[18] Saltaire's plainness and geometric purity were virtues for him as they must have been for Sir Titus.

Salt was a man who made a fortune by using the alpaca wool which others passed over, according to Dickens' portrayal of "The Great Yorkshire Llama" in his *Household Words*. Salt could seriously contemplate buying part of the London Crystal Palace (where Salt, Akroyd, and Crossley had exhibited in 1851) as a weaving shed and as reasonably reject it when, upon inspection, it did not appear able to withstand the weight and vibration of machinery.[19] He had also been an alderman, mayor (1848–49), chief constable, president

17. Hitchcock, *Early Victorian Architecture in Britain*, p. 461.

18. Hole, *Homes of the Working Classes*, p. 67.

19. Balgarnie, p. 120.

of the Bradford Chamber of Commerce (1856–57), and Member of Parliament from Bradford (1859–61).[20] Shortly before he undertook Saltaire, he was considering retirement. But, as he later explained to Lord Harewood, the Lord Lieutenant of the West Riding, he changed his mind because, while a nobleman may make his influence felt on society through his rank and estates, a manufacturer has only his business. Saltaire, a factory town, thus became the medium for his social self-expression.[21] The architect Lockwood said Salt wished to secure the "health, intellectual culture and rational recreation of the operatives."[22] He celebrated his fiftieth birthday on September 20, 1853, at the grand opening of his stupendous works with 3,750 guests present.[23] A poem read then undoubtedly reflects something of his own feeling as seen through the shining eyes of his admirers:

> The Peer who inherits an ancient estate,
>   And cheers many hearts with his pelf,
> We honour and love: but is that man less great
>   Who founds his own fortune himself?
> *Chorus*
> For this is his praise—and who merit it not
>   Deserve no good luck should o'ertake them,—
> That while making his thousands, he never forgot
>   The thousands that helped him to make them![24]

Although an avowed and active Congregationalist, as his biographer and friend the Congregationalist Reverend Robert Balgarnie often took occasion to remark, he tried whenever possible to encourage other churches at Saltaire by donating land and money. He believed in both religious and secular education as a method of improving the workingman's approach to life, and he went about providing for these assiduously. On the main street above the factory were the schools and the Institute, containing a number of recreational and educational facilities. There was a health officer for overseeing the medical requirements of the town, and an infirmary was placed opposite the almshouse green on the same Victoria Street, conveniently near both the factory, in case of industrial accidents, and the elderly. Cholera, typhus, and rheumatic fever were materially reduced by the planning. The doctor's re-

20. *Leeds Mercury* (Dec. 30, 1876) and Holroyd, *Saltaire and Its Founder*, p. 81.

21. Balgarnie, p. 122.

22. *Illustrated London News* (Oct. 1, 1853), p. 288.

23. *London Times* (Sept. 22, 1853). *Builder,* *12,* 437–38.

24. Holroyd, pp. 16–17. Holroyd was the keeper of the news and book shop at Saltaire. The poem was by Mr. Robert Storey, the Craven poet.

port to the Paris Exposition of 1867 observed that the closeness of the factory to the houses helped to eliminate tuberculosis, since long, wet, cold journeys were avoided between work and home.[25]

One form of enjoyment that Salt would not tolerate in his town was alcoholic beverages. He and his son Titus tried to "supply the advantages of a public house, without its evils" through the recreation rooms at the Institute.[26] According to Balgarnie, Salt had early served on the grand jury in Leeds and had come away convinced that "drink and lust" were at the bottom of all human crime and misery.[27] That he was not without a sense of humor, despite his deep conviction in such matters, is evident from the fact that when he handed out cigars to distinguished guests he always placed an anti-smoking tract on top of the box.[28] He had been able to give up the habit himself.

 Akroydon

Akroydon in Halifax (Fig. 17) was the second venture of Colonel Edward Akroyd. The principles on which it was established are of more than incidental interest because they show that he was well aware of the reform movements of his era. In the North these were aimed essentially toward the abolition of the Corn Laws, promotion of universal suffrage, and cooperative movements. All three model village builders at some time spoke for a wider distribution of the vote. The desire for a larger voice applied to cities as well as individuals, and it was the commercial phase of political reform that came first. The Parliamentary Reform Bill of 1832 and the Municipal Corporations Act of 1835 meant that the towns of the West Riding would have a greater opportunity to determine their national role. Bradford, Halifax, and Leeds shortly before the model villages were undertaken, had sought and obtained charters of incorporation. Salt, Akroyd, and the Crossleys were able to become mayors and M.P.s as a result.

The novelty of Akroydon was that it sought to promote home ownership among the workers. The Halifax Union Building Society, more popularly known as the "Go-a-head Society," had been founded in 1845. Part of its purpose was to enlarge the number of forty-shilling freeholders and thus increase the local vote. Mortgages had been issued by it in the name of three trustees, two of whom were Colonel Akroyd and Mr. Frank Crossley. The Akroydon

25. Balgarnie, pp. 224–25.
26. Holroyd, p. 51.

27. Balgarnie, p. 227.
28. Ibid., p. 215.

Fig. 17. Akroydon Model Village, Halifax; G. G. Scott and W. H. Crossland, 1861–63. The hollow central park was a step toward the single garden and was oddly prophetic of Letchworth.

Building Association of 1860 was capitalized by the Halifax Permanent Benefit Building Society which had been founded in 1852. The latter was to provide the same service for West Hills Park, following the policies of the earlier Union Building Society.[1] In practice, the building association put up three quarters and the future owner one quarter of the cost of a house. In the event the new purchaser was unable to furnish the down payment, Akroyd himself underwrote the quarter for a period of three years.[2] His personal capital had previously been tied up by Copley, hence his appeal to the Halifax Building Society in this instance.[3] The average run of a mortgage at the time was twelve to thirteen years. The possibility was also discussed by Hole of a new advance, equal to the original sum lent, in case of sickness or unemployment.[4]

The building association thus acted as a savings bank and a benefit society. But, as Akroyd observed, the previous experience of the "Go-a-head" "also elicited the defects of their plan, exposing the natural tendency to build cheap and flimsy houses devoid of architectural proportion and beauty, thereby indicating to me the mode in which I might work with them, and assist them to help themselves in this praiseworthy direction, if they would allow me the privilege."[5] Yet because of the rapid increase of population in the town, it had been possible to resell even these "cheap and flimsy" houses at a 30 or 40 per cent profit. He envisioned a similar occurrence with his own houses at Akroydon. The figures of the census of 1871, when compared to those of 1861 (when Akroydon was started), would appear to bear out his prediction. By annexation and other means the parish was enlarged by 25,325 inhabitants during that decade, the greatest gain of the century.[6]

Encouraging the freehold privilege for the lower economic levels in the North was practicable because the workers lived in row houses instead of in large tenements, as in London, where there were numerous flats under one roof. Akroyd was ready to admit that a modification of his idiom would be necessary in London because of the high land values, but he felt that the absence of the development of the ownership and savings principle was unfortunate.[7]

1. Enoch Hill, *The Faith of Fifty-Three: A Brief History of the Halifax Permanent Building Society* (Halifax, 1921), pp. 37–41. The Mt. Pleasant District of Halifax was originally called "Go Ahead" because of its financing by the Union Building Society. D. Taylor, "Halifax Streets and Buildings," *Trans. Halifax Antiquarian Society* (April 7, 1959), p. 64.

2. Hole, *Homes of the Working Classes*, p. 73.

3. Akroyd, *On Improved Dwellings*, p. 6.

4. Hole, p. 88.

5. Akroyd, p. 7.

6. *The Victoria History of the Counties of England: Yorkshire, 3* (London, Constable, 1913), 533.

7. Akroyd, pp. 14, 15.

The site for Akroydon was on the hillside sloping down to the edge of the
Hebble Valley. The rows were to consist of only eight to ten units, to facili-
tate access to the service alleys between. There were to be no back-to-back
houses this time. Already the vision, pursued through the whole garden city
venture like a holy grail, is in evidence. *The Builder* observes, "Mr. Akroyd
is very desirous of keeping up the old English notion of a village—the squire
and the parson, as the head and centre of all progress and good fellowship;
then the tenant-farmers; and lastly, the working population."[8]

Such was the social vision. Connected with it again was the aesthetic admiration for the native cottage architecture. Akroyd relates:

> In 1859 I consulted the eminent architect, Mr. George Gilbert
> Scott, and commissioned him to furnish plans and designs in the
> domestic Gothic. This type was adopted not solely for the gratifica-
> tion of my own taste, but because it is the original of the parish of
> Halifax, over which many old houses are scattered of the date of the
> Commonwealth, or shortly after, and retaining the best features of
> the Elizabethan domestic architecture. Intuitively this taste of our
> forefathers pleases the fancy, strengthens house and home attach-
> ment, entwines the present with the memory of the past, and prom-
> ises, in spite of opposition and prejudice, to become the national
> style of modern, as it was of old England.[9]

Akroyd's view differed from that of the architects of Saltaire in that he
preferred a "native" to a "foreign" style. He was anxious to heal the breach
in feeling between the ancient village and the new industrial age. Yet the
medieval picturesque incident, of which Fletcher was so fond, could not actually be revived in a nineteenth-century neo-Gothic village any more than it
could be in a neo-Renaissance one like Saltaire. It was still a vision from a
book, a product off the drawing board, set down in a very literal environment. A building could not sag, a roof line waver, or a wall bulge. The streets,
the sidewalks, the lintel, ridge, and cornice lines must remain sharply defined
and parallel. As at Copley and Saltaire, the multiplicity of the units caused
the straight lines to repeat and reinforce each other. The speed and scale of
construction and precise units of measurement strengthened the uniform

8. (Feb. 14, 1863), p. 110.

9. Akroyd, p. 8. W. H. Crossland, a pupil of
Scott finished the designs. A booklet describing
St. Stephen's at Copley (Halifax, 1865, p. 4)
states that Crossland was only able to proceed
with the plans after Scott and the Rev. B.
Webb, editor of the *Ecclesiologist*, approved
them. Perhaps some such arrangement was also
in force for Copley and Akroydon.

effect. The tightness and coarseness of the whole are more marked today in the houses that have been repointed. The white grid of the joints makes one overly conscious of repetitive striations in the facades and the street and building lines of the whole village (Fig. 18).

Fig. 18. York Terrace, Akroydon. The white grid of mortar brought out by the repointing betrays the Victorian artifice. The houses could not be authentically medieval in appearance, as Akroyd hoped. The dormers are tokens of status, and were bitterly argued.

We learn from Akroyd's report that the imposition of a conscious style was a struggle. He says:

> In my own case the public battled stoutly against the Gothic for some time; although they liked the look of it, they considered it antiquated, inconvenient, wanting in light, and not adapted to modern requirements. The dormer windows were supposed to resemble the style of almshouses, and the independent workmen who formed the building association positively refused to accept this feature of the Gothic, which to their minds was degrading. This point I was obliged to concede.[10]

10. Akroyd, p. 8.

As compensation for this first *gaffe,* Akroyd had a new feature added, a stone shield over each front door with the owner's monogram or device imprinted upon it, by which they were "much gratified." It was a time that introduced many such tokens, the supreme one being, of course, the royal couple, Victoria and Albert, to whom so many objects are dedicated in the North, including the central park and monument at Akroydon.[11] The range of social fluidity was enormous in contrast to earlier days. The mother of the Crossleys liked to recount that when she was in service with a Miss Oldfield and informed her family in 1800 she was about to marry a Crossley, her yeoman father sent word that he would disown her if she married a weaver, even if he were a foreman of weavers.[12] Three of her boys by the weaver were to become millionaires, one was knighted, and all were conversant with nobility and men of large affairs. Ultimately a coat of arms was applied for and received by the Crossleys, and it appeared thereafter on the family's philanthropic buildings.

Akroydon employs dormers and gables to relieve the monotony of the row house, as did Copley. Like Saltaire it has projections in some units which reflect a difference of internal plan. These plans alternate between pairs of houses of the parlor-plus-kitchen and the single-living-room types. One writer had misgivings about the parlor house out of fear that the workman might dwell only in the kitchen, especially in winter, and keep the larger and better room idle for "Sunday best." On the other hand, as the argument always runs, "More gifted workmen have been driven from their homes to places of less profitable resort, through the want of a quiet room in their own houses, than perhaps by any other circumstance."[13]

The absence of ground about the houses should also be considered in this connection. The case for the individual garden is put forth later on exactly these terms, as a device that could generate a sense of pride and attachment and that might also keep the owner more healthfully occupied than the corner pub. The substitute for the individual garden at Akroydon was the central park and a group of allotments for cultivating vegetables, just outside the plan. Akroyd perceived the need to relate the occupant to the ownership of the house in order to promote social and psychological stability. But he had

11. On the south side of the monument was a figure of Queen Victoria and the inscription "Erected as a monument of Christian reverence for the emblem of the Cross and of Loyalty to our sovereign Lady Queen Victoria, by Edward Akroyd, the founder of Akroydon, 1875, Fear God: Honour The King," and on the opposite side a long quotation from Wordsworth's *Excursion,* Book VI (*Halifax Courier,* Nov. 26, 1887). See also *Building News* (May 11, 1877), p. 464.

12. Bretton, "Crossleys of Dean Clough," Part I (1950), p. 5.

13. *Builder* (Feb. 14, 1863), p. 110.

not arrived at the same conclusion in regard to the land. That he also had no wish to take advantage of the old English device of establishing a green square in order to boost the value of houses built around it is suggested by a much more crowded drawing without a park, published in *The Builder* of February 1863.[14] Akroydon gives the impression of being built from the outside, and there is evidence that the outer houses did not sell fast enough.[15] A disintegration of the logic of settlement takes place as one moves in toward the park. This belies any previous realization by Akroyd of the advantage of what contemporaries were pleased to call, in savoring its unusual worth, "circumjacent" land. The best-known contemporary example of this effect would be Joseph Paxton's Birkenhead Park, near Liverpool (1844–45). There, as Olmsted noted, one third of the property surrounding, or sixty acres, was held out for villa sites in anticipation of the rise in land values from the new park.[16]

Financing for individual ownership was one innovation at Akroydon. Establishing a positive aesthetic environment that would provide more durable social values was another. A third theme was mixing classes by grading the costs and varying the location of the homes. They had four price levels: £100 (equivalent to the standard at Copley), £140, £170, and £250. The last, if we are to judge from figures of the period, approached the expectation of the lower middle class. This was done "so that the better paid and better educated might act usefully on the desires and tastes of others in an inferior social position."[17] The purpose enunciated was not charity, but cooperation—working with, rather than for, the working man—as the success of the other great product of Akroyd's fertile mind, the highly successful Yorkshire Penny Bank, also demonstrated. The workman was to be encouraged to save and own, to lay up and look forward for himself, no matter how modest his beginning.

 West Hill Park Estate

The West Hill Park Estate in Halifax (Fig. 19) was begun in September 1863, two years after the start at Akroydon. It was the project of John Crossley the younger, but as R. Bretton, the modern biographer of both men, has indicated, the inspiration came largely from Akroyd.[1] That the personal influence

14. Ibid., p. 116.
15. They originally planned for 350 houses (Akroyd, p. 12).
16. F. L. Olmsted, *Walks and Talks of an* *American Farmer in England* (New York, Putnam, 1852), p. 81.
17. *Builder*, p. 116.
1. Bretton, "Crossleys of Dean Clough," Part IV (1953), p. 7.

Fig. 19. West Hill Park Estate, Halifax; Paull and Aycliffe, 1863–68; a four-class grouping developed by the Crossley family, with small front gardens throughout. The inner service alleys are screened from the main streets by houses at right angles.

also ran in the other direction is evident from Sir Francis Crossley's decision to make his new Square Congregational Church (1855–57) of architectural value to the town. This apparently caused Akroyd to contemplate a much more impressive church for Haley Hill in his All Soul's (1856–59).[2] This in turn led to the unusual complaint of Sir George Gilbert Scott in his autobiography that the client had poured too much money into the church which at first "was never meant to be so fine a work as it is."[3] Scott nevertheless considered it his best church and Akroyd his great good friend (who later backed him in the national dispute with Lord Palmerston over the Foreign Office designs).

West Hill was another freehold estate, and it offered an even higher range of prices than Akroydon, with class 4 costing £160 per house, class 3 £270, class 2 £320, and class 1 £500. The last two classes, fairly expensive for the

2. Bretton, "Colonel Edward Akroyd," June 5, 1948, p. 82.
3. *Personal and Professional Recollections*

(London, Sampson Low, Marston, Searle and Rivington, 1879), p. 176.

time, were conceived for foremen and a higher type of clerk. The dates of its development (1863–68) identify it as the latest of the model villages. The layout has a more subtle approach than the others, with a better feeling for the site and for the house, with its individual front garden. It was the outcome of a competition in which several Halifax firms and Paull and Aycliffe of Manchester were invited to submit, first premium going to the latter.[4] Instead of attempting a square on the side of a hill, as at Akroydon, they cleverly ran the major rows of twelve to twenty-two houses north and south along the dale in the older manner. Each row was exclusive to one of four price categories. There was less reason for the breakup of fronts than at Akroydon since fewer of the houses could be seen at a distance in silhouette. Nevertheless, the neo-Gothic gables were still present at wide intervals.

The new landscape feature of these houses was that six of the rows did face inward on individual front gardens. These green strips with walks alternated with back streets for service. To screen the service roads, a few of the more expensive houses were run east and west at right angles across the ends of the development. They were arranged so that the gardens and walks, but not the service roads, would be visible from the major streets of Hanson Lane and Gibbet Street as they descended the slope into the town.

   The People's Park

This was a neighborhood abounding in Crossley benefactions. A few streets away and six years earlier, in 1857,[1] the People's Park of Sir Francis Crossley had been finished, adjoining his mansion of Belle Vue and his almshouses of 1855 (Fig. 20). The People's Park may have influenced the outline of the housing estate. The design approaches are remarkably similar. Both mirror a wish to attain seclusion by screens within a densely mixed neighborhood of mills, workshops, stores, and houses, on the northern edge of which stood the twenty-five acre Dean Clough mill of the Crossleys. The elements used for the purpose of concealment in the People's Park are rows of trees, huge stone blocks, and artificial mounds. That Paull and Aycliffe could have made a study of the design of the People's Park by Joseph Paxton before undertaking their own project of the West Hill Estate appears likely from the similarity of

4. R. Bretton, "Crossleys of Dean Clough," Part IV (1953), pp. 7–9.

1. Dates of construction May 1856 to Aug. 1857 (T. Tiffany, *Description of the People's Park Halifax on the Opening Day* (Halifax, Wormersley and Stott, 1907), p. 13. The architect of the terrace and stonework was G. H. Stokes, the son-in-law of Paxton.

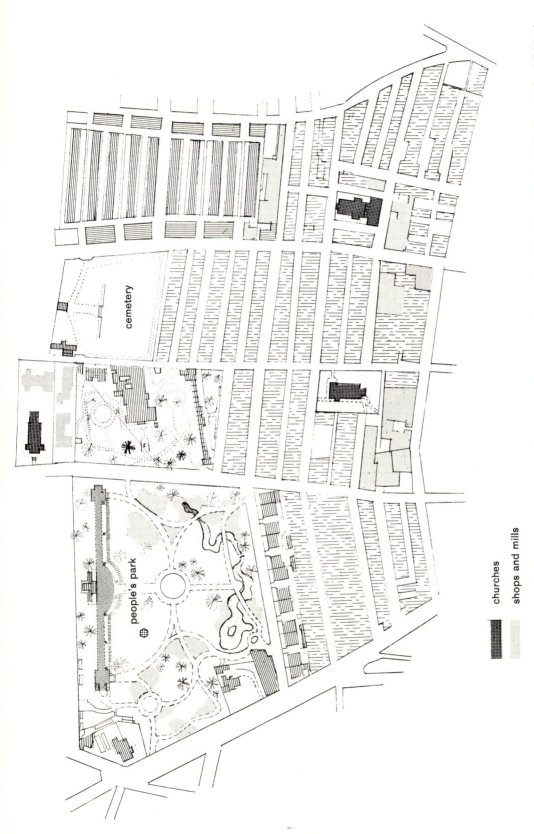

churches

shops and mills

Fig. 20. Map of People's Park, Halifax; Joseph Paxton, 1856–57. Belle Vue, the mansion of Sir Francis Crossley, is to the right of the park. Farther to the right is the West Hill Park Estate. On the lower edge are the Crossley almshouses. Beyond to the right in a valley would be the Crossley mills, covering twenty-five acres. A mixture of multiple-use mills and machine shops, churches, and row houses fill the immediate area.

orientation, with the rows of houses blanking out the important roads descending into the town.

In the illustration of the West Hill Park Estate, the handkerchief-sized gardens in front of the row houses are composed in the most romantic manner, full of curves and sinuosities. They contrast with the stiff linearism of the facades. The instant one steps within the People's Park the same effect on a much larger scale applies. The curving of the serpentine lake, the winding paths and the artificial mounds are symptomatic of a rebellion against the tyranny of the straight line and continuous plane found everywhere else in the congested environment.

The park is generously furnished with the bric-a-brac of Victorianism. It is a measure of the ability of the landscape architect that this variety never goes beyond the limits of the primary pattern. By the same token, it is to gauge the wealth, vitality, and cosmopolitan interests of the age; or at least of its leaders, to thoroughly comprehend the objects and episodes within it (Fig. 21). From Italy there are eight statues of Roman deities to represent Classical

Fig. 21. Promenade, People's Park. Paxton conceals the crowded town with trees and mounds, but opens the view above them out to the distant moor.

culture. There were two Russian guns captured at Sebastopol to symbolize the British Empire.[2] There was a central fountain which threw out 113 jets, the central one rising to 26 feet, to demonstrate the marvels of modern piping and pressure.[3] Iron-posted summer houses exploited a new material. Paxton is also supposed to have done the small metal and glass conservatory attached to Belle Vue, and certainly his son-in-law, G. H. Stokes, remodeled the house under his supervision in 1856.[4] The serpentine lake is said to have had two waterfalls, two bridges, and an island with weeping willows, rhododendrons, ferns, and briars with blocks of stone and roots of trees, a characteristic Paxton treatment, forming a shelter for water fowl.[5]

The diversity of Victorian objects in the park is rivaled only by the number of organizations marching in the parade on the day of dedication, Friday, August 14, 1857. In it were ten bands and the United Order of Ancient Druids, the Halifax Temperance Society, the Order of the Peaceful Dove, Odd Fellows, Halifax Horticultural Society, the Ancient Order of Foresters, Early Closing Association, the Mayor and Corporation, and the Sixth West Yorkshire Militia Staff and Band, escorting the two Russian guns. Singing was provided by 130 selected vocalists from the local churches and the "Yorkshire Nightingale," Mrs. Sunderland.[6]

At a luncheon preceding the formal dedication, Sir Francis Crossley revealed the source of inspiration for the People's Park. In 1855 he and his wife had been for several months in America. He relates that on the 10th of September,

> I left Quebec early in the morning for the White Mountains of the United States. I remember passing through some of the most glorious scenery on that day which I ever saw in my life. I remember that, when we arrived at the hotel at White Mountains, the ladies sat down for a cup of tea, but I preferred to take a walk alone. It was a beautiful spot. The sun was just then reclining his head behind Mount Washington, with all the glorious drapery of an American sunset, which we know nothing of in this country. I felt that I should like to be walking with my God on the earth. I said, "What shall I render to my Lord for all his benefits to me?" I was led fur-

2. Ibid., p. 24.

3. The present fountain statue of marble is not original, but was given by Lord Somerleyton, Sir Francis' only son, from his winter garden at Somerleyton: *Halifax Courier and Guardian* (Aug. 13, 1932).

4. George F. Chadwick, *The Work of Sir Joseph Paxton 1803–1865* (London, Architectural Press, 1961), p. 195.

5. Tiffany, p. 24.

6. Ibid, p. 17.

ther to repeat that question which Paul asked under other circumstances—"Lord, what wilt thou have me do?" The answer came immediately. It was this:—"It is true thou canst not bring the many thousands thou hast left in thy native country to see this beautiful scenery; but thou canst take this to them; it is possible so to arrange art and nature that they shall be within the walk of every workingman in Halifax; that he shall go take his stroll there after he has done his hard day's toil, and be able to get home again without being tired."[7]

Crossley had the inspiration for his park while watching a colorful American sunset over Mount Washington in the early New England fall, the most poignant season in that part of the world, with the air crisp and the trees turning to brilliant hues. Visible acknowledgment of Crossley's moving experience lies in the purposeful slope of the People's Park toward the east where no buildings or other man-made objects are allowed to impede the splendid view out to Beacon Hill. As with Maslen's earlier vision of this same hill bedecked with oriental pavilions and kiosks, the inspiration had come from another, more distant land. Romanticism had inspired these Victorians to see spontaneously. The Hanover Park Zoo development stands at the beginning of the sequence and the People's Park at the end. What makes the People's Park more Victorian, however, is that Crossley would take this intimate revelation, translate it promptly into a public spectacle in the midst of a dull and tedious environment, and then relate exactly why he did it. It is the ability to learn from the *other* experience and the "intense moment" that identifies the Romantic and the act of wearing his aesthetic heart on his sleeve that proclaims the Victorian.

In the same novel by Disraeli that may have influenced Salt, we discern this quality of observation, and see that Crossley's "unique" revelation need not have been unique after all. Disraeli muses on the fact that "Time passes with a measured and memorable wing during the first period of a sojourn in a new place, among new characters and new manners. Every person, every incident, every feeling, touches and stirs the imagination. The restless mind creates and observes at the same time."[8] Crossley arrived in New Hampshire already receptive to the meaning of what he was to see.

From the elevated promenade at the top of the park the eye can sweep the entire valley. This grand promenade is 30 feet wide, 720 feet long, and 8 feet

7. *Sir Francis Crossley, Bart.* (London, Religious Tract Society), p. 13.

8. *Sybil* (New York, Collier, 1845), p. 202.

above grade level. The foreground too loses nothing in the looking if one knows that the first soil was extremely thin and that loam had to be carted in and a great deal of the underlying gritstone had to be excavated for the lake and fountain pipes and drainage. Original trees were also very few.[9]

The whole display at the People's Park recommends consideration of Paxton's much earlier work for the Duke of Devonshire at Chatsworth, not many miles away. A. J. Downing, the American landscape architect from the Hudson Valley, who visited it in August 1850, gives almost as striking and personal a picture of the Chatsworth grounds as Sir Francis Crossley gave of the White Mountains. He passes into the estate through Edensor gate and observes Paxton's model housing for rural workers which, together with Nash's Blaise Hamlet of 1811 near Bristol, constitute the two original romantic villages of the nineteenth century. Downing writes:

> There may be thirty or forty cottages in all, and every one most tasteful in form and proportions, most admirably built, and set in its appropriate framework of trees and shrubbery—making an *ensemble* such as I saw nowhere else in England. There are dwellings in the Italian, Gothic, Norman, Swiss, and two or three more styles; each as capital a study as you will find in any of the architectural works, with the advantage which the reality always has over its counterfeit. From this little village to Chatsworth House, or palace, is about two miles, through a park, which is a broad valley, say a couple of miles wide by half a dozen long. It is indeed just one of those valleys which our own Durand loves to paint in his ideal landscape.[10]

He notices the emerald green of the park and the mild and tempered gray of the sky and altogether the painterly nature of the scene. The difference in the Victorian attitude from the Hudson River School of Durand is, however, that the Romanticism of Crossley and Paxton was not going to be recollected in tranquility but was to be fitted to some immediate and practical purpose. In that respect, of course, Paxton's Crystal Palace in London would be the final monument to Romanticism, properly appreciated in its own time as something remarkable to look at, arising from a sudden, personal vision, and in the same moment, supremely useful. Downing also notes and admires, as only a trained American observer would, the Emperor Fountain, 267 feet

9. Tiffany, p. 13.
10. A. J. Downing, *Rural Essays* (New York,   Leavitt, 1869), pp. 499–500. Prof. Peter Hornbeck of Harvard called this to my attention.

high, the terrace with its Italianate balustrade "where you take in, without moving, all this magical landscape," and the paths with their "rocks of vast size."[11] No further description is needed to realize that many of the basic elements at Chatsworth were to be re-employed at Halifax.

Sir Francis called upon Paxton to apply the full power of his art to nature. His seriousness can be measured by the amount of Crossley money spent, £30,000, with a later endowment of £6,300. The park was to go to the city, but it was by no means the outcome of typical municipal finance. Individualism set the standard over against public indifference for once. Crossley stated that an annual sum of £315 would have to be guaranteed by the town for maintenance before he would deed the park over. It combined, with great artistry and sufficient backing, two keen perceptions. One, already mentioned, depended on the recognition that although Halifax itself was visually dull and congested, its natural setting was not. The other was that while this particular area of the town appears on a map like a confused patchwork, anarchistic and overwrought, the contradictory surroundings can be detected from within the People's Park itself only by random spires and factory chimneys rising over the treetops. These perceptions were not exclusive to Crossley and Paxton, of course. When Akroydon Park was similarly dedicated in 1876 a newspaper reporter observed that, "Such a facility is indeed a boon in a manufacturing town like this, which, although surrounded by charming and romantic natural scenery, is nevertheless not so conspicuous for its horticultural beauty in the centres of population."[12] But Crossley and Paxton put their ideals firmly together and pushed them as far as money, skill, and nature allowed.

Internal urban space was at a premium. So was time. John Crossley in reminiscing in 1878 said that in his youth the mill at Dean Clough had started at 5:30 in the morning and carried on until 8 P.M.[13] At Copley the work hours had been only an hour shorter, from 6:00 in the morning until 7:30 at night, with a forty-minute break for dinner.[14] But in 1847 the Ten Hours Bill had been passed by Parliament. Robert Baker, the factory inspector and former town councillor of Leeds, in *The Present Condition of the Working Classes* (1851), drew an early conclusion from this event in regard to leisure. "Time, then," he writes, "for mental and moral improvement, is now what is required to be determined, time for relaxation; time for

11. Ibid., pp. 502–04.

12. *Historical Almanack and Literary Companion* (Halifax, Guardian, 1906–08), p. 141.

13. *Halifax Courier* (April 19, 1879). The People's Park opened at 6 A.M. and closed at sunset during Francis Crossley's time.

14. Turner Clippings, "Copley," Part 1.

the evolition [sic] and direction of thought; time for social and domestic conversation, for religious exercises, and for sober and rational enjoyments."[15] The idea of "sober and rational" enjoyment was incorporated in the program of the People's Park. Strolling was the most strenuous exercise allowed by Crossley's regulations. No cricket, bowls, hockey, or refreshments were permitted, and no music on Sunday. That it belonged within the strict decade of the fifties is shown by a comparison of these rules with those of Saltaire Park in 1871.[16] By then cricket, croquet, bowling, and other sports were actively encouraged. Yet the basic land form of a terrace on the side of a hill with winding paths is much the same. These parks offer additional proof that the problems of the model dwellings and villages in relation to open spaces were gradually being recognized as inseparable. What is undeniably English about this development is that there appears to have been little or no hesitation when intuition suggested that a transition should be made from one specialty to another—from architecture to planning to landscape. Paxton's brilliant amateurism was the epitome of the national genius in this regard.

 Report on Public Walks

With all due credit to the initiative of philanthropy, it appears that national discussion of these problems of beauty and rest had begun with the Parliamentary report on public walks of 1833 and continued through the later government documents and proposals on the state of general health in the most populous towns.[1] R. A. Slaney and James Silk Buckingham, as Parliamentary reformers, were in the forefront of this movement. They in turn had been singularly impressed by the antienclosure campaign of J. A. Roebuck, the friend of J. S. Mill and then at the height of his Parliamentary influence:

> As early as 1828 he had outlined a programme of "town planning" and town development in accordance with Benthamite principles, in a speech before the Utilitarian debating society. He had advocated tree-lined boulevards, grass lawns open to the public, and flower-bedecked parks; while outside the towns, and if possible

15. (London, Longman, Brown), pp. 10–11.
16. The designer of Saltaire Park was William Gay, a surveyor of Bradford (Holroyd, *Saltaire and Its Founder,* p. 69). He had laid out the Undercliffe Cemetery of 1852 in Bradford, according to Thomas Baines.

1. *The Report on Towns* of 1845, for instance, says that "The great towns of Liverpool, Manchester, Birmingham, Leeds, and very many others, have at present no public walks," (p. 123).

ringing them round, large tracts of common land varying in size according to population and maintained by the town authorities or the State itself for town dwellers.[2]

He appeared to be much before his time in recommending "greenbelts," municipal acquisition of land, compensation for "utility loss," and taxes on the increased value of land brought by the expansion of towns.

The earliest government paper on the subject dealt mainly with the areas around Manchester, Birmingham, and the Bradford–Halifax–Leeds region. Its first assumption was that there had been an enormous growth of population in the larger towns during the last half century (60 per cent to 150 per cent according to its figures). The effects of this were extremely detrimental, "more especially as regards those classes who are, with many of their children, almost continually engaged in Manufacturing and Mechanical employments." Its second premise was that "During the same period, from the increased value of Property and extension of Buildings, many inclosures of the open spaces in the vicinity of towns have taken place, and little or no provision has been made for Public Walks or Open Spaces."[3] Healthful outdoor exercise was seldom taken any more. The main recreations had become drinking, dog fights, and boxing matches. "The reason of this state of the people is, that all scenes of interest are remote from the town, and that the walks which can be enjoyed by the poor are chiefly the turnpike roads, alternately dusty or muddy."[4] Within the towns the people were "lodged, for the most part in narrow courts and confined streets."[5] Since the work people had little free time, it was desirable that they be able to reach an open space in a comparatively short walk. To satisfy this need, the report suggested the establishment of recreation spots within the town as well as public walks outside. The People's Park was a late but cogent answer in 1857 to the main problems raised by the government report of 1833. It had quick accessibility from the working-class district of Halifax. At the same time its grand promenade for exercise offered an opportunity to at least view and contemplate the distant countryside. It had been noted also by the committee that well-regulated walks improved the cleanliness, neatness, and personal appearance of those who frequented them. Here alone might be found the explanation for Crossley's wish to employ an outstanding practitioner like Paxton, as well as for his restrictive rules for action within it.

2. Francis E. Hyde, "Utilitarian Town Planning," *Town Planning Review* (*19*, Summer 1947), 155–56.

3. *Report from the Select Committee on Public Walks* (June 27, 1833), p. 1.
4. Ibid., p. 4.
5. Ibid., p. 5.

The assessment of recreational facilities by the committee appears to have had a long and nearly continuous response in the Bradford–Halifax–Leeds area.[6] Within the testimony of the committee itself already appears the name of Ellis Cunliffe Lister, M.P., who stated that he customarily allowed the people of Bradford to view his deer park on Sunday and that this and similar observations had convinced him that a more effective means of public recreation ought to be found at once.[7] In 1870 the corporation purchased the family estate at Manningham for the sum of £40,000 and renamed it Lister Park.[8] The Lister firm had also, like John Foster at his Black Dyke mill, built housing near its factory, but the lack of imaginative touches have caused it long since to recede into its drab surroundings. Peel Park of 56 acres in Bradford, dedicated in 1863, was similarly purchased through the initiative and support of Sir Titus Salt.[9] It had a terrace walk 400 yards long and 30 feet wide, much like the one in the People's Park.[10] The fact that the Aire River was artificially widened at Saltaire to afford the workers bathing, boating, and fishing privileges also follows the general demand in the report of 1833 for more recreational opportunities on the rivers and especially for more swimming tanks.[11] Colonel Akroyd, besides placing the small Victoria Park in the center of Akroydon, persuaded Mr. Savile to devote a likely site in Halifax to the creation of Shroggs Park and paid for its execution partly out of his own pocket.[12] Akroyd and John Crossley were partially responsible for the purchase and layout of the Albert Promenade of 1861 (Fig. 22) overlooking the Calder Valley in Halifax.[13]

 The Degree of Self-Seeking

Since we are examining the work of the Bradford–Halifax School of model village builders in terms of its broader implications for the future, it may be worthwhile in conclusion to consider these men for what they were not, as

6. That the manufacturers' concern for public walks was by no means confined to the Bradford–Halifax–Leeds area is evident from the following: "Mr. Joseph Strutt, of Derby, has presented to that town a public garden of eleven acres, which has been so laid out by Mr. Loudon as to give the advantages of a walk of two miles, and the interest afforded by an arboretum, displaying the specimens of 1000 shrubs and plants: *Inquiry into the Sanitary Condition of the Labouring Population of Great Britain for the Poor Law Commissioners* (London, Clowes, 1842), p. 276.

7. *Report from the Select Committee on Public Walks*, p. 53.

8. Samuel Smiles, *Fortunes Made in Business, 1* (London, Sampson Low, Marston, Searle and Rivington, 1884), 85.

9. Balgarnie, *Sir Titus Salt*, p. 110.

10. T. Baines, *Yorkshire Past and Present, 2*, Part 1, 313.

11. Holroyd, pp. 62–63.

12. "Death of Colonel Akroyd," *Halifax Courier* (Nov. 26, 1887).

13. D. Taylor, "Halifax Streets and Buildings," *Trans. Halifax Antiquarian Society* (April 7, 1959), p. 57.

Fig. 22. View from Albert Promenade, Halifax, 1861. This walk overlooking the Calder Valley was also partly conceived and paid for by Akroyd and John Crossley. The concentration of buildings along with the smoke in the valley contrasts with the older farms, higher up, and reflects the original sequence of settlement.

well as for what they were. It appears difficult for modern authors to write of the Victorians without implying that there was an element of hypocrisy in their every deed. It has been suggested that the model village builders were sanctimoniously carrying out their plans and accepting approbation while taking advantage of their workers by renting or selling them homes at a large profit.

Although there was bitterness to spare between capital and labor during the lifetime of these men, as testified by the editor of the *Halifax Courier*, Thomas Latimer, whom John Crossley brought in to start a Liberal paper in 1853, it is hard to believe that an honest admiration did not exist for them among the townspeople.[1] The last of the Crossley brothers to die was John. His funeral was on April 22, 1879. It is reported in *The Standard* of the 23rd that all work stopped in the city and shutters were closed for the day. The paper goes on to remark that at the end of his life his wealth was wiped out because he fell into the hands of speculators. It concludes:

1. Bretton, "Crossleys of Dean Clough," Part IV (1953), p. 5.

> Now that he is gone, we see from the testimony borne by the organs
> of both political parties, and by the great public demonstrations of
> yesterday, how deep and wide-spread was the affectionate respect it
> entertained for him; and how little popular sentiment has been al-
> tered, even by that great reverse which had converted him from the
> prosperous millionaire, whose good word meant fortune, into the
> penniless invalid.

Even the elderly Benjamin Wilson, who might be expected to harbor resentment toward manufacturers, since he had been an early Chartist in Halifax,
had nothing but good to write of John Crossley. "What he, along with his
two brothers Mr. Joseph and Sir Francis, has done for the town will long be
remembered."[2]

There is evidence that with his many benefactions Crossley helped to un-
dermine his fortune, much as Akroyd and Salt also did.[3] Single-handed (no
doubt to rival Bradford) he undertook to purchase and redevelop most of
downtown Halifax; he widened the streets and replaced the hovels, backyard
workshops, stables, and piggeries with the Town Hall by Scott, the Joint
Stock Bank, the Mechanics' Institute, the Princess Buildings, and the White
Swan Hotel. "Unhappily," another newspaper reports, "he accomplished all
this with no permanent benefit to himself, except the satisfaction of having
conferred a great good upon the people among whom he dwelt."[4]

It seems inaccurate also to assume that profits on the model villages were
beyond the bounds of reason. The average landlord of the time expected a
return of 8 to 10 per cent on his investment. No less a person than Prince
Albert, who was so deeply interested in social questions, advocated a rate of
7 to 8 per cent as the only realistic one for London model housing. Alderman
Waterlow was acclaimed a great benefactor of society when he built tenements there which yielded a net of 8½ per cent.[5]

By way of contrast, Saltaire was said to have returned only 4 per cent on its
capital[6] and Copley brought in 4½ per cent according to Colonel Akroyd.[7]

2. Benjamin Wilson, *The Struggles of an
Old Chartist* (Halifax, Nicholson, 1887), p. 38.

3. "Death of Colonel Akroyd," *Halifax
Courier* (Nov. 26, 1887), says, "His subscriptions
to charities at one time reached £5000 or £6000
per annum; and indeed it was his fault—a fault
that leaned to virtue's side—that in one way
and another he spent and gave away his whole
income." Likewise in J. Horsfall Turner (see n.
9 under "Saltaire"), p. 49, "It was generally reported that Sir Titus had exceeded his posses-
sions, or at least seriously crippled the estates
by these munificent gifts and endowments."

4. "Death of Mr. John Crossley," *Halifax
Courier* (April 19, 1879).

5. Hole, *Homes of the Working Classes,* p.
56.

6. Ibid., pp. 67, 93.

7. Ibid., p. 71. *Builder* (Feb. 14, 1863, p. 109)
also reports 4½ per cent for Copley.

A newspaper of 1880 stated that the rents of Copley had always been "most reasonable."[8] Akroyd lost money on the first units at Akroydon, for which he had to give a premium. He hoped later proprietors might gain as much as 6 per cent.[9] West Hill Park was supposed to return 5 per cent over thirteen years until the mortgages were discharged.[10]

Salt and the other manufacturers held a viewpoint approximating that of some modern social scientists—that healthy and contented workers are more productive. Salt and the Crossleys were both interested in finding methods of avoiding layoffs during slack periods,[11] and a portion of the stock of the Crossley and Akroyd companies came ultimately to be sold to the workers, premonitions of the guaranteed annual wage and profit sharing. It was said that one of the main purposes of turning the Akroyd firm into a joint stock company in 1871 was "to obviate the antagonism between capital and labour, and to give to those who had contributed to the past prosperity of the business an opportunity of obtaining as proprietors an interest in its future success."[12] We tend to denigrate the early manufacturers as a group today because we suspect that they possessed too much wealth and power and too little vision and social conscience, whereas the question may now be raised whether just the opposite inference could not be drawn from the model village episodes in Bradford and Halifax, which might be taken as the most characteristic, substantial, and well-considered housing in Britain evoked by early paternalism.

8. Turner Clippings, "Copley," Part 2.
9. Akroyd, *On Improved Dwellings*, p. 12.
10. Hole, p. 78.
11. Balgarnie, p. 164. Also *Sir Francis Crossley, Bart.* (London, Religious Tract Society, undated), p. 12.

12. *Halifax Courier* (Nov. 26, 1887). A similar offering had been made to the workers of The Crossley Company in 1864. Salt was also interested in such a move but his partners dissuaded him, according to Balgarnie (p. 219).

3. THE BAD EXAMPLE OF LEEDS

Hole's Book

Of the three cities of Halifax, Bradford, and Leeds, it was Leeds that finally became the true metropolis of the West Riding of Yorkshire. It also became a center on the east, like Manchester on the west, for discussion of social reform.[1] No document exemplifies this better than James Hole's *The Homes of the Working Classes*. It contains a quantity of information about the region and is dedicated to Colonel Edward Akroyd of Copley and Akroydon. The book grew out of an essay competition proposed by the Mayor of Leeds to accompany a national conference of the Society of Arts on housing, held in Leeds in 1864. Hole's prize-winning effort was publicly read in January 1865 and subsequently published in the local press.[2] These events aligned it with another civic trait of Leeds, an ability for searching self-examination. That process began in 1839 when the town council issued a statistical report "upon the condition of the Town of Leeds and its inhabitants" as a first response to the self-governing powers granted by the Municipal Corporations Act of 1835. Action did not accompany realization, however, then or later. As late as 1874 *The Builder* was still plaintively asking, "What progress have the Town Council of Leeds made since we pointedly drew their attention to the disgusting state of their town in 1860?"[3]

Leeds typifies English urbanism under the direct pressures of the industrial revolution, as contrasted to the smaller sideshows of the model villages in this same area. However little headway was made in urban problem solving during the last century, it is apparent that the problems, once set, remained remarkably constant. The persistent tension between the need and its solution

1. J. F. C. Harrison, "Social Reform in Victorian Leeds, The Work of James Hole 1820–95," *The Thoresby Society*, Monograph III, 100 (Leeds, 1954), p. 2.

2. *The Homes of the Working Classes* (London, Longmans, Green, 1866), Preface.
3. (Oct. 10, 1874), p. 844.

became more and more unnerving as technology advanced. First to be no-ticed in Hole's book is the guilt provoked in the middle-class conscience by the sight of slums in what was without hesitation then called "the richest country in the world." Progress taught one lesson, Victorian morality an-other. As Robert Baker had put it earlier, "Individuals may be rich, but the nation, never. Our commercial greatness may be a world's wonder, but unless we maintain our moral character as a nation, that greatness will decay."[4]

There is also registered in the book an acute awareness of the physical stress put upon these slums by semisymbolic acts of progress, such as the railroads cutting ruthlessly through them (Fig. 23). "Lord Shaftesbury stated in the House of Lords, that during the present year the Railways and other Acts had been the means of pulling down 3,500 houses in London, and displacing 20,000 persons, chiefly skilled artisans and day labourers, and for whose ac-commodation no provision has been made."[5] In our own century sudden slashes through the urban fabric result more often from new expressways than from the rails, but the anxiety of some experts about where to put the dislocated families and institutions, after progress has been served, remains much the same.

Then we hear the call of the "fighting" ecologist, clear and indisputable as at present, and as little heeded: "Fish who cannot live in a stream show it is unfit for human consumption. So also we have a danger signal showing that we are infringing the laws of health in trying to live where the air will not support plants."[6] Some do-gooders may be concerned with air pollution. They are then confronted with the timid official, the inevitable companion of the indifferent citizen: "If, to satisfy the outcry of those who object to it, a smoke inspector is appointed, he, as a subordinate officer, soon learns not to come into collision with his employers. 'Not too much zeal' is the safe rule for him."[7] As so often in the twentieth century too, the opposition is fore-armed with catchy slogans. The tacit motto of the do-nothing or "Voluntary-ist" group in the North was, "Where there's muck, there's money," which was later to be translated in the United States to, "A smoky city is a pros-perous city."

Pro- and anti-suburban thinkers were already much in evidence too. A com-posite opinion was that the suburban trend could be halted if only the poor were removed to the country and given cheap commuting fares and the rich en-

4. *The Present Condition of the Working Classes* (London, Longman, Brown, 1851), p. 12.
    5. Hole, pp. 64–65.

6. Ibid., pp. 30–31.
7. Ibid., p. 32.

Fig. 23. Over London by Rail: Gustave Doré, 1870. The railway viaducts entering the bigger cities displaced houses and led to increased crowding of families. The scale of the scene began to shift, displaying greater contrasts in size; note the tiny, minimal, repetitive units here in the channel-back houses with their walled yards.

ticed back into town. "The migration of the better educated, better conditioned inhabitants to the outskirts of the town, makes the case of the poor who are left even worse than it otherwise would be."[8] Today we still hear this lament coupled with another assertion in the interest of augmenting the centripetal force of the city, namely, that the urban environment alone can offer culture in its purest and most rewarding form. Hole says:

> It has also been objected that such a plan [for building model villages outside with rapid communication by train back into town, in purpose much like modern Vällingby or Farsta around Stockholm] would tend to remove the working classes from those civic influences which, after all, compensate for many of the evils in town life. The sight of noble buildings, public amusements, when they are rational, the collision of mind with mind through meetings, lectures, and other stimulants to intellectual activity offered in towns, contrast favourably with the dulness of village life, and especially if the village be not a *model* village, but simply one of those ugly, misshapen collections of houses, too common in Lancashire and Yorkshire, combining the worst features of town and village life, without their advantages, and where ignorance, stupidity, and filth reign supreme.[9]

One only misses the presence of the service occupations in these discussions, the white collar and professional groups which are now everywhere in evidence in the flight to the suburbs. Could the survival of these problems and attitudes be partially due to the cultural astigmatism which Maslen already perceived in the first half of the nineteenth century? "The changes which have taken place in the state of society in England during the present century, were so different from the ordinary circumstances under which great social revolutions take place, that men's attention was not sufficiently directed to enquire into the new wants to which they gave birth."[10] This criticism would refer more directly to public intuition than expert analysis if Leeds is any sign. Surely no city was more thoroughly researched, quantified, and commented upon in its own most difficult times. This opens to further speculation whether our age may not be some day characterized in planning history

8. Ibid., p. 4. On this see also Rev. J. S. Jones, "On Certain Contradictions or Abnormal Phenomena of the Age," *Proceedings of the Literary and Philosophical Society of Liverpool*, 22 (1867–68), 47–63.

9. Ibid., p. 64.

10. T. J. Maslen, *Suggestions for the Improvement of Our Towns and Houses* (London, Smith, Elder, 1843), p. 93.

as one in which the excellence and topicality of intellectual formulation was accompanied by an absolute inability to do anything effective with the knowledge once it had been accumulated because of the constant increase in size and complexity of the basic urban units.

What was the city that could give rise to such speculation actually like? What conditions in Leeds typified, as Hole and his associates seemed to believe, the position of a rapidly expanding industrial urbanism not only in the West Riding of Yorkshire but also in London, Liverpool, Birmingham, and Manchester?

 Air and Water Pollution

The greatest change brought on by the concentration of West Riding industry at Leeds was the pollution of air and water. As early as 1823 there were complaints about smoke in the town and hope for its immediate alleviation. Edward Baines remarked in his *Gazetteer* of that year, "On the Aire and its tributary streams are numerous mills for grinding corn, dyers' wood, rapeseed, & c. as well as for fulling cloth, and turning, carding, and spinning machines. These works are, however, principally wrought by steam, the numerous furnaces of which, for want of the general application of the smoke-burning apparatus, contaminate the air, and impair the beauty and healthfulness of a well situated town."[11] He observes also that the condition is similar in Bradford and other centers of the West Riding, although as late as 1831 a Miss Lister of Halifax on a journey to York confides to her diary that, "In passing along, I could not help observing on the comparatively fine, clear air of Halifax. Never in my life did I see a more smoky place than Bradford (Fig. 24). The great, long chimneys are doubled I think, in number within these two or three years. The same may be said of Leeds."[12] The abundance of waterpower in Halifax seems to have been the chief reason for the greater clarity of the atmosphere there. But by 1837 in returning from a weekend at Bolton Woods, Miss Lister was ready to concede that even Halifax was "brightening into the polish of a large smoke-canopied commercial town."[13]

In his report of 1842 on Leeds to the Poor Law Commissioners, Robert Baker continued to write of the smoke as being especially bad, although he

11. *History, Directory & Gazetteer of the County of York, 1* (Leeds, *Mercury* Office, 1823), 30.

12. T. W. Hanson, *The Story of Old Halifax* (Halifax, King, 1920), p. 239.

13. Ibid., p. 240.

Fig. 24. View of Bradford. The rapid multiplication of factories produced a veritable forest of chimneys, each with its plume of smoke. There was no room within the city for the enlargement or consolidation of factories.

believed it arose from the dye-houses and tobacco-pipe furnaces more than from the engine chimneys. The latter at least carried their fumes above the town while the two former filled the streets with dense clouds carried on every breath of wind. Only on Sundays, he said, was it possible to view the entire city from an elevation.[14] What may not be entirely understood now is that there were not only active critics of the atmospheric situation but also numerous inventions available to assist their cause.[15] At Saltaire the architects were "expressly enjoined to use every precaution to prevent the pollution of air by smoke, or the water by sewerage or other impurity."[16] By the time T. J. Maslen published his idealistic but sensitive *Suggestions* in 1843 he

14. "Report on the Condition of the Labouring Classes in the Town of Leeds," in *Local Reports on the Sanitary Conditions of the Labouring Population of England* (London, Clowes, 1842), pp. 356, 406.

15. Thomas Baines in his *Yorkshire Past and Present*, 2 (London, Mackenzie, 1871–77), Part 1, 275–76, reports that a Mr. Buckley of Bradford was dissuaded in 1793 from introducing steam power into his mill by the threat of a lawsuit from some "very respectable, but not very far-seeing inhabitants of the town, on the ground that the smoke from the engine furnace could be a nuisance." In the shadow of later events it could be claimed that their vision was altogether too keen.

16. *London Times* (Sept. 22, 1853). *Illustrated London News* (Oct. 1, 1853), p. 287.

was prepared to list ten patent smoke consumers as well as to report the foundation of societies in London and elsewhere for the prosecution of owners of furnaces that did not consume their own smoke.[17] Two of the inventors came from Leeds, a number surpassed only by London with three. Maslen added that the inhabitants of the more valuable houses in the town might soon be driven out into the country by the smoke and soot, since "they are not obliged to stay." Baker in his report on Leeds of a year earlier mentions that three patents were most in vogue there, Hall's of Leeds, Hall's of Nottingham, and Williams' of Manchester.[18] The common principle was the introduction of secondary air in order to provide more thorough combustion. Smokeless fuel was also in existence and many railroads were "required" to stoke with it.[19] Numerous local acts had been exhorting owners of furnaces for years "to use the best practicable means for preventing or counteracting the annoyance from smoke."[20] But as Baker and Baines ruefully observed, the final remedy was yet obscure and people were still suffering from air pollution.

In the countryside under the old cottage system the proximity of work and home could be a distinct advantage. Here the opposite was apt to be the case. The river Aire and its contributing becks received so much industrial and domestic waste as to be "offensive in the first degree." The water was so discolored and the temperature raised enough to make it useless for the purposes of condensing and dyeing. In the spring of 1839 the river overflowed its boundaries during the night and regurgitated so powerfully into petty drains as to float many of the inhabitants from their beds and cause a great deal of fever.[21] For Baker this much-discussed catastrophe was only part of a larger picture. He noted that the lower parts of the city, "which lie contiguous to the river and the Becks or rivulets are dirty, confined, ill ventilated, and in many instances self-sufficient to shorten life."[22] Diseases of the upper respiratory tract, tuberculosis, and cholera were endemic. Other causes of death officially and statistically recorded might be as fatal today but are less easy to identify pathologically. They included Decay, Decline, Visitation of God, Old Age, Complicated Disease, Want of Food, Inanition, Found Dead, and Sudden and Natural Death.[23]

There was no way out from the basic grind, no physical or mental relief

17. P. 235.
18. P. 407.
19. *Second Report of the Commissioners for Inquiry into the State of Large Towns and Populous Districts* (London, Clowes, 1845), p. 81.
20. Ibid.

21. *The Statistical Report Issued by the Leeds Corporation, 1839.* A reprint with a foreword by Mr. Councillor Hawkyard, M.D. (Leeds, 1932), p. 13.
22. *Report on Leeds*, 1842, p. 349.
23. Ibid., p. 377.

from the constricting environment except by "the shortest route out of Manchester," and Leeds as well—by drinking until numb. The Leeds report concluded that

> in the broad fields and pure air of villages, the necessity for room
> wherein to imbibe oxygen into the lungs, physical enjoyment, and
> of promenading where the beauties of nature can add to the moral
> happiness of the people, is not felt; but in smoky atmospheres,
> where pure air is an unknown luxury, and amid the pent areas of
> mill walls, where there is no vegetation visible, every means is re-
> quired to keep up the bodily strength and enlarge the mental.[24]

However, the industrial revolution was not alone to blame for thwarting the impulse for wholesome recreation and the unspoiled countryside. The earlier agricultural revolution had also contributed. Two causes were here visibly related in one effect. Thomas Baines, the son of the earlier chronicler of Yorkshire, Edward Baines, wrote in the 1870s that, at the beginning of the nineteenth century, Leeds

> did not cover the fifth part of the ground which it occupies at pres-
> ent [Fig. 25], when vast and apparently interminable lines of streets
> extend in all directions from the centre of population, and render it
> difficult to find either fresh air or a pleasant walk, within any reason-
> able distance of the more thickly-peopled parts of the town. This
> evil was very much aggravated in the beginning of the present cen-
> tury and the close of the preceding one, by the rage that everywhere
> prevailed for inclosing commons and waste lands. This originated
> in a great degree in the excessive dearness of corn, and of all the
> products of the soil, caused by the rapid increase of the population,
> the cost of military and naval operations abroad, and the impossi-
> bility of obtaining any adequate supplies of food from abroad,
> either from the continent of Europe, which was wasted by continual
> wars, or from America, which at that time only contained a few mil-
> lions of inhabitants, unable to supply the urgent wants of the
> thickly-peopled countries.[25]

Baines declared that in compensation for the disappearance of the traditional commons near the towns it had been necessary to contrive public parks and

24. Ibid., p. 402.
25. *Yorkshire Past and Present,* 3 (1871–77), p. 163.

other means of recreation. He believed that these facilities were made possible by the increase of wealth and public spirit accumulating from the industrial revolution. Nevertheless, he noted (as many would who came after) that this process required a heavy subsidy to replace artificially features which had been naturally available in the older environment. The enclosures also meant that the small clothiers could no longer keep one or two cows for their families, bringing a further hardship upon them and compelling a radical dietary change, with tea substituted for milk and white wheat bread for havercake.[26]

   ## The Space Famine

As the English city of the industrial revolution may be described as evolving more from an accretion of difficulties than from a successful formulation of new principles, so its specific appearance at various stages could be generally catalogued as rising from an increasingly concentrated use of space, no matter what its designated purpose, shape, or location.

The usual back-to-back dwelling in Leeds consisted of three rooms—a cellar, sitting room, and chamber above. The average size of the rooms was 15 feet square.[27] The day of the typical poor family in or out of one of these houses was not a pleasant sight.

> Let the poor family, consisting of a man, his wife, and five children, two or three of whom are adolescent, be imagined occupying one of these chambers, in a *cul-de-sac*, or in an undrained and unpaved street, seven human beings, each requiring 600 cubic feet of breathing room, shut up in a chamber not containing more than 1000 feet for the whole . . . both parents and children rising in winter and summer at five o'clock in the morning, and labouring in other unhealthy atmospheres with occasional intermissions, from six a.m. till half-past seven p.m., in a temperature, probably, of 70, 80, or 90 degrees, tasting flesh-meat once a-week, and returning to the limited atmosphere of the night, unchanged, because unable to be improved, owing to the defective sanitary regulations, or an entire absence of them;—and the mind that so thinks, draws a picture which the theatre of any large manufacturing town could pourtray [sic] in a thousand instances.[28]

26. Hanson, p. 235.
27. *Statistical Report on Leeds, 1839*, p. 17.
28. Baker, *Report on Leeds*, 1842, p. 359.

The extension of the working day left no time for relaxation and the enlargement of the town no place for it, but possibly the gravest hardship was caused by the extreme concentration and parsimony with domestic space. The price of building land in Leeds in the early 1840s was from 1 shilling a yard up. As soon as it rose above 3 or 4 shillings it was considered too valuable for cottage purposes.[29] Such dwellings, yet to be built, were inevitably shunted onto the dampest and smokiest sites, predestined to be slums. As with running the railroad tracks through the city, what is witnessed here is one of the most unfortunate phenomena of the future city, established by a general increase in urban activity and value. It was not only the blindness to what was actually occurring in the urban environment that was causing the distress but also the disposition to assume that the evident improvement of the larger economy assured the health of all of its parts.

The cost of a worker's house might be £80, including the land at £10 or £15. It would then rent for something in the vicinity of £4 to £7 per year.[30] The minimal cost of a cottage at Copley and Akroydon of £100 and up, without the land, suggests that there was a considerable gap between the lowest *possible* standard of urban housing and the lowest *decent* standard, with no obsolescence yet involved. This economic difference was precisely what worried both Baker and Hole. The former remarked, "Were the houses built upon a much larger scale, therefore, and with a much larger quantity of land appropriated to them, the annual value would be beyond the income of the labourers."[31] For him the presence of front gardens was undesirable for this reason, although he readily acknowledged the beneficial "effect which an attention to the architecture and order of cottage houses and the good arrangement of streets has upon the health and habits of the people."[32] A quarter of a century later Hole, after participating in a scheme at Leeds modeled after Akroydon, was likewise of the opinion that the laboring class was too poor to build houses for itself even with the aid of a building society.[33] It would be unable to attract sufficient capital into the field unless the cause were to be continuously subsidized by men like Salt, Akroyd, and the Cross-

---

29. An interesting contrast to rising land values is provided by the decline in the price of stalls for the home weavers in the Leeds cloth halls. In the Coloured Cloth Hall they had begun at 3 guineas in 1755 and dropped to 50 shillings by 1823. The White Cloth Hall had charged 30 shillings in 1775. This had gone as high as £16 to £24 about 1800 but then dropped to £1 by 1823. E. Baines, *Gazetteer*

(n. 11 above) *1*, 20.

30. Baker, p. 358.
31. Ibid., p. 60.
32. Ibid., p. 61.
33. Hole, pp. 87–88, 94–97. See also Harrison, p. 46; E. Akroyd, *On Improved Dwellings for the Working Classes* (London, Shaw, 1862), pp. 12–13; *The Builder* (April 27, 1861), p. 289.

leys, of whom there were too few. His ultimate recommendation was that government building loans be supplied at a rate of 3 to 3½ per cent for this purpose.[34]

This conviction appears to have grown apace during the nineteenth century and to have become municipal theory by the 1890s, when it touched Lord Leverhulme, George Cadbury, and others. D. B. Foster in his *Leeds Slumdom* of 1897 attempted to prove that slum clearance could be made first and foremost profitable for the city. He recommended that it buy slum property in East Leeds, demolish the houses upon it, and erect new ones to be let at an annual all-over profit of £7,000. This would have the advantage of eliminating such losses as the difference between the £150,000, which the city was in the process of paying for the East Leeds Clearance Scheme, and the £50,000 it expected in return for the cleared land. It could, furthermore, borrow money at the rate of 2½ per cent, while a private developer would have to pay 4 per cent. The process would at the same time enable the city to maintain some control over the character of neighborhoods, particularly in regard to the frequency and conduct of public houses.[35]

Whatever the merit of this proposal, it appears that the construction of speculative cottages could in some instances hardly have been less substantial. Comments on the astonishing speed and carelessness of construction at mid-century are recurrent in the literature. In Manchester some walls were only half a brick thick, and a whole row of houses was said to have blown down there in a heavy storm. Baker was convinced that, "the law fell far short of its object when it limited the size of bricks, put a tax upon light, and neglected to enforce a minimum size of sites for houses in which to lodge the population."[36] Although the window tax (1695–1851) would not appear to have had a directly adverse effect upon the worst area of Leeds because dwellings with less than eight windows were exempt, it appears indirectly to have restrained builders from placing ventilators in cellars, roofs, privies, and passageways. Any opening visible on the exterior, glazed or not, was recorded as a window and charged at the rate of 8s. 3d. per annum.[37] For this reason some builders urged that the cubic content be used as a basis of assessment rather than the number of windows, but it was naturally easier and quicker to count windows than measure walls.

---

34. Harrison, "Social Reform in Victorian Leeds," p. 48.

35. *Leeds Slumdom* (Leeds, Halliday), pp. 20–24.

36. *Present Condition of the Working Classes,* p. 46.

37. *First Report of the Commissioners for Inquiring into the State of Large Towns and Populous Districts, 1* (London, Clowes, 1844), 238–39.

Around and about the poorer houses of Leeds there were two basic spatial elements, the court and the street. The court, or yard, was obviously contrived from the medieval "burgage." These were originally strip lots along the Briggate, the main street of the town. Woledge has suggested in his study of medieval Leeds that, "The site occupied by each of these yards and the buildings opening off it is no doubt a very early unit of land which has been developed by building over what was originally a back garden."[38] The original burgages totaled thirty on the east side of the street and thirty-five on the west. The average frontage was estimated as 3 perches, or 49½ feet, with a depth varying between 10 and 18 perches. He regards the breakdown from the original land divisions into the "dark and airless yards" as having already begun by 1341, when eighteen burgesses still held a burgage apiece, but twenty-three owned only fractions ranging from an eighth to five sixths of a unit.[39] The advantage of owning a burgage in the thirteenth and fourteenth centuries (besides the fact that it faced on the chief market street) was that it was free from villein disabilities and hence easy to buy and sell.[40]

The Giles map of Leeds of 1815 (Fig. 25) also shows that the town even then had expanded by only a few streets to the east and west of the Briggate. The curves and turns of the old roads winding out of town with their few houses were about to provide the larger pattern for an enormous filling process by what was essentially a medieval mode, the elongated court, or yard. The resulting congestion was classic.

> The courts and *cul-de-sac* exist everywhere. The building of houses back to back occasions this in great measure . . . In one *cul-de-sac,* in the town of Leeds, there are 34 houses, and in ordinary times, there dwell in these houses 340 persons, or ten in every house; but as these houses are many of them receiving houses for itinerant labourers during the periods of hay-time and harvest, and the fairs, at least twice that number are then here congregated.[41]

This description referred specifically to the so-called Boot and Shoe Yard off Kirkgate, which had one of the worst cholera records in the town and was supposed to have paid the best interest to its owners. Many of these courts were several feet below street level and could be reached only through a narrow door and steps. The sense of isolation was affecting. "The inhabitants of

38. "The Medieval Borough of Leeds," *The Thoresby Miscellany,* 2 (Leeds, 1945), 294.
39. Ibid., p. 299.
40. Ibid., p. 301.

41. Baker, *Report on Leeds,* p. 353. The houses used for lodging and the cellar dwellings created even greater problems of congestion.

courts and alleys can never see what is passing along the adjoining street, and this is one reason why so many groups of poor men and women are always standing at the ends of the courts and alleys in a town, staring at the passengers as if they had never seen a man before in their lives."[42] The feeling of confinement was supposed to be one undesirable result of the court. The concealment of vice, depravity, and misery was another.

> If you hear a quarrel between two women, it is sure to be up some court or alley. If you see a fight between two men, it is sure to be up some court or alley . . . If you hear of a barbarous murder committed upon some unsuspecting youth, it will turn out that he was decoyed to a public house up some court or alley to see some cheap silk handkerchiefs. . . . So [says Maslen], I strongly recommend, for the good of all classes, that courts and alleys be abolished; and let men live in wide streets, and act openly and honestly in the sight of all.[43]

A changeover in emphasis from court to street was to be the primary recommendation for the rehabilitation of Leeds. Yet it was more easily spoken of than accomplished. The dense land coverage had previously forced many of the house functions out into the narrow streets which tended to become adjuncts to the houses and courts rather than thoroughfares. Horsemen were constantly dismounted by forgotten clotheslines, and broken legs were occasioned by the unprotected entrances to cellar dwellings. The inhabitants threw refuse and ashes into the street, which sent up a black and irritating dust or left the surface soft and spongy in wet weather.[44] The dependence of the house on the street was nowhere more in evidence than in the lack of out-offices. What the twentieth century considers a private necessity, the nineteenth century in Leeds thought of as a casual public convenience, to be fitted in if and where other buildings permitted:

> A great many of the privies of the cottages are in small passages, between clumps of houses, which are different properties; others, with the ash entrance open to the public streets; and others at a little distance from, and open to, the front of the houses; whilst some streets are entirely without. The inhabitants, to use the language of an old woman, of whom inquiry was made, say "that they do as they can, and make use of the street itself as the common receptacle."[45]

42. Maslen, p. 213.
43. Ibid., pp. 212–13.

44. Baker, *Report on Leeds*, p. 350.
45. Ibid., p. 356.

Fig. 25. Netlam and Giles map of Leeds, 1815. The center shows the medieval Briggate with its moot hall, houses, and market runn
down the middle and on each side the elongated medieval yards or courts which were to become such a vicious feature when they w
rapidly multiplied during the nineteenth century.

The use of the street to obtain additional living or work space had already been typified by medieval Briggate. Until 1825 it had a row of houses attached to its moot hall, running down the middle for approximately a quarter of its distance, dividing on the east into a narrow alley called the Shambles (the former wool market) and on the west into the Back of the Shambles.[46] The habit of conceiving of the street as a "place" more than a right-of-way was undoubtedly as much of a holdover from the Middle Ages as the courts of Leeds or the tall slum houses of Glasgow. The abuse of the archetypes derived from the fact that there were no restraints, no ground rules, with which to modify the effects of the flood of population pushing in upon them. It shows clearly enough the futility of desiring a restitution of the "true" Gothic city, since the forms that were inherited had been so often perverted. One can understand, therefore, that the neo-Medievalists were not so much romantic searchers for some distant mirage but were striving to retrieve a tradition whose remains, as in Leeds, were still readily discernible in the actual environment. In 1842 only 86 of nearly 600 streets in the town came under municipal control, and few of these were both sewered and paved.[47] In 1896, after an outbreak of fever had revived the perennial interest in the subject of housing there, a witness observed that, "It is a curious fact there are hardly any two streets in the old part of the town that ever make connection with one another."[48]

 The Street Becomes Predominant

However, an urge toward light, air, and mobility in cities was soon to burst forth all over England, culminating in the Public Health Act of 1875. Its chief instrument was to be the straight, wide, continuous way—the "bye-law" street. The second report (p. 55 n.) on the state of large towns of 1845 considered it a distinct benefit to enable a circulation of the population through courts and yards. Their disgraceful condition had been concealed from the passerby, which provided the local authorities with an excuse for not exercising jurisdiction over them. It was also believed that the time had come when the width of streets might be regulated. In Leeds it had been largely left to each landowner to please himself in the matter.[49] Private opinion out-

46. E. Baines, *Gazetteer, 1,* 18.

47. Baker, *Report on Leeds,* pp. 350, 352.

48. *Minutes of Proceedings Taken Before the Select Committee on Private Bills,* Group F, On the Local Government Provisional Orders (Housing of Working Classes), Leeds Order Bill (Monday, June 13, 1896), p. 3.

49. P. 106. By 1871 when the Bradford Improvement Act was passed, streets in that town were required to have a clear width of 42 to 60 ft., with the dwelling not to be higher than the width of the street. "Bradford," *Architect* (March 4, 1876), p. 139.

side the government was beginning to hold that not only might the width and direction of the streets be controlled but that such rules would also furnish an opportunity to move on to a rudimentary master plan.

Maslen, for example, had originally considered Halifax a cleaner city than Leeds and, because it was both ancient and opulent, took a lenient view of its failings. "We must not quarrel with the relics of times," he said tolerantly, "when regularity of plans, and utility, health, comfort, convenience and beauty in buildings and streets were things far from the thoughts of men."[50] But the annoying fact was that the modern inhabitants of Halifax, like those of Leeds, simply would not mend their ways. They kept on laying out pitiful little streets. A bit later we find Maslen losing his temper entirely and his hard-won historic perspective into the bargain:

> Halifax is a mass of little, miserable, narrow, ill-looking streets, jumbled together in chaotic confusion, as if they had all been in a sack, and emptied out together upon the ground, one rolling this way, another rolling that way, and each standing where chance happened to throw it: there is not one handsome or long street in the town, and the cause of this is the want of previously surveying the ground for the town.[51] . . . I have, myself, gone up one or two of the new streets, and have been called out to by some good woman— "there is no passage that way, Sir; you must return, and go down that lane, then turn to the right into a lane, at the bottom of which you will get into the street you want."[52]

His best advice to all towns was to set up hundred-year programs in which the widening and straightening of streets should be done in concert, rather than leaving improvement to an occasional widening project alone.[53] The determining feature in each street would be an imaginary center line drawn on an official map from which all building lines could be controlled in the future. As the old houses became ruinous they would be pulled down and new structures erected farther back. This century-long "gradualism" would bring a greater efficiency and cleanliness to the urban scene and also encourage the beauty which, theoretically at least, derives from being constantly under public scrutiny.

> A long straight street can be more easily drained than a crooked short street; and a wide street enjoys more sun, is lighter, more

50. Maslen, pp. 115–16.   52. Ibid., p. 116.
51. Ibid., pp. 116–17.   53. Ibid., p. 109.

cheerful, more airy, easier of thoroughfare, and possesses greater
capabilities of improvement and beautifying than a narrow street.
One that is both straight, wide, and long, can scarcely fail of becoming handsome in the course of years, however humble its inhabitants may be originally, as some of the owners of the property
therein will, from time to time, acquire wealth, and improve the
houses they live in.[54]

An appearance of orderliness and uniformity is advocated which turns up
a decade later in the model villages like Saltaire, where still later, at the end
of the century, it was to be deplored by Fletcher and other romantically inclined visitors.

There were, naturally enough, those who already had misgivings about
urban dynamics in a rigid frame—such as Henry Austin, architect and past
engineer for the Blackwall Railway. His work in laying track through London had persuaded him that as far as population density was concerned, this
brand of progress had only made a bad situation worse. He estimated that the
usual size of the rooms in the districts in which he had pulled down houses
was 8 x 10 or 10 x 12 feet and by his own admission concluded that his actions
had caused the population to become even more crowded, since large numbers of the displaced inhabitants had ended by doubling up. From his railroad experience he wished to urge caution in cutting thoroughfare streets
through densely crowded districts.[55]

Nevertheless, the image of the long, wide, straight street had successfully
captured the attention of the authorities. Even problems that were not residential but circulatory came to be solved by the "philosophy" of the new
street. In Leeds this was illustrated by the improvement of the Camp Field
Insanitary Area. The Housing of the Working Classes Act of 1890 allowed
the Corporation either to buy whole areas and clear them or to condemn individual buildings that detracted from surrounding structures.[56] The Camp
Field Improvement was an instance of the second power.

Because the field in which the houses were laid out was approximately rectangular, the original outline of the complex was also regular and consisted
essentially of four rows of back-to-back houses (Fig. 26). However, even before these basic rows had been completed, secondary courts and yards were
being tucked in among them.[57] There appears to have been no logical reason

54. Ibid., Preface, p. v.
55. *First Report on the State of Large Towns, 1* (1844), 355.
56. F. M. Lupton, *Housing Improvement, A*

Summary of Ten Years Work in Leeds (Leeds, Jowett and Sowry, 1906), p. 4.
57. See the Giles Map of 1815.

for this beyond local custom, since the fields surrounding it were open. Under the 1890 act the 238 inhabitants in 59 dwellings were swept out from between the main rows, and two streets were run through.[58] There was no vehicular traffic permitted on them and they were closed at either end by iron posts (Fig. 27). Yet they were plainly streets in form, if not function. A curious sidelight on current semantics is that these revamped streets or walks were still sometimes referred to as "courts."[59] After the improvement all the interior houses received as much sunshine and ventilation as those facing the original outer streets.

The progression in dominant spatial shape from court to street can be illustrated as well, if not better, by photographs. Woodhead's Yard in Leeds of the early nineteenth century was so sealed off from the city outside as to create its own microcosmos (Fig. 28). Quite typically for Leeds, a slightly higher saw-tooth building rises at the rear, and what amounts to half a back-to-back house projects into the court. For all its drawbacks, the court does convey a picturesque and cloistered feeling which the external, bye-law reform of the streets would abruptly end. And there is a hint of eighteenth-century grace still lingering in the architecture. One can imagine that newly arrived rural groups might even welcome its sense of temporary shelter and security from the huge and impersonal city. On Clark Street (1850–60) the characteristic Leeds closure of buildings at the end still keeps the street within visible limits, but all else has changed. The street is now open and straight and almost empty of incident (Fig. 29). The wall planes are flatter and harder, the windows and doors deeper set and more harshly outlined. The heavy lintels exaggerate their essential form and set up a horizontal rhythm. The cornice and chimney line, like the sidewalk it repeats, is notably insistent too.

 The Interminable Street

When this new insistence on the priority of the line and continuous plane in Leeds was carried out in the full-fledged bye-law street of Birmingham (1880–90) the street and house achieved a mutual reformation (Fig. 30). The greater width and directness of the street were rendered necessary for municipal health and efficiency, but the price has been tremendous. Nothing remains of the intimacy of even the poorest courts of the past. Nor are there as yet any mitigating effects from nature—no intervening grass or trees between the

---

58. G. F. Carter, "Operation of the Housing of the Working Classes Act in Leeds," *Journal* *of the Sanitary Institute* [c. 1890–95], *18*, Part IV, p. 471.

59. Lupton, p. 10.

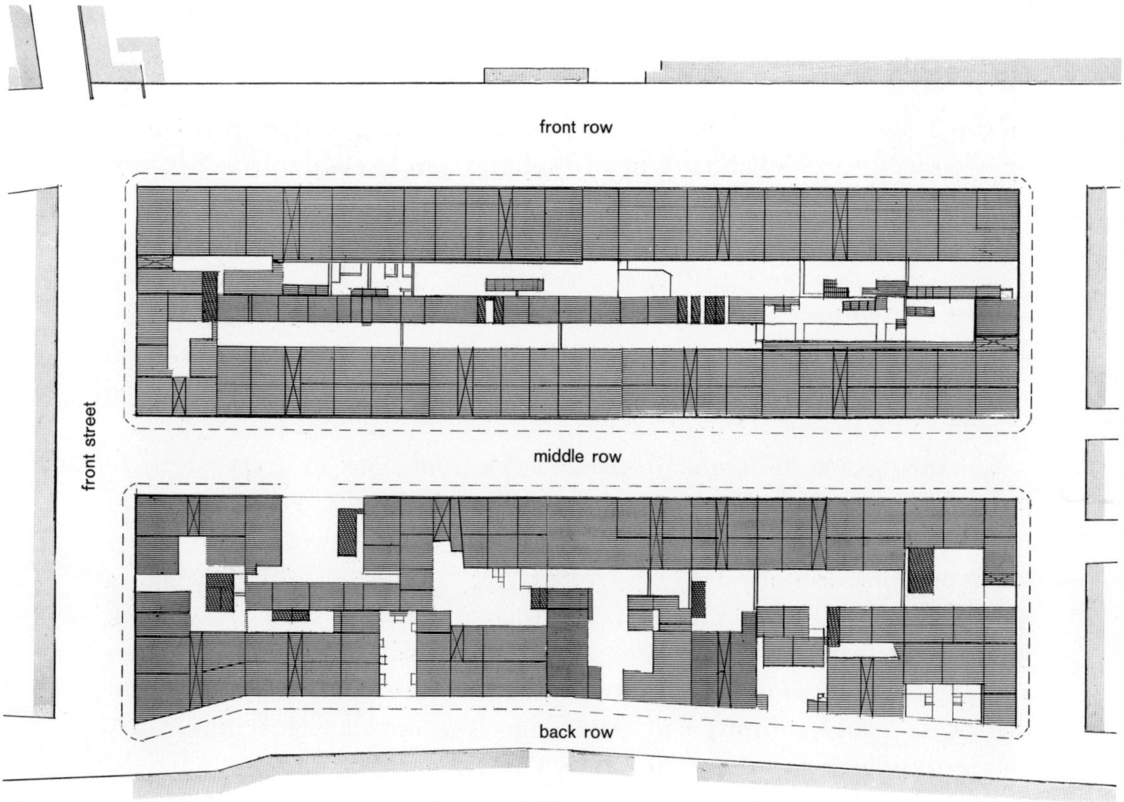

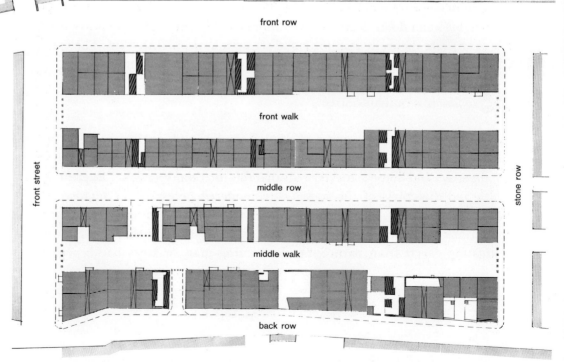

front row

front street

middle row

back row

Fig. 26. Camp Field, Leeds, before improvement.

front row

front street

front walk

middle row

stone row

middle walk

back row

Fig. 27. Camp Field, Leeds, after improvement. At Camp Field, southwest of the town, bye-law streets were substituted for the older courts or yards, but they had no destination—instead, they were used as tidier, more open, courts, with posts at either end, continuing the conviction that a street should provide auxiliary living space for the houses, always too small in themselves.

Fig. 28. *Woodhead's Yard, Leeds, c. 1820. Half of a back-to-back house is visible in the background.*

Fig. 29. *Clark Street, Saynor Lane, Hunslet District, Leeds, 1850–60. Back-to-back houses with a single downstairs living room and two bedrooms up represent a more orderly but more monotonous and harsh idiom than the courts. If anywhere, sanitary conveniences were at the end of the row.*

Fig. 30. Bye-law street, Bournbrook, Birmingham, 1880–90. The width and straightness of the street follow the reform embodied in the Public Health Acts of 1872–75. The lonely children playing at the left appear to typify the whole progression of the nineteenth century, with the people remaining the same size but the cities getting larger and longer.

street and houses. These latest streets are so cold and impersonal, so sterile, that they appear to aggravate the original loss of identity and personal locus which the town and factory had brought at the outset of the industrial revolution. One might even welcome some petty crime or misdemeanor if only to demonstrate that the culture which produced them was subject to human error and emotion.[60] To see children playing in them, as here, is to experience a great loneliness. The street space is swept so clean as to approach emotional emptiness and complete negation. "Englishmen," observed the Hammonds in *The Town Labourer,* "thought of their great towns not with hope, or pride, or ambition, but with a haunting fear."[61]

It could be assumed that their naked ugliness placed these streets beneath serious aesthetic consideration in any event. But a comparison with other

60. Karel Čapek, as quoted in Francesca M. Wilson, *Strange Island* (London, Longmans, Green, 1955), p. 245, says "no revolutionary throngs will ever march through the streets be-cause these streets are too long. And also too dull." Čapek coined the word "robot."

61. (London, Longmans, Green, 1920), p. 53.

European pictorial statements of the eighteenth and nineteenth centuries offers evidence that these were as much a result of the essential spirit of the time
as were the more conscious images. The main difference was of degree rather
than character. If the Birmingham bye-law street be compared with the
Lange Strasse project for Karlsruhe in Germany (Fig. 31) of the first decade
of the nineteenth century, we see that the lack of architectural stylism in the
English street bears some resemblance to the German neo-Classic project,
which was not influenced by the industrial revolution. Both manifest a desire
to bring surfaces, volumes, and open spaces under a more thoroughgoing control. Weinbrenner, the architect of the Lange Strasse, hoped to pull a number
of earlier and irregular house facades into a new unity by employing long,
neo-Classic arcades. There were to be few architectural pauses from towers
or pavilions along the way. It was a street that found its significance in uniform direction rather than in volumetric modulation or in final spatial resolution.

It could be argued that this kind of compulsive order is inherent in the
form of a through street whenever a town begins to grow rapidly, as Karlsruhe and Birmingham certainly did in the nineteenth century. Therefore the
bye-law street as a total form still fails to qualify for the broader and higher
realms of artistic discussion. But if we retrogress again to some such example
as Boullée's interior for a French national library (Fig. 32) of the 1780s, it becomes still more evident that the generators of form for the English streets are
not to be found among economic, hygienic, and sociological causes alone. In
this huge room individuals have lost much of their pertinence, just as they do
in the corridor street. Inanimate objects, like the lines of books, contribute
much more to its spatial articulation. The rows of shelves, the columns above,
and the coffers of the great arched vault flatten the planes and have in addition sharp horizontal separations between them. The objects within the space
have become highly classified. The quick repetitive rhythms of the Ionic columns equate with the arcades of the Lange Strasse and the repeating windows, doors, and chimneys of the bye-law streets. The converging perspective
lines draw the eye into the picture but reward it with no final, focal accent.
The architectural situation is altogether detached and uncompromising. This
effect is heightened by the evenness of the cool neo-Classic light which floods
in from above and discourages any attempt at Baroque modeling.

The implication again is that the English street cannot be ascribed solely
to minimal reform interacting with basic economic forces. Although its peculiar features arose out of local conditions, it also had a relationship to the in-

Fig. 31. Lange Strasse Project, Karlsruhe, Germany; F. Weinbrenner, 1808. The neo-Classic street preceded the bye-law street with its interminability.

Fig. 32. Project for the French National Library; E. Boullée, 1788. The unifying impulse behind the English bye-law street may have appeared first in the grandiose neo-Classic dreams of the French Revolution, with their novel building types. Interior urban forms correlate with exterior spaces because of the double need for order and concentration of large numbers of people and systems of knowledge, as in Imperial Rome.

ternational mood and scene, having been anticipated by several decades in the imagination of the neo-Classic architects of the Continent. The sheer rationality of neo-Classicism signaled a release from traditional disciplines and amenities—social, economic, and spatial. The typical reaction was one of release after compression. So it might rebound all the way to fantasy, as with the Ledoux and Boullée drawings, or Hubert Robert's imaginary painting of the artificially ruined long gallery of the Louvre at the end of the eighteenth century; or it could descend into stark reality as with the Birmingham bye-law street. Besides the intellectualism the important change was the increased contrast of scale. The consideration of forms at a great scale was a counterpart to the new abstraction, through urban statistical studies, of human beings as units.

What is so eternally damning about the bye-law street is that the first re-form or "improvement" brought in by rationalism, working through the industrial revolution, should turn out to be so urbanistically cold, harsh, and desolate.

High Flats or Low Houses

In order to miss none of the issues of urbanism, which each generation appears to prefer to discover anew, it should be pointed out that the great twentieth-century debate about high and low, single or multiple, dwellings went on in a subdued vein throughout the nineteenth century as well. G. F. Carter came out for flats in Leeds at the end of the century, although he readily admitted that only one unit had ever been built there. He proposed that it be no more than two to four stories in height under any condition.[62] He claimed that suitable housing could not otherwise be provided at a decent price for the lower classes; he followed Baker in advising against gardens because of their marginal expense, and stood with Akroyd and Thomas Cubbit against the abolition of back-to-back houses on the same principle.[63] He was opposed by F. M. Lupton, the chairman of the Unhealthy Areas Committee which improved Camp Field (Figs. 26, 27), who abhorred such flats or "barracks." He felt they lacked privacy, it was difficult to supervise children from them, and that they were unnecessarily hard on the aged and infirm. Besides, cheap land was still available within a mile of the most crowded parts of the city.[64] But Maslen, writing sixty years earlier, better typifies the more enduring attitude. He sat firmly on the fence, debating with himself meanwhile:

> I never wish to see the English people live in houses with more than
> four or five stories; yet if they did, I am persuaded it would make
> all our cities and towns incomparably more compact, and very much
> more beautiful. I, however, succumb to the old custom of separate
> dwellings; but I deny that it is the cause of more health or more
> cleanliness.[65]

62. Carter, p. 469.
63. For Cubbit see *First Report on the State of large towns*, 2, 264.
64. Lupton, p. 3.
65. Maslen, p. 241.

4. THE OASIS AT BEDFORD PARK

 Bedford Park (1875–81) was tied to London by its artistic and intellectual life and by the surveillance of both of these by the popular press. The relationship was sharply delineated on maps by the railroad tracks which connected it with Charing Cross Station in London. Even now the best approach to it from London is along the railroad embankment, from which one can comprehend at a glance the verdant basin of trees in which it rests. The importance of the railroad is further demonstrated by the Bedford Park stores, inn, church, and schools, which are adjacent to the station.

A newspaper of 1880 presented the picture much as it can still be observed:

> On approaching Turnham Green Railway Station the red-tiled roofs of the Bedford Park Estate, as it is called, are seen gleaming through the delicate leafage of the trees. The charm of the scene has been greatly enhanced by the loving tenderness with which every possible tree has been preserved. . . . [here are] neither mansions nor mews but comfortable dwellings fitted for persons wishing to live within 30 minutes of town.[1]

Two of its determining features were thus clearly recognised even before it was finished. It was to provide the first sylvan setting for the commuting middle class "where the nightingale and the skylark could still be heard."

The beginning issue of the *Bedford Park Gazette* announced that the story of the suburb had opened in 1875 when Jonathan T. Carr, the developer, acquired twenty-four acres of land adjoining an old Georgian manse known as Bedford House. The property took its name from the brothers Bedford to whom it had belonged. The intermediate owner was Dr. John Lindley (1799–1865), Curator of the Royal Horticultural Society Gardens at Chiswick

1. *Daily News* (May 5, 1880).

nearby (the same gardens in which Joseph Paxton had worked from 1823 to 1826). It was Lindley's trees which the plan of Bedford Park (Fig. 33) was calculated to save.[2] Moncure D. Conway (1832–1907), the Anglo-American clergyman and community leader of Bedford Park, in describing it for the

Fig. 33. Plan of Bedford Park, Chiswick; Maurice B. Adams, 1896.

American *Harper's,* explained the character of the street pattern as follows: "It is said some of the streets of Boston, Massachusetts, followed old sheep paths; and it may now be entered in the archives of Bedford Park, against its becoming a city, that its streets and gardens have largely been decided by Dr. Lindley's trees."[3]

2. July 1883, p. 2. By the time of this report, 113 acres had been obtained, with 490 houses built.
3. 62 (March 1881), 486.

The visual impact of the setting and its abrupt contrast with the more conventional suburbs around London were everywhere discussed. *The Pictorial World* of 1880 said, "The pretty houses are dotted among the trees, and even when there is the least approach to a hard line of frontage, there is always some group of greenery to break the ugliness of the mere thought of a dead level."[4] *The Illustrated Sporting and Dramatic News,* after entitling it "a novelty in suburban dwellings," remarked that, "Here too the houses stand in rows and are all more or less alike, but the sentiment of dull uniformity and monotony of which we complain is ingeniously destroyed by the variety of form and design introduced into the buildings themselves, the arrangements of thoroughfares, and changes in the relative positions of the houses."[5] The perspicacity of the observations in these popular, nonprofessional media can only be explained by the depth of the response which its novelty aroused. Another reason why it may have been so easily assimilated at the outset comes from *The Pioneer:* "It is hardly four years since the first brick of the first house was laid, and the last houses were only completed yesterday; yet the whole place has the snug, warm look of having been inhabited for at least a century."[6] The English dual requirement, the seeking of new images through the restoration of old values, was cogently expressed.

The street picture was what attracted the attention of the earliest commentators. One said, "The peculiar characteristic of these streets is the utter absence of that stiffness which always seems to attend the chilly, regular, and hideous house-rows of our other suburbs."[7] Another wrote, "All the others [except one straight road] appear closed at the end by trees and houses, and form a succession of views, as if the architect had taken a hint from Nature, who, when in a pleasant lazy mood, will dispose such mighty rivers as the Rhine and Hudson to form a series of lake views."[8]

The streets were different and followed a natural feature of plantation. But the block system of land division, long and narrow, was more conventional and disqualifies Bedford Park from serious consideration as a garden suburb, even though it has often been so described. What harmonized these disparate elements, and indeed all the features of the Park, was the new and revolutionary consciousness of space brought alive by light filtering through the trees. The streets were wide and had fifteen- to twenty-foot setbacks. This represented the beginning of the essentially modern and middle-class search for some effective compromise between street and home, dynamic and static,

---

4. July 17.
5. Supplement (Sept. 27, 1879), p. 27.
6. March 22, 1881.

7. *Chamber's Journal* (Dec. 31, 1881), p. 839.
8. *Daily News* (May 5, 1880).

public and private, big scale and little elements in the suburban picture, in a delayed and removed reaction to the larger problems of the bigger city.

There were a few single and row houses, but the majority were semidetached. They were placed on lots fifty feet wide and seventy-five feet deep. Pleasing vignettes could be caught down the streets and across the blocks through the open side yards (Fig. 34). Along the roads, in addition to Dr. Lindley's original trees, were planted limes, poplars, and especially willows; in the gardens there were apple, pear, and plum trees.[9] The *Ballard of Bedford Park,* modeled on Gilbert and Sullivan's operetta, *Patience,* by taking up an actual incident for satirization,[10] conveyed perhaps more clearly than intended the atmosphere of the environment:

> And Abbey (he, the artist,
>   Malicious little wretch)
> Said it made him feel like walking
>   Through a water-colour sketch![11]

There was a quality of luminosity in Bedford Park that did suggest a watercolor sketch but, as with the earlier romanticism of Hanover Park in Salford, there is also the temptation to draw analogies with contemporary French oil painting (Fig. 35). Pissarro, Daubigny, and Monet had fled to London with the outbreak of the Franco-Prussian War in 1870, and the mid-1870s in France and England marked the beginnings of Impressionism. Its shimmering light, its preoccupation with out-of-doors scenes (as was also to some extent the case with the Pre-Raphaelites), and above all the rich and colorful charm within a positive and beneficent nature, invites the comparison.

It will also be recalled that, although Colonel Akroyd at Akroydon had no thought of putting his row houses on independent lots, he did seek to give each owner identity through a monogram over his door. At Bedford Park the lot itself became a badge of distinction. John Betjeman has noted that Bedford Park, "the most significant suburb built in the last century," belonged to a period when "the middle classes were riddled with subtle distinctions." Each person literally aspired to be his own squire at the Park. "The railway could take him to his work and he could be at home with his wife and chil-

9. "Death of Mr. Jonathan Carr, Founder of Bedford Park," *Chiswick Times* (Feb. 5, 1915); *Daily News* (May 5, 1880); *Building News* (Dec. 22, 1876, and Nov. 9, 1877, p. 451).

10. Edwin Abbey did not live in Bedford Park but took great interest in it and came to look at it soon after its completion, remarking, pleasantly enough, that he "felt as though he were walking through a water-colour" according to Moncure Conway, *Autobiography,* 2 (Boston and New York, Houghton, Mifflin, 1905), 375. He and Conway were jointly employed by *Harper's.*

11. *St. James Gazette, 3* (Dec. 17, 1881), 11.

Fig. 34. Newton Grove Road, Bedford Park; J. Nash, 1882. Views through the side yards from street to street distinguished Bedford Park as a new and middle-class suburb.

Fig. 35. La Route de Sydenham; Camille Pissarro, 1871. Driven from Paris by the Franco-Prussian War, Monet and Pissarro settled in London, where Pissarro painted in the suburbs of Norwood and Sydenham. In the same decade of Impressionism in painting Bedford Park was laid out. The English house was externalized and the light was modulated through shimmering trees. Artists of the time noticed the "sketchiness" of Bedford Park streets.

dren in the evenings in what seemed like country. The suburb was the fulfill-
ment of every man's dream—a house of his own in the country,"[12] a symbol of
upward transition. The modern tendency of a lesser class to aspire architecturally to the emblems of those above provides the same answer to the often
heard criticism that side yards and single lots are wasteful and uneconomic—
that was to be the splendor and glory of them at Bedford Park!

From the circumstances surrounding its creation developed what might be
called, because they appear in some respect insoluble, the three mysteries of
Bedford Park. The first concerns how the "Queen Anne" style with its red
brick, thick sash bars, white trim, and semi-elliptical pediments and scrolls
should be interpreted. Professors Pevsner and Hitchcock and Mr. Dudley
Habron have greatly enlarged our knowledge of the course of the style, but
in this setting it offers some special difficulties.[13] The Quennells in their *History of Everyday Things in England* would deny even the courtesy of the
term, Queen Anne, to Bedford Park because they feel it illustrated a revival
of the early Renaissance rather than the later, which they preferred to call
Queen Anne.[14]

However, if we refer to the speech in 1861 of the Reverend J. L. Petit, "On
the Revival of the Styles," instead of to John Stevenson's talk in 1874 which
is more often taken as the beginning of the acceptance of the style, we understand why the problem of definition as Queen Anne would exist, particularly
in connection with middle-class houses.[15] Petit recommends its consideration
as a national style because it could be used through the whole range of monumental to vernacular buildings, as Gothic and Classic could not. It had a
solid, dignified, and convenient air about it which eliminated the preoccupation with insignificant decoration. And it promised, Petit said, to give "gran-
deur, and some picturesqueness to many of our street views."[16] It was the
greater adaptability of the Queen Anne style that drew such men; they would
rather concentrate on the opportunities for further eclecticism of the single

12. "Suburbs Common or Garden," *Daily
Telegraph and Morning Post* (Aug. 22, 1960), p.
11.

13. Nikolaus Pevsner, "Richard Norman
Shaw 1831–1912," *Architectural Review* (March
1941), pp. 41–46; Henry-Russell Hitchcock,
Early Victorian Architecture in Britain (New
Haven, Yale University Press, 1954), p. 332;
Dudley Habron, "Queen Anne Taste and Aes-
theticism," *Architectural Review*, 64 (July,
1943), 15–18.

14. Vol. 4, 1851–1942 (London, Batsford,
1941–42), p. 105.

15. Petit, *Builder* (May 25), pp. 350–52.
Stevenson, "On The Recent Reaction of Taste
in Architecture," *Builder* (June 27, 1874), pp.
537–40. (Also *Building News*, June 26, 1874,
pp. 689–95; *Architect, 12*, 1874, 1; *Building
News*, March 13, 1875, p. 285.) Professor Peter
Collins of McGill University kindly called my
attention to the precedence of the Petit reference. See his valuable essay "Aspects of Ornament," *Architectural Review* (June, 1961), pp.
374–75, for connections with eclecticism and the
domestic style.

16. Petit, p. 351.

style than on its accurate interpretation. In many ways the Queen Anne in Shaw's hands was to become the overture to that simultaneous stylistic and technical event that could be described as inventive or dynamic eclecticism. It passes over into H. H. Richardson's works in the United States and then to architects like Stanford White, John Calvin Stevens, Bernard Maybeck, and even Frank Lloyd Wright. That this heralded no mere research for greater academic correctness or a more sophisticated substyle is demonstrated by a letter written two years before his death by Shaw in which he spoke, somewhat grumpily, of his disillusionment with the neo-Gothic, "there was any amount of tall talk as to what it was to do, but it didn't do a thing."[17] Sir George Gilbert Scott in 1878 saw the Queen Anne as a reaction rather than a revival, since he believed he had been more consistent in following the true path to what he termed "Modernism" through the neo-Gothic, but his remarks show that he was well aware of an increasing impatience with the formalities of the earlier style.[18] As still another writer observed just a few months before Stevenson, "The bondage of strict gothicism was becoming intolerable, the unfailing accuracy of its movements seemed oppressive on occasions not the most serious."[19]

Stevenson preferred the more embracing term, "Free Classic," in order to include within it the various phases of the brick architecture of the time of Queen Anne and the early Georges.[20] He was depressed by the prospect of what might happen if it were to be taken up by the general public, or at least those who normally built for these classes. "Tags and shreds of the style will doubtless appear in speculative builders' houses, and we may even see street rows in it, violating its best characteristic of freedom and spontaneity by repeating the same fantastic gable or the same elaborate porch as many times over as there are houses in the row."[21] This prophecy was delivered only a year before Bedford Park was begun. The "public" was in substance to take up there the Queen Anne style and, owing to Shaw's skillful treatment of its "freedom and spontaneity," to achieve an effect too good to be true, according to Stevenson. This is why the Park must have carried so much conviction and appeared at first so timely. As a later author was to express the stylistic advantages in 1896, "It is this power of blending certain features hitherto deemed irreconcilable that gave the Queen Anne the vitality of a new

17. As quoted in Sir Reginald Blomfield, *Richard Norman Shaw, R. A. Architect, 1831–1912* (London, Batsford, 1940), p. 31.

18. Scott, *Personal and Professional Recollections* (London, Sampson Low, Marston, Searle and Rivington, 1879), pp. 374–76.

19. *Building News* (Jan. 16, 1874), p. 79.

20. Stevenson, p. 540.

21. Ibid.

growth."[22] In one phase at Bedford Park this adaptability extended so far beyond style as to present an entirely new picture of street composition, in another it took on a more honest use of materials. "Here brick is openly brick, and wood is openly wood, and paint is openly paint. Nothing comes in a mean, sneaking way, pretending to be that which it is not."[23]

We entertain this notion gladly until we recognize that the assertion was made against the "new" cast iron and plate glass. However, this attitude was not directed toward the greater potential of the new materials but against their more common misuses. The social and technical innovations were there, yet they served different purposes from those we have so far been trained to observe. Even though the public image of the Park was to become decidedly that of an aesthetic colony, it was also an effort to bring the merchant and the retired officer into sympathy with "artists, authors, men of science, and members of professions, whether their profession be that of the Bar or that of the Stage."[24] The broader aim might be described as one of re-establishing the artistic individualist, the Bohemian, within the society and linking him with the growing middle class. For that reason it might also be looked upon as more "modern" than the working-class villages of the North. But like them it sought primarily to reintegrate occupational groups, which had been dispersed, by invoking the memory of the ancient village. And, as *Building News* put the matter, it really attempted to do for the middle class what the Shaftesbury Park Estate of 1874–75 had just done for the artisan class.[25] The latter was, along with Baroness Burdett Coutts' Bethnal Green of 1860, the closest equivalent in the London area to the model villages of the North, if its later date, lack of direct contact with industry, and relationship to the London residential square, terrace, and tenement may be discounted.

A later essay by Shaw was entitled, "That an Artist Is not Necessarily Unpractical." His claim was backed by Bedford Park. As the local paper stated, commercial success at the Park was duly subordinated to the purpose of establishing a settlement that should possess "artistic and sanitary advantages superior to those to be found in any other suburb of London."[26] This bipolar declaration of intent, stretching from art to hygiene, apparently found its reflection in the daily life of the community, documented by a slightly later

22. "G.," "The Revival of English Domestic Architecture, II, The Work of Mr. Norman Shaw," *Studio*, 7 (1896), 102.

23. *Illustrated Sporting and Dramatic News* (Sept. 27, 1879), p. 27.

24. *Bedford Park Gazette* (July 1883), p. 3.

25. (Dec. 22, 1876), p. 621. I owe this reference to Miss Dora Wiebenson's excellent paper, "City Planning 1850–75," from Professor Henry-Russell Hitchcock's class at New York University of May 1, 1957.

26. Bedford Park Gazette (July 1883), p. 3.

announcement in the paper that the two public lectures for December of 1883 were to be on "Goethe and His Forerunners," followed shortly by "Digestion, Circulation and Respiration."

In 1871 the Prince of Wales nearly succumbed to typhoid fever which had been traced to defective drainage. According to Shaw's biographer, Blomfield, it was he who then began the custom of placing the soil and waste pipes on the outside wall of houses, with free ventilation and intercepting traps, thus initiating the abstract pattern of external plumbing which never fails to catch the foreigner's eye.[27] Devey, Webb, and Shaw were also responsible for bringing the kitchen up out of the basement, an innovation which seems to have made a singular impression in Bedford Park because of its nearness to London where basement kitchens were the rule.[28] Each dwelling rested on a solid bed of concrete with only a ventilating space beneath.[29] These features were advertised as following the "well-known" views of Dr. Benjamin Richardson (a sanitary reformer and the man who proposed the town of Hygeia in 1875) on the construction of modern houses. Hot and cold water and interior toilets were also part of the equipment of each house. Because of soil difficulties, in 1882 the proprietor had to lay a second and deeper sewer system with pumping stations.[30] This expense, plus the fact that the excavators accidentally came upon the graves of victims of a London plague, which had to be transferred, no doubt hastened the court petitions of 1886 to wind up the company.[31]

The technology, like the sociology and aestheticism, was more concerned with improving the general environment for mental and physical health than with the distinctions of special materials. The Dr. Gordon Hogg residence by E. J. May is another illustration of how this applied indoors as well as out. The windows and fireplaces were hermetically sealed and the air in each room changed every twenty minutes. In winter the air was sent over hot water pipes and in summer through water or over ice. It was cleaned by pass-

27. Blomfield, pp. 41–42.

28. The Quennells, op. cit., 4 (1941–42), 94.

29. M. Conway, "Bedford Park," Harper's New Monthly Magazine, 62 (March 1881), 484. John Brandon-Jones, "The Work of Philip Webb and Norman Shaw," Architectural Assn. Journal (June 1955), pp. 10, 17, points out that Shaw was much interested in reinforced concrete and exposed steelwork as well.

30. Bedford Park Gazette (Nov. 1883), pp. 49–50, 59. See also "Bedford Park" in Lady's Pictorial (June 24, 1882), p. 314, and Building News (June 2, 1882), p. 685.

31. Building News (Sept. 10, 1886), p. 407. Sir Arthur Comyns Carr, nephew of Jonathan Carr, told the author in a telephone conversation in July 1960 of the financial difficulties. The Ballard of Bedford Park seems to suggest in one of its last stanzas that by 1881 Carr had already "sold out to a company" in some manner. Building News (July 22, 1881), p. 121, reports that shares were then being offered by Carr.

ing through canvas. Perimeter heating was run around the nursery. Unnecessary moldings for catching dust were eliminated and the principal rooms separated by curtains instead of doors. But, being English, the authorities thought that later it might be desirable, "and even necessary, as a matter of sentiment," to open up the fireplaces.[32]

The second mystery of Bedford Park concerns the primary responsibility for its creation. The credit for the basic idea appears to belong to the developer, Jonathan (or John) T. Carr (1845–1915). He had "been connected with many architectural schemes in and near London, and was best known as the pioneer of the Garden Suburb."[33] His major business was as a cloth merchant, but his family had a reputation for artistic activity.[34] His better-known brother (from a family of ten children) was Joseph W. Comyns Carr (1849–1916), the art critic and editor of the *English Illustrated Magazine*.[35] Together they were instrumental in founding the art school in Bedford Park.[36] The brother was a close friend of Burne-Jones for over twenty-five years and an acquaintance of William Morris. Another friend was Rossetti.[37] For many years Jonathan was a member of the Arts Club in Hanover Square and the Reform Club. "An enthusiastic Radical, with many original views on social questions, he took an active part in politics, and was in his early days engaged as political secretary to Mr. John Stuart Mill, the famous political economist, when the latter stood as a candidate for Westminster."[38] Art and social reform were thus complementary interests.

The original architect of Bedford Park was the colorful and ill-starred E. W. Godwin.[39] His efforts were concentrated on eighteen houses, the first one being occupied in the autumn of 1876.[40] However, a dispute over his competence soon developed in the architectural press and he was replaced by Norman Shaw.[41] Essentially it seems correct to regard Shaw as the architect of Bedford Park, if one can accept the fact that he neither began nor finished

32. Ibid. (Nov. 3, 1882, pp. 532–34, and Feb. 2, 1883, p. 126).

33. "Death of Mr. Jonathan Carr, Founder of Bedford Park," *Chiswick Times* (Feb. 5, 1915).

34. The Quennells, p. 104, and Moncure D. Conway, "Bedford Park," *Harper's New Monthly Magazine, 62* (March 1881), 483.

35. See J. Comyns Carr, *Some Eminent Victorians* (London, Duckworth, 1908), pp. 71, 209; J. Comyns Carr, *Coasting Bohemia* (London, Macmillan, 1914), p. 42; *Mrs. J. Comyns Carr's Reminiscences*, ed. Eve Adam (London, Hutchinson, n.d.), p. 71.

36. Sir Arthur Comyns Carr told the author

in July 1960 that this was one of their major purposes in founding Bedford Park.

37. Carr, *Some Eminent Victorians*. Also told the author by Sir Arthur Comyns Carr, son of J. Comyns Carr, in July 1960.

38. Obit., *Chiswick Times* (Feb. 5, 1915).

39. *Bedford Park Gazette* (July 1883). See also Dudley Habron, *The Conscious Stone: The Life of Edward William Godwin* (London, Latimer House, 1949), pp. 113, 118, 157.

40. Ibid. It appears that Messrs. Coe and Robinson, architects, assisted with these first eighteen houses (see *Building News*, Feb. 23, 1877, p. 192, and March 9, 1877, p. 253).

41. Carr obit., *Chiswick Times* (Feb. 5, 1915).

the building campaign. The first communal structure completed by Shaw was the Club in 1879. This was to constitute a genuine social center.[42] The largest dwelling, the Tower House of Jonathan Carr, was finished in the same year.[43] The church was constructed in 1880, as were the stores and the Tabard Inn (Fig. 36).[44] Then a break occurred between Carr and Shaw and

Fig. 36. Houses, the church, art school, Tabard Inn, and stores of Bedford Park from Acton Green; E. Hargitt, 1882. The figures are dressed in Queen Anne costume, as they actually were in the community on occasion. The railroad embankment is just behind the inn to the right but was omitted from the picture so as not to spoil the pastoral effect.

the latter handed over his design for the church, S. Michael and All Angels, to Maurice B. Adams.[45] Adams added the parish hall and chapels to the church and carried out the Chiswick School of Art completely on his own in 1881.[46] E. J. May designed the vicarage and other houses and enlarged the Club.[47]

The furor over the Godwin houses is instructive insofar as it reflects the contentious atmosphere in which the whole Park evolved. It is duly recorded in *Building News,* which was edited at the time by Adams. On December 29,

42. *Bedford Park Gazette* (July 1883).
43. Ibid.
44. Ibid.
45. Ibid. See also the Quennells, p. 105.

46. *Building News* (May 30, 1884, p. 832; Sept. 10, 1880, p. 316).
47. Ibid. (June 17, 1881, p. 706; May 29, 1885, p. 850). See also the Quennells, p. 105.

1876, a letter criticizing Godwin's first house appeared in that periodical, signed by W. Ravenscroft. The objections were centered on the alleged deficiencies of planning. The fault most often mentioned was the location of doors. The kitchen door opened into hall traffic. The drawing room door was too close to the bottom of the stairs and too near the fireplace for comfort on a winter's night. The dining room and kitchen were too small. Half the treads of the staircase were winders and the bedrooms above did not permit a convenient arrangement of beds.[48]

This bill of particulars appeared to spring from one cause: too avid a pursuit of economy on the part of the client. The explanation of deficiency can be traced through two later communications to *Building News,* one from Godwin and the other from the proprietor, Carr, who adopted the pertinent pen name of "The Freeholder" for the occasion. He gave his primary reason for employing Godwin in a letter of January 25, 1877.

> I said I wanted plans of houses that a gentleman would be glad to live in, which would be as perfect architecturally as the most splendid house, but that the extreme cost of a detached house should be £700, and for a pair of villas £1,100. Now, while I found, as I said above, every member of the profession with a sneer for "Camden Town Gothic," as the efforts of a speculative builder to be picturesque are generally called, there were few who could suggest a remedy as long as people were so inconsiderate as to want houses at such a price. Now, sir, I looked up an old file of the *Building News,* and I came across Mr. Godwin's design for a country parsonage for £500: and I felt that he, at least, was able to arrange plain bricks and tiles in a thoroughly artistic manner, and so I secured from him designs which I maintain make the Avenue-road, Bedford-park, unrivalled around London.[49]

After further derogatory discussions of his designs in the *Building News* and a final report on the visit of the Architectural Association to the Park in which the interior detailing of the houses was described as tasteless,[50] Godwin was evidently stung into a late reply. On November 23, 1877, he wrote to the journal:

48. P. 679. The Ravenscroft letter followed publication of a corner house by Godwin in *Building News* (Dec. 22, 1876), p. 621. His semi-detached villa was published Jan. 5, 1877, p. 36.

49. P. 134.
50. "The Villas on the Bedford Park Estate" (March 9, 1877), p. 253, *Building News* (Friday, Nov. 9, 1877), p. 451.

BEDFORD·PARK· is ·within· 50·Yards· of·
TURNHAM· GREEN· RAILWAY·STATION
Rents £45 to £85 per·Annum· Good·Drainage· & Gravelly·Soil·
Architect·to·the·Estate· R·Norman·Shaw· A·R·A·
for PARTICULARS· for·Houses· & Plots· apply· to· The·Office·on·the· ESTATE
or·to· Mr· Wilson· 57· Norfolk· St·Strand ; Messrs Carr·Fulton& Carr· 17· Vigo·St
Regent·Street· or·to·Messrs· Terrell· & Honey· 70ª Aldermanbury· City· E·C·

※·Bedford·Park·Estate· TURNHAM·GREEN· ※ Perspective·View· of·VILLAS· R·Norman·Shaw· A·R·A· Arch.

PRINT OF ORIGINAL POSTER·1877·ADVERTISING THE PROPOSED FIRST GARDEN CITY IN ENGLAND COMMENCED THEN BY JONATHAN CARR ORIGINATOR OF BEDFORD PK
THIS VIEW WAS MADE BY MAURICE B. ADAMS IN COLLABORATION WITH R·NORMAN SHAW TO SHOW 3 TYPES OF HOUSES DESIGNED BY HIM. THE LAST ON THE LEFT WAS BY E·W GODWIN F·S·A·
PROBABLY THE LAST EXISTING COPY OF THIS PHOTOLITHOGRAPH. PRESENTED TO THE PUBLIC LIBRARY CHISWICK BY M·B·A· 1937·

Fig. 37. Original poster advertising homes in Bedford Park; Maurice B. Adams, 1877. This was placed in the train stations. The house at the far left is the controversial one by E. W. Godwin.

Sir,—Permit me to say that I have had nothing to do with the super-intendance of any building on the Bedford-park Estate. I was asked for two designs, which I furnished, and for nothing else am I respon-sible. Seeing a curious caricature of them at some of the metropoli-tan stations [posters were displayed for advertising in the train stations. The original poster (Fig. 37) was drawn by Maurice B. Adams, in collaboration with Shaw in 1877, and shows a Godwin house at the far left] I was induced to visit Bedford-park Estate, where I found that my designs had been carried out with as much knowledge of the details of architecture as that exhibited in the railway caricature.[51]

It is difficult to determine the precise role which Shaw played after this. Some authorities write as if he, in contrast to Godwin, was given a free hand. But Blomfield, whose statements often have the advantage of firsthand acquaint-

51. P. 526.

ance even when they are partisan, reports that Shaw also made the designs but did not superintend the construction, parting company with Carr at the earliest opportunity.[52]

The third mystery of Bedford Park surrounds the question of how much of an Arts and Crafts or Pre-Raphaelite colony it was. From E. J. May we have it that Carr was acquainted with Morris and De Morgan and they might have recommended Shaw to him.[53] Moncure Conway reports that those inhabitants who purchased or leased were allowed to choose their wallpapers and interior paint and that "most have used wallpapers and designs of Morris."[54] Yet, as Professor Pevsner has pointed out in a short speech on the architectural tastes of William Morris, the great craftsman was inclined to damn Shaw's Queen Anne with faint praise, and he referred to Bedford Park as "quaint and pretty."[55] Pevsner thought that Morris did not like Shaw, "Yet Shaw and Shaw's clients liked him." Here some allowances must evidently be made for the inconsistency of greatness. According to Shaw's son, as transmitted through Blomfield, the architect felt that Morris' Socialism was just a pose and his only object had been to make money. If he had wanted to help the poor he might better "have devoted himself to the manufacture of cheap chests of drawers, and wallpapers at 10½ d. a piece, with which the poor man might adorn the walls of his tenement."[56]

In an essay in 1904, "The Home and Its Dwelling Rooms," Shaw suggests that a wallpaper should provide a quiet background for the room, plain or with only a discreet and unobtrusive pattern and color. "The art teaching of to-day gives but little consideration of this fact. It follows in the steps of William Morris, a great man who somehow delighted in glaring wallpapers." His revulsion from Morris wallpapers appears by this time to have reached a physical pitch. "We all know from sad experience, when ill and in bed, what it is to have always in evidence a patterned wallpaper, a thing that transforms a wall into a labyrinth of curving lines, by which the mind is fascinated and rendered anxious and feverish. Surely we might be spared this distraction!"[57] As Pevsner has observed in another article on Shaw, "it becomes alarmingly obvious that Shaw was a brilliant artist but not a thinker."[58] This

52. Blomfield, pp. 36–37.
53. Quennells, pp. 104–05.
54. Conway, "Bedford Park," *Harper's* (March 1881), p. 485); also Walter Hamilton, *The Aesthetic Movement in England* (3d ed. London, Reeves and Turner, 1882), p. 133.
55. "Architecture and William Morris," *Journal of the Royal Institute of British Archi-* *tects* (March, 1957), p. 174.
56. Blomfield, p. 12.
57. R. Norman Shaw, "The Home and Its Dwelling Rooms," *The British Home of To-day*, ed. W. Shaw Sparrow (London, Hodder and Stoughton, 1904), pp. cii–ciii.
58. "Richard Norman Shaw, 1831–1912," *Architectural Review* (March 1941), p. 41.

distinction is brought out by the fact that although W. R. Lethaby was Shaw's chief draughtsman, and considered him a "delightful man," his intellectual allegiance appears chiefly to have gone to Ruskin, Webb, Morris, and Gimson.[59]

Yet Shaw did design furniture, and when we discover him writing the following he seems only a little apart from Morris.

> Why is it that country cottages and farms are often such pleasant places, so aptly furnished and so rich in comfort and in homeliness? It is not only because the cottages frequently belong to fine old periods in English architecture; it is also because their owners are natural and modest, and never attempt to do more than they can afford to do well. They are not ashamed to be humble. If this were remembered in our towns and cities, the ordinary householder would have a far better and more comfortable house than he has at present.[60]

This demonstrated considerable insight into the more unfortunate effects of status seeking through home design and recalls the story of Morris who, when asked by a wealthy lady how the cottages he had just finished for her might best be decorated, replied, "with a flitch of bacon."[61]

Furthermore, it was Shaw's pupils, Prior, Macartney, Newton, Horsley, Lethaby, and Blomfield—"The Family"—who were most active in the Art Worker's Guild and the Arts and Crafts Society and who went on to establish the general reputation of English domestic architecture. Shaw joined them in 1892 in a book of thirteen essays against the proposal for registration of architects by the Royal Institute of British Architects. "What enthusiasm can ever be raised by mere professionalism, or the parade, so constantly made, of being above all things 'practical men'?" asks Shaw.[62] Throughout the essays runs the theme of the architect as the master builder and artist and the fear that he may be cut off from painters, sculptors, and craftsmen through an excess of professionalism.

59. A. R. N. Roberts, "The Life and Work of W. R. Lethaby," *Journal of the Royal Society of Arts, 105* (March 29, 1957), p. 358, and John Brandon-Jones, "W. R. Lethaby 1857–1931," *Architectural Assn. Journal* (March 1949), pp. 170–71.

60. Shaw, "The Home and Its Dwelling Rooms," pp. cv–cvi.

61. This story was told to me by Mr. Gilbert McAllister in August 1960 in London. He was unable to indicate the source.

62. *Architecture, A Profession or an Art*, co-ed. T. G. Jackson (London, Murray, 1892), p. 5. Reginald Blomfield in *Memoirs of an Architect* (London, Macmillan, 1932) and Barrington Kaye in *The Development of the Architectural Profession in Britain* (London, Allen and Unwin, 1960) document the background of this dispute more thoroughly.

The book is curious in that it is the last plea of a group for the individualistic artist–craftsman who is so typical of the last quarter of the nineteenth century. Can it be that because of the avowed independence of these men we strive overly hard in retrospect to match up their thoughts and link their purposes? Relationships among them have a way of appearing when least expected. A small illustration of this is the genesis of the famous Studio House for Mrs. J. Wilson Forster by C. F. A. Voysey. The architect lived briefly at the Park when he was first married. It has been observed that the Studio House was unique in Bedford Park and proved Voysey's youthful determination to separate the essence of his first work from that of Shaw. Certainly it had in its turn an influence on the houses of Olbrich and Behrens at the Darmstadt colony in Germany. An early study for the house, dated August 19, 1888 (Fig. 38), makes it obvious, however, that Voysey had looked long and hard at Shaw's Tabard Inn (Fig. 39), built some eight years before, which was a part of a consciously architectonic street picture, devised as an alternative to the tree-shaded roads elsewhere in the suburb.[63] The second-story band of plaster is much taller than that of the brick on the ground story in both instances, already suggesting a manneristic proportion. The window bands with tiny leaded panes are likewise similar at the third story. The contrast in window shape, size, and location which is associated with the Voysey house as finally built (Fig. 40) is already recognizable in the Shaw facade, particularly in the juxtaposition of the two large, shallow bay windows with the small rounded windows at either side. On the ground floor the flat-arched entrance doorway with a bay to the right reinforces the similarity. The over-all impression of "blouse over petticoat," of contrast between rough and smooth, dark and light, is notably similar, although some of the patchiness and tautness goes out in Voysey's work and only the tall-over-short mannerism remains. One might claim from this design that it was Voysey, not Shaw, who displayed the more conservative temperament. Shaw sought to utilize the full palette of eclecticism, while Voysey looked primarily for contrast in the sketch and, in the finished house, for a new simplicity and purism already predicted in the earlier drawing. Simultaneous attraction and repulsion seem to have been present among the artists toward the end of the century.

We know that the developers and architect of Bedford Park were acquainted with William Morris and that several of its inhabitants visited him

63. Dr. Pevsner has noted other similarities between Shaw and Voysey's work in "Richard Norman Shaw 1831–1912." John Betjeman informs us that Voysey admired most of all Norman Shaw: "Honour Your Forebears," R.I.B.A. Journal (Jan. 1954), p. 87.

Fig. 38. Early study for the J. W. Forster House, Bedford Park; C. F. A. Voysey, August 1888.

Fig. 39. Tabard Inn and stores, Bedford Park; R. Norman Shaw, 1877–80.

"The STORES"   Private House   Yᵉ HOSTELRY

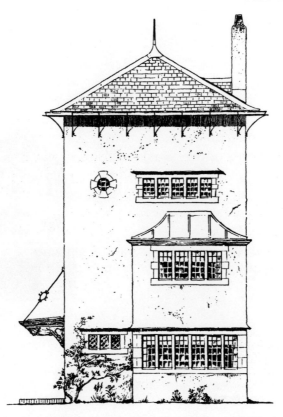

*Fig. 40. Forster House as completed; Voysey, 1891. The Shavian high-low proportions are exag-
gerated into mannerism, but the roughcast surface, the ribbon windows, and the circular window,
as on the Tabard Inn, suggest the source of inspiration.*

regularly at nearby Hammersmith.[64] We understand also that he spoke in
favor of attempting to save original trees on any building site (which Bedford Park had exemplified) and that he declared the future of art should not
be contemplated until all city streets could be made decent and orderly.[65]
But perhaps the quickest way to qualify the entire progression is to adopt the
words of Professor Pevsner on the whole Arts and Crafts Movement for Bedford Park. He has described it as "spiritually the work of Morrisites though
physically of Norman Shavians."[66]

Besides a hectic shortage of capital and the gratuitous frictions between
owner and architects, the later failures of Bedford Park can probably be attributed to its very conspicuousness. What a profound change the Park repre-

64. W. B. Yeats, *The Trembling of the Veil*
(London, Laurie, 1922), p. 84.
    65. N. Pevsner, "Architecture and William

Morris," *R.I.B.A. Journal* (March 1957), p. 175.
    66. Ibid., p. 174.

sented cannot be understood until the maps and pictures of it are thoughtfully examined. The map (Fig. 33) shows clearly that the layout was more a
loose assemblage of streets than a total site plan; in this it conformed to convention. The new aspect was typified in the re-evaluation of the character of
the street itself, which represents a distinct cultural break. The Bedford Park
chronicler, Moncure Conway, felt that London's ugliness derived from a
Puritan strain still dominant among the British. As an American, he could
speak with some authority on the survivals of Puritanism. It was embodied
for him in mile upon mile of streets of yellow-gray and sooty brick houses.
But, he noted, those of the middle class were large and comfortable and one
might pause before any of them and be fairly certain that inside there would
be good music, English, French, and German literature and pictures of noble
men and heroic deeds. "Between all that and a fine outside they have chosen
the better part," he concludes.[67] Or as another foreigner was to put it later,
"The poetry of the English home exists at the expense of the English street
which is devoid of poetry."[68]

Bedford Park was in substance an attempt to move the inner poetry of the
urban house out of doors and to reintegrate it with English nature. However,
what at first blush may have appeared stimulating and attractive soon began
to pall. Perhaps it stirred too quickly the middle-class sense of propriety in
becoming identified as the "showplace" of the Aesthetic Movement, of which
Oscar Wilde was by then the most conspicuous figure.[69] While the Park today
seems rather inoffensive and muted, contemporaries had no such reaction.
They literally saw red in their resentment of the appearance of the streets.
G. K. Chesterton called it Saffron Park in *The Man Who Was Thursday*. "It
was built of bright brick throughout; its skyline was fantastic, and even its
ground plan was wild."[70] One could not regard it normally, he said. To be
appreciated, it had to be seen as a work of art, a dream, or a comedy.

In order not to attribute the opprobrium too exclusively to the middle
class, *The Ballard of Bedford Park* in its entertaining way brought two hypothetical members of a lower stratum out from London to look at it as well.
Blomfield helped things along in his transcription of the poem from the *St.
James Gazette* by exaggerating the punctuation and the spelling a trifle. The
original read:

67. Conway, *Travels in South Kensington* (New York, Harper, 1882), pp. 176–77.

68. Karel Čapek, quoted in Francesca M. Wilson, *Strange Island* (London, Longmans, Green, 1955), p. 245.

69. Hamilton, *The Aesthetic Movement in England*, pp. 125–36.

70. *A. G. K. Chesterton Omnibus* (London, Methuen, 1936), p. 205.

> Now he who loves aesthetic cheer
>   and does not mind the damp
> May come and read Rossetti here
>   by a Japanese-y lamp.
> While 'Arry shouts to Hemma
>   "Say, 'ere a bloomin' lark!
> Them's the biled lobster 'houses
>   as folks calls "Bedford Park!"[71]

Horace Lennard in his *Carol of Bedford Park,* a somewhat milder parody of the next year, reiterated the conscious pursuit of quaintness, the search for an impression of durability and "taste, taste, taste," as among its most doubtful aspects.[72]

However, for a moment it did capture the sympathetic imagination of at least one poetic child. W. B. Yeats has written, "We went to live in a house like those we had seen in pictures, and even met people dressed like people in the story-books. The newness of everything, the empty houses where we played at Hide-and-seek, and the strangeness of it all, made us feel that we were living among toys."[73] By 1887, roughly a decade after its founding, when the Yeats family returned and again settled in Bedford Park at a different address, the Pre-Raphaelite illusion had vanished:

> But now exaggerated criticism had taken the place of enthusiasm, the tiled roofs, the first in modern London, were said to leak, which they did not, and the drains to be bad, though that was no longer true; and I imagine that houses were cheap. I remember feeling disappointed because the co-operative stores, with their little seventeenth century panes, had lost the romance they had when I had passed them still unfinished on my way to school; and because the public house, called the Tabard after Chaucer's Inn, was so plainly a public house; and because the great sign of a trumpeter designed by Rooke, the Pre-Raphaelite artist, had been freshened by some inferior hand.[74]

His experience appears to have accorded with the whole adult response; first of surprise and delight, even of affection, and then of mounting embarrass-

71. *3* (Dec. 17, 1881), 11. Blomfield, p. 36.
72. *Lady's Pictorial,* Supplement (June 24, 1882).
73. Joseph Hone, *W. B. Yeats, 1865–1939* (London, Macmillan, 1942), pp. 26–27. The

Yeats family lived first at 8 Woodstock Road (1876–80) and on its return at 3 Blenheim Road (1887–1902).
74. W. B. Yeats, *Trembling of the Veil,* pp. 3–4.

ment and rejection. Habits of sight trained on mile after mile of London streets and the grimness of much of the Gothic revival, were not to be changed overnight by one meretricious experiment despite the fact that the London streets themselves had sprung up in only a matter of decades. The ability of the nineteenth-century metropolis by authority of its sheer volume and bulk to assume the guise of a permanent and well-nurtured tradition is astonishing, as anyone who has to deal with the revision of its actual planning well knows. Does it suggest that the specialized visual experience of each generation in our age tends to nullify traditional lessons, no matter how well recognized the historic continuity may appear to be? If so, either a frantic search for singularity could result or, under slightly different circumstances, a monumental self-satisfaction and complacency would evolve. What seems to have happened at Bedford Park is a direct collision of these two attitudes, with the rare intrinsic beauty of its architectural vision being finally forgotten.

5. NEAT AND CLEAN AT
PORT SUNLIGHT AND BOURNVILLE

The ultimate issue at Port Sunlight was to be whether a great industrialist, whose affairs and responsibilities were constantly broadening, could continue to have an effective understanding of the daily needs of his workpeople. The negative opinion was advanced by the Secretary of the Bolton Branch of the Engineers' Union who wrote the founder of Port Sunlight in 1919 that, "No man of an independent turn of mind can breathe for long the atmosphere of Port Sunlight. That might be news to your Lordship, but we have tried it. The profit-sharing system not only enslaves and degrades the workers, it tends to make them servile and sycophant."[1] And indeed, Lord Leverhulme himself seemed more than a little bewildered by the events that followed in the wake of the international success of his business. In a speech before the Birkenhead Literary and Scientific Society in 1900 he expressed a nostalgia for the return of the "office, factory and workshop to that close family brotherhood that existed in the good old days of hand labour."[2] While this was manifestly impossible, the wish appears to have released the same impulse that motivated the earlier Halifax model village builders. In the smaller village, as opposed to the huge manufacturing town, responsibility between man and master might be humanely and honestly expressed. So it had been, too, Lever thought, in the old paternalistic craft shop as opposed to the modern manufactory.

Ability and time elevated Lever and George Cadbury of Bournville far above their workers and neighbors. Subconsciously they appear to have resented the change as much as their workers. Perhaps the two garden villages would never have been undertaken if the industrialists had yielded easily to

1. As quoted in Charles Wilson, *The History of Unilever, 1* (London, Cassell, 1954), 150.
2. "Prosperity v. Profit Sharing in Relation to Workshop Management," reprinted from *Birkenhead News* (Nov. 24, 1900), p. 47.

their rapid elevation in status. Cadbury especially had a passion for overseeing the smallest details of his employees' lives. His advice to them on health would have been amusing were it not for the sincere spirit in which it was offered. And it is distinct in its environmental emphasis. He recommended that they wear stout shoes for wet weather and he lent them bed warmers until the damp had worked itself out of their new houses. He promoted the "Savo-Spaco" bath among them, a sort of Murphy bed of plumbing. Possibly his least-heeded admonition was that they sleep with their mouths closed.[3]

These villages of the last quarter of the nineteenth century are characterized by the generous assignment of land by the owners to whatever purpose: architectural, agricultural, recreational, or even aesthetic. In 1887, at the age of thirty-six, Mr. Lever had become dissatisfied with his rented factory at Warrington and the impossibility of rapid expansion there.[4] He and his chief architect, William Owen, began to scour the countryside for an advantageous open building site. The location decided upon was chosen primarily for its cheap land, water frontage, good labor supply, and transport facilities. Bromborough Pool was on the south, the New Chester Road to the east, and a main line of the Birkenhead-to-Chester railroad passed on the west. By July of that year fifty-two acres had been bought at £200 per acre.[5] Twenty-four acres, or a little less than half, were to be allocated to the works and the rest to a model village.[6] The first sod for the works was cut on March 3, 1888, and the village itself was begun in the spring of the following year.[7]

Most of the later garden communities followed the gentle roll of the English countryside, which lent an underlying unity to every aspect of the man-made plan. And Lord Leverhulme built his London residence overlooking Hampstead Heath because of his "great love of panoramic vistas."[8] But the Port Sunlight terrain proved to be an exception. It was relatively low, flat, and deeply penetrated by tidal wash—roughly the shape of a capital E (Fig. 41). The Gothic curves and flourishes of the E gave the flavor to the final layout. All the ravines, except the Dell in the southwest corner, were one day

3. George Cadbury, *Suggested Rules of Health and Other Information for Youths at Bournville*, reprint by the Youths' Committee, Bournville (1924), pp. 6, 8. "Warming Pans," memorandum from George Cadbury (Bournville Village Collection).

4. Second Viscount Leverhulme, *Viscount Leverhulme by His Son* (London, Allen and Unwin, 1927), p. 48.

5. Clifford Powell, "Redevelopment of Port Sunlight," unpublished thesis, University of Liverpool (May 1952), Introduction. Lever himself said that the original purchase was 56 acres and that by 1902 it had reached 230 acres: "The Buildings Erected at Port Sunlight and Thornton Hough," paper read at a meeting of the Architectural Association, London, March 21, 1902, p. 7.

6. Viscount Leverhulme, p. 48.

7. Thomas H. Mawson, *Civic Art* (London, Batsford, 1911), p. 280.

8. Thomas H. Mawson, *The Life and Work of an English Landscape Architect* (London, Richards Press, 1927), p. 129.

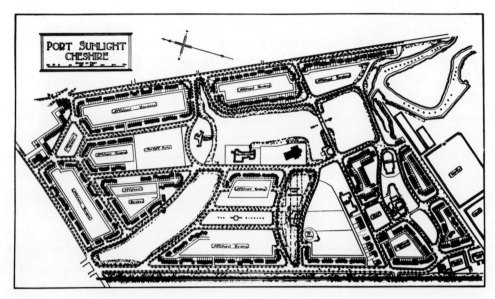

Fig. 41. Earlier plan for Port Sunlight, 1888–1934. The tidal wash which influenced the whole scheme has receded to the upper right. The original Dell settlement is at the lower right.

to be filled for recreational purposes, thus concealing the primeval pattern from the casual visitor. The Dell was the first area occupied and demonstrates the difficulty of squaring rigid building lines with the free shapes caused by the twenty-five acres of tidal estuaries. The final solution was a compromise, where the introduction of a kind of superblock with fifty to a hundred cottages around its rim minimized by its very size the effect of both curves and straight lines. It also, incidentally, permitted a reduction in the number of serving streets. Both conditions anticipated two of the later conscious principles of Parker and Unwin: low density on the land (five to eight houses per acre at Port Sunlight as against seven to eight at Bournville and twelve in Unwin's writings) and a reduction in the length and number of streets necessary for residential development. In the larger blocks at Port Sunlight the central area was filled in with allotment gardens (the northern idiom) instead of the old-fashioned service alleys as in the Dell. This also anticipated the increasing importance of land for the cultivation of food in the greenbelts of the garden cities that were soon to be established. Mervyn Macartney believed that the allotments were to be filled up by houses when the "need comes for denser housing," with additional streets driven through the superblocks, but the basis for his assumption is not evident.[9]

9. Mervyn E. Macartney, "Mr. Lever and Port Sunlight," *Architectural Review* (July 1910), p. 43.

Bournville's architect, W. Alexander Harvey, reflected the progressive attitude of his day toward better layout when he suggested that "it is nearly always better to work to the contour of the land, taking a gentle sweep in preference to a straight line."[10] Unlike the modest legion of architects whom Lord Leverhulme engaged at one time or another, Harvey had favorable ground upon which to start his plan.[11] Old field boundaries, country lanes, a shallow valley running east and west were minor elements to cope with compared to Port Sunlight's tidal ooze on a flat landscape (Fig. 42). In the Bournville situation all features appeared to converge easily toward the final goal. This harmony of contour, varying only between 450 and 500 feet, undoubtedly militated against the establishment of a formal village center at Bournville. An article in *The Studio* at the turn of the century remarks the tree-bordered roads and concludes that this "has greatly enhanced the beauty of the village, and, added to the undulating nature of the land, which is dotted with coppices and bosky dells, and through which a pretty winding stream runs, gives the special charm that is always connected with old English village scenery."[12] A significant index of the garden village and city can be presented in terms of subdued earth sculpture alone.

In 1879 the Cadbury works had been removed from Birmingham, also because of a need for expansion and for cleaner conditions for food production. Twenty-four double tunnel-back houses, typical of Birmingham, were soon erected on open lots for key personnel.[13] Despite this early start, the later main development of the domestic building campaign, in 1895, undoubtedly assisted in the establishment of the generous house lot for gardening and recreation, instead of the allotment in the center of the superblock for gardening, as at Port Sunlight.[14] This single plot of residential green, which seems so hallowed by custom today, claims our attention here as an innovation for working-class houses. In his deed of gift of 1900 Mr. Cadbury specified that

10. W. Alexander Harvey, *The Model Village and Its Cottages: Bournville* (London, Batsford, 1906), p. 63.

11. Architects of Port Sunlight were William Owen, who designed the works and negotiated the purchase of the land, and his son Segar; the firms of Douglas & Fordham, Talbot & Wilson, Grayson & Ould; T. T. Rees; and Maurice Adams. Lever's old school friend Jonathan Simpson also designed some cottages, and his son James L. Simpson did some work before 1910 and a good deal of the work after 1910. One group of houses was designed by Charles Reilly. Josephine Reynolds, "The Model Village at Port Sunlight," *R.I.B.A. Journal* (May 27, 1948), p. 495; Viscount Leverhulme, p. 87.

12. J. H. Whitehouse, "Bournville: A Study in Housing Reform," *Studio* (1901–02), pp. 170–71.

13. Harvey, p. 9.

14. By 1900 there were 313 houses built at Bournville. By contrast, the works were moved to Port Sunlight in January 1889, 28 model houses were up there by 1890, and eight years later the number had risen to 278 (Charles Wilson, p. 144). By 1907 there were 720 houses and finally 892 (Clifford Powell, op. cit.).

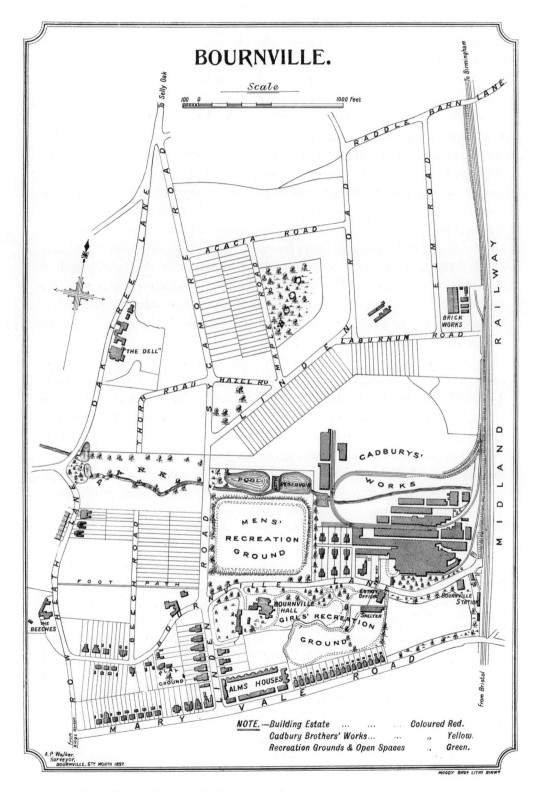

Fig. 42. Map of Bournville; A. P. Walker, 1897. The original twenty-four tunnel-back houses for overseers are at lower left, facing Linden Road.

a dwelling might not occupy more than 25 per cent of its site. In the larger setting he required that one tenth of the land exclusive of roads be devoted to parks and recreation ground. No more than one fifteenth of the estate could be occupied by factory buildings.[15] Ultimately a continuous system of parks would be woven through the village, although this was not originally stipulated. This greater freedom of layout testifies not only to an advance in social theory but also to the increase of capital wealth which the latter part of the century brought with it. What is so striking about the two villages is that the wealth was directed inward to the general welfare almost before its accumulation. At least one reason was given when George Cadbury deeded the bulk of his property, outside of his business, to the Bournville Estate: he had considered whether he was justified in giving away the heritage of his children, but decided that they would "be all the better off for being deprived of this money. Great wealth is not to be desired, and in my experience of life is generally more of a curse than a blessing to the families of those who possess it."[16]

If one were to oversimplify the industrial problems of the nineteenth century he might claim that the basic difficulty of the worker was the constantly increasing specialization of function demanded of him, while the entrepreneur's greatest problems arose from the unwieldy units which he had helped to create—great cities, great factories, and great fortunes. An industrialist of good will in the early days, like Akroyd, might have trouble in identifying the powerful economic forces bearing in upon him. One at the end of the century, like Cadbury, would be overwhelmed by the difficulty of administering the establishment which mass demand, investment capital, and faster communication and transport had enabled him to build up. From this it might be inferred that Cadbury and Lever would find their greatest satisfaction in constructing model villages as a means of insulating their workers and themselves from the surprisingly mutual feeling that they were adrift among social tides which neither party was fully capable of controlling. In the sense of satisfying a need for a refuge in the present out of the distant past, the villages were probably more romantic than utopian.

The accounts in the *Birmingham News* of the second and third annual gatherings of the Bournville tenants make it evident that Cadbury, like Lever, did regard factory labor as over-specialized, in that it was "unnatural and confining." His chief means of compensating for it he said at the second

15. Harvey, p. 8.
16. "Model Village of the World," *Our Day* (April 1902), p. 2.

meeting would be by work in the garden, by "labour on the soil," in the wholesome air and open space. This was made necessary by the "altered conditions" of contemporary life.[17] In his speech to the third gathering the paper reported that "for himself he was largely vegetarian, and he believed the mere fact of men having gardens would tend to the consumption of more vegetables and less meat, which he was perfectly sure would improve the general health of the country."[18] The indefatigable English spirit shows up most regularly in the garden city movement in the openness and convertibility of its arguments. They are more inclusive than exclusive, running on together and only occasionally swinging apart. No set of discussions illustrates this better than those centering around Bournville. In addition to its hygienic and dietary aspect, the individual garden might be regarded as completing the long development toward the freehold privilege for the poorer citizen, although for various reasons that ideal was never fully attained at Bournville.[19] In the same way, the single lot could be described as a further advance toward a lower land density which was to become a cardinal principle of the garden city movement. In his speech of 1901 to the third annual gathering, Mr. Cadbury also implied that work in the outdoors and the elimination of slums had a direct bearing upon the military posture of the country. He cited the fact that of ten thousand men who had applied to enlist at Manchester in the previous year, only 10 per cent were found fit to serve. This national deficiency was mentioned merely by way of illustration, for Cadbury was a Quaker and a pacifist, who went so far during the Boer War as to buy up a newspaper, the *London Daily News,* in order to publicize his distaste for military adventures.[20]

Cadbury could focus his garden line of thought as easily on children as on war in his effort to realize all spheres of responsibility. He frequently declared that children ought to be raised among beautiful surroundings.[21] Lever also maintained that the young cut off from the sight of nature "grow up depraved, and become a danger and terror to the State; wealth-destroyers instead of wealth-producers, compared to whom the South Sea islander, the Maori, or Zulu is an educated intelligent citizen."[22]

17. Feb. 10, 1900.

18. Feb. 16, 1901.

19. Original Prospectus of Bournville, item 4; Harvey, p. 12; *Bournville Housing: A Description of the Housing Schemes of Cadbury Brothers Ltd., and the Bournville Village Trust* (Publication Dept., Bournville Works, 1926), in the Bournville Village Collection, pp. 11–12.

20. A. G. Gardiner, *Life of George Cadbury* (London, Cassell, 1923), pp. 210–37.

21. *The Garden City Conference at Bournville: Report of Proceedings* (London, Garden City Assn., 1901), p. 45.

22. "Land for Houses," a paper read before the North End Liberal Club on Tuesday, Oct. 4, 1898. Reprinted from the *Birkenhead News* (Oct. 8, 1898), p. 33.

In the back gardens at Bournville flowering trees were planted and there was also a place for flowers in each. In this emphasis on beauty conveyed by natural forms the builders anticipated, or perhaps more accurately, rein-forced, Raymond Unwin's future approach to the design of the garden city. This, among other things, made Unwin's appointment in 1911 to the lecture-ship in civic design endowed by Cadbury at Birmingham University seem entirely fitting.[23]

The most old-fashioned argument Cadbury employed was that the garden might keep the husband away from the pub and closer to his family. His most significant prediction was that the gardens would pay their own way by pro-ducing more food per acre than open field farming did. For these considera-tions the full prestige of the new science of statistics was brought to bear. Neither Cadbury nor Lever ever wearied of quoting figures to prove how much lower the death and disease rate was in their villages than in Birming-ham or Liverpool, or how much more food they might grow than ordinary farmers if only all their tenants would cultivate the house plot as intensively as the few who carried off the local prizes. A man working two or three days a week in the factory, said Cadbury, could devote himself with actual eco-nomic profit to work in his garden.[24] He had received a pamphlet from a Captain J. W. Petavel (an early advocate of linear cities and a lecturer at Calcutta on ways to fight poverty), who had "tried to show that an acre of land under spade culture, and with feeding the poultry on the refuse from the garden, would produce £102 a year. He rather thought that was an over-estimate, but he himself knew of a road scavenger who had produced vege-tables worth about £14 from a quarter of an acre of land, which showed that under spade culture there was a vast amount of wholesome food to be pro-duced by the land. If the same land had been used for pasturage it would not have produced more than £7 or £8 an acre."[25]

This assumption was soon to be backed by definite policies. Classes were begun in gardening and the advice of experienced gardeners was made read-ily available. Six gardens were tested for a year, according to Budgett Meakin, writing in 1905, and found to average a yield worth nearly £60 per acre.[26] A few years later when the American horticulturist Wilhelm Miller visited Bournville he learned that in a competition among nineteen householders

23. *Bournville Village Trust 1900–1955* (Bir-mingham, Bournville Village Trust, n.d.), p. 94.

24. *Birmingham News* (Feb. 16, 1901).

25. Ibid.

26. *Model Factories and Villages* (London, Unwin), p. 438. These tests appear to have been begun in 1901. *Bournville Village Gardens*, a booklet in the Bournville Village Collection (n.d.), p. 2.

the average yield of fruit and vegetables had been $23.45 per garden, or $278.25 per acre, compared with the less than $25 per acre resulting from ordinary farming in the vicinity.[27] The results were much the same at Port Sunlight, where the vegetable allotments within the hollow superblocks produced an average of £4 to £5 per plot, or £60 to £80 per acre, contrasting to yields of £6 to £7 per acre in Cheshire as a whole.[28] The Port Sunlight arrangement was possibly the more efficient in that allotments were rented only to those clearly interested in cultivating them. The older device of a walled and paved court, with privy and coal storage immediately behind the cottages, made back yards there impractical. At the annual flower and vegetable show, cash prizes and cups were given by firms of seedsmen, "a special prize of two tons of manure being well worth winning."[29] The dimensions of the plots were comparable in the two places—usually 100 feet long by 25 to 30 feet broad at Port Sunlight and 120 feet long and 30 feet wide at Bournville.[30]

In more recent years the lively discussions by Osborn, Wibberley, Stamp, and their respondents of the agricultural potential of land covered by low-density housing have tended to revolve around the question of whether high-rise flats should not be more extensively employed throughout the country.[31] What fascinates the stranger is how these associated ideas can be constantly connected and disconnected in British thinking. We know, for instance, from our study of Leeds that the debate about high or low housing could be carried on entirely without reference to agriculture or garden villages. At Akroydon the principle of individual home ownership was supposed to have stimulated a more responsive citizenship. Now at Bournville a similar argument was used for the existence of the private garden. It had been suggested in the original prospectus on Bournville that the cultivation of the garden might cover the cost of rates. These were to be paid by the tenant instead of the landowner, so that the former would consciously relate his own interests to those of his government. The policy was especially noted in a critical essay on Bournville by J. A. Dale in *The Economic Review* of 1907, with the additional caution that, "It is not safe to set the value of garden produce in every

27. *What England Can Teach Us About Gardening* (New York, Doubleday, Page, 1913), p. 136.

28. W. L. George, *Labour and Housing at Port Sunlight* (London, Alston Rivers, 1909), p. 103.

29. Ibid., p. 125.

30. Ibid., p. 62, and *Interesting Social Scheme, The Model Village of Bournville,* Bournville Collection (n.d.).

31. See Lionel Brett, "Town Planning and Architecture, 1945–65," *Listener* (Oct. 6, 1955), pp. 539–40, for a popular discussion of the issues involved.

case against the rates, owing to variations in soil (which are very considerable), and in the tenants' skill, leisure, and industry; but in nearly all cases there is a substantial return, and in many of the smaller houses sufficient to cover the rates."[32]

Yet the knack in garden city thought is to know how far to carry one idea before going on to the next. And it is apparently a mistake to break the principles down into such a variety of parts that the conception as a whole is lost sight of. This precept may be applied to the aesthetic framework as well. The single, private garden is the basic horticultural unit at Bournville, but it is not allowed to disrupt the overall visual effect of the community, any more than private ownership of the houses could be. The land, the houses, and the gardens have to be evaluated as cohesive elements, supplementing each other wherever possible, in order to understand what the owner and architect were after by way of total result.

Miller, in his book entitled *What England Can Teach Us about Gardening,* came as close as any foreign observer when he noted that despite the encouragement of individual initiative in the gardens at Bournville, the chief reason for the uniformly high quality of the planting was the clause written into every house contract requiring high standards of neatness and beauty.[33] He felt that this achieved even better results than at Port Sunlight, where only the front gardens were subject to professional attention, or Letchworth, where there was not such a strong effort to get plants, seeds, and bulbs at reduced prices into the hands of the householder.

Lord Leverhulme found it necessary to take over the front gardens and maintain them at company expense because his tenants occasionally used them as fowl runs and dustbins. He was always anxious to keep them unobstructed.[34] Sometimes this continuum is referred to in the literature as the "American open front" system. We have to be grateful to the American, Miller, for also supplying the reason why this system has nearly always failed in England, and will no doubt continue to do so. He reports with approval that the inhabitants enclosed their front yards with hawthorn hedges because they wanted flowers there "and you cannot have flowers if dogs, cats, and children are allowed to enter."[35] Americans do not, of course, grow many

32. "Bournville," *Economic Review* (Jan. 15), p. 17.

33. (New York, Doubleday, Page, 1911), p. 137. Another very perceptive account of Bournville planting is contained in the Bournville Village Trust, *Landscape and Housing Development* (London, Batsford, 1949).

34. W. L. George, p. 62, and W. H. Lever, p. 14. See also *Liverpool Daily Post* (March 25, 1902) for report of this talk as given to the Liverpool Architectural Society.

35. Miller, pp. 140–41.

flowers in their front yards even today, and the pet census in a United States city would undoubtedly be much lower than in a comparable English city.

Miller believed that the gardening at Bournville was perhaps the finest in the world at the time. The reasons for his high opinion were contained in what he termed the "seven lessons" of Bournville. They included the planting of smaller ornamental trees and dwarf bushes to suit the scale of the homes and streets of the town, the use of only one kind of tree to each street (also a practice at Letchworth), the seasonal modification of the environment which well-chosen trees and plants conferred, the decorative effects that climbing plants can give to inexpensive architecture, and the comprehensive benefits to be derived from community spraying.[36] Since Miller was an advocate of regional schools of landscape within the United States, being especially active in promoting a prairie style when he was a professor at the University of Illinois, the lessons were recommended with ample acknowledgment of those things that could be accomplished only within the climate of the British Isles.

The out-of-doors, the setting, was to become increasingly important as the model village passed into the twentieth century. At Bournville even the semi-detached houses had begun to be modified to suit the needs of the garden (Fig. 43). The house plans were widened "by arranging the staircase of each house, not between the back and front rooms, but between the houses. This will bring the outside houses nearer to the extremity of the land, and will not only give each garden the desired straightness and breadth, but afford a greater breadth of view upon it from within."[37] There is a considerable difference in Bournville between the earlier Elm, Willow, Maple, and Linden Road area, completed mostly between 1898 and 1905, and the district of Weoley Hill (Fig. 44), begun about 1914.[38] The first section remains close to the old rectilinear block and corridor street plan, brought out from the city like the Dell area at Port Sunlight. Weoley Hill adjusts itself with finesse to the slope of the ground and includes cul-de-sacs, hollow superblocks with a cricket field, woods, bowling green, and park within them, and a road system that takes account not only of the rise and fall of the land and of ancient trees but also of the difference in function between major and minor roads. It comes as no surprise to learn that Raymond Unwin submitted a plan for

36. Ibid., p. 139.
37. Harvey, p. 68.
38. Earlier date from letter of Nov. 28, 1956,

from F. R. Barlow, Secretary and Manager, Bournville Trust; Weoley Hill date from *Bournville Village Trust 1900–1955*, p. 72.

Fig. 43. Elm Road, Bournville; W. A. Harvey, 1898–1905. The width and direction of the street follow the bye-law type of Birmingham, although shorter and with a setback of houses. The picturesque features, such as gables and bays, and the differentiation of materials are held to a minimum, in contrast to Port Sunlight.

Weoley Hill when he lectured at Birmingham University from 1911 to 1916, although Samuel A. Wilmot carried out his own scheme ultimately.[39]

The norm for roads became an 18-foot carriageway with a grass verge and path of 6 feet each and with a setback beyond amounting to 20 feet. From house front to house front across the road was 82 feet.[40] Some care was taken also to stagger the alignment of the houses so that no two would face each other directly.[41] The proportions of these elements at Port Sunlight were much the same, with a distance stretching across from house front to house front of some 70 to 80 feet.[42] The street picture was a constant preoccupation with the architects and owners in establishing the type of community life

39. *Bournville Village Trust 1900–1955,* p. 94, Bournville Notes. Other architects working on Bournville besides Harvey and Wilmot were H. Graham Wicks, C. B. Parks after 1920, and J. R. Armstrong for the larger buildings.

40. *The Bournville Village Trust: An Account of Its Planning and Housing Schemes in Suburban and Rural Areas* (Bournville, n.d.), pp. 11, 15.

41. Harvey, p. 67.

42. Budgett Meakin, p. 430, and Viscount Leverhulme, p. 87.

Fig. 44. Weoley Hill District, Bournville; Samuel A. Wilmot, 1914–. In this later section of Bournville the roads follow more naturally the contour of the land and the corners have oblique setbacks. The roofs exhibit a longer slope and the gables and bays a greater amplitude, to echo the land and tree forms. These features derive from Parker and Unwin and the domestic school to which they belonged.

they wished to support. The most prominent outgrowth of this concern at Port Sunlight was on Greendale Road where some of the best cottages were deliberately faced across a wide street toward the railroad embankment—considerably different from backing them up against it that characterized Railway Terrace at Akroyd's Copley several decades before.[43] The counterpart at Bournville was along Elm Road where the backs of the cottages were given

43. W. H. Lever, p. 7. Viscount Leverhulme, p. 88, and Thomas Mawson, *Civic Art*, p. 280.

special treatment so that they might also appear attractive from the passing trains on the Midland line (Fig. 45). The visual impact was always paramount with Lord Leverhulme, and one notices this particularly in his attitude toward road patterns. In a lecture to the Architectural Association in 1902 he said, "The roads have been so planned that whilst making directest and shortest ways to important points, such as the railway station, the ferry, the tramway terminus, and to the office and works, they still form wherever possible

Fig. 45. Backs along Elm Road, Bournville. The backs of the houses were given special treatment because passengers on the Midland Railway could view them. The unusual width of the semi-detached houses is the result of the Bournville effort toward wider house lots so that each unit might have an adequate garden.

curves and sweeps following the lines of the ravines."[44] He constantly sought to enhance utility with beauty. He readily admits in a letter of 1918 to his landscape architect, Thomas Mawson, that he projected the streets at the outset over ravines whose water rights he did not control and through land he did not own, because he already had an impression of the basic outline for his village. The spans of the ravines were to be permanently left open for

44. W. H. Lever, p. 7.

parks and recreation. He firmly believed "in town planning that the convenience and life of the people can be achieved without any sacrifice to beauty or inspiring vistas."[45]

At Bournville the houses came chiefly in pairs or groups of four or eight. At Port Sunlight the clusters ran even higher, up to ten units per row with three to seven as an average. In angling them at the street corners and forming rudimentary U-shaped courts out of the larger combinations, Lever's architects effectively forecast certain devices to be incorporated in the garden cities. The most important advance was in the use of the houses on both sides of the road to characterize and punctuate the space between, rather than simply to limit it. At Port Sunlight they were so designed that little or no distinction could be perceived among the individual houses of each group externally. What it amounted to visually was a street of mansions in which the volumes held up remarkably well, a need increasingly felt as the thoroughfares grew wider under the pressure of circulatory reform.

The wish for diversity in the street picture was expressed even more directly in the variation of textures and colors. At Bournville brindled Staffordshire bricks were used instead of pressed stock brick, giving a cherry red tint blended with blue and purple. The roofs were covered with handmade tiles of thick green slate. Roof ridging was to have careful attention because it was "wiser to suppress than sharpen, the better to obtain that rustic appearance suitable to a cottage."[46] The effect of the bye-law streets in Birmingham was evidently causing a salutary reaction.

The variation of materials is even more impressive at Port Sunlight. While it may be claimed that Bournville exhibited the highest level of horticulture, the domestic architecture at Port Sunlight seems definitely superior. W. L. George in his study of the latter estimated that there was an average of ten or eleven different house styles within each superblock, since there were ordinarily that many or more "mansion" units in each.[47] In this place the superhouse equated with the superblock at last. The Shavian country house had become the multiplex. George felt, nevertheless, that the good use of materials in the Shavian manner had offset the disintegrating influence of the many styles. He enumerates the materials as "brick, roughcast, tile, slate beams (brown or green), plaster (white) or sandstone (red)."[48] Whitecast and plaster were widely used with occasionally a lower story of brick or red sand-

45. Lord Leverhulme, pp. 86–87.
46. Harvey, p. 57.
47. W. L. George, p. 66.
48. Ibid., p. 67.

stone in Queen Anne fashion. And there is a measure of the bright, affirmative appearance of Bedford Park still at work leavening these garden villages, together with a provincial extension of Shaw's dynamic eclecticism. We gather this also from the writing of contemporaries. George remarks that white roughcast (an indication of a later date than Bedford Park) "is extensively used at Port Sunlight, and anything fresher and more charming than the little white houses, spotlessly clean with their French windows, leaded panes, and gaily painted woodwork I cannot imagine."[49] Similarly, in J. H. Whitehouse's study of Bournville of 1901–02 we learn that, "From the outside these houses present a charming appearance. The woodwork is painted green, and the whitewashed bricks, the blacktarred plinth, the long, sloping, tiled roof, and the green woodwork form a most effective combination of colours."[50] Such spontaneity and exuberance would always remind one of Bedford Park, necessarily omitting the virtuosity of Norman Shaw. But there is another trend, too, which might be described as a search for a more ornamental and patently pretty effect. The trend could also be shown by contrasting the smaller and more exotic trees of Bournville such as the white-beam, thorn, Japanese crab, Hizakura and Amanogowa cherry, almond, mountain ash, silver birch, and laburnum with the larger, heavier, and more common limes, poplars, and willows along the streets of Bedford Park. It can be exemplified as well by the vivid patterns of half-timber, roughcast, and brick at Port Sunlight. The sense of stylistic eclecticism and artificiality which, to be sure, began in Bedford Park, grows almost rampant in Port Sunlight and Bournville. The only other possible way to explain Port Sunlight visually is as a kind of last, ruddy glow of high Victorianism, with all its little dignities and affectations, its prosperity and expansiveness. This eclecticism of forms, styles, and surfaces was to swell until, as W. L. George put it, each street exhibited its own "local nationality."[51]

The actual link with Bedford Park was provided by Maurice B. Adams, previously Shaw's assistant there. In his book of 1904, *Modern Cottage Architecture,* three plates are devoted to groups of cottages at Port Sunlight (Fig. 46). The five-cottage combination by Adams himself is described as of "red brick, with tile-hung walling to the first floor of the end houses, the three intermediate ones being rough-cast in lime stucco left in its own natural cream

49. Ibid.
50. J. H. Whitehouse, p. 170.

51. W. L. George, p. 63.

Fig. 46. Five workmen's cottages, Port Sunlight; Maurice B. Adams, 1904. This is a translation of Shaw's mansion type into cottage units, for economy and better proportion to the widening street and the superblock which originated at Port Sunlight.

colour."[52] This is a typical Port Sunlight house. The three-unit model is described as being "so grouped as to give a largeness of external treatment."[53] Thus, in conformity with the other houses, it was intended to count from the road as one huge, picturesque mansion.

The architect Harvey stated that his aim was to strike a balance between art and economy at Bournville.[54] He believed that only every third or sixth cottage needed ornament.[55] Stock sizes of building materials were to be used along with standardized windows and doors. Roof lines were to be uninterrupted and chimneys grouped, to avoid the expense of costly trimming and flashing.[56] The interior fittings should be of the simplest and most inexpensive kind; the inglenook was to be distributed with restraint, and the ancient parlor completely discouraged as an unnecessary indulgence for the laboring

52. (London, Batsford), Pl. IV, p. 22. J. Lomax Simpson, one of the architects of Port Sunlight, has reported in a letter (Sept. 3, 1961), "It was at this time, about 1899—that Lever engaged several architects, each to design one block of cottages 5 or 7. (I think with the idea of finding one whose designing he liked.) Among those that built a block each were

Maurice B. Adams, Lutyens, Curtis Green, Douglas & Fordham and my father." Mr. Simpson believes the original plan of Port Sunlight itself was entirely Lord Leverhulme's own idea.

53. Ibid., Pl. III, p. 22.
54. Harvey, p. 6.
55. Ibid., p. 65.
56. Ibid., pp, 14, 21.

class.[57] His greatest warning was reserved for the use of half-timbering. He said it "should be used sparingly. While the bye-laws insist on a 9-in. wall being at the back, an unwarranted present and future expense is incurred by its use; and an effect equally as good, moreover, may be obtained with rough-cast, weather boarding, or white-wash. Half-timber one lives to regret, for the weather tells sadly upon it, and it demands constant repair."[58] At Port Sunlight, on the other hand, half-timber was to provide a visual leitmotif, much as it had done in Shaw's earlier country houses. It appeared first here and then there, but one could never lose consciousness of it no matter where he might find himself in the village. As Josephine Reynolds has described it, "The houses are designed in many styles, the predominant one being Tudor, half-timbered with brick or plaster infilling. The half-timbering is structural and there is no doubt that the effect of permanence which Lever wished to establish in his business relations is given expression in the housing of his work people."[59] The land had been bought cheaply and shrewdly to exploit, but it had then been tempered and tailored with the utmost care. The oak half-timbering of the houses was similarly executed with mortise and tenon, fixed with wooden pegs and accompanied by the carving of wood and molding of plaster. Lever was like the rich father making up for the hardships of his youth by lavishing every luxury and comfort on his work family. They would no longer have to walk out to the countryside to experience a more beautiful world. It would surround them. Some of the half-timber houses cost £300 to £400 apiece. By 1910 the land and buildings were estimated to have absorbed £350,000. Although repair and maintenance bills rose as high as 20 per cent of the rent rolls (when they should have been kept down to 10 per cent or less),[60] and the later speeches of the owner make it apparent that even he had occasional doubts on this score (Fig. 47), the practice is nevertheless revealing.[61] As Leverhulme's son noted in his biography, Port Sunlight was by no means the first village in the vicinity. Price's Candleworks had built model housing in 1853 on Bromborough Pool (Fig. 48) and, at the time Port Sunlight was coming into existence in 1888, the Hartley jam and marmalade interests offered a prize for the best design of a workers' settlement a few miles

57. Ibid., pp. 22, 24.

58. Ibid., p. 59.

59. Josephine Reynolds, "Model Village at Port Sunlight," p. 495.

60. W. L. George, pp. 86–98. See also for costs Mervyn E. Macartney, "Mr. Lever and Port Sunlight," *Architectural Review* (July 1910), p. 45.

61. W. H. Lever, *The Buildings Erected at Port Sunlight and Thornton Hough*, pp. 10, 12, 19.

Fig. 47. Houses on Corniche Road, Port Sunlight. The three painters on ladders show the extraordinary maintenance standards, which in the early days went as high as 20 per cent of income. The ideal of cleanliness at Port Sunlight because of soap manufacture and at Bournville because of chocolate production was ever-present. Unwin called this mood the cleansing, lighting, and paving enthusiasm of the nineteenth century.

Fig. 48. Housing at Price's Candle Works, Bromborough Pool, 1853. This model housing of the mid-century was not far from Port Sunlight.

north of Liverpool at Aintree.[62] This five-acre project, like Bromborough, was laid out with an enlarged hollow block in the center which today contains a bowling green (Fig. 49).[63]

Lever and Cadbury had been actively interested in the preservation of ancient half-timbered structures. Lever had been the donor of funds to stabilize the fifteenth-century Hall i' th' Wood near Bolton where Samuel

Fig. 49. Housing for Hartley's Jams and Marmalades at Aintree near Liverpool; William Suyden and Sons, 1888. Although resulting from a competition and built at the same time as Port Sunlight, Aintree exemplifies the older tradition of flat surfaces and uniform street lines.

Crompton had invented the spinning mule in the eighteenth century, and Cadbury had gone so far as to purchase and rebuild at Bournville two ancient half-timber buildings.[64] The urge to validate their villages by associating them directly with the past was strong. In 1887 while Lever was making prep-

62. Viscount Leverhulme, p. 87. See also Alan Watson, "The Price's Bromborough Village," *Progress: The Unilever Quarterly, 3,* 1964, 138–44; J. N. Tarn, "The Model Village at Bromborough Pool," *Town Planning Review* (Jan. 1965), pp. 329–36.

63. "Aintree," *Building News* (July 6, 1888, p. 29; Sept. 7, illust., 14, 21; pp. 324, 336, 390–91). William Suyden & Sons of Leeds were the architects.

64. Selly Manor and the Minworth Greaves House, *The Bournville Village Trust: An Account of Its Planning and Housing Schemes in Suburban and Rural Areas* (n.d.), p. 45.

arations to build Port Sunlight, the Royal Jubilee Exhibition was held in Manchester, not far away. It contained a temporary village which in its feeling and appearance bore a notable resemblance to the more permanent community. The intellectual similarity lies in the principle of collecting and concentrating historicisms. "Old Manchester and Salford" was meant to depict "the many aspects of the town from the time of the Roman occupation to about the middle of the Georgian era." It ended up, the catalogue proudly stated, as "a wonderfully delightful jumble of incongruities," and "its popularity was immense."[65] In the animation of the forms and the patterns of half-timbering of Cheshire and Lancashire inspiration, Old Manchester and Salford and Port Sunlight possessed many resemblances. The buildings of the two villages, one temporary and one permanent, were intended to display the possibilities of communal life. On the ground floors of the Manchester exhibit houses all types of craftsmen were at work in their shops (Fig. 50). Yet what reminds one most of Port Sunlight is the presence of a bevy of bright and charming maidens, dressed in Queen Anne costume, selling ices, creams, and chocolate in front of the replica of old Hulme Hall. It was considered that the merchandising of refreshments, soap, and history called for similar display methods, because the demand for all of them was growing out of the rising standard of living, as Lever well knew. Port Sunlight had replicas of Kenyon Old Hall on Greendale Road (Fig. 51) and Shakespeare's birthplace in the Poet's Corner. There was a Hulme Hall at Port Sunlight too, although it was not a copy of the original and seems to have obtained its name from Lady Lever's family.[66] Of some interest also is the fact that both Hulme Halls exhibited paintings of indigenous subjects in the upper rooms to complement the architecture.[67] Altogether, Port Sunlight, like so many of the architectural events of the 1890s, became tantamount to a permanent exposition. In 1910 at the Brussels Exhibition, the first block of cottages, built in 1888–89, was rebuilt and received the Grand Prix.[68]

The tendency nowadays is, of course, to dismiss both villages as a kind of theatrical sham. But before they are too shortly dismissed, two other features ought to be considered. As the century drew to a close, the history of domestic architecture became much better known than it could have been in the

65. Walter Tomlinson, *The Pictorial Record of the Royal Jubilee Exhibition, Manchester, 1887* (Manchester, Cornish, 1888), p. 127. The architects were Alfred Darbyshire and Frederick B. Smith. There is no evidence that they worked at Port Sunlight.

66. The Kenyon Old Hall replica was by Talbot & Wilson and Shakespeare's birthplace was by E. Kirby, according to the Leverhulme biography, p. 87. Told to the author by F. A. Lawman in July 1959.

67. Tomlinson, p. 129.

68. Stanley Gale, *Modern Housing Estates* (London, Batsford, 1949), p. 204.

Fig. 50. Old Manchester and Salford, Royal Jubilee Exhibition, Manchester, 1887.

Fig. 51. Reproduction of Kenyon Old Hall, Greendale Road, Port Sunlight; J. J. Talbot, 1902.
Kenyon Old Hall reflected the influence of the Royal Jubilee Exhibition. It also faced the railroad
embankment so was made particularly attractive, as were the backs along Elm Road at Bournville.
The indented court is characteristic of Port Sunlight and anticipates the arrangement of houses
around greens in Hampstead Garden Suburb of a few years later.

1850s and 60s, or even in the 70s when Bedford Park was begun in its broad, free classic style. Port Sunlight would be in this evolution a more accurate reflection of the desire for the expansion of the historical vernacular, which was first noticed in Bedford Park. It is most important to realize that this eclecticism generated antiquarianism of the more careful kind, and not vice versa. The use of a variety of revival styles within one village was made for the same reason as the employment of half-timber, roughcast, brick, or hung tile. It was to move the elements forward to appear simultaneously more abstract and more animated, to heighten, brighten, and intensify the visual by emphasis and juxtaposition. There can be little doubt that Lord Leverhulme was determined to take advantage of every possible means to achieve this emphasis, because the industrial and commercial urban North, which was everywhere about him and his associates, was so indescribably dull and oppressive. The city had been indifferently created with only an occasional thought for the arts of spatial amenity, architectural beauty, or circulatory convenience and almost no regard for the possible modifications and harmonies of nature. The need for a feasible alternative to the agglomeration of the city was pressing, since the often asked question in architecture, planning and, for that matter, all the arts, had been—Is it convincing, does it look real? And certainly nothing could have looked more solidly real in its unnatural state than the northern industrial city. Thus the abstract planner of garden villages, like the abstract painter of post-Impressionism, was driven to extremes of intensity by the very excesses of realism he encountered in the conventional, everyday urban environment.

With its perfection of the details of workmanship and its high standard of maintenance, Port Sunlight became likewise a "shrine for the worship of cleanliness."[69] As Unwin was to mention later, most of the urban reforms of the nineteenth century derived from the enthusiasm for lighting, cleansing, and paving. Some regarded this particular instance as a manifestation of the soap industry. Angus Watson, star salesman of Skipper Sardines and later a director of the parent Lever company, wrote in his autobiography: "The whole village was dominated by the spirit of Soap. All of its occupants were employed in the industry; not only were they engaged in it all day, but it was a constant source of conversation at night."[70] The visible promotion by a giant corporation of the clean and neat in architecture for public relations looks toward the future as well as the past. So in the Lever House of 1952 in New York City the pleasure of a fresh and pristine appearance was again appreciated, along with a sympathetic attitude toward low-density zoning and the amenity of a street. The accompanying theme in New York was a further exploration of the structural possibilities of a new material, which leads one to wonder whether this third element was also present at Port Sunlight. It inevitably was, for it was highly characteristic of these men to go on collecting approaches to any multiphased problem. Lord Leverhulme declared in 1902:

> Modern domestic architecture requires to adapt itself to the requirements of the twentieth century in the same way that naval architecture has done in shipbuilding, and to accomplish as much by disregarding traditions as to building materials in supplying the demand for dwellings for the masses of the people as naval architecture has done by disregarding traditions as to ship-building materials in supplying our present-day demands for ships.

69. W. L. George, p. 177.

70. *My Life* (London, Nicholson and Watson, 1937), p. 137. Watson also seems to believe that Lord Leverhulme obtained his inspiration from Bournville (p. 136).

He wished moreover to build houses which would last only for fifty or sixty years.[71] This recalls what John Brandon-Jones has significantly pointed out about Norman Shaw (which Reginald Blomfield evidently chose to ignore in his biography of the architect) that Shaw was always ready to see what might be done with reinforced concrete and the exposed steel frame.[72] By the second decade of the twentieth century Bournville actually had experiments under way with cottages of wood, rammed earth, concrete, and Telford steel.[73]

The next step at Port Sunlight shows plainly that when abrupt changes in viewpoint were to be made, they followed the lead of planning theory rather than material or structural potentialities. Charles Herbert Reilly, who designed a crescent terrace house of white stucco at Port Sunlight and conceived the Reilly Green, a form of garden settlement, was Director of the nearby School of Architecture at the University of Liverpool from 1904 to 1929.[1] His advent there coincided nationally with a reorientation of architectural education from office pupilage to university training. In order to demonstrate to the profession that academic leadership was well informed, and thus worthy of its new role, he sought a definite standard for his students to follow. Liverpool became "the first of the great architectural schools to which the new race of office-liberated students flocked."[2] At the outset the training was in the direction of the neo-Grecque, tempered with some inspiration from the Adam brothers, but this quickly gave way to a more systematic course based on the Beaux Arts. This was in turn supplemented by a strong American influence. "Liverpool as the chief port for Americans in this country was peculiarly susceptible to American influence, and Reilly was, architecturally speaking, one of the first to cross the Herring Pond."[3] In his reminiscences of 1932 about Reilly's career at Liverpool, Stanley C. Ramsey notes that fifteen to twenty years previously, publication of the work going on in America caused intense excitement among the students. "It seemed to have all the breadth of the French with the refinement of the Italian, and yet was somehow wonderfully Anglo-Saxon."[4] When Thomas Hastings arrived in

71. W. H. Lever, pp. 24–25. Also "Port Sunlight and the Housing Question," *Liverpool Daily Post* (March 25, 1902).

72. John Brandon-Jones, "The Work of Philip Webb and Norman Shaw," *Architectural Assn. Journal* (June 1955), pp. 10, 17.

73. *The Bournville Village Trust Publication Department: An Account of Its Planning and Housing Schemes in Suburban and Rural Areas,* p. 32.

1. Stanley C. Ramsey, "Charles Herbert Reilly," *The Book of the Liverpool School of Architecture,* ed. Lionel Budden (Liverpool, The University Press, 1932), pp. 26–27.

2. Ibid., p. 27.

3. Ibid., and the *Liverpool Architectural Sketch Book,* Introduction, by C. H. Reilly (London, *Architectural Review,* 1910), p. 13.

4. Ibid.

London from New York to build his block of modern flats in Piccadilly, known as Devonshire House, he asked Professor Reilly to become his associate.[5] And Reilly himself was, of course, to write a book on the work of McKim, Mead, and White.

The peculiar significance of the American Beaux Arts style in regard to Port Sunlight is that it would necessarily carry the seeds of the City Beautiful movement, first made evident in the Chicago Columbian Exposition of 1893. It was in the era when admiration ran strongest for American architectural modes at the University of Liverpool that the Department of Civic Design was established within the School of Architecture. This occurred in 1909 after Lever had recovered £100,000 in damages from a group of newspapers which had accused him of amalgamating firms in order to reduce competition. He presented the sum gained from the court action to the University for improving the School of Tropical Medicine and to establish a department of town planning, the first in Britain.[6] In the same year he offered prizes of £20, £10, and £5 to the students for the best suggestion for the future expansion of Port Sunlight and the accommodation of a high school, gymnasium, museum, and art gallery. Ernest Prestwich was named first prize winner in 1910.[7] His Beaux-Arts scheme (Fig. 52), with slight modifications, was to be carried out by the firm of Thomas Mawson, the friend of Lord Leverhulme, and a lecturer at Liverpool in landscape design from 1909 to 1924.

That Mawson, like Reilly, was intrigued by America is evident in his esteem for Charles Mulford Robinson, who wrote "the most delightful works on modern civic art in the English language," and his acquaintance with Daniel Burnham of Chicago, the leader of the City Beautiful Movement.[8] In his two published studies for the replanning of Bolton, also financed by Lever and often called "The Bolton Beautiful Scheme," the same influence is to be observed, along with a certain dissatisfaction with earlier civic ideals such as those formerly represented by Port Sunlight.

> Do what we will [he writes in his study of 1916] we cannot express any great civic ideal in terms of cottages however few we allow to the acre, nor can we express our national or civic pride in terms of ornamentation. Both are required to complete the civic edifice, but they only can be successful if they are considered as parts of a policy

5. Ibid.
6. Mawson, *Life and Work of an English Landscape Architect*, p. 177.

7. Ramsey, p. 51. Mawson, *Civic Art*, p. 284.
8. Mawson, *Life*, pp. 172, 249–54; *Bolton: A Study in Town Planning and Civic Art*, 1910.

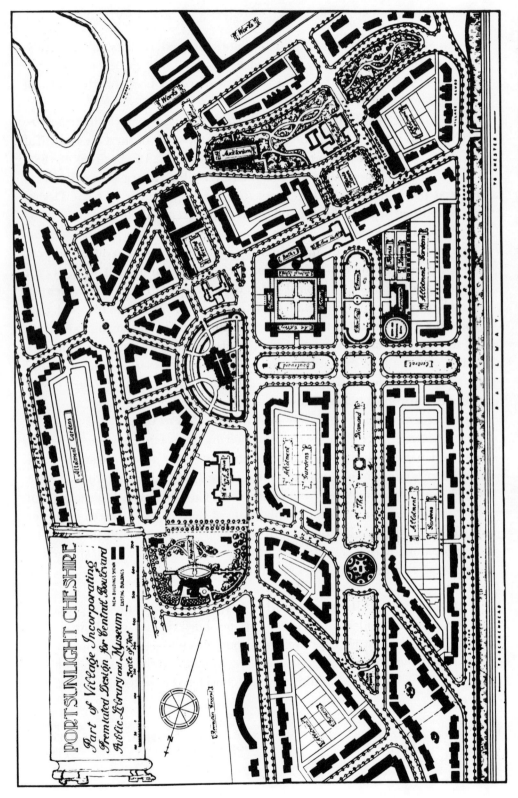

Fig. 52. Revised plan of Port Sunlight, incorporating the premiated plan of Ernest Prestwich; Thomas Mawson, 1910. An axial plan has been developed and monumental buildings introduced, in emulation of the American City Beautiful movement.

which will include the solutions of all the larger problems incidental to the subject.[9]

Or as he had written in his report of 1910, "America, with its more modern
ideas of civic art, never loses sight of the spectacular possibility in arranging
civic centres."[10]

His visualization of the effect of the new plan on Port Sunlight depended
upon cross-axes to be adapted from the student's prize-winning layout.

> First and foremost of these fine effects will be the two new boule
> vards running at right angles to one another, with their central
> lawns and gardens and their avenues of shade trees. As already men
> tioned, the one running east and west will form a vista along which
> persons passing along the railway will view the new church, stand
> ing among its greenery and supported by the statuary with which it
> is proposed to adorn the avenue.[11]

The east and west axis was an elaboration of Lever's original intention of
making the community presentable from the railroad on the west. The
Prestwich–Mawson plan indirectly reflects the enthusiasm of Lever for the
picturesque vista and the initial act of seeing (Fig. 53).

Mawson goes on to say, "The other boulevard, known as 'The Diamond,'
a portion of which already exists and is graced by the classically treated bandstand . . . will, when completed, be six hundred yards long by sixty-five yards
broad, and therefore of imposing proportions."[12] The scale of this grand
avenue, which was no longer required to adapt itself to swampy ravines or
to proceed in a menial or sluggish way from one service point to another,
was also the cause of its appearing less than satisfactory to such later critics as
Josephine Reynolds who noted: "Supposedly, and on the plan, the main core
of the village is the wide causeway with Christ Church at one end, but the
grand planning of the causeway is reduced by the lack of surrounding buildings of suitable scale."[13] Ironically enough, the problem of relating the scale
of buildings to the wider street, which Port Sunlight had surmounted in a
domestic vein better than the other garden villages, was thus raised again in
a different and less promising way on the mall.

9. *Bolton As It Is and As It Might Be*
(Bolton, Tillotson, 1916), p. 14.

10. *Bolton: A Study in Town Planning and
Civic Art*, p. 29.

11. Mawson, *Civic Art*, p. 287.

12. Ibid.

13. Josephine Reynolds, loc. cit., Viscount
Leverhulme, p. 87, says that the houses flanking the Diamond were by J. L. Simpson.

Fig. 53. *Elevation of revised plan of Port Sunlight; T. Mawson. The view east from the railroad embankment shows the formality of the axial plan and boulevard but with a focal point at the church, as would be expected in an older English village.*

It was singularly appropriate then that the final large building at Port Sunlight, the Lady Lever Art Gallery, should be at the northern end of the Diamond. Although Prestwich has written that it was not thought of in this position when his plan was first proposed,[14] it is in the Beaux Arts style and is placed where a building in the American City Beautiful tradition ought to go, at the end of an axial vista. It was begun in 1913 and opened in December of 1922 with a speech by Lord Leverhulme on what art had meant to him.

What a radical break in the philosophy of Port Sunlight's planning this shift in stylistic preference represented cannot be thoroughly understood unless one considers it in the immediate setting. Locally it was an American influence transmuted through the University of Liverpool, and its larger meaning was involved with a renewed interest in urban monumentality, just as it was in the United States.[15] In one way the Diamond was an exaggerated statement of the civic and ecclesiastical centers of Letchworth and Hampstead, but more conspicuous as an afterthought. Prestwich also informs us that, although Reilly admitted his respect for Americans like Burnham, McKim, Hastings, and Cret, he would never concede the English superiority in smaller domestic work.[16] Places like Port Sunlight and Bournville, and Bedford Park before and Letchworth and Hampstead after them, were made important in history by the manner in which they adapted the achievements of the contemporary English domestic school of architects, the best in the world at the time, to the earlier concern for the housing of the working classes. The conviction that the surroundings of the lower classes deserved any aesthetic treatment at all was revolutionary. But the new realization expressed through the incorporation of the Beaux Arts viewpoint was that the model communities had begun to attain such a size that it was more fitting to regard them as complete towns than as overgrown residential districts. Up to that time they were virtually without centers in respect to planning. Again this represented a kind of logical progression, for where Lever's architects had first hollowed out the individual blocks for gardens, they now hollowed out the whole settlement for axial malls.

Whether such an active mind as Lord Leverhulme's would have been aesthetically or socially satisfied, even if he had inherited an authentic Tudor

14. Letter to the author of July 24, 1956.

15. Viscount Leverhulme, p. 288, also *Progress: Unilever Quarterly* (Jan. 1923). The architect of the Gallery was Segar Owen, son of William Owen. The last house units in Port Sunlight appear to have been the Duke of York Cottages opened in May 1934 (letter from Mr. F. A. Lawman, Aug. 13, 1960). See also C. H. Reilly, Introduction, in *The Liverpool Architectural Sketch Book* (London, *Architectural Review*, 1910), p. 12.

16. Prestwich letter July 24, 1956.

village in excellent repair for his workers at Port Sunlight, seems doubtful. His son testifies that he was most content when seated at his drawing board with a ruler and T-square.[17] A few years after he bought Thornton Manor in 1891 he was busily pulling down old houses and farms at the village of Thornton Hough and putting up new ones which he and his architects, Grayson & Ould, W. & S. Owen, and Douglas & Fordham, considered more picturesque and, hence, ipso facto, more original than the originals. "The cottages Lever replaced by others more attractively designed, and he built a new smithy in the Old English half-timbered style, planting in front of it an appropriate chestnut-tree,"[18] apparently still another fortuitous scrap of American influence via Longfellow. Lever did salvage some of the original houses, he tells us, but gave most of them up as a bad job.[19] The result is that the old village of Thornton Hough appears as another and still quainter version of Port Sunlight except for the fact that the natural contours and associations have had more effect, and the manor holds the socially dominant off-center position which the factory has in Port Sunlight (Fig. 54). At the same time with its church at the top of a rise before a long green it recalls especially such old Cheshire villages as Astbury. The un-English aspect of Lord Leverhulme's thought is that he appears to have had little conception of the mellowing possibilities of time and aspired instead to recreate the past and all its patina with one master stroke, much as the Manchester Jubilee Exhibition had done. Yet this attitude of enlarging responsibility to history and the desire to capture its meaning within a moment is undeniably Modern and Romantic.

How fast and far such ideas were traveling at the time and how composite their application was likely to be is brought to mind in far-away Seattle, Washington, where we read that, "The Beaux Arts Society was founded in 1908 with the idea of establishing a community in many respects similar to the Garden Villages of England, and to advance the arts and crafts, as related to home building."[20] The resultant "Beaux Arts Village" because of its location on Lake Washington, the effort to preserve the trees and natural cover, and the character of its organizers (among whom was Sidney Lawrence, the painter of Alaskan landscapes), contained some extremely attractive rustic

17. Viscount Leverhulme, p. 86.
18. Ibid., p. 100.
19. W. H. Lever, *The Buildings Erected at Port Sunlight and Thornton Hough*, p. 27.
20. Frank Calvert and T. Ross Ditty, *Homes*

and Gardens of the Pacific Coast, *1* (Seattle, Beaux Arts Society, 1913), no page. Mr. James O'Gorman called this settlement to my attention.

Fig. 54. Cottages beside the church, Thornton Hough, c. 1891. The image of Old Salford at the Manchester Royal Jubilee of 1887 was imposed on Port Sunlight and, shortly after, on the authentic Tudor village of Thornton Hough after Lever had purchased it in order to live in the manor. The street composition is given careful attention as it ascends the hill, showing it to be still in the Norman Shaw vein, but more precise in its historicisms and more wedded to the Cheshire vernacular.

houses in a landscape setting.[21] This colony helps to show that the garden village movement with its pronounced eclecticism, as manifest at Port Sunlight, was both fundamentally aesthetic in its inspiration and almost too easily able to absorb coincident movements. This whole mood of amenity and conciliation was to disappear with World War I.

After Lord Leverhulme and Mr. Cadbury had wrapped up tradition and housing problems to their own satisfaction, they went on to the really staggering question of the land and its ownership and occupancy. Leverhulme wanted municipalities to purchase peripheral land which would be then offered without charge to private builders. With the urban high-rise, high-density, reform block as his age knew it, he had no sympathy. He says as much in a speech of 1898 while making his recommendation for the land,

21. *American Guide Series: Washington* (Portland, Binford and Mott, 1941), p. 323.

But, it may be asked, is it absolutely necessary to provide free land? Cannot we leave this question of free land alone, and proceed in some other way? Believe me, ladies and gentlemen, there is no other way than first dealing with the question of land for houses. All other methods are simply tinkering with the evil we would remedy. Corporations, and notably Liverpool, have built blocks of workmen's dwellings—so-called—and anything more hideous, more undesirable for the rearing of a family, or more wasteful of the public money, it would be impossible to find.

Moreover, he said, "Every public improvement, such as the demolition of old property, widening of streets, etc., has increased the overcrowding."[22] Liverpool tenements were usually four to six stories high and back to back.[23] His basic argument for the municipal ownership of land was simple and supposed to be appealing to the taxpayers. If an acre cost the city £200 and the annual interest upon it was 2¾ to 3 per cent, twelve houses built by private developers and together yielding rates of £30 would provide a steady income on the investment, even though the land itself was given away. In the overcrowded slums where a single owner might pay the tax bill for all the tenants of his building, the per-family return to the city was bound to be lower than if they all lived separately in houses on the outskirts at a comparatively low density. He failed to reckon, of course, with any kind of municipal service costs such as today plague the light, power, water, and sewage agencies of suburbs. The chief contention was that at the same time the landlord was obtaining his full profit from abusing the land by overcrowding it, the municipality was being deprived of its rightful income by the representation of too many citizens by one landlord. The city merely supported the fundamental error when it built flats within slum areas. The nominal owner of land held only a lifetime interest in it, according to his view, and the municipality was therefore to be considered as the "real" owner over any longer period. The evidence for this priority was that in the eyes of the law, the claims on taxes preceded those on rents and interest. The city's "ownership" therefore entitled it to seek profit from the land benefiting both itself and its poorer citizens in the process, since "the cheapening of the land will be the most powerful factor in reducing cottage rentals."[24]

The arguments are attractive. George Cadbury matches them in his

22. W. H. Lever, "Land for Houses," pp.   23. Ibid.
35, 36.   24. Ibid., p. 37.

speeches and writings. In a letter of 1906 to Walter Runciman, the ship-owner and Northern Liberal leader, he declared that, "I could only wish that municipalities held land around every town and city, so that we might have a belt of garden villages like Bournville all round them."[25] And two years later he also wrote to John Burns, then President of the Local Government Board, "I know by conversation with leading conservatives that they are quite prepared to help an efficient measure on the German plan where municipalities have full control over the areas around them."[26] It is probable that Cadbury, like others of his generation, had been influenced in this direction by Thomas Horsfall's *The Improvement of the Dwellings and Surroundings of the People: The Example of Germany,* which had been published in Manchester in 1904. But it seems equally likely from such examples as Lever's speech of 1898 and D. B. Foster's argument in 1897 for profitable municipal investment in downtown land for Leeds, that public land ownership was being generally discussed in England before Horsfall's publication, although Horsfall has hitherto been accepted as the only source of such views. The nature of this ferment is particularly indicated by the conference at Bournville in September 1901 on the ripening garden city concept. The avowed purpose of meeting was to consider the implications of the Cadbury village for the future. Ebenezer Howard was often to acknowledge his debt to Bournville.[27] Besides Howard, the two men who stand out among the three hundred delegates are Raymond Unwin and J. [sic] Bernard Shaw.[28] Unwin was to offer a resolution that until a garden city could be realized, local authorities should be urged to buy land on the outskirts of towns, which shows he was evidently under the influence of Lever.[29]

George Bernard Shaw, who came as a London Borough Councillor from St. Pancras, was typically engaged in mental gymnastics during the meeting and brought up the following hypothesis as a challenge to his host and the assembled company.

> This notion that you are going to found a Garden City in order to make the inhabitants of it the absolute properitors [sic] of it would undoubtedly lead to this: If by accident, owing to the development of industry, it became very valuable, you would enable the inhabit-

25. April 28 (Bournville Village Collection).

26. Jan. 27, 1908 (Bournville Village Collection).

27. Ewart G. Culpin, *The Garden City Movement Up-to-Date* (London, Garden Cities and Town Planning Assn., 1914), p. 24.

28. *The Garden City Conference at Bournville: Report of Proceedings* (London, Garden City Assn., 1901), frontispiece.

29. Ibid., pp. 13–14.

ants to retire practically as landowners, and if you did that they would do just as other owners do: sell their property, live at Monte Carlo, and realise the whole value of their increment as unearned increment, and you must, if you want to get this experiment through, be prepared to meet that objection, and to show that your deed of trust does provide for that contingency.[30]

To which frivolity Mr. Cadbury soberly replied that

I may say that we sold 140 of the first houses we built on lease for 999 years, but we soon found that the tenants who had bought at, for example, £250, were selling at £300 and more, the demand was so great, and we felt that it was not right to put that money into the hands of a few, and that it ought to go to the Trust for the benefit of those who need it most. Mr. John Burns, who came to the village, said, "How foolish you are! You are giving a present to these men. You will soon find that this is so." We did soon find that they were actually making 20 to 30 per cent. profit when they sold their houses.[31]

The program of encouraging individual ownership and responsibility at Bournville was thus reluctantly dropped in favor of rentals. The means and skills to produce higher property values had increased by leaps and bounds during the nineteenth century, as had the population to consolidate the demand for them. While the potentialities belonged to the whole age, they became acutely visible in the model villages, because these communities concentrated all the possibilities of value enhancement within them, the heavy capitalization and the wholesale purchase of land, the improvement of these by good planning, full municipal services, attractive landscaping and superior architecture, and the presence of people in fairly large numbers. Cadbury and Lever discovered through their villages that no matter how altruistic the purpose, the employment of these means inevitably created monetary rewards along with intangible benefits. The question then became, who was to receive the by-product of the good intention, an individual or an agency representing a group? The foundation was set for the land ownership policies of the garden city itself as much by this side effect and its unintended results as by the reform theory of Howard and his predecessors. While individualism and pri-

30. Ibid., pp. 34–35.
31. Ibid., p. 35.

vate ownership were advocated wherever it seemed feasible, from Akroydon to Bournville, when it offered a threat to the whole community, it was as promptly and objectively discarded. This instinct for self-control was what distinguished the growth of the model village from that of the great cities during the nineteenth century and suggests the way in which the movement made use of the best side of the British temperament.

So again it becomes inaccurate to label the garden city movement as one which was irrevocably against the big city and all its advantages. What these men were fundamentally calling for instead was a new method of communal regulation to offset the greater problems of the industrial and urban revolutions. So long as they saw no signs of adequate control within the metropolis, they would build self-contained communities, but this did not mean that they rejected out of hand the possibilities of a new richness and variety evolving from urban life. Lever frankly admitted in his speech on the land, for example,

> But just as surely as the country is made by God, so surely is it that man is also made by the same Creator—who constituted him a social being, loving to live in towns and cities where he finds the greatest scope for his social instincts, and where his genius and abilities have the fullest opportunities for development. Therefore it is an established fact, and one that all past history of the human race confirms, that men prefer city life to country life; hence the great importance to the well-being of the race that city life be carried on under proper conditions as to housing, with a view to securing surroundings the most favourable to health. It is for the citizens themselves as a body to control this matter through their municipal organisations.[32]

And, of course, up to that point, they had failed miserably to do so.

32. W. H. Lever, "Land for Houses," p. 33.

6. MORRIS AND HOWARD—BOSTON AND CHICAGO

Since the influences of Ebenezer Howard (1850–1928) and William Morris (1834–96) merge in the work of Barry Parker (1867–1947) and Raymond Unwin (1863–1940), the actual designers of the first garden city of Letchworth, it is rewarding to consider one or two aspects of this relationship which have gone largely unnoticed. Ebenezer Howard willingly described the impulse to action that seized him as he read Edward Bellamy's book about a utopian Boston in 1888.

The next morning as I went up to the City from Stamford Hill I realised, as never before, the splendid possibilities of a new civilisation based on service to the community and not on self-interest, at present the dominant motive. Then I determined to take such part as I could, however small it might be, in helping to bring a new civilisation into being. At once I called on Reeves, then in Fleet Street, and suggested that he should publish an English edition of *Looking Backward.* This, on my offering to dispose of at least a hundred copies, he agreed to do. Shortly afterwards, and before writing my book, I joined with a few friends in discussing Bellamy's principles. We gradually discovered some of the author's weak points, the most outstanding being the assumption that such a tremendous change could be effected at once. Thus I was led to put forward proposals for testing out Bellamy's principles though on a very much smaller scale—in brief, to build by private enterprise pervaded by public spirit an entirely new town, industrial, residential and agricultural.[1]

Howard adds that his own scheme, published first in 1898 as *To-morrow: A Peaceful Path to Real Reform,* might be characterized as a continuation of

1. Dugald Macfadyen, *Sir Ebenezer Howard and the Town Planning Movement* (Manchester, University Press, 1933), pp. 20–21.

three other projects as well: "(1) The proposals for an organized migratory movement of population of Edward Gibbon Wakefield and of Professor Alfred Marshall; (2) the system of land tenure first proposed by Thos. Spence and afterwards (though with an important modification) by Mr. Herbert Spencer; and (3) the model city of James Silk Buckingham."[2] As W. A. Eden has indicated in his important essay on the sources of Howard's thought, these influences, together with that of John Stuart Mill, were to impart to his diagrams a peculiarly archaic, geometric, mid-century appearance. This was accentuated by his use of the title, Crystal Palace, for the shopping arcade around his Central Park, perhaps reflecting Paxton's suggestion for the Great Victorian Way to encircle London or possibly William Moseley's similar Crystal Way, both of 1853.[3] Yet Howard denied having knowledge of the visions of either Wakefield or Buckingham when he produced his own. There appears to be a quiet insistence throughout his life upon the independent nature of his own process of reflection. Although generous to a fault in acknowledging earlier ideals when he was conscious of their influence, it was evidently more difficult for him to identify those elements that came with the general culture. He was neither an intellectual nor a systematic reader in the field, we are told.

For that reason Eden's erudite analysis and theoretical study is especially useful. He presents Howard's views as a series of clear-cut positions assumed under specific circumstances.[4] He notes, for example, that while the mid-century diagram of the City of Victoria may have represented Buckingham's inherent distrust of a new age and a manifest will to confine it within bounds, Howard had a more generous and optimistic "faith in men, believing that whatever they seek after is a component of the highest good, which therefore presents itself as a combination of the objects of human desire."[5] His vision was essentially a projection of "the somewhat earnest, chapel-going, or chapel-emancipated, lower middle class which had lately acquired political power, and was destined to inaugurate a revolution by returning the Liberal Party with its huge majority to the General Election of 1906."[6]

Eden appears to be interpreting the role of Howard mainly through the aspirations of a single class. He also believes that Howard's personal wandering, lack of attachment to London, and concern for the well-being of others

2. Ebenezer Howard, *Garden Cities of Tomorrow* (London, Faber and Faber, 1946), p. 119.

3. See George F. Chadwick, *The Works of Sir Joseph Paxton 1803–1865* (London, Architectural Press, 1961), pp. 207–12, for an excellent description of this route. Also John Gloag,

Victorian Taste (New York, Macmillan, 1962), p. 115.

4. W. A. Eden, "Ebenezer Howard and the Garden City Movement," *Town Planning Review* (Summer 1947), pp. 123–43.

5. Ibid., pp. 134–35.

6. Ibid., p. 134.

may have arisen from the early bankruptcy of his father in London, an in-
triguing theme in view of the similar financial failure of Raymond Unwin's
father and the difficulty Unwin had in adjusting to Oxford. But for the same
reason, Eden feels, Howard never could rise above the intellectual limitations
of that same lower middle class. Freedom for country life and freedom for the
values of the class to operate were not full freedoms because they were not
vested by the whole society. Eden identifies Howard's fatal weakness as not
being able to distinguish between the "desires" of a culture and its true best
"interests." His garden city was thus predestined to become only a beggars'
opera. To emphasize his point, Eden requotes Browning's "Italian person of
quality" as saying,

> And so, the villa for me, not the city!
> Beggars can scarcely be choosers.

Eden shrewdly observes that Howard's program was dependent upon the
use of land as a form of indirect and overall control. This was to grow more
relevant as recreation and leisure became increasingly possible with the
shortening of factory hours toward the end of the century. The larger question then reduced itself to whether the rapid and centralized piling up of
land and building worth was a more appropriate reflection of the age than
any proposal for dispersing the values. Eden objects that in both Buckingham's Victoria and Howard's Garden City the centers would be devoid of the
pageant and bustle of urban life. He notices too that the cores of the actual
towns of Letchworth and Welwyn exhibit the same "reversal of traditional
values" in their emptiness and passivity, unlike the centers of the great cities.

This theme of emptiness is further worked out when reference is made to
Howard's question whether children can be better taught where school sites
cost £9,500, as they did in London, or £40 as they would in a garden city.
Eden's answer is that it depends upon what one considers a worthwhile education, for,

> if the opportunity to observe all sorts and conditions of men counts
> for anything in education, or if proximity to museums, art galleries,
> historic sites and buildings, concert halls, zoological gardens, to say
> nothing of shipping, commerce and the seat of government, is of any
> value to a child in its formative years, then the advantage would ap-
> pear to lie with the site costing £9,500 an acre.[7]

7. Ibid., p. 136.

Eden's conclusion has to be that the increased worth of land and buildings would not have resulted except in legitimate response to the "convenience of commerce." London, by this commerce, was made not only a British capital but a world capital. Howard had hoped to drain off London's hard-earned treasure to subsidize his lower middle-class communities out in the country. Perhaps the deepest insight one gains from Eden's theoretical discussion of Howard's views is the sudden realization that Eden cares more for the position and power of national wealth than for what it can actually buy or produce. The issue is patently one of the possible overthrow of "a seat of power" for the whole British culture. For planning theory in general this article by Eden has an acute interest because it poses the idea of a modern city as a brain and nerve center for a civilization, with its prestige emanating from the process of decision as much as from money making.

Given these attitudes, it is additionally instructive to realize what Eden apparently did not, that the other most often cited document on communal utopias of the 1890s, William Morris' *News from Nowhere*, was also chiefly inspired by Bellamy's *Looking Backward*. John Bruce Glasier, architect friend of both Morris and Raymond Unwin, gives an informative account of how this happened. Casually, and somewhat by accident, Glasier's brother-in-law, Sam Bullock, had asked Morris on a Saturday to lecture in the Kelmscott meetingroom at Hammersmith to a local group.

> Morris objected that he had nothing new to lecture about, and had already spoken there on any subject upon which he could find anything to say. Bullock suggested that he might make a few comments on Bellamy's book—which Morris told him he had just read. Morris brightened at the suggestion and on the Sunday evening gave a running commentary on the book, incidentally introducing by way of contrast some of his own ideas of how people might live and work in "a new day of fellowship, rest, and happiness." Doubtless it was this lecture which gave him the idea of writing "News from Nowhere," which immediately afterwards began to appear in weekly instalments in the *Commonweal,* and was intended as a counterblast to "Looking Backward." . . . Morris never intended, however, "News from Nowhere" to be regarded as a serious plan or conspectus of Socialism, and was both surprised and amused when he found the little volume solemnly discussed as a text-book of Socialist politics, economics, and morality.[8]

8. J. Bruce Glasier, *William Morris and the Early Days of the Socialist Movement* (London, Longmans, Green, 1921), pp. 150–51.

There is a Bank Holiday air about the dream it recounts. The title alone suggests this: *News from Nowhere, or, An Epoch of Rest, Being Some Chapters from a Utopian Romance.* A few incidents, such as gifts to the public of carved and bejeweled tobacco pipes, eerily forecast the provision of free dentures and spectacles under the twentieth-century national health acts. It is difficult to give sober consideration to his semisymbolic designation of the Parliament buildings as a dung market, although it is this that most offended the later reviewers of the book. Morris' grievance was the double one of misrule from what he thought to be an ugly building, but it was impossible to tell which abuse he objected to more—the political or the aesthetic. Dickens too had called Parliament the "national dust-heap." What would be more held against Morris today is that he would not linger in the city and grapple with "the tough urban realities." Instead he indolently took a tour up the Thames, his boating party becoming more idyllic as it proceeded. Morris tried to simulate through this a heightened sense of well-being, a living consciousness of the environment, enhanced by greater and greater beauty the farther the party got from the city. Having once experienced the dream of *News from Nowhere,* it seemed hard for future generations to shake off, all evidence of waking reality to the contrary. It appears to have haunted Parker and Unwin all their lives. Unwin copied the following from Morris in his last notes: "We must turn this land from the grimy back yard of a workshop into a garden. If that seems difficult, I can not help it: I only know that it is necessary."[9]

In his early review of *Looking Backward* in the *Commonweal* of 1889, Morris puts down his serious objections to the book. He describes Bellamy's temperament as the thoroughly modern one, "unhistoric and unartistic." The American author wished to rid the world of "injustice, misery, and waste," which struck Morris as only half an improvement. The latter followed the main stream of British thought from Pugin and Ruskin in believing that economic, social, and moral uplift would be futile unless accompanied by a drastic change in the intrinsic quality of the physical environment. He was convinced that these aims should be undertaken simultaneously, not one after the other. For him the logical person to lead the reform was, of course, the socially oriented artist, an artist actually in residence in the nineteenth century. Thus the artist and his productions would be more in evidence and the city less, reversing the normal sequence of nineteenth-century daily experience.

9. From "Art and Beauty of the Earth," by Morris. In the Unwin R.I.B.A. papers.

Morris distrusted the dependence of Bellamy's scheme on the great metropolis which was to be directed by a national monopoly and the superstate. These institutions could only breed personal irresponsibility within a militaristic, tightly drilled society. He also resented the fact that although Bellamy mentioned villages, he apparently regarded them as strictly subordinate to the great urban centers. The metropolis was already a place where the populace tried to shuffle off responsibilities "on to the shoulders of an abstraction called the State," thought Morris. The reconstituted village would be much more satisfactory as an administrative unit because it would be "small enough for every citizen to feel himself responsible for its details, and to be interested in them."[10] In *News from Nowhere* he imagines the villages of the future first equaling, then surpassing, those of his favorite fourteenth century: "the difference between town and country grew less and less; and it was indeed this world of the country vivified by the thought and briskness of town bred folk which has produced that happy and leisurely but eager life,"[11] also anticipating in some measure the principle of double magnets of town and country elaborated by Howard.

It was a similar search for a more efficient, yet more humane, environment which later activated Unwin. This restraint helped to protect him, the greatest planning technician of his age, from the danger of technical absolutes. Planning was for him, too, only an instrument by which other desirable goals might be attained—never a complete end in itself. He stretches the theoretical limits of urban population by keeping Morris' basic principle always before him. Half a century after Morris' critique of Bellamy's *Looking Backward* we find Unwin still declaring that the size of a model city, "must vary widely; it may be 30,000 as Howard suggested, or 50,000, or even 100,000; but at some point the limit is reached beyond which the good relations can no longer be maintained."[12] When the point of breakdown in good relations was reached, new satellites with federal ties to the mother city should be founded.

Morris did not share Bellamy's optimistic opinion either that more leisure could be bought from the machine or that the working years for an individual ought to be over by age forty-five. There are always new wants to be satisfied, he says, and the human race has consistently tended to work up to capacity. Machines would make possible only other and newer machines which in turn would have to be as carefully watched and tended. The final goal of

---

10. William Morris, "Looking Backward," *Commonweal* (June 22, 1889), pp. 194–95.

11. William Morris, *News from Nowhere* (London, Reeves and Turner, 1891), p. 79.

12. Raymond Unwin, "Syllabus, School of Architecture, Columbia University," Course I, Lecture 9, Feb. 23, 1939.

society should not be to escape from labor into leisure, but to find a deeper joy through work, by fostering conditions so pleasant and varied that everyone would have the desire to keep at it. Invention would concentrate on taking care of the most "irksome" tasks by improved machinery. Once the proper employment was found for the machine, mankind as a whole could emerge again into the true artistic activity, or "work-pleasure."

Howard found much to praise in Bellamy's book, Morris more to condemn. Yet, as in any similar attempt to contrast the views of Norman Shaw and Morris, it is the resemblance between the premises of the two contemporary figures, rather than the diversity of their conclusions, which is most arresting. Time enthralls their individualism. Both Howard and Morris based their discussions upon an imaginary community which would draw its coherence from a limit of population and the consequent desire for cooperation based on personal acquaintance. They were rebels, but in a distinctly conservative way. Both had little faith in state initiative or control.[13] Howard differed from earlier reformers like Owen and Buckingham in that he visualized a more "open" and permissive economy within a less self-sufficient social unit.[14] He did not have in mind the regulation of either agriculture or industry except by location. Morris' aversion to the swollen state and commercial monopoly resembled Howard's attitude in that it expected the individual to assume certain responsibilities when brought face to face with them. But the closest similarity lies in their willingness to risk all on a single turn of the wheel. In a sense, they both tried to take exception to the anarchy of uncontrolled urban growth by a single grand gesture. Howard wished to exercise final power through the municipal ownership of land, while Morris hoped to restore the primacy of art in determining the environmental quality and texture of the community.

Howard was better equipped by experience, however, to cope with the American technocratic vision of the 1880s, when *Looking Backward* was written. He had lived in Chicago from 1872 until 1876, as a shorthand clerk after his failure at homesteading in Nebraska. He was in his early twenties at the time and, as Osborn has astutely put it, "It is a pity that only brief flashes of light on Howard's life in Chicago are available, because it is likely that the pattern of his lifelong interests was set during those four years."[15] No city or its hinterland could have better persuaded him of the advantages that Amer-

13. F. J. Osborn, "Ebenezer Howard, Father of the Garden City," *Listener* (April 27, 1950), p. 736.

14. F. J. Osborn, "The Garden City Movement," *Britain Today* (Dec. 12, 1941), pp. 4–5.

15. Ebenezer Howard, op. cit., Preface by F. J. Osborn, p. 19.

icans were obtaining from the mechanized implements introduced after the Civil War. His sensitivity to the rapid rise of land values and his concern with land as the root of the communal problem could easily have been acquired there, although there is no doubt that the writings of the American Henry George on the subject influenced him later as well. The skyscraper, invented by William Le Baron Jenny in Chicago by the early 1880s, was a visible enough manifestation of the compression of these forces. Chicago, in the midst of hundreds of square miles of unoccupied and easily accessible prairie, crowded in upon itself to send land prices skyrocketing. This was a glaring inconsistency which few sensible men could fail to observe. And Howard was more than an ordinarily sensible person. He carried the late Victorian ability to relate multiple causes to a diversity of effects far beyond its usual limits.

Howard's awareness of the time and expense necessary to deliver agricultural products to the ultimate consumer might also have been acquired here, for Chicago was rapidly becoming the agricultural transport center of the nation. Finally, and perhaps most significantly for the future, he could have been brought to realize in Chicago that the nineteenth-century metropolis was the creation of men, after all, and not of some vast and intransigent system of economic laws which it was the duty of the best intellects only to uncover and obey. As his biographers point out, Howard was pre-eminently a person of action, even up to purchasing the land for Welwyn without sufficient funds or prior consultation with his advisors, thus forcing them willynilly to build a second garden city. Chicagoans, too, were men of action and indefatigable builders.

In reviewing the earlier history of the term "garden city" in the United States and New Zealand, Osborn remarks that, "Howard was not conscious of deriving his term Garden City either from Chicago or from the name of Alexander Stewart's industrial suburb or village on Long Island, N.Y. (1869), but I cannot doubt that it was from Chicago that he got it, though he gave quite a new meaning to the term." Again there is reticence about the possibility that other, unrecognized sources influenced Howard. Chicago was full of dramatic suggestion at the time and the garden city aphorism and the living experience could have been effortlessly and even unconsciously joined in the young stenographer's mind. Osborn also remarks in passing that, "Chicago (surprising as it seems at a distance) called itself the Garden City, through pride in its magnificent surroundings."[16] This is correct in substance but slightly mis-

16. Ibid., p. 26.

directed by allusion. The reference was actually to the city itself, not to a projected circle of parks nor to the great sweep of the wild prairie or of Lake Michigan, and the before and after sequence in the use of the title is of singular importance to Howard's residence there.

U. P. Hedrick in his history of horticulture in America up to 1860 notes that, "Probably in no other city west of the Atlantic seaboard were grounds about private homes more enthusiastically cared for or better planned."[17] Frederick Francis Cook in a volume which he subtitled *Recollections of the "Garden City" of the Sixties* describes a view of Chicago of 1862 from the Court House under the heading, "Why Chicago Was Known As the 'Garden City.'"

> What we now behold is a magnificent natural forest in the midst of a city,—or is it not better to say that the city here plays hide and seek in the forest? Either way, it is a dream. The noble, lake-bordered expanse is divided into lordly domains, embellished with lovely gardens . . . Not only is every street shaded, but entire wooded squares contain each only a single habitation, usually near its centre, thus enabling their fortunate owners to live in park-like surroundings. . . . And to think that in a single night all this wealth of nature disappeared as if it had never been![18]

The single night on which this occurred of course was October 8, 1871, the night of the Chicago Fire. According to Cook's expert testimony, Chicago was appropriately called the Garden City before and never after. Or, as architect Louis Sullivan nostalgically put it in his autobiography, "The Garden City had vanished with its living story. That tale could not be twice told, that presence could not be recalled. It had gone forever with the flames."[19] Since Howard came to live in Chicago the year after the fire, he is not likely to have experienced it personally. Yet it is not beyond possibility that he went through Chicago on his way to Nebraska the previous year and he would, in any event, have been familiar with the legend of a verdant city which had vanished overnight. Cook was a star reporter for the same *Chicago Times* for which Howard did some shorthand reporting.[20] In the nomenclature of Howard's Garden City diagram, Fifth Avenue adjoins Central Park, as it does in New York. From such signs one is inclined to believe that Howard carried

17. (New York, Oxford University Press, 1950), p. 235.

18. *Bygone Days in Chicago: Recollections of the "Garden City" of the Sixties* (Chicago,

McClurg, 1910), p. 178.

19. *The Autobiography of an Idea* (5th ed. New York, Dover, 1956), p. 244.

20. Macfadyen, p. 10.

a penchant for American terms with him for decades after he left the country in 1876.

The American landscape architect, Frederick Law Olmsted, was deeply impressed by Paxton's Birkenhead Park across from Liverpool when he visited it in the early 1850s. He confessed himself "ready to admit that in democratic America there was nothing to be thought of as comparable with this People's Garden."[21] There is some cause to believe that the cultural compliment was returned by Howard when he observed Olmsted's suburban town of Riverside, four miles west of the outskirts of Chicago. The Riverside Improvement Company was organized in April 1869 and most of the layout was completed by 1871.[22] Of the 1,600 acres it covered, no fewer than 700 were devoted to roads, borders, walks, recreational grounds, and parks (Fig. 55). The fortunate inhabitant "[has] plenty of elbow room, and can dig to his heart's content, raise his own fruit and vegetables, keep his own cow, and even make his own butter. And he can do all this without the sacrifice of the urban comforts which long use has made necessary to him."[23] The advantages of a new combination of town and country, so germane to Howard's garden city promotion, were already being advertised in the Riverside prospectus. Riverside was an avowed suburban community and was to be tied directly to the city by twelve passenger trains a day and a tree-lined parkway, 150 feet wide, across open country, with separate paths for pedestrians, carriage traffic, horseback riders, and heavy drays, not too different in general intent (except for self-containment) from Howard's circular Grand Avenue which was to have been 420 feet wide. One sees also from this that Riverside stood completely free from the edge of the larger city, as did Letchworth from London. Many of the inner features of the designs of Parker and Unwin also recall those of Olmsted, such as the desire to be rid of back alleys, and particularly the cul-de-sacs modeled to the contours of the land, which first showed up in Roland Park in Baltimore in 1891 with Olmsted and at Letchworth in 1903 with Parker and Unwin.

Howard was no designer. He was fundamentally a purveyor of ideas. Yet he would have found considerable food for thought if he had taken the trouble to visit the suburb developed shortly before his arrival. The entire plat was to be planted with groves of trees not exceeding four hundred feet in

21. *Walks and Talks of an American Farmer in England* (New York, Putnam, 1852), p. 79.

22. *Charter and By-Laws: Riverside Improvement Company* (Chicago, Beach and Barnard, 1869); and A. T. Andreas, *History of*

Cook County, Illinois (Chicago, Andreas, 1884), p. 876.

23. Anon., *Riverside in 1871* (Chicago, Blakely, 1871), p. 21.

Fig. 55. Rustic bridge to Pic-Nic Island, Riverside near Chicago; Olmsted, Vaux Company, 1871. This was an Indian camp ground until 1836, and it is this fact, along with the importation of thousands of trees to give the prairie a more forested effect, that shows the American impatience to remake land and nature as fast as possible. The buildings in the background are by Wm. Jenney, the inventor of the skyscraper.

width, anticipating to some extent the screening functions of the greenbelt. Noteworthy in this relation too is a sentence from Olmsted's *Preliminary Report* of 1868.

> There are two aspects of suburban habitation that need to be considered to ensure success; first, that of the domiciliation of men by families, each family being well provided for in regard to its domestic in-door and out-door private life; second, that of harmonious association and co-operation of men in a community, and the intimate relationships and constant intercourse, and interdependence between families.[24]

These were interlocking considerations of which Morris, Howard, and Un-

24. "Preliminary Report upon the Proposed Suburban Village of Riverside Near Chicago,"   Olmsted, Vaux & Co., Landscape Architects, 110 Broadway, New York, Sept. 1, 1868, p. 17.

win together must surely have approved. Parker and Unwin would have appreciated particularly the emphasis on the family and its integrity (Figs. 56, 57). Morris would have liked the thought of rewarding personal relationships, supported by the environment. Undoubtedly Howard would have been attracted by Olmsted's mention of "harmonious association and co-operation."

It could be assumed merely by virtue of Howard's residence in Chicago that he would be cognizant of Riverside. But there was a secondary reason why he might not have been overly eager later to acknowledge acquaintance with it. After the fire of 1871, refugees and workmen crowded into Riverside. Fever and ague broke out, giving it a reputation for unhealthiness. Then the panic of 1873 placed it in financial difficulties[25] which led to a civic scandal of more than usual proportions. The suburb had originally been the vision of Emery E. Childs, but a large portion of the property on which it was built, known as Riverside Farm, belonged to David A. Gage.[26] He was the proprietor of the Sherman Hotel and had been a popular municipal treasurer. In 1874 the new treasurer, who had been swept into office by an unexpected upsurge of the People's Party, inconveniently asked Gage to turn over $500,000 of public funds, which he was in no position to do. As reporter Cook delicately put the matter, "If only the broad, finely wooded acres on the Desplaines had remained Dave Gage's farm to the end of his days, how differently would the history of its whilom owner now be written!"[27] By the custom of the time and place, Dave fled to Denver, Colorado, where he took up hotelkeeping again, sending back occasional greetings to his old Chicago friends who loyally introduced a "motion to quash" the indictment for misappropriation against him. The legal action on this defection and its otherwise tangled affairs which finally projected it into bankruptcy, lasted from 1874 to 1876. These are precisely the years in which the Chicago directories carry the name of Ebenezer Howard as a court stenographer for the firm of Ely & Burnham.[28]

Whatever Chicago may have lacked by way of adequate stimulation for

25. *The Riverside–Brookfield Community Historical Pageant* (Riverside, Brookfield High School, 1916), pp. 28–29.

26. "Riverside," *Chicago Tribune* (Feb. 25, 1900). William Jenny and his partners were the architects and engineers of Riverside. Jenny invented the skyscraper (the Home Insurance Building in Chicago, 1883–86). He lived in Riverside, was a stockholder, and designed the

108-foot water tower, the hotel, and many of the houses, including that of the proprietor, E. E. Childs. (See Andreas, pp. 876–77 and *Riverside in 1871*, pp. 6, 25–26.)

27. Cook, p. 302.

28. *Lakeside Directories of Chicago* 1874–75 and 1876–77, pp. 558, 521. The office of Ely & Burnham was at 206 La Salle, and Howard boarded at 374 Michigan Ave.

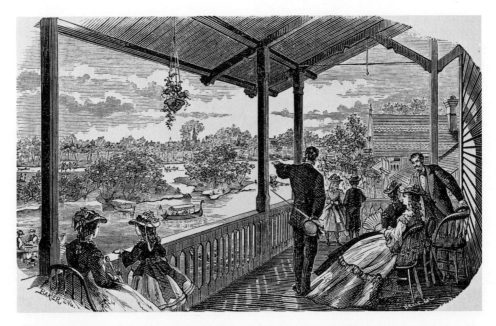

Fig. 56. *View of the Desplaines River from the verandah of the Refectory, Riverside, 1871. The Refectory was an amusement pavilion offering card games and billiards, but the figures emphasize the felicities of family life and the association of one family with another, just as was planned for Riverside.*

Fig. 57. *The Luncheon of the Boating Party; Pierre Renoir, 1881. Although it features young men and women rather than family groups, the famous Impressionist painting by Renoir of exactly a decade later reflects much the same mood as Riverside. The desire to get out of the city and take pleasure in less crowded, less dirty, and less formal surroundings was an international one in the 1870s and 80s, and growing leisure and affluence were making it possible, for the middle classes at least.*

molding the character and mind of an ingenuous young British stenographer, the dramatic events of the destruction of the original "Garden City" by the fire of October 1871 and the Riverside scandal of January 1874 ought to have left some impression. Osborn believed that Howard's residence in Chicago must have "insensibly educated him in the variety and fluidity of urban re-development, the phenomena of rapid growth, and the contrast between the life in the city and on the farm," despite the fact that Howard himself re-called in after years that he was occupied with "religious speculations" at the time.[29]

Might he not have been highly sensitive to the urban color around him, but later a trifle reluctant to admit it, even to himself? And there could con-ceivably have been embarrassment to an idealistic youth and mature man who more than once launched similarly precarious financial ventures. He might also have wished to dissociate himself from the kind of flamboyant midwestern promotion that was often followed by poor or weak execution, so heavily satirized by Sinclair Lewis in *Babbitt*. Frank Lloyd Wright claimed that earlier it had ideologically killed Louis Sullivan and had nearly mangled himself. It finally drove Jens Jensen out of the city's park system. In essence, such promotion represented a rapidly accumulated technical and financial power unshaped by any communal vision, except what an occasional great architect or landscape architect might briefly lend it. Howard wanted his new community to be at liberty also, but not at the price of a total absence of discipline and coherence. The newer and larger Chicago had been built on the charred remains of the older, soon to be forgotten "garden city" on Lake Michigan. It is possible that the elderly Howard had built his own con-cept of the garden city on foundations which he could not, or did not, wish to recall.

29. F. J. Osborn, "Sir Ebenezer Howard, The Evolution of His Ideas," *Town Planning Review*, *21* (Oct. 1950), 227.

7. PARKER AND UNWIN

Antecedents

William Morris and Ebenezer Howard had the dreams—Parker and Unwin in the next generation helped them to come true. For a young man who began his academic career in an inauspicious manner, having been unable to interest himself in Magdalen College School at Oxford where he grew up, Raymond Unwin was to collect in later life his fair share of international degrees. They were awarded him by Prague, Manchester, Trondheim, Toronto, Columbia, and Harvard Universities.[1] One wonders in retrospect whether they were not given more immediately for his ability to achieve, to act with obvious assurance and bold resolve, in a society paralyzed by the destructive forces of wars and depressions, than out of any deeper recognition of the consistency and subtlety of his planning thought. But there is justification for this more popular appreciation too. Unwin was apparently determined to cast himself as a leader long before he made his first mark as an author, architect, and planner.

He was President of the Royal Institute of British Architects from 1931 to 1933, and one of the peaks of his career was reached when he was awarded its Gold Medal in April 1937. On that solemn occasion he broke his custom of plodding ahead and glanced back for a moment to the individuals who had influenced him most in choosing a career. In his acceptance speech he noted,

> One who was privileged to hear the beautiful voice of John Ruskin declaiming against the disorder and degradation resulting from the *laissez-faire* theories of life; to know William Morris and his work; and to imbibe in his impressionable years the thoughts and writings of men like James Hinton and Edward Carpenter, could hardly fail to follow after the ideals of a more ordered form of society, and a

1. Barry Parker, "The Life and Work of Sir Raymond Unwin," *Town Planning Journal* (July–Aug., 1940), p. 160.

better planned environment for it, than that which he saw around
him in the 'seventies and 'eighties of last century.[2]

Unwin's childhood drawings were corrected at Oxford by Ruskin, according to family legend.[3] His father, William, was a private tutor there.[4] He had
retired to the university town on the failure of the family textile business
when he was already over fifty years old.[5]

Mrs. Havelock Ellis in her book on Hinton, Nietzsche, and Carpenter,
Three Modern Seers, observes that although the two English members of the
triad were in reaction against Victorian social convention: "All meet on the
common ground of a striving towards perfection of individual character as
the chief factor in social progress."[6] Regardless of the self-sufficiency of British
thought during the 1880s and our own reluctance to entertain the Nie-
tzschean brand of theory after its corruption in the 1920s and 1930s by the
Fascists of Central Europe, there is within the career of Unwin considerable
evidence for the appropriate association of Nietzsche with the other two seers.
David Gebhard has also pointed out that Nietzsche's *Thus Spake Zarathustra*
was probably the greatest influence on Louis Sullivan's thought as well.[7]
Stuart Hughes has captured the attitude of that age in explaining Nietzsche's
similar effect on Spengler:

> A new élite must create the fresh values that the herd was incapable
> of conceiving. This élite—a master race in the sense of common
> ideals rather than a common blood inheritance—would practise the
> virtues of personal daring and intellectual honesty. Secure in the
> knowledge of their own superiority, they would breathe the pure
> air of mountain tops and tread proudly on the bleak summits of
> lofty thought and action.[8]

What would moderate the lofty position (although not the drive) in Unwin's
case was his enthusiasm for democratic or socialistic equalities and a family
habit of Christian compassion. The Unwin family training enlarged on personal "gifts and talents and opportunity" as a "strong feature in true Christianity."[9]

Dr. James Hinton (1822–75) was an aural surgeon at Guy's Hospital in Lon-

2. "The Royal Gold Medal," *R.I.B.A. Journal* (April 1937), p. 582.

3. Mrs. William Sully Unwin, letter to
author, Aug. 9, 1956.

4. *Garden Cities and Town Planning, 1*
(March 1911), 35.

5. Mrs. Barry Parker, personal interview,

also Mrs. Unwin, op. cit.

6. (London, Stanley Paul, 1910), p. 7.

7. *Journal of the Society of Architectural
Historians* (March 1964), p. 52.

8. *Oswald Spengler, A Critical Estimate*
(New York, Scribner's, 1952), p. 21.

9. Mrs. Unwin.

don, who became progressively more immersed in ethical and aesthetic problems. He felt that animals attained a natural harmony by their mode of existence while humans lived in a contradictory and self-defeating situation.
Here one catches the drumbeat of anthropological interest that grows louder
toward the end of the century. Hinton's life is strangely reminiscent of that
of the painter Paul Gauguin, with its early social and financial success, the
increasing restlessness and dissatisfaction with urban and civilized ways, and
the final flight into death in a simpler and more idyllic setting. For Hinton
this last refuge was the Azores rather than Tahiti.

Hinton's views were chiefly opposed to the "hypocrisy" of Victorianism.
He was, moreover, disturbed by the specializations of this society, of which
his own, aural surgery, was but one example. To bring nature and human
passion into a more direct and less destructive alignment in order to more
effectively pursue "goodness" was the major lesson of his writing. What may
have been especially different about his ideas, and attractive to Unwin, was
his unwillingness to discard nature as a benevolent force. He thought that
inner personal adjustment preceded outward social improvement and that
the state of the arts was a sensitive index to the progress of any culture, including the contemporary one.

Edward Carpenter (1844–1929) was born a little over two decades after
Hinton. Unwin was thus able to form a personal relationship with him,
which he could not with Hinton. Unwin's son Edward was named after Carpenter, who was also his godfather, "if," as the latter drily remarked, "an
atheist can be a god-father." Carpenter writes in his autobiography of Unwin
as "a young man of cultured antecedents, of first-rate ability and good sense,
healthy, democratic, vegetarian . . ." while the latter was working for the
Staveley Coal and Iron Company at Chesterfield, near which Carpenter had
his own little colony of Millthorpe.[10]

A book-length appreciation of Carpenter, published two years after his
death, included essays by G. Lowes Dickinson, Havelock Ellis, E. M. Forster,
Katharine Bruce Glasier, Laurence Housman, J. Ramsay MacDonald, Henry
W. Nevinson, Evelyn Sharp, and Raymond Unwin and testifies to how widely
the intellectual net can be cast in Britain. In a chapter significantly titled,
"Edward Carpenter and 'Towards Democracy,'" Unwin states that beginning in 1881 at Oxford, Carpenter became a great influence on him.

> He was then giving one of the last of his courses of University Lec-
> tures on Science. These were dropped when he was driven in to the

10. *My Days and Dreams* (3d ed. London, Allen and Unwin, 1920), pp. 131–32.

country to find himself, and to write *Towards Democracy* as the
expression of his disentanglement. A year or two later, when intercourse with working people and close contact with their lives
brought home to me the contrast with all that I had been used to in
my Oxford home, I turned again to Edward Carpenter for help, as
the overwhelming complexity and urgency of the social problem
came in upon me.

    During 1883 and 1884, after his move to Millthorpe, I spent help-
ful and happy week-ends with him and his companions there. In
October of the latter year, on the occasion of my leaving the district,
he gave me the first edition of *Towards Democracy*. The feelings
compounded of mystification, escape, and joy with which I read it
through on the journey to Oxford, are still a vivid memory.[11]

Unwin writes eloquently about the sense of liberation the book conveyed to
a person of his generation. "Carpenter uses all the arts of literature and poetry. The religious philosophies of the world are drawn upon; the history of
races, the lives of men and animals furnish illustrations. The reader is
charmed, astonished, mystified, shocked, comforted, and enlightened by
turns!"[12]

The extravagant language and the sudden, apocalyptic vision recall the relationship of the older Louis Sullivan to the younger Frank Lloyd Wright in
Chicago, which was to take place at the beginning of the next decade. We
remember the similar moment when Sullivan came silently up to Wright's
desk and laid his drawing of the Wainwright Building on it, and the latter
suddenly realized what modern architecture ought to be as the "scales fell
from my eyes."[13] Both of the older men, the teachers, drew inspiration from
the American poet Walt Whitman.

Unwin remembered that the title of Carpenter's poem *Towards Democracy* had derived from Whitman, but felt that the former's expressions were
"more intimate and mature, better balanced."[14] Carpenter had visited Whitman in 1877 and again in 1884. He had known him since 1874 and when in
the United States had called too on Emerson, William Cullen Bryant,
Holmes, Lowell, Charles Eliot Norton, and John Burroughs the naturalist,
who also appears to have had a strong influence on Wright.[15] Unwin notes

11. Gilbert Beith, ed., *Edward Carpenter, In
Appreciation* (London, Allen and Unwin, 1931),
p. 234.

12. Ibid., p. 236.

13. F. L. Wright, *Genius and the Mobocracy*

(New York, Duell, Sloan and Pearce, 1949), p.
79.

14. Beith, *Edward Carpenter.*

15. Ibid., pp. 146–47.

that Carpenter, in contrast to Whitman, made only occasional reference to democracy as a political institution. He was more aware of a need "to give body to the fresh sense of freedom and equality of place and partnership in the universe, and unity with its Great Spirit."[16] The possibility that democracy was more appropriate as a moral and spiritual exercise for the individual than as a massive political ambition and leveling agent attracted Unwin's attention in Carpenter's writing. The reverberation set going between the improved individual and the improvable society would bring about its own reward. The portions Unwin selects to quote from Carpenter's *Towards Democracy* make this especially evident:

> I see a great land poised as in a dream—
> Waiting for the word by which it
> May live again.
>
> . . .
>
> Ah, England! Have I not seen, do
> I not see how, plain as day,
> through thy midst the genius of
> thy true life wandering—he who
> can indeed, who can alone save thee—
> Seeking thy soul, thy real life,
> out of so much rubbish to disentangle?[17]

Unwin did not feel obliged to choose between honest arrogance and hypocritical humility and to play the enfant terrible as Frank Lloyd Wright did. Nevertheless, he was determined by an early age to become a public leader. He believed the truly gifted individual had no need to wait in false modesty for the people to call him, to be elected to some democratic office. He had only to begin by showing a better way to accomplish more desirable ends. The key to the missing environmental order and discipline must first be provided through personal excellence.

Years later, at the zenith of his reputation as a private architect and planner, he still reflects the original position.

> There seems no need to wait until the development of corporate life and feeling has reached the stage at which it would seem natural for the community to carry out for itself through its own officials the entire development of its towns and homes; it may be better that

16. Ibid., p. 236.
17. Ibid., p. 239.

smaller bodies, more responsive to the initiative of individual pioneers, should deal with the more detailed work.[18]

All the circumstances were present to duplicate the American tragedy of Sullivan and Wright, the brilliant architects within a democracy struggling to formulate its outward expression and being rebuffed and crushed for their pains (the story of *The Genius and the Mobocracy* play by Wright), but there was a significant difference. Unwin started with the social problem and gradually fused it with the aesthetic possibilities, whereas the two Americans began more with their pride in individualism and originality and attempted to superimpose these on the given physical and economic situation. Then too, the path had been better cleared for Parker and Unwin by a highly vocal line of British authors running as far back as the beginning of the nineteenth century and dealing more often with architectural subjects than the more literary Emerson, Thoreau, and Whitman. Eventually, public approval of Parker and Unwin was to provide another handicap, for as their principles were in a measure accepted and their administrative record became better known, their drive lost some of its verbal clarity and directness. This never happened to Sullivan and Wright. Remaining rebels to the last, they could not easily be blamed for the errors that followed them. Thus Parker and Unwin were to be often and mistakenly condemned for suburban sprawl and urban escapism, while Sullivan was never held to account for the excesses of the skyscraper for which he supplied such a beautiful form, nor was Wright ever castigated for the follies of the suburban house to which he gave such a handsome model. To succeed in the popular or democratic eye also seemed to mean the submission of aesthetic decision to lower juries.

Unwin was not blind to this eventuality. It worried him, as it worried the Americans, that democracy was not developing its own backlog of visual traditions. "Hitherto the growth of democracy," he notes, "which has destroyed the old feudal structure of society, has but left the individual in the helpless isolation of freedom."[19] It is also interesting to see that he, like Sullivan, assumed that feudalism was immediately followed by democracy in the historic stages of culture.

One other resemblance between the English and the American viewpoints is worth consideration because it also arises from the common roots of Whitman, Emerson, Bryant, and Burroughs: the precept that architecture and the

18. Raymond Unwin, *Town Planning in Practice* (London, Unwin, 1909), p. 376.
19. Ibid., p. 375.

settlements it comprises should appear to belong to the land. Hinton and Carpenter hoped to draw the people back into a closer harmony with nature, not to assert their ascendancy over it. This was to call attention to the fact that the only true permanence, even with all the benefits of modern technology, lay in the works of nature rather than those of man. The term "realities," used in this connection, stands out in Unwin's summary of Carpenter's *Towards Democracy*. He observes that, "Love of the land, of the natural life in close contact with the fields, the flowers, the animals, and the belief that here may be found a basis on which to build up a less artificial civilization in close touch with realities, pervades the whole book."[20] It is the opportunity to extend the awareness for the body politic of the life force within the universe, as represented by visible nature, which appears to intrigue him.

One senses the difference between the old warrior who deals head on with the problems of industrialization and urbanism and the leader who seeks a permanent reconciliation and refreshment from the verities of nature in William Morris' terse comment on his visit to Edward Carpenter in 1884, just when both of them were having their greatest influence on Unwin.

> I went to Chesterfield and saw Edward Carpenter on Monday, and found him sensible and sympathetic at the same time. I listened with longing heart to his patch of ground, seven acres: He says that he and his fellow can almost live on it: they grow their own wheat and send flowers and fruit to Chesterfield and Sheffield market: all sounds very agreeable to me. It seems to me that a very real way to enjoy life is to accept all its necessary ordinary details and turn them into pleasures by taking interest in them: whereas modern civilisation huddles them out of the way, has them done in a venal and slovenly manner till they become real drudgery which people can't help trying to avoid. Whiles I think, as a vision, of a decent community as a refuge from our mean squabbles and corrupt society; but I am too old now, even if it were not dastardly to desert.[21]

Only once more is there an opportunity to compare the statements of these two men. That occurs in the short volume, *Forecasts of the Coming Century*, which was actually published in 1897, shortly after Morris' death, by the Labour Press of Manchester. Alfred Russel Wallace and the ever-present Bernard Shaw tried their hands at prognostication in it too. Morris declares

20. Beith, p. 238.
21. J. Bruce Glasier, *William Morris and* *the Early Days of the Socialist Movement* (London, Longmans, Green, 1921), p. 145.

that the general absence of beauty in modern civilization is a social malaise, deriving from an aesthetic deficiency.

> Art was once the common possession of the whole people; it was the rule in the Middle Ages that the produce of handicraft was beautiful. Doubtless, there were eyesores in the palmy days of mediaeval art, but these were caused by destruction of wares, not as now by the making of them: . . . Ruin from wars bore on its face the tokens of its essential hideousness; today, it is prosperity that is externally ugly . . . we sit starving amidst our gold, the Midas of the ages."[22]

It is the typical Morris viewpoint, concisely stated. Then comes a passage which has more direct bearing on Unwin's future.

> Art is kept alive by a small group of artists working in a spirit quite antagonistic to the spirit of the time; and they also suffer from the lack of co-operation which is an essential lack in the art of our epoch. They are limited therefore, to the production of a few individualistic works, which are looked upon by almost everybody as curiosities to be examined, and not as pieces of beauty to be enjoyed. Nor have they any position or power of helping the public in general matters of taste (to use a somewhat ugly word). For example, in laying out all the parks and pleasure grounds which have lately been acquired for the public, as far as I know, no artist has been consulted.[23]

Unwin was then making up his mind to be consulted in the future, to become the super-artist, as Morris wished.

The last chapter of the book is by Carpenter and is entitled, "Transitions to Freedom." He hoped that the next century would witness a more widely based production of objects "of use and beauty." He predicted that "As William Morris points out in his foregoing paper, and elsewhere—that 'work' in the new sense would be a pleasure— . . . And, your work being such, its product is sure to become beautiful; that painful distinction between the beautiful and the useful dies out, and everything made is an artistic product. Art becomes conterminous with life."[24] Carpenter goes on to describe the creative, cooperative, house-building, crime-free society of the Marquesas Islanders, as reported in Herman Melville's *Typee,* and we detect similarities to the

22. *Forecasts of the Coming Century,* p. 64. 24. Ibid., p. 182.
23. Ibid., p. 68.

earlier thoughts of James Hinton too. He concludes anthropologically that, "if modern man, with his science and his school-boards and his brain culti- vated through all these centuries, is not competent to solve a more complex problem than the savage, he had better return to savagery."[25]

The three older men, Hinton, Carpenter, and Morris, put the problem squarely before the youthful Unwin. As a person proposing to create he must either become a historian and anthropologist, devoting himself to ancient or distant cultures to discover what is fundamentally wrong in his own, or he must expand the contemporary function of the artist, enlarging his responsi- bility and scope until by assimilation he becomes the total leader, the com- plete planner. Artistic intuition is no longer enough, although it is as basically necessary as it ever was. In his last lectures at Columbia University Unwin makes it apparent that in his estimation no single man can ever en- compass all the skills necessary to plan a city. He therefore urges the appren- tice to cultivate his feeling for the first principles of the urban situation in order that he may later synthesize his specific knowledge. It appears that the bridge between concrete information and imaginative inspiration is the critical construction for Unwin, as it was also in some degree for Ebenezer Howard.

Once Unwin had resolved the main direction of his life, he set out to trans- late it into action. Carpenter gave the larger frame to his thought, but it was Morris who put him in motion. While still in the North he began to use his spare time to preach in Labour Churches on "The Life and Work of William Morris."[26] He also wrote in the late 1880s articles for Morris' magazine, *The Commonweal,* with such unseasoned titles as, "A Tramp's Diary" and "Down a Coal Pit."[27] In his Columbia lectures and in Steen Eiler Rasmussen's book, *London: The Unique City,* Unwin appears as the Nestor, the mellow and moderate old sage of planning. As he grew older he did learn to dissimulate his intentions and restrain his barbs. His writing became broader and more replete with legal, financial, and statistical information. But the gift of de- scription, the ability to see life as a series of vivid personal episodes, caused him to look often in Ruskinian anger as a young man. His partner, Barry Parker, remarked after his death that his influence on planning had been "largely due to his sympathy with everyone in trouble and with the under- dog," which Parker felt was the quality "least understood and appreciated

25. Ibid., p. 187.
26. Barry Parker, "Obit of Raymond Un- win," *R.I.B.A. Journal* (July 15, 1940), p. 209. See also E. R. Thompson, *William Morris: Ro-*

mantic to Revolutionary (London, Lawrence and Wishart, 1955), p. 644.
27. *Commonweal* (Jan. 12, April 22, 27, June 15, 1889; June 7, 14, 1890).

about Unwin."[28] In one early incident in particular, reported by Unwin in *Commonweal,* this sense of righteous indignation and personal involvement bobs suddenly to the surface.

> The other day as I looked out my office window into the yard of a large ironworks, I saw a man standing; his face attracted my attention, there was such a look of anxiety on it, a nervous impatience to know the result of the interview he hoped to get with the manager of the yard. . . . Presently the manager comes along; I watch the man as he steps up to meet him, for a moment a ray of hope beams in his face as with beating heart he begins to stammer out, "Please, sir, could you find me—" "Don't want any one to-day," and the manager is gone. But that man's face![29]

Unwin, the young mining engineer, cannot get it out of his consciousness. He objects to the callous assault on the dignity of the worker, and he cannot reconcile the treatment with his understanding of Christian brotherhood.

His mood of indignation caused him to view the landscape in much the same way. He writes of Sutton Hall near Chesterfield with its estate of four thousand acres where he was then taking recreational walks. He did like "the prosperous look of the prettily situated farm-houses and cottages; all the gates are painted white, and the roads and paths seem well kept, and the whole estate has rather the air of being a continuation of the park."[30] But he did not appreciate the fact that the Hall itself was empty and the erstwhile owner away. He and his friends found themselves imagining how it might function if utilized by them.

> Plenty of room in that large house for quite a small colony to live, each one having his own den upstairs where he could go to write, or sulk, or spend a quiet evening with his lady-love or his boon companion; and downstairs would be large common dining-halls, dancing halls, smoking rooms—if indeed life shall still need the weed to make it perfect. And we chatted on, each adding a bit to our picture; how some would till the land around and others tend to the cattle, while others perhaps would start some industry, working in the outbuildings or building workshops about the park, and taking

28. Typescript in the Barry Parker Collection with pencil notes apparently by Osborn, p. 1.

29. *Commonweal,* 5 (April 22, 1889), 132.
30. Ibid., June 15, 1889, p. 190.

care not to spoil our view with a hideous building or blight our trees with smoke.[31]

This article too appeared in *Commonweal* and obviously relates to Morris' own vision of "guest houses" or communal dwellings for sociable learning. Morris also speculated in *News from Nowhere* during the same years upon the potentiality of large country houses for such groups, "who are not necessarily husbandmen; though they almost all help in such work at times. The life that goes on in these big dwellings in the country is very pleasant, especially as some of the most studious men of our time live in them, and altogether there is a great variety of mind and mood to be found in them which brightens and quickens the society there."[32] Like Morris, Unwin hypothesizes a distinct pattern of intellectual association within a rural rather than an urban setting.

Unwin's daydream must also have derived from Carpenter's actual agrarian colony of the early 1880s at Millthorpe in the Cordwell Valley. As Professor W. H. G. Armytage has shown in his *Heavens Below,* Carpenter in turn gained much of his active theory from Ruskin's slightly earlier St. George's Guild Farm (1877–80) at Totley. Both groups based their income on hand-made shoes and sandals, and the sale of vegetables in the nearby Sheffield market.

These affinities simply suggest how often the men who influenced Unwin overlapped in their activities and intentions. Their previous experience in Yorkshire, Derbyshire, and Lancashire in the industrial North prepared Parker and Unwin for the garden city programs which they undertook after 1900. The advantage in being aware of this lies in the larger perspective it offers of a group of thinkers working in one direction and the realization that the garden cities and new towns did not appear solely as a sudden and mysterious reaction to the megalopolis of London around which the majority of them now cluster. The industrial cities of the North and Midlands were an intrinsic part of the background as well.[33]

The philosophic antecedents of Parker and Unwin's efforts further demonstrate a projection of the ephemeral image to the solid accomplishment. The utopian theory, the romantic vision, the democratic plane, and the pose of the rebel and the superman were developed to the point where building the

31. Ibid.

32. *News from Nowhere* (London, Reeves and Turner, 1891), p. 81.

33. W. H. G. Armytage, *Heavens Below,*

Utopian Experiments in England 1560–1960 (London, Routledge and Kegan Paul, 1961), pp. 293–301, 310.

kind of environment gradually outlined by these century-long dialogues could be undertaken. Hence it becomes abundantly evident that it is not the idiom or technique of building a garden city or new town that matters so much as the British capacity to link original theory with active practice over a comparatively long span of time. Parker and Unwin implemented a consistent reform tradition, filled in the lacunae, worked out the specific problems, embodied the existing principles. The basic themes had already been to some extent developed for them, as Unwin readily acknowledged when he received the Gold Medal of the Royal Institute of British Architects in 1937.

The individuals who had a direct influence on them are discernible, as are also the methods and devices by which Parker and Unwin forwarded their architecture and planning. But what is not quite so obvious is a set of underlying principles and assumptions which served a kind of middle range, supporting function and gave further dimension and purpose to their accomplishment, sounding within the two careers the resonance of many. Several of these, naturally enough, reveal a further dependence on William Morris' views.

1. The village as an animate symbol. For Parker and Unwin the village ideal offered two great opportunities for the future. One was social and the other aesthetic. Akroyd, long ago, had subscribed to the revival of the village as a social stabilizer, and so did Unwin. "The landlord and tenants, parson and flock, tradesman and customers, master and servant, farmer and labourers, doctor and patients; all were in direct relation and shared common interests forming a network of community life," Unwin says: "these linking relationships exist today and must be considered in planning."[34]

Unwin further observed that here social unity could best be interwoven with physical beauty. "It is the crystallisation of the elements of the village in accordance with a definitely organised life of mutual relations, respect or service, which gives the appearance of being an organic whole, the home of a community, to what would otherwise be a mere conglomeration of buildings."[35] The people of the ideal village not only existed together, they lived together through a heightened sense of place. The local building materials helped to make the social experience more complete and convincing. "The sense of unity is further increased in most old villages by a general harmony

34. Sir Raymond Unwin, *Housing and Town Planning Lectures* (mimeo.), Columbia University, 1936–37 (Washington, D.C. Sub-Committee on Research and Statistics, Central Housing Committee), p. 5.

35. Unwin, "Building & Natural Beauty," in *The Art of Building A Home* (London, Longmans, Green, 1901), p. 93.

in colour and style of the buildings themselves, due to the prevalent use of certain materials which are usually found in the district."[36]

2. *The necessity for understanding the past.* The partners followed Morris also in not being antihistorical—in expecting a positive awareness of history from the social artist because his responsibility was not only to himself and his client but to his entire cultural heritage. In this they seemed to owe likewise some inspiration to their friend, Patrick Geddes, who studied carefully the historic origins of a region in order to revive its best life. "Of special importance to the planner are the faculties of memory and association, resulting in tradition, and of imagination, the power to conceive new orders as the basis of planning," Unwin informed his Columbia students.[37] In another year he said to them, "It is easier to get away from tradition than to create new values worthy to be the foundation of a fresh tradition."[38] Parker similarly told the Oxford students, "The greatest geniuses have never attempted to evolve something new. Their contribution has been the improvement and carrying further of traditional methods. Tradition has created for us a language in which to express our ideas."[39]

A renewed consciousness of tradition was thus to accompany the whole creative process. In this context it was meant to be a catalytic agent, a paramount necessity for the individual artist working on such a broad scale as the future town plan. In this manner a brittle epoch would become fluid once again and begin to move in a consistent direction.

3. *The Middle Ages as the historic standard.* Morris' favorite century had been the fourteenth, but it is an error to consider this period as remote in Britain as on the Continent. Town planning and a great deal of building outside London were in substance medieval right up and into the nineteenth century. Anyone who wished to return to the village as the model social unit would have to take this into account, regardless of debate on the relative merits of neo-Classic, neo-Gothic, or neo-Renaissance stylization. Socially we see this reflected in the contrast between the industrial squirearchy successfully imposed by Lever at Port Sunlight and Cadbury's paternalism at Bournville (with very little profit margin) and the bitter resentment by workers of Pullman's model village near Chicago of the 1880s and 1890s. The tradition of noblesse oblige was much thinner in the American Midwest. Besides the depression of 1893 and the famous Pullman strike, we hear of 20 per cent

36. Ibid., p. 94.

37. Sir Raymond Unwin, *Planning and Housing History and Theory Lectures* (mimeo.), Columbia University, 1938–39, n.p.

38. *Housing and Town Planning Lectures,* 1936–37, p. 18.

39. Barry Parker, *A Lecture on Art in Industry,* Balliol College, Oxford, Oct. 3, 1925 (Letchworth, Letchworth Printers, 1925), pp. 5–6.

overcharges in rent in the village, wage deductions, a failure to reduce charges in time of slack, and a ten-day eviction clause by the company, in addition to the more usual complaints about diminutive room sizes. Titus Salt's employees, on the other hand, regarded him with great respect in the 1850s as the latest version of the feudal lord, as was stated in the song about him. Lever, for another, was constantly emphasizing that Port Sunlight ought to pay its own way, like any other business enterprise, but he never seemed to be ready to force it to the degree that occurred in Pullman.

Left to themselves, the arts were bound to retrogress toward the Middle Ages in Britain. Unwin observed:

> So long as the few have the leisure, the trained intellectual capacity, and the refined appreciation, while the many are dulled by drudgery, our civilisation must be admitted to be a partial failure, and all those artists who appreciate life as well as art, will continue to look back with longing to the days of the mediaeval craftsman, in spite of the narrowness in many ways of his life, and the limited extent of his intellectual opportunities.[40]

Until the industrial age could evolve its own vocabulary of favorable manifestations and appearances, the Middle Ages would have to provide the standard. An authentic "new style" would result only when the artist was often and liberally commissioned to create and the people were made ready to accept him. Medievalism was helping to set the mark.

4. The indispensability of beauty. Much of the misunderstanding of the garden city has arisen because it has not been realized that it was in large measure the product of the 1890s. The means were secondary to the idealistic end of achieving a comely town, like Chicago's City Beautiful Movement, also from the 1890s. This is essentially why, although the stylistic vocabularies were so different, the two streams merge so easily and naturally at Port Sunlight and Letchworth and later in the planning of such men as John Nolen in the United States. Unwin felt it had been finally acknowledged in the nineteenth century that the average citizen was entitled to improvements pertaining to public health, and the logical step at the end of one century and the beginning of the next would be to accord a similar recognition to the necessity for mental health and beauty everywhere.

Unwin writes often of a return to the individual of a renewed sensibility

40. Raymond Unwin, "The City Beautiful from Converging Views of Social Reform," *Lectures on Land and Labour*, Swanwick, Interdenominational Summer School, June 20–29, 1914 (London, Collegium, 1914), p. 103.

to a community, through affection for his home; "in short to aim at building up little communities of people who will have some sense of locality and will acquire the ties which spring from common interests, and enjoyments shared with those around them."[41] This instinctive reaction against urban anonymity, rootlessness, and harshness motivated a great number of his utterances. Beauty was the balm with which the loneliness and uncertainty of the nation might be eased. Achievement of this was far more important than the restoration of excellence in any one of the arts alone. In his estimate, the specialization of creation and consumption had become merely the convenient escape hatch for the artist and connoisseur alike. Crafts, painting, architecture, landscape architecture, and planning would gain little ground unless they could be calibrated against the whole range of contemporary society. He said:

> It is characteristic of the civilisation of the last century to ignore beauty in connection with useful productions, and to disregard it in the expression of its public life. Where beauty has been appreciated at all in this period there has been a tendency to regard it as something separate and apart from life, to be provided in the form of ornaments or easel pictures made or retained for the sole purpose of being beautiful. Hence we have seen the well-to-do individual living in the ugly house in which all his useful articles are devoid of beauty, while his drawing-room is filled to overflowing with the beautiful bric-a-brac of other lands or other days; and the people we find living in the squalid slum or the dreary suburb, so characteristic of the modern town, while the Municipal Picture Gallery is erected and stocked as an acknowledgment of our lurking suspicion that art is, after all a matter of some importance.[42]

Or, as Parker had put it, "If we realise what is a living art, we shall find it but an easy and natural step to grasp the fact that when art was alive in other spheres the art of Town Planning also lived; that this was the case in Egypt, in Assyria, in Greece, in Rome, in mediaeval times and in Renaissance times."[43] Unwin wished this realization to become a working part of the new search for environment because, "substantial as are the material boons which may be derived from such powers for the control of town development as

41. Ibid., p. 107.
42. Ibid., p. 99.
43. Parker, "Horizontality and Verticality in   the Architectural Treatment of Town Planning Schemes," *Town Planning Journal*, 3 (1916), 137.

we hope our municipalities will soon possess, the force which is behind the movement is derived far more from the desire for something beyond these boons, from the hope that through them something of beauty may be restored to town life."[44]

Parker and Unwin thought that art had become too withdrawn during the nineteenth century. The populace might have it in a museum and the well-to-do in their houses, but as soon as they step out into the streets, as Morris once put it, they are again in the midst of ugliness and squalor which baffles or blunts their senses. The wealthy had acquired power to command in every realm except that in which their greatest need lay—the public environment. At the advent of the Second World War and only a year before his death in the United States, Unwin still writes in a memorandum for a governmental conference that one of the chief functions of planning must be to satisfy "the natural aesthetic hunger of mankind."[45]

5. *Twelve houses to the acre*. Parker and Unwin's best-known professional innovation, upon which all their other technical suggestions to some extent depended, was the principle contained in the slogan, "twelve houses to the acre." Like Howard's garden city scheme, it looked to the development of land as the key to the combination of architecture and planning. Yet it sought to take advantage of a low development cost rather than to cash in on rapid increment later, as Howard had intended. The specific figures and arguments for this were amply treated in Unwin's pamphlet with the long but informative title, *Nothing Gained by Overcrowding! Or How the Garden City Type of Development May Benefit Both Owner and Occupier*.[46]

Lest the impression grow that his method consisted mainly of amassing dry columns of figures, it is useful to ask in what respects this way of attacking a problem was typical of Unwin's general philosophy. All his life he sought diligently to find "clinchers," unanswerable arguments, to support his favorite policies. At the same time he nurtured a powerful imagination, and his statistical outlines often come up at last as huge and abstract mental pictures. It is evident that he enjoyed making this kind of exposition to the widest audience. As his partner once wrote, possibly in an effort to distinguish between their two personalities, "Some can express themselves better when

44. Raymond Unwin, *Town Planning in Practice* (London, Unwin, 1909), p. 4.

45. Sir Raymond Unwin, memorandum for Proposed Forum, Unwin-Tugwell, Moses-Hey- decker, Lyme, Conn., Sept. 9, 1939.

46. (London, Garden Cities and Town Planning Assn., 1912), reissued in 1933 as leaflet no. 13 by the same group.

writing to a sympathetic and understanding friend than they can more publicly. To Unwin the wider appeal was always the greater inspiration."[47]

Parker also explained that there was nothing "magical or sacrosanct in the
number twelve. It is simply that we found, by a long process of trial and error,
there is inevitably sufficient loss of frontage where there are more than twelve
houses to the acre to cause the cost of roads to outweigh the saving in cost of
land which results from there being more than twelve houses to the acre,
except where land is unusually costly."[48] Actually, in 1902, just the year before they began Letchworth, they were still advising no more than 20 to 30
houses to the acre, "except under very great pressure."[49]

In *Nothing Gained by Overcrowding* Unwin took one plot of ten acres
with 34 houses to the acre (slightly over his 1902 "ideal" density) and contrasted it with another of 15.2 houses per acre (slightly over his prescription
of 12 to the acre). The raw land cost the same in each case, £500 an acre. In
the first scheme only 83½ square yards of ground are available for each house,
while with the second and lower density, 261½ square yards are possible. The
first would require an expenditure of £9,747 10s. for roads, whereas the second would need only £4,480 10s. And, "Although the number of houses has
only been reduced by rather more than half, the area of the plot has been
increased more than three times."[50] It is not actually a principle of costing less
then, that counts, so much as obtaining more for the money per family unit.

There are, obviously, all sorts of exceptions to the argument. Where land
is expensive and road building relatively cheap, crowding will become highly
profitable. As one moves toward the center of a great city this situation tends
to prevail, and little can be done. Unwin admits, "When you are putting
houses one on top of the other, you are not necessarily increasing your road
space and cost, as with cottage building. However, you are only gaining in
flats by ignoring the supply of open area for garden or recreation."[51] The
burden of providing amenities is then passed on to the public. The owners
are rewarded twice for their selfishness, according to Unwin.

But the argument seems solid enough if he is granted his preference for the
cottage as the basic unit instead of the flat or row house. This would, of
course, be an indispensable assumption for Unwin because the cottage was
identical in his mind with healthy family life. His slogan makes much more

47. Parker, "The Life and Work of Sir Raymond Unwin," *Town Planning Journal, 26*
(July–Aug., 1940), 160.
48. Ibid.
49. Raymond Unwin and Barry Parker,

Cottage Plans and Common Sense (London,
Fabian Society Tract 109, Buxton, 1902), p. 5.
50. *Nothing Gained by Overcrowding*, p. 8.
51. *Columbia Lectures*, 1936–37, p. 32.

sense as "twelve families to the acre" than twelve houses. The ultimate yield would be a desirable environment consonant with "(1) the nature and needs of a full life for the individual and the family; (2) the quality and extent of the relations which constitute healthy community life; and (3) the opportunities which spring from the character of the land, allowing for the technical requirements that must govern any developments upon it."[52]

He realized that his own claims had a more immediate appeal to the tenants than the landowners, so he tried to attract the latter by demonstrating that more land would be required if a lower density were adopted, thus making larger total profits for the group. He reminded them that it would be better to sell two acres each year for £300 than one for £500, and that land values are never lost, they merely migrate.

Howard's approach was one of sweet reason. Unwin liked a dash of the contentious when he dealt with economics, because he was forever tilting against the fiscal windmill. Usually his tendency was to demonstrate that things are seldom what they seem. Once the listener was receptive to such a possibility, he devoted his effort to proving that well-planned space cost surprisingly little, considering the great gain in amenity. The more comprehensive the planning, the more efficient it would turn out to be. He wished to promote "planned order over unregulated pushing."[53] Parenthetically, and somewhat prophetically in view of the utility of the principle during World War II, he observed that a queue was much to be preferred over a crowd in any given space.

In a speech of 1936 he reported that since 1918 nearly three million dwellings had been built in England and Wales. "The whole three million houses, at an average density of ten to the acre, would barely fill a space measuring twenty-two miles each way; which represents almost a negligible patch on the map of England and Wales."[54] This argument furnished the core of defense against those who claimed that low density consumed valuable agricultural land. The difficulty was, however, that he was seldom content with putting forward only a "clincher." It often had to be a "shocker" as well. This must have induced a certain subconscious resistance on the part of at least some of his audiences. For example, he told an assembly of real estate men, builders, and architects in New York in 1933, at the depth of the Depression and the height of his own reputation as a statistician, that the whole population of

---

52. Raymond Unwin, "Housing and Planning," paper read at the Health Congress of the Royal Sanitary Institute, Southport, July 6–11, 1936, p. 2.
53. Ibid., p. 4.
54. Ibid., p. 2.

the United States could be housed at ten families to the acre on a parcel of land little more than seventy miles by seventy miles, "and it can leave in the center a space larger than Manhattan Island for your public buildings."[55] A few years later he was informing a Columbia University audience that the whole population of the world at ten houses to the acre "would not occupy the State of Kansas."[56] Either he did not realize what pictures his estimates would conjure up in the American mind, or perhaps he was emulating his old heroes Ruskin and Morris with his shock technique. It is not likely that commercially engaged and financially distressed New Yorkers would be too pleased to imagine valuable Manhattan occupied exclusively by unprofitable public buildings or of the whole population of the world being deposited in Kansas.

Back in England, instead of leaving his negligible square patch of low-density floating over the countryside like a harmless cloud, Unwin finally determined to bring it in directly over London. Then he got what may have appeared to him as his most brilliant idea (Fig. 58). "The facts that the area of circles expands as the square of the diameter, and that in urban centers important distances are generally radial, have practically solved the physical space problems of the planner; apart, of course, from man-made difficulties of existing congestion through land values, and so forth."[57] He forgot to mention, unless it was somewhere in the "so forth," the total absence of control in the overall use of urban land. The low-density, floating square, had metamorphosed into a circle and was to be stuck down on the least receptive point, London. Furthermore, the "crystallising" concept of Unwin (Fig. 59) by now bore an uncomfortable resemblance to Ebenezer Howard's concentric garden city diagram, which had been supplemented in his book by another drawing showing a central unit with satellites around it (Fig. 60), "illustrating correct principles of a city's growth."

Frederic Osborn, the devoted publicist of the garden city, didn't like all this. It made him nervous because he felt it would make others even more apprehensive. Years later he complained to Parker about Unwin's "propaganda tactics." He revealed that on the subject of population densities versus agricultural needs, "I never liked Unwin's examples. They made people

55. Address of Sir Raymond Unwin to the Real Estate Board of New York, Slum Clearance Committee of New York, New York Building Congress, Architectural League, New York Chapter A.I.A., and New York Society of Architects, Dec. 28, 1933, p. 4.

56. *Columbia Lectures*, 1936–37, p. 14.

57. *Columbia Lectures*, 1938–39, Oct. 17, 1938. See also Unwin, "Regional Planning with Special Reference to the Greater London Regional Plan," *R.I.B.A. Journal* (Jan. 25, 1930), p. 11.

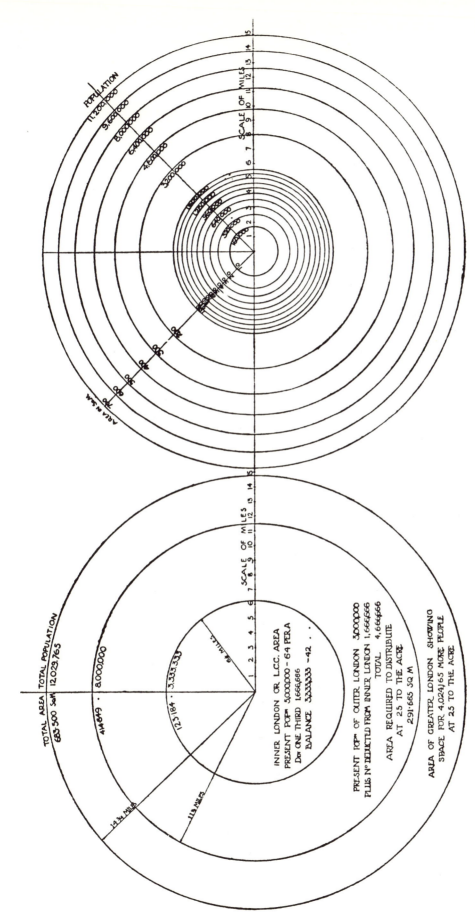

Fig. 58. Circular diagrams showing London at the left and an abstract formulation at the right; Raymond Unwin, 1912. These diagrams were intended to demonstrate how the outward push of the suburban movement could be accommodated by concentricity without destroying the form of the city. It typifies Unwin's gift for grand abstractions.

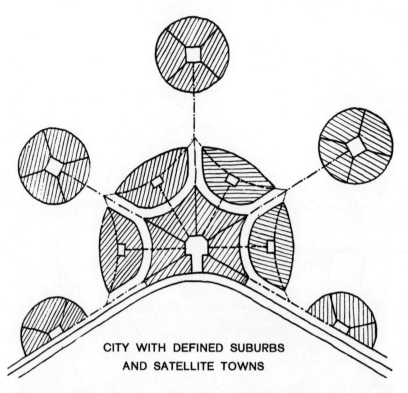

CITY WITH DEFINED SUBURBS
AND SATELLITE TOWNS

Fig. 59. Satellite diagram showing crystallizing principle of Unwin. The intention was to bring further order out of chaos in London by forcing the decentralizing forces into definite nuclei or "crystals." Open land in the proper places would then be readily available.

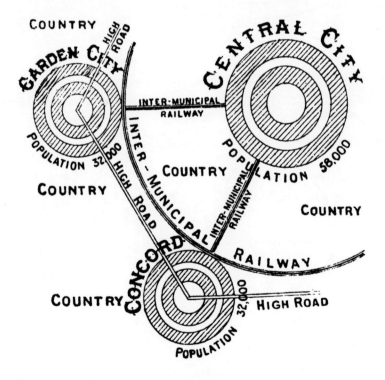

Fig. 60. Ebenezer Howard's diagram of satellite cities. The implication of Howard's utopian diagram extended to Unwin's generalizations about London and thence on to his actual work on the London Regional Plan and seems to have caused some to suspect that his major effort was toward making the great metropolis one huge garden city.

think we wanted to expand London to one continuous urban tract." Osborn declared that it would have been "far better to say that you can house the whole population of Great Britain on 2½% of the land of G. B. at 10 houses to the acre,"[58] than to pick on London alone. To remain detached was safe. To focus on London or such a place as New York was to invite the wrath of its intelligentsia, authors, and administrators.

Unwin sought to cover himself by repeating that it was with family life that he was first occupied and once that was taken care of, the city pattern would permit an almost unlimited variation.

> This movement proposes that every dwelling, whether central or not, should have enough ground for healthy family life, and should be within reasonable distance of some open land. With this secured, the need for excessively low density to obtain further protection is greatly diminished. There is nothing in garden city principles that calls for scattering, or even semi-detachedness; nor is there anything with which the crescents of Bath or the squares of Bloomsbury would be inconsistent.[59]

In the final analysis he yields to the inevitable and remarks wistfully (but with some insight into human nature) that what logic and persuasion may not accomplish in reducing the density of great cities, the threat of bombings will.[60]

It is in several ways appropriate that Raymond Unwin's career should end where Ebenezer Howard's began—in Chicago and the United States. His last article, published posthumously, was "Land Values in Relation to Planning and Housing in the United States."[61] The Loop area of Chicago was especially interesting to him in the article. He had already employed it in 1924 to demonstrate that now familiar corollary that, if the buildings in it suddenly emptied their office workers into its streets, there would not be enough room for the workers and the automobiles. Nor could they all get onto the streetcars. This was another of the abstract yet dramatic forms of exposition he had developed.[62] The coincidence is more striking when it is noticed that

58. Typescript in Barry Parker Collection, Letchworth, with marginal notes by Osborn, p. 11.

59. Raymond Unwin, address to Section B, Architecture, Town Planning and Engineering, Royal Sanitary Institute, Portsmouth, July 11–16, 1938, pp. 16–17.

60. Unwin, "Planning and Education," *R.I.B.A. Journal, 44* (1937), 5.

61. *Journal of Land and Public Utilities Economics, 17* (Feb. 1941), 1–9.

62. Unwin, "Higher Buildings in Relation to Town Planning," *Journal A.I.A., 12* (1924). 124–31.

Unwin emphasizes too the human determinants in creating an undesirable situation. Like Howard he believed that a metropolis like Chicago was man-made and, to some extent therefore, mythmade.

The Depression had only heightened his interest in land values. In 1932 he expressed the belief that economics would share a "growing intimacy" with planning.[63] He pointed out that the American city had been built on the assumption that values should be heavily concentrated at the center. He recognized that the distinction between taxes on land and buildings made it easier in the United States to pile up values in one area and thin them out in another than in Great Britain where land and buildings tended to be kept together. Unwin agreed it was commercial use that held the potential of heavy yields in the central areas, but the moment had arrived to reassess the whole picture. Because of the rapid expansion of the United States during the nineteenth century it had become customary to inflate tax values. At the same time, the wide ownership of automobiles was causing central areas to decay more rapidly than they ever would in England. What had now appeared, under the stress of the Depression, was an acute "scarcity in the supply of value," or faith in the future.

Chicago was the prime example of his thesis. Between 1923 and 1936 its commercial area had increased by only 3.79 square miles. By 1936 there were 44 square miles of blighted land surrounding this commercial nucleus. It would take 146 years of steady commercial growth to redeem the blighted district at the present rate. As an alternative to commercial expansion he proposed that an effort be made to reverse the trend of population to the suburbs. The program would include the redevelopment of the blighted area downtown for residential rather than commercial use. With 100 families per acre, as in a New York scheme, the pre-Depression annual rate of increase of 60,000 people would not absorb the land until 187 years were up, slower than commercial occupation. But if, in consequence of a deflated and more realistic land value policy, the density could be lowered to 25 families, or even 10, it would require only 46.7 or 18.7 years respectively to fill the blighted space. The purpose is ostensibly the old one of spreading the increment for the benefit of the landowners as a whole for, "Where land is not used or where buildings are not occupied, no actual value is being created, and no real land value exists." It was self-deluding to "prize the unreal hope or expectation more highly than the real and realized value."

63. Unwin, "Town and Country Planning and Land Values," *Contemporary Review* (April 1932), p. 11.

What Unwin sought to provide was other forms of urban abstraction that could talk louder than the tax base. With his gift of imagery he was also anxious to forge these into active planning concepts. In the garden city movement itself the generalized slogans of "twelve houses to the acre" and "nothing gained by overcrowding" were to open up the further specific possibilities of the side path and internal circulation, the cul-de-sac, the superblock, the curving street, the tree-lined verge, the closing and opening vista, the varied setbacks, climatological and focal siting, and any number of other refinements in the disposition of houses and buildings within a given setting. The loosening of the land pattern conferred four broad benefits in addition to those allowing for better family adjustment: (a) It called attention to the ground as a distinct entity in itself, not merely a quantity waiting to be "improved" by structures; (b) it meant that the sequence of planning, from the house to the community, to the region and thence to the whole country could seem a more apposite process and that the planner's skill ought to be increasingly needed as the units enlarged; (c) it proved that the petty tyranny of the street over the home, or the opposite, as happened in early Leeds, could be restrained if other elements of urban composition could be better interpreted; (d) it indicated that visual planning was at its best when it was understood as an adjustment of solids, voids, edges, planes, and directions.

This last brought Parker and Unwin's planning maps and elevations very close to the relativism of the outdoor paintings of the great artists of the 1890s and early 1900s like Cézanne, Seurat, Utrillo, and even Van Gogh, where a two-dimensional canvas gained its fullest meaning from its three-dimensional inference of spatial movement and resolution of tension among many solids (Figs. 61, 62, 63), none of which would ordinarily be too dominant. In this respect it was the logical step beyond Bedford Park and Impressionism with its out-of-door emphasis. The urban artist was to take the strength of his social conviction and somehow translate it into an organizing force on the land or in the cityscape. Moreover, he would inject a habit of informal variety and personal identity guided by educated decision in places where only impersonal accidents had previously occurred. A new balance was about to be struck.

 The Beginnings of Form

Raymond Unwin was born in 1863 at Whiston, near Rotherham, northeast of Sheffield; Barry Parker was born in 1867 at Chesterfield, south of Sheffield.

Fig. 61. The Village of Gardanne; Paul Cézanne, 1885–86. A leading English art critic, Roger Fry, used illustrations such as this to bring to the public an awareness of the greater significance of the French painter, who was, he said, the "totem" of artists formed before World War I.

They were half-cousins, and their relationship became even closer when Unwin married Parker's sister Ethel in 1893. If a wide swath be drawn from Sheffield westward through Buxton, Chapel-en-le-Frith, Macclesfield, Altrincham, and thence up to Manchester, the chronological and geographic sequence of their early lives can be easily followed.

Chesterfield is in the coal-mining district of Derbyshire which supplied the steel mills of Sheffield. Unwin's first job was as apprentice engineer at the Staveley Coal and Iron Company, a few miles northeast of Chesterfield, in the early 1880s. It is likely that he was involved with the model housing built by the Staveley Company at nearby Barrow Hill. It is known that he designed St. Andrew's Church there in 1895.[1] The settlement itself had been begun by the company in the 1850s. The houses have brick fronts and stone sides and backs. The building stones, according to local legend, are old rail-

1. Letter from P. J. Lamb, City Librarian of Sheffield, June 21, 1956. Mr. Lamb also says that Barrow Hill was laid out on rather advanced lines by the Staveley Co., beginning in the 1860s. Emeritus Professor Stephen Welsh of the University of Sheffield has corroborated this in a letter of March 1963. He also suggests that the progressive attitude of the company toward housing was due to Mr. Barrow, an enlightened industrialist. The company built a school as early as 1856. For St. Andrew's Church, Barrow Hill, see also *Builder* (Dec. 7, 1895), p. 426.

Fig. 62. A small French market place; Unwin, 1909. Unwin's buildup of forms to a final tower, the merging and re-emerging of houses and trees, and the use of shed roofs to establish diagonal planes are all similar to the treatment of planes and shapes in Cézanne's work.

Fig. 63. An imaginary irregular English town; Unwin, 1909. To communicate awareness of the exact position and amazing diversity of multifaceted solids in space was an absorbing exercise for Unwin, just as it was for the French Post-Impressionists (see also Figure 80). In contrast appear the simple, flat foregrounds in each picture, a typical modern differentiation between plan and elevation.

road sleepers. The earlier houses are laid out in terraces; the later units are semidetached, four-square in shape with hipped roofs. Strips of garden run along the hill between them. The solid shapes, smooth walls, and small casement windows with white frames vaguely suggest the introvert and substantial quality of the later domestic work of Parker and Unwin.

At the Bolsover and Creswell collieries, a few miles south, model housing had an even longer tradition. Emerson Bainbridge, one-time M.P., chairman and director of the Bolsover and Creswell Colliery, had first conceived of a model village scheme at Bolsover in 1888.[2] Both villages had workingmen's clubs and cooperative stores. G. L. Morris regarded the larger settlement at Creswell as comparable in quality to Port Sunlight, Bournville, and Aintree.[3] From 1896 to 1900 Percy B. Houfton supervised the construction of 250 houses there. The general plan was a huge eight-sided layout of a double row of attractive houses surrounding a green. A tram line to take the workers to the colliery ran between the two rows of houses. The architect's brother, John B. Houfton, was the general manager of the colliery, which employed 1,500 men. There is no more evidence that Percy Houfton influenced the thought of Unwin than that G. Faulkner Armitage influenced Barry Parker, but it is interesting that Houfton's house, Brookside, was only two miles out of Chesterfield on the Chatsworth Road and that in it he tried to revive the local Derbyshire building tradition by the use of thin beds of sandstone of a gray-brown color, richly stained with reddish ocher. On the roof were Barton-on-Humber tiles, which weathered quickly to approximate the tone of local stone slates from quarries which were no longer accessible.[4]

Houfton won the first prize of £100 for a design which was built at the Letchworth Cheap Cottage Exhibition of 1905.[5] This exhibit, and another in 1907 organized by J. St. Loe Strachey of the *Spectator* and Thomas Adams, the first manager of Letchworth, conveniently satisfied both the call for less expensive houses at Letchworth and the English version of the back-to-the-land movement. Houfton also laid out, beginning in 1907, the Woodlands mining village near Doncaster, which was cited several times for the excellence of its planning and housing.

In 1896 Barry Parker asked Unwin to join him in an architectural partner-

2. "Creswell Colliery Model Village, New Workmen's Club Opened," *Sheffield and Rotherham Independent* (April 2, 1900), p. 7.

3. G. L. Morris, "Evolution of Village Architecture in England," *Studio, 10* (1897), 181, 183.

4. Mervyn Macartney, *Recent English Domestic Architecture* (London, Architectural Review, 1909), p. 109.

5. Lawrence Weaver, The *"Country Life" Book of Cottages* (2d ed. London, Country Life, 1919), p. 8.

ship at Buxton, which lasted until 1914. Parker had started his own office there the previous year to be near his father Robert, who had been head of the bank in Buxton but was in failing health. The partners did a number of houses in the vicinity, which is between Sheffield and Manchester. Among the earliest and best were those on College Road dating from 1897–98. Parker's father had helped the young men financially, to get them started on this particular effort.[6] Parker writes that shortly before this period, while he had been living with Unwin, the latter "was planning many miners' cottages, houses for managers, and others, schools and other buildings, in mining villages. Among these was a small church for which I designed a glass mosaic reredos."[7] Unwin was then known for his early introduction of pit-head baths. Parker himself was mainly active before the partnership as "a designer of carpets, wall papers, pottery, printed cottons, linens and silks."[8]

Opportunity for wider recognition came with their exhibit, "Cottages Near A Town," at the Northern Art Workers Guild in Manchester in 1903. Since they had already been dealing in practice with model mining cottages, the plan of the house was more enlightened than that of the land, which was presumed to be thirty acres near the edge of a town (Fig. 64). "The high value of land and the cost of road making determine that cottages so near a town must be closely packed in streets," is their concession to the contemporary state of urban affairs. But there is a new day coming, says Unwin: "The essential thing is that every house should turn its face to the sun, whence comes light, sweetness and health. The direction of roads and the fronting to streets are details which must be made to fall in with this condition, or to give way to it."[9] The long, narrow block, usually admitted to be a great disadvantage, is turned to advantage in this scheme by being oriented in one direction. The standard dwelling units are double or semidetached. A checkerboard pattern is set up with green plots alternating front and back. The passerby would see a continual change of light and shade, of building and garden, "instead of the long, monotonous rows with its strip of sky above and no nature to modulate the harshness." They hoped to outface the atmosphere of monotony and gloom and to eliminate the back alley and the enclosed service yard with its clutter and dirt. They believed that it would "be freely admitted that few

6. Information from Mrs. Barry Parker. Other houses in Buxton were on Lightwood Road, Cavanaleck, Overlaw, Lightwood Ridge, and Woodlea (letter from Borough Librarian of Buxton, Ivor E. Burton, July 10, 1956).

7. Barry Parker, "Sir Raymond Unwin," obit., R.I.B.A. Journal (July 15, 1940), p. 209.

8. Edward W. Gregory, "The Work of Mr. Barry Parker," House Beautiful (Sept. 1911), p. 117.

9. Sir Raymond Unwin, Cottage Plans and Common Sense (Buxton, Fabian Tract no. 109, 1902), p. 3.

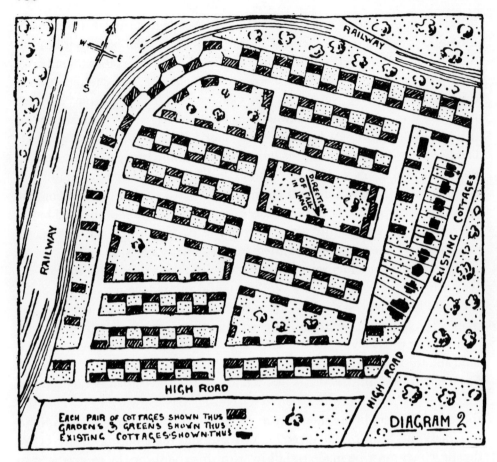

Fig. 64. Plan of cottages near a town; Parker and Unwin, 1903. This scheme was an important part of the exhibit of the Northern Art Workers Guild and proves how better land planning was in many respects the inevitable outcome of the Arts and Crafts movement.

spots on earth are so depressing as the back premises of the rows of cottages which form the outskirts of most towns, and no outlook so saddening as that from their back windows."[10] It was the same attitude that on the middle-class level led to the popular campaign against "the Queen Anne front and the Mary Anne back," and which turned Olmsted away from the domestic alley at Riverside in 1869.

It is instructive that when their first map for the Hampstead Garden Suburb appeared in 1905 (Fig. 65) they were still engaged with this checkerboard, for three rows of it still appear on the western fringe of the Hampstead

10. *Cottages Near a Town,* Catalogue of Works Exhibited by Members of the Northern Art Workers' Guild at the City Art Gallery (Manchester, Charlton and Knowles, 1903), p. 36.

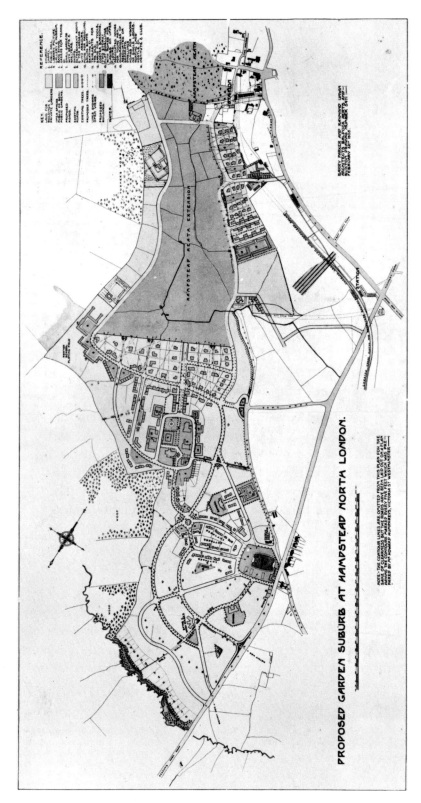

PROPOSED GARDEN SUBURB AT HAMPSTEAD NORTH LONDON.

Fig. 65. Proposed garden suburb at Hampstead, North London; Parker and Unwin, Feb. 22, 1905. This was the original plan for Hampstead Garden Suburb, and was considerably modified later. Its looseness and complexity show it, like Earswick, to be among the architects' earliest works.

Heath Extension. Yet they could not easily take advantage of the view of the Heath without splaying the end of the street, and the block was too short anyhow to make the checkers count (Fig. 66). So it was abandoned. However, the checkerboard served as a token of transition in Unwin's thought for the special law he got passed for Hampstead to eliminate the bye-law street in favor of the short cul-de-sac. A progression from the bye-law street to the tiny green plot, to the cul-de-sac, and on to the large green court and quad was noticeable in their work when he said in 1906, just at the right moment, that the medieval forefathers, "knew full well that a degree of simplicity in design which would be wearisome if spread out in a long straight row may be extremely pleasant when the buildings are grouped round a square, or green."[11]

It is evident from Unwin's resolution for the purchase of ground on the outskirts of cities, put forward at the Bournville Conference of September 1901, that he believed the immediate struggle for land would manifest itself on the urban fringe. Their 1903 scheme for "Cottages Near A Town" was a further acknowledgment of that situation. But they never liked the "feeling" of the suburb, any more than that of the slum. Unwin designated the "squalid slum" and "the dreary suburb"[12] as equivalent evils.

> There is nothing whatever in the prejudices of people to justify the covering of large areas with houses of exactly the same size and type . . . It is due to the wholesale and thoughtless character of town development, and is quite foreign to the traditions of our country; it results very often in bad municipal government and unfair distribution of the burdens of local taxation; misunderstanding and want of trust between different classes of people, and in the development and exaggeration of differences of habit and thought; it leads, too, to a dreary monotony of effect, which is almost as depressing as it is ugly."[13]

Instead he felt that each part of a town ought to have its own significant form. "In the arrangement of the spaces to be devoted to dwellings, as in the laying down of the main city plan, a complete acceptance of natural conditions must be combined with some definite design."[14] Thus, in 1901, Unwin himself,

11. Unwin, "Cottage Building in Garden City," *The Garden City, 1* (June 1906), 109.

12. "The City Beautiful from Converging Views of Social Reform," *Land and Labour,* Swanwick Summer School, Darbyshire (London, Collegium, 1914), p. 99.

13. Unwin, *Town Planning in Practice* (London, Unwin, 1909), p. 294.

14. Unwin, "On the Building of Houses in the Garden City," *The Garden City Conference at Bournville* (London, Garden City Assn., 1901), p. 70.

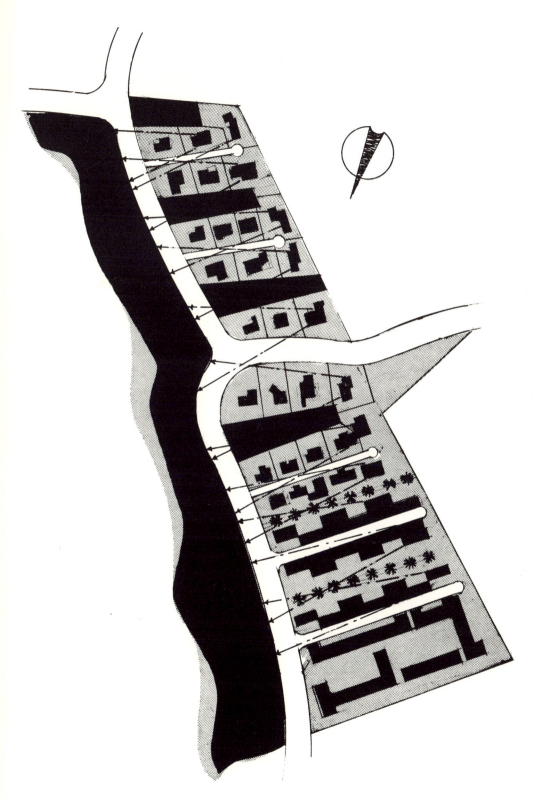

Fig. 66. Detail of south edge of Heath Extension from first plan of Hampstead Garden Suburb, 1905. The checkerboarding illustrates plainly that this pattern, which was not executed, was influenced by the plan for the Northern Art Workers Guild of 1903. The central green has to be slightly splayed in order to look out on the Heath. This is also the beginning of the cul-de-sac theme for which a special Hampstead law had to be passed. Every element is in transition.

before he had even built a garden city, anticipated the argument that would be used against it and him many times by those deploring suburban scatteration.

Parker, like Unwin, thought that the "present ideal" of having "each house standing alone in the middle of its own little plot" was architecturally disastrous. He likewise found the habit of considering "the facade of each building apart from its relation to its neighbours" highly disturbing. He abhorred the contradictions in scale which came out of this. He noticed that the sequence in which the suburb was built was wrong too. First appeared the residences, lying at the end of a long daily journey from the city, he records, then the hotels, shops, workshops, churches, and public buildings, "in that order," which had to be fitted in without forethought among the smaller buildings already there.[15]

However, there can be no denial that the partners sometimes withdrew from what they considered an impossible situation, like Howard and Lever shortly before. Unwin particularly avoided the suburban commitment because, "The social stability and well being of the community require that the tendency to segregation of the people's dwelling-places according to the depth of their pockets, should be resisted."[16] The older villages alone retained the set of social and architectural values that could offer useful suggestions for the future. The Englishman living either in isolation in the country or anonymously in the suburb had no better opportunity than the city dweller to share in a communal spirit. And that was really what they were after— some new form of community that would rise up out of the land, clear, clean, honest and alive. This was the essential quality of the medieval town, Unwin claimed, an "honest" place, "confessed, which does not seek to look half-countrified," like the suburb.[17] In an open and comely spot, surrounded by nature, the people could respond by willing new beauties and more effective social relationships, so that once the initial effort of communal creation rather than modification was made, the progress toward realization should be that much more rapid.

15. Parker, *Town Planning* (Letchworth, Herts., 1907), pp. 10–11, 15.

16. Unwin, *Columbia Lectures*, 1938–39, Nov. 1, 1938, Lecture 6.

17. Unwin, "Building & Natural Beauty," *The Art of Building a Home* (London, Longmans, Green, 1901), p. 84.

8. NEW EARSWICK

Although it can be fairly said that the architecture of Parker and Unwin belongs to one branch of the thriving British domestic style, their planning activity defies assignment to any school. Hence any description of their communal work as an evolutionary process would require a more intensive examination of their principal settlements in chronological order.

Planning in Britain, as Parker put it in discussing their first commission at New Earswick, hitherto "was the almost undisputed realm of the Speculative Builder," whose forte was "pinching and paring the house itself, and saving every penny he could,"[1] rather than enlarging his responsibility to include the best use of land. Parker felt that the builder was a useful member of society, and often maligned, but his outlook was simply not broad enough.

In order for the artist to attain a legitimate position in planning, he had to be responsive to the more informed stratum of his society, while preparing himself to surpass the builder at his own difficult game through increased inventiveness. Commissions like the Earswick development from an educated and wealthy Quaker family extended an opportunity to demonstrate both qualities. It was the underlying drive of restless energy and experimentation in planning that brought Parker and Unwin most quickly to fruition as artists. As onetime utopians, they were about to set themselves the task of becoming convincingly useful rather than transparently perfect in a very imperfect world.

In 1901 Joseph Rowntree purchased the estate of New Earswick near his cocoa works, three miles northeast of York. The earliest sector of twenty-eight houses (Fig. 67) was mapped out and built between 1902 and 1903 by Parker and Unwin.[2] These were, of all their communal houses, perhaps the

1. Barry Parker, "A Lecture on Earswick Delivered Before the Town Planning Institute," Parker Collection, Oct. 6, 1923, pp. 3–4.

2. *One Man's Vision: The Story of the Joseph Rowntree Trust* (London, Allen and Unwin, 1954), pp. 3, 32.

closest to the style of C. F. A. Voysey, who had built multiple cottages with great success for landed proprietors in several places (Fig. 68), but had dismissed both the suburb and the garden city as an affront to individualism. He considered that the garden city encouraged a "colony of flanneled faddists all prying into each others gardens."[3] Nevertheless, the resemblance to Voysey's mode gives an appearance of uniformity to the older part of Earswick which, when combined with the detail of the boarded gables and the rhythm of the arched doors and windows, establishes a tranquil yet varied look along the street. The steady rhythm is not unlike that of Saltaire, while the variation comes in a measure from Shaw's intended break in the monotony of the street picture.

New Earswick resembles Port Sunlight in that it was flat, but it did not exhibit the same rich architectural electicism. Nor was there room left for the development of the key architectural or landscape features, which had occurred later at Port Sunlight. Moreover, documents clearly show that the financial and social details were modeled more closely on Bournville than Port Sunlight. The Quaker families of Cadbury and Rowntree were in direct correspondence on the subject, and the New Earswick Trust Deed of December 1904 exhibits many similarities to the Bournville deed—for example a provision for all profit above $3\frac{1}{2}$ per cent to be returned for the maintenance and extension of the village. The Rowntrees also refrained from selling their houses to the tenants, because of the unfortunate experience of the Cadburys with rising values and consequent speculative turnover.

The older half of the settlement east of the Haxby Road contains staggered rows of houses of two, four, and six units (Fig. 69). These rows were calculated, as at Port Sunlight and Bournville, "to avoid producing the spotty restless effect in the village which would result from using pairs only."[4] The names of the "places" or service roads in this area also recall those of Bournville—Sycamore, Hawthorn, Rose, Almond, Lilac, Crab, Cherry. Wherever possible the places were connected with short footpaths.

The first step at Earswick was rethinking the relationship between house and street. The speculative builder was blamed for not considering this. "Back projections will nowhere be found in Earswick," observed Parker. "The narrow frontage was the fetish of the Speculative Builder, and it was curious he never realised he could eliminate all the useless passage-way and

3. C. F. A. Voysey, "On Town Planning," *Architectural Review, 46* (July 1919), 25, and Thomas Adams, "A Reply to Mr. C. F. A. Voy-sey," *Architectural Review* (Sept. 1919), 75–77.
4. Parker, "Lecture on Earswick," p. 8.

Fig. 67. A few of the original twenty-eight houses at Earswick, near York; Parker and Unwin, 1902–03. The breaking of the building line away from the street was already indicated at Earswick.

Fig. 68. Houses for Whitwood Colliery, Normanton, near Leeds; C. F. A. Voysey, 1905.

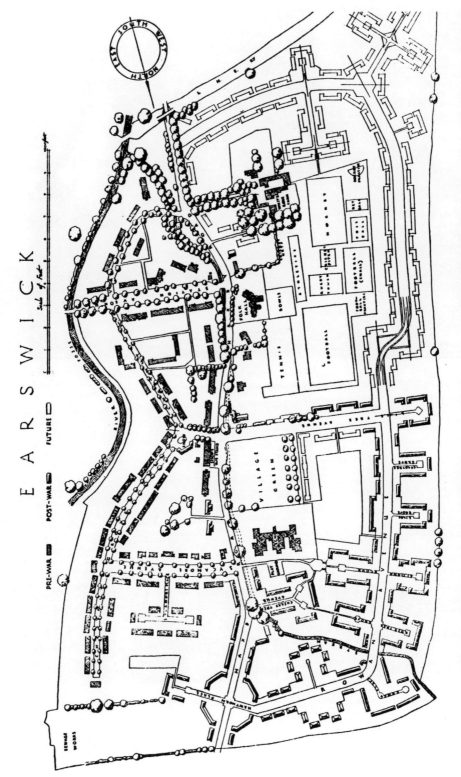

Fig. 69. Map of New Earswick. Footpaths are visible in the oldest, upper right quadrant, vaguely anticipating the internal circulation of the later Radburn Plan by Stein and Wright. The interior of the superblock was utilized for some houses, in contrast to Port Sunlight. It was also a step toward the cul-de-sac, which appears fully developed in the post–World War I sections.

retain his narrow frontage if he adopted a front projection instead of a back projection."[5] From the front the house and street could be linked in causal relationship. "Everyone overlooked the fact that the depth from front to back of the narrow fronted cottage necessitated a waste of space in internal passage-ways costing more than was saved in road costs."[6] A few of these tunnel-back houses had been originally built at Bournville. However, the pattern of the first sector of New Earswick was not wholly successful, being rather too in-formal. This was due partially to the River Foss and the Haxby Road, be-tween which the site was squeezed into the shape of an hourglass. Yet the final effect is primarily the result of a personal response of Parker and Unwin to the initial street-versus-house problem. In this first work they were so con-cerned with a direct attack upon glaring abuses of the street that they forgot to look for the inner opportunities of the blocks. It was first necessary in their eyes to break the rigid convention of the hidden back as well as the monoto-nous front. Unwin was particularly rabid on the subject. In 1902 he re-marked, "By no means the least advantage which will arise from giving to aspect its due weight will be the consequent abolition of backs, & back yards, back alleys and other such abominations, which have been too long screened by the insidious excuse of that wretched prefix *back*."[7] The upshot was that in concentrating upon the removal of this two-faced evil they failed for a time to comprehend what the total prospect of the blocks would be. In view of the short pedestrian paths between the roads, it would be interesting to speculate whether their early indifference to internal possibilities, regardless of the automobile, did not inhibit them from arriving sooner at a formula for consistent internal circulation similar to the Radburn Plan in America by Stein and Wright.

It is therefore even more fitting that the newer half of Earswick, west of the Haxby Road, should contain some of the best examples of the cul-de-sac device which Parker and Unwin employed to get around the awkwardness of irregular sites. In his much later "Site Planning as Exemplified at New Earswick," Parker developed his classic argument for the cul-de-sac.[8] The gist of his economic position was that it was always cheaper to leave small areas of "back land" (Figs. 69, 70) undeveloped by through crossroads unless the purchase price was fairly high (over £300 an acre). These odd segments

5. Ibid., pp. 4–5.
6. Parker, "The Life and Work of Sir Ray-mond Unwin," *Journal of the Town Planning Institute* (July–Aug., 1940), p. 161.

7. Raymond Unwin, *Cottage Plans and Common Sense* (Buxton, 1902), p. 3.
8. Parker, "Site Planning at New Ears-wick," *Town Planning Review* (Feb. 1937), pp. 2–9.

usually resulted from old field boundaries or other natural features. For Parker the cul-de-sac was the perfect instrument with which to penetrate these small parcels of back land and at the same time thwart the development of ribbon houses along primary roads (Fig. 71). Its length, width, and shape were conveniently adjustable. It also offered greater safety for children, easier police control (since it was open to view) and, of course, was less expensive to pave, maintain, and provide with utilities. Since the back lands would require short off-angle roads for their development anyway, that necessity was additionally served by clustering houses around the cross arm of the capital-T-shape of the usual cul-de-sac. As an ultimate refinement, Parker and Unwin turned the ends of the four-unit house so that its U shape would wrap neatly around the cross arm of the T.

What is most striking about the cul-de-sac as Parker and Unwin developed it is the suggestion of retirement into the back land in order to convert all disorderly backs, in a sense, into orderly fronts. This layout seemed to them to be compatible with the times. And it provided enough living space so that the inhabitants could withdraw from the presence of the automobile which was beginning to fill the roads with noise, fumes, and danger. Later, when the automobile increased in numbers and speed, compromises became less possible, especially when it entered the cul-de-sac. It is symptomatic that the second half of Parker's definitive essay on New Earswick, written in retrospect in 1937, is devoted to the new concept of the automotive parkway versus the ribbon development, without specific reference to Earswick or its cul-de-sacs. The tragic implication for his generation lay in the circumstance that, while striving so hard for complete synthesis and interrelation, the planners found it ever more difficult with the passage of time to reconcile the car with any other element, try as they might.

Within the Earswick houses the most significant novelty is the front-to-back living room. In writing about Earswick for the chief organ of the English domestic style, *Country Life,* Lawrence Weaver observed: "Mr. Parker has always before his mind the following facts: a tuberculosis germ will live for two years out of the direct rays of the sun and not more than ten minutes in the sun. He regards a 'through living room'—i.e., one with a window at each end—as indispensable in a non-parlour cottage."[9]

Another novelty at Earswick was the second-story bathroom. Although Parker gives credit to Unwin for championing the separate bathroom in all English cottages, his own local enthusiasm for it appears to have been con-

9. Lawrence Weaver, "Cottages at Earswick," *Country Life* (Oct. 31, 1925), p. 681.

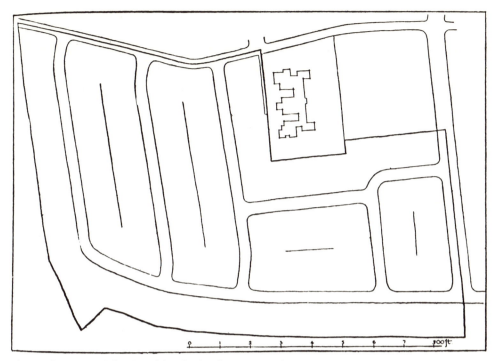

Fig. 70. *Area around the Earswick School as if penetrated by crossroads.*

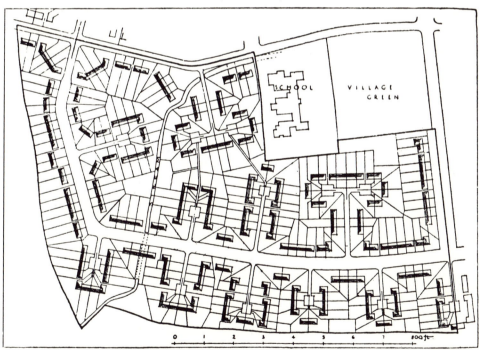

Fig. 71. *Area around the school as actually developed. The cul-de-sac offered great advantage in penetrating odd-shaped land plots. The reduced number, length, and width of roads were to reduce development costs. This principle was also the basis of the well-known Parker–Unwin slogan "Nothing gained by overcrowding."*

siderable. The partners wished to skip the intermediate step of placing the bath off the scullery, because they feared this location would be out of date in a few years. The tenants seem to have protested the abrupt improvement, as usual, but they were undemocratically and correctly overruled by the trustees.

Other devices introduced sooner or later were the turned stairs without winders (for safety) in houses two rooms deep and, after World War I, small sheds in the body of the house accessible from outside for the storage of fuel, perambulators, cycles, and garden tools. "Sites on which 'Housing Schemes' have been carried out since the war are being disfigured and spoiled by the erection of Bicycle and Perambulator Sheds, and the promoters of these schemes are at their wits end to prevent this from happening,"[10] wrote Barry Parker. The inner ground is still cluttered in the older portion at Earswick with hedges, sheds, and greenhouses (Fig. 72), so a historic cause and effect is still plainly visible there.

In time the architects resolved the building volumes more happily too, introducing open passages through the multiple houses for better front-to-back access and, after 1912, brick walls between the terrace houses to give them visual unity and accentuate country pictures under arched entrances.

The log of costs is fairly legible at New Earswick. It gives an unusual opportunity to gauge the inflationary effect of World War I. This catastrophe brought an end to the building of great country houses. Its interruption likewise reached down to the humble cottage. The founder of Earswick, Joseph Rowntree, openly voiced his disappointment at the appearance of the houses built there after the war. This was but one incident in the national building chronicle, yet three general postwar conditions are particularly in evidence at Earswick. They all run somewhat counter to the previous direction of garden city development. The first is a new emphasis on cost rather than amenity, as when the older, outside soil and vent pipes were put down the front of houses instead of the back. Weaver reports that the basic house unit after the war was a brick oblong with a hipped roof (Fig. 73), instead of the more picturesque and expensive gabled house of the earlier period, although this reflected a style change toward the Georgian, as well as economy.

The second condition, closely allied with the first, was a renewed interest in the technical possibilities of materials other than the traditional stucco or brick. When Parker was about to resume building, "the Trustees said they

10. *Architecture and Home Organization,* Foreword by Barry Parker (London, Assn. of Teachers on Domestic Subjects, 1926), p. 4.

Fig. 72. Inner space in the older portion of Earswick. Debris, hedges, and sheds tended to build up within the blocks, which resulted in the provision of sheds within the house itself for storage. This was due to the lack of careful layout of inner land at the beginning.

wished me to be able to say there was no alternative to bricks for the walls of cottages offered by anyone anywhere which I was unaware of or which I had not thoroughly investigated."[11] After exhaustive research and tests with a full-time assistant, and a report on the subject to the Ministry of Health (in Unwin's charge), it was concluded that bricks were still the best material. Aesthetics, economics and the conservatism of labor very likely assisted toward this conclusion, as they had in the Bournville experiments with wood, rammed earth, iron, and steel cottages. Even after the next disrupting experience of World War II, Louis de Soissons, architect of Welwyn Garden City, was as adamant in his role as consultant to New Earswick when he declared, "I am convinced that cottages cannot be suitably built in what are called the 'new materials' and that the traditional materials are inevitably right. Logically this must exclude all flat roofed cottages which, in this country, are completely upright!"[12] The compelling social desire to see the villages as spatially cohesive units, temporally stable, also appears to have militated

11. Parker, "Lecture on Earswick," p. 6.   12. *One Man's Vision*, p. 28.

Fig. 73. Almond Grove cul-de-sac, Earswick; Barry Parker, post-World War I. The identifying trees for each street follow the earlier Bournville practice. The runs of brick are now straighter, the window frames more standardized, and the hipped roofs more prevalent, because of postwar economy.

against specialized and isolated experiments with new materials. The wish for communal harmony and containment and the earlier inspiration from Shaw and his Queen Anne style for an integrity in the disposition of all materials, old or new, appear to have outweighed the urge toward innovation.

The third general condition that altered the appearance of Earswick was the need for building subsidies from the government between 1919 and 1936. The achievement of a higher housing standard which, ironically enough, was in large part due to the efforts of Raymond Unwin as head of various official bodies, had a tendency to freeze all improvements through official regulation. By way of contrast, Parker and Unwin in private practice were never satisfied in their explorations. Parker asserts in 1923, that, "If ever the time comes when I have nothing to offer as a cottage plan for Earswick better than the last I offered it will be a sad time for me."[13] But after the war it was not with the houses that he made most progress. His main goal had always been to reduce street expenses in order to have more money for the houses, and he was now able to get on with this. The prewar cost for roads, sewers, and other services amounted to £56 13s. per house while the third postwar plan dropped

13. Parker, "Lecture on Earswick," pp. 6–7.

Fig. 74. Earswick Primary School; Raymond Unwin, 1912–21. One of the earliest "open-air" schools.

this to £43 15s. 11d.[14] But he was simultaneously obliged to cut the number of house designs, standardize the building components, and look for straighter runs for the bricklayers.

There are two other projects of some significance at Earswick. Clifton Lodge Estate was begun in 1926 and completed in 1936 on land that became available from the estate of Joseph Rowntree. This was to represent an unusual feedback, as did Hampstead Garden suburb, of land patterns and house types devised for working-class groups into a middle-class, freehold development. The houses were valued between £1,500 and £1,650. The density was diminished to four and a half houses per acre, and certain refinements were added such as screen planting along Shipton Road, an ornamental pond, tennis courts, and an inner secondary road between cul-de-sacs. Parker controlled both house designs and the site plan, but only four of the homes found purchasers and the remainder were let. He ensured that each sitting

14. Ibid., p. 8.

room would have three exposures and that garden views in several directions
would be promoted. "About the planning of the houses themselves, the chief
thing to be said, is, that it has been done with the object of securing an unusual amount of sunnyness, cheerfulness, brightness and openness."[15]

In the Earswick School of 1912–21 (Fig. 74) by Raymond Unwin, class-
rooms were provided with long windows toward the southern exposure,
which could be folded back against the inner walls. This produced a one-
story, open effect, looking onto a green that preceded by many years the
similar school designs of Richard Neutra for Los Angeles or those of Eliel
and Eero Saarinen, associated with Perkins, Wheeler and Will for the Crow
Island School near Chicago in 1939. Yet it is evident from various allusions
in the literature that Unwin was already aware of yet earlier open-air schools
in America before his own.

15. Brochure of Clifton Lodge Estate, p. 8.

9. THE FIRST GARDEN CITY OF LETCHWORTH

The broad license that Ebenezer Howard was willing to issue to his ideal community made its unique growth possible. His final outline was presented at the garden city conferences at Bournville in 1901 and at Port Sunlight in 1902. W. H. Lever of Port Sunlight, like Howard, had also begun to make suggestions on the subject of land control in 1898, the year Howard published his *Garden Cities of Tomorrow*. Lever proposed that towns purchase their outlying areas, which could then either be sold at cost or, better, leased for 99 years.[1] The precocity of his views on "free" land led to his final withdrawal from the councils of the garden city. They felt that he went too far. Both he and Edward Cadbury were on the original board of directors of Letchworth, but "he wanted sites for houses and factories to be virtually given away to attract builders and others to come to the town."[2] Unwin must have been supporting Lever's idea when he made the motion at the Bournville Conference of 1901 that cities buy up fringe land until the garden city principle itself could be realized.

Letchworth in theory was to consist of 6,000 acres, about 3.3 miles square. The interest on the capital invested should run between 4 and 5 per cent, "all profits beyond this to be applied in local improvements and for the benefit of the community to be formed," in Howard's words.[3] Approximately seven years after the incorporation of the joint stock company a body of trustees would be entitled to purchase the stock at par for the community so that it might then guide its own destiny.

1. "The Garden Cities Association," 7th Annual Meeting, *The Garden City*, 1 (April 1906), 71. Actually Lever had once attempted to sell an estate of 1,530 acres to Birkenhead at cost, to which the Corporation agreed, but the local government board would not allow it. "An Adverse Decision," *Garden Cities and Town Planning* (March 1913), p. 79.

2. C. B. Purdom, "At the Inception of Letchworth," *Town and Country Planning*, Letchworth Jubilee Issue, 21 (Sept. 1953), 429–30. Purdom's *The Garden City: A Study in the Development of a Modern Town* (London, Dent, 1913) is the most complete single source for the early history of Letchworth. See also his *The Building of Satellite Towns* (London, Dent, 1949) for later developments.

3. Ebenezer Howard, "Outline of Garden City Project," *The Garden City Conference at Bournville* (London, 1901), p. 75.

One significant use to be made of the authority of the joint stock company was to prevent unreasonable profits in building operations. The company would undertake to build houses whenever industry, private individuals, or building societies failed to satisfy the numerical need adequately. This initiative could be employed as a check or stimulus for private enterprise, as the occasion demanded. However, the action would have to depend upon whether the company possessed "sufficiently large funds," and, of course, it never did.

This was the real source of the architectural inconsistency of Letchworth. In the period from 1906 to 1916, when the inherent originality of the English domestic school could have contributed so greatly to the appearance of the town, there was not enough money to bring it to bloom, despite the fact that the architects, house plans, and materials of cream, gray, white and yellow plaster, stucco, and roughcast (sometimes in half-timber and sometimes with brick visible) were the absolutely appropriate ones. For a similar reason a complete civic center of public buildings was not possible at Letchworth (Fig. 75). By abandoning private philanthropy, as followed in the garden villages, Howard in a measure deprived his garden city of the immediate architectural orchestration that made the earlier efforts harmonious. What was gained in freedom of development of the land was lost to creative pride and discretion in the architecture, and Parker and Unwin found themselves in a compromised position which made them vulnerable to both the perfectionists' and the pragmatists' criticisms. The latter were soon heard from: "One of the great difficulties in connection with the provision of cottages for labourers is that standards of comfort and of architecture aimed at, is beyond the reach of the labourer earning less than 25s. per week," wrote one of the practical people as early as the spring of 1906. "Cottages must be provided for the labourers at rents they can afford to pay, and the sooner the better for the Garden City Scheme."[4] Such truculent statements had led shortly before to the Cheap Cottage Exhibition at Letchworth and caused Unwin to refine his standards and to renew his plea for a cottage that was decent in every respect, including beauty. That this was a more personal issue with Unwin than Howard seems clear from the latter's declaration that "Healthy homes in healthy areas must be provided if we are to maintain our position among the nations,"[5] which relates more directly to the nineteenth-century preoccupation with public health and seems to mirror the concern of Cadbury and Horsfall for the position of the country's working and fighting forces vis-à-vis that of the other leading industrial nations.

4. "Great Need for Labourers' Cottages," *The Garden City, 1* (April 1906), 55.

5. Howard, p. 54.

Fig. 75. The center of Letchworth in 1930–35. Critics like W. A. Eden used the void in the center of the city as evidence of the emptiness and lack of vitality of garden city ideals. What they missed was the civic and ethical content of the age and the hope of creating an effect through a void. This space was meant to enhance the dignity of only one or two public buildings within the area outlined by the poplars. The actual commercial area was on Leys Avenue in the upper part of the picture.

The central issue in judging Letchworth could be whether a town that is more comprehensively planned and less thoroughly executed than an earlier type of garden village is more, or less, acceptable. Howard, and along with him, Parker and Unwin, simply could not impose their wills on the community as effectively as the old-time industrialists. The amount of green space for the community also fell below the standard set. In his book and outline Howard had recommended that a ring of agricultural land, five times the area of the center, should lie around it. He was forced to be content at the outset with a little less than three times the central area. The first purchase was of 3,826 acres, of which Parker and Unwin took 1,300 for the town. The greenbelt had for Howard both a utilitarian and an aesthetic aspect. He wanted it to furnish milk, fruit, and vegetables directly to the inhabitants of his garden city—combining the advantages of freshness and the absence of transport and handling charges. His observations also demonstrate that he was already aware of the recreational parklands around Adelaide, Australia, which derived from the colonial movement led by Edward Gibbon Wakefield.

He was as anxious to avoid internal as external crowding. Minimal lot sizes were to be 20 by 100 feet. Frontages were later expanded to 32 and 40 feet. Parker and Unwin took it as a rule of thumb that not more than one sixth of the site should be covered with buildings. Dwellings costing less than £200 should not exceed twelve to the acre, those costing from £200 to £300 should not exceed ten to the acre, houses costing from £300 to £350 should not exceed eight to the acre, and so on.

At the Bournville Conference Howard had emphasized that the plan in his book was "a diagram only." In his speech he asserted, "Of course, no actual plan for the laying out of the town can be presented until an estate has been selected."[6] He would not attempt any town, anywhere, without "the best expert advice." Halsey Ricardo and Professor W. R. Lethaby were accordingly invited to submit one scheme for Letchworth and Parker and Unwin another. This invitation should not have come as a complete surprise to Unwin. At the Bournville Conference of 1901 he had already indicated what his approach to such a hypothetical city would be:

> The successful setting out of such a work as a new city will only be accomplished by the frank acceptance of the natural conditions of the site; and, humbly bowing to these, by the fearless following out of some definite and orderly design based on them . . . such natural features should be taken as the keynote of the composition; but beyond this there must be no meandering in a false imitation of so-called natural lines.[7]

Parker and Unwin adapted this principle to the boundaries of the old fields and the rise and fall of the Hertfordshire countryside, 34 miles north of London (Fig. 76), more directly than to Howard's anachronistic, but admittedly tentative, diagram.

There was a loose and informal aspect to the actual town which was to be periodically noted by friend and foe alike. This reflects the self-conscious aim of Parker and Unwin to avoid any suggestion of nineteenth-century utopian rigidity, Beaux-Arts formality or overly opportunistic romanticism. Sir George Pepler, for example, surely favorable to the movement and an excellent designer himself, wrote in his 1953 "Salute to Letchworth" that "The town square may be rather too large, and the emphasis upon a series of street

6. Howard, p. 52.   the Garden City," *The Garden City Conference*
7. Unwin, "On the Building of Houses in   *at Bournville*, p. 69.

pictures—rather than upon a major composition—may be a point of criticism. On the other hand the street pictures, which in many cases are achieved without terraces, are charming. A small, self-contained, and self-sufficient homely town was the admirable aim."[8] The undulations and blending of the town into the countryside were the special qualifications, rather than the symbolic assertion of the public buildings or the town form itself.

Howard had said that he wanted to make it possible for his people to "enjoy the combined advantages of town and country life" for all time. His planners likewise determined to make this a working thesis. Besides setting the density at twelve or fewer houses per acre, they turned the dwellings on the lots so that they commanded the sunniest aspect and pleasantest prospect available, instead of merely aligning them along the street. Reminiscent of Bournville, each street was supposed to have its own species of tree (forty-five in all) as part of a campaign to reinforce the sense of place (Fig. 77). Unwin observed in 1904 that "The Japanese have special holidays to celebrate the flowering time of certain trees; and even the English workman might be tempted to vary his route home, if in one street he would find the earliest blossoming trees, in another the first spring green, and in a third the last bright colour of autumn."[9] In recommending an overall program for any young planner to follow, Parker said: "He will possibly so contrive as not to cut down a single tree; he will arrange to leave the view of anything which has beauty or interest in the surrounding landscape unobstructed from as many points as possible, and will arrange his street vistas to include these."[10] Parker took a lifelong pride in building Letchworth with the destruction of only a single tree. Additional shrubs and trees might be kept low, emphasized, or omitted in order to build up or blot out views. Unwin too was beginning to think less exclusively of houses and streets and more of distant prospects. He says, "The six to ten feet gaps so common between villas are of little service, but if the villas were united into groups of four or six, and a gap of some thirty feet then left between the groups, this would be a pleasing break, and might afford a view of garden, country, or building beyond, that would add distinct interest to the street."[11] Parker called these windows out to the landscape "driftways," thus characteristically depreciating his active role in their conscious arrangement.

The idea that the people at large were somehow cut off from the country-

8. *Town and Country Planning,* Letchworth Jubilee Issue, p. 472.

9. Unwin, "The Improvement of Towns," paper read at the Conference of the National Union of Women Workers of Great Britain and Ireland, Nov. 8, 1904, p. 3.

10. Barry Parker, *Town Planning* (Letchworth, Herts., 1907), pp. 7-9.

11. Unwin, "The Improvement of Towns," p. 5.

Fig. 76. General view of Letchworth in 1930–35. Letchworth has a little of the utopian diagram, something of the City Beautiful axiality, and a sloping off to the countryside from the earlier Romantic outlook. But Parker and Unwin hoped these influences could be unself-conscious, acting in the manner of a new and rejuvenated tradition. Although there were courts and cul-de-sacs at Letchworth at an early date, the more usual form is the odd-shaped superblock. The forested area of Norton Common at the upper left is interesting in that both here and at Hampstead, Parker and Unwin were careful to preserve an internal woods even though a greenbelt surrounded the settlement.

Fig. 77. Broadway, Letchworth; Parker and Unwin, 1903–05. Lime trees were used along this major street to give it identity. The trees, hedges, and grass verges furnish a living and spatial screen for the houses and family life, which Parker and Unwin considered paramount.

side, from a birthright, had been implanted in the English reform mind since the beginning of the enclosure of the common lands, but Ralph Neville, Chairman of the Letchworth Board, presented the problem in a more topical light when he remarked in his speeches that the worker had by some device to be brought back to the presence of nature because the number of people living on the land had already been reduced to a much smaller proportion than in either Germany or America.

The real criticism that can be made of the program at Letchworth is that eventually nature swung out of balance and became something of a burden. The trees, bushes, and flowers were quickly planted, while the buildings lagged. This is especially noticeable around the central square of the town. The older inhabitants were acutely conscious of the general effect during the jubilee year of 1953. "From being rather bare of trees in the early days it has become rather overgrown and a good deal of thinning should be done," said one.[12] "Now, like so many Letchworth cottages and houses, whose elevations were designed with so much care and patience by the architects to the company, they are almost completely lost to view," observed another.[13] And a third, "In places there are too many trees so that in midsummer the continual contrast of strong sunlight and shade is slightly disturbing. Many of the trees are overshadowing houses and robbing them of light and view."[14]

The abundant green served not only as a blending agent but also as a distraction, Osborn felt.

> Naturally, when I visit Letchworth, it is its external appearance that most compels my attention; and though many of the early housing schemes are perfectly charming, I am displeased, as other observers are, by what seems a lack of control of architectural design in some of the later parts of the town that, in the second garden city of Welwyn, we found it possible to maintain. A few Letchworth people, sensitive to architecture, agree with the critics on this; but most are not troubled by it at all. The mantling of the trees, the vistas in every direction of gardens and flowers, give them a constant pleasure that means more to them than good architecture. . . . It is a defence, but not a complete one, that Letchworth

---

12. R. W. Tabor, "Need of Better Balance," *Town and Country Planning*, Letchworth Jubilee Issue, p. 486.

13. Editha M. Berry, "The Howard Family in Letchworth," ibid., p. 463.

14. Barbara Hill, "Architectural Influences," ibid., p. 424.

had at times a hard struggle to attract developers, and could not be too strict in this matter.[15]

The fault should not be entirely excused, for the planners had set out to produce a community which would not only harmonize with the past but also be capable of programming itself as it grew in the genuine "organic" tradition. At the Bournville Conference Howard had observed that the "Garden City will not come into being except as the result of a great outburst of moral enthusiasm and human sympathy."[16] That enthusiasm and sympathy had been present with the first generation, all agree, but whether it was effectively carried beyond was a question asked by many of the older inhabitants. Nature, in which they had sought psychological refuge, now threatened to smother the visible ideal and blot out the sunshine, which had originally been so important to the architects and inhabitants from the grayer North (Figs. 78, 79).

The desire for architectural control had always been strong with Parker and Unwin and their colleagues. As late as World War II Parker says, "I look forward most keenly to there being far more architectural control exercised by exactly the right man."[17] The compositional method was always supposed to have a certain spatial rhythm too, much like that of the informally disposed trees and shrubs. The ideal planner "will also study to make the most of any fine buildings he may hope to have, and to make any beautiful features he may expect in these, terminate his street vistas. He will arrange to allot to these buildings not only the most convenient sites he can give them, but also the sites which will give them dignity, majesty, and beauty."[18] The difficulty was that eclecticism and the abundance of material possibilities were constantly breaking down the limits of their assumptions. Of these two dangers, the first was the greater. A style, any style, was conventionally acceptable for a building, but no styles for whole new cities were then recognized. Moreover, they were caught in an age that did not furnish aesthetic answers easily. The intuitive exercises had lain dormant too long. Like Sullivan, with his moratorium on architectural decoration, Unwin thought that the problem might be solved in a negative way by postulating a "non-stylised" environment (Fig. 80). He could not visualize any city becoming completely Classical, Palladian, or Gothic, he said. The nineteenth century

15. F. J. Osborn, "Letchworth's First Fifty Years," ibid., p. 404.

16. Howard, p. 57.

17. Parker, "The Future of Letchworth and the Garden City Movement," *Letchworth Citizen* (March 1944).

18. Parker, *Town Planning*, pp. 7–9.

Fig. 78. Norton Way South, Letchworth, 1910.

Fig. 79. Norton Way South, Letchworth, 1960. The great complaint of the inhabitants in later years was that the trees overshadowed the houses and robbed them of light and view. Norton Way was a main north–south artery.

Fig. 80. Rushby Mead, Letchworth. This street captures the originally intended balance between nature and architecture, with the plain gables rising at unusual angles to the road line to give shape and direction to the space. The architects did not usually employ the S-curve, preferring to be more subtle, but this street happened to follow an old stream bed, and so was a response to a natural feature.

had tried this approach and failed. Instead, "It is possible perhaps to revive an old natural limitation to which much of the beauty of ancient cities was due, and to regain, by some regulation of building materials, that general harmony of effect which was so often due to the prevalent restriction of local materials."[19]

Public health was conveniently measured through statistical levels. Public beauty had no such graph. And as the precepts of democracy gained influence, the requirements of beauty became even more difficult to describe and widely enforce. Yet the painter William Townsend in examining Letchworth in 1950 discovered much in it still to praise. He mentioned particularly the open planning in the houses, the interplay of inside with out, and the domesticity of the public buildings. "There is not a trace of 'ye olde.' If we find

19. Unwin, "On the Building of Houses in the Garden City," *The Garden City Conference at Bournville*, p. 73.

a harking back to medieval types of furniture like benches or settles, or houses designed in all sorts of cottage styles, that was because these forms seemed best to serve some perfectly sensible need of the day. All was made new for the day"; and hence remained durably fresh and original.

On the other hand, Townsend thought he recognized the last faint impulse of the Arts and Crafts movement in the ornamentation. "Its feebleness was not only in its well-wrought yet somehow flabby manner, but in the extreme weariness of its subject matter. It gathered in the last weeds from the Pre-Raphaelite garden—one might say the lilies and languors made healthy." Sinuous tulips, daffodils, and water lilies were among the favorite decorations on the finger plates and chimney pieces, while Lombardy poplars waved gently in the breeze outside. Yet it was not the end-of-the-century exhaustion in the decorative arts that disturbed him so much as the disconcertingly naive quality of the place. There is something "dauntingly wholesome, almost too healthy-minded," about it, he says. "It is like living on wholemeal bread all the time. These neat little houses in nursery procession are like toy models in their tidiness and cleanliness." Townsend claimed that the current lack of popular appreciation of Letchworth was not clouding his view. "There is at times a brisk buoyancy, a light coloured brightness in the scene, that is tonic . . . but it does lack the marks of tension, of doubt, of struggle of any kind. It misses on the other hand the large acceptance of life. As a prospect, as urban landscape, it is just miles and miles of pleasant cosiness."[20]

The painter has written very intelligently of Letchworth. It only remains to combine his observations with what is known of recent history to make them more significant. The architectural pedigree of the town goes back, of course, to Morris' idealized London, "small and white and clean, / The dear Thames bordered by its gardens green,"[21] and to Voysey's studio house in Bedford Park of 1891, and thence on to the Josef Olbrich house at Darmstadt, Germany, of 1905. Baillie Scott had been asked in 1898 to decorate two rooms in the new palace of the Duke of Hesse-Darmstadt, and Peter Behrens undertook his first domestic effort there. In a word, in Darmstadt and Letchworth we are simultaneously close to the future mainstream of Continental architecture and not far from the hearth of the English domestic school.

Letchworth was smaller in scale and more refined than the Georgian Hampstead Suburb or the postwar (and also more literally Georgian) sec-

20. William Townsend, "The Garden City," *Listener* (Nov. 23, 1950), p. 590.
21. "Prologue," *The Earthly Paradise*.

ond garden city of Welwyn. Letchworth was architecturally an event in the hunt for a more deeply rooted and authentic folk life, which was going on in other countries as well at the time—most notably in Austria, and in Finland with its research into the Karelian district in which Eliel Saarinen and his partners were so involved.

What Townsend forgot in his excellent critique was that the outlook before World War I was generally cheerful and optimistic, regardless of how much struggle was involved in achieving a specific project. His *ex post facto* wish for the marks of tension, doubt, and struggle in the town also shows that he did not fully realize the primary reason for the garden city. The fact that the world was suddenly to grow grimmer after the war could be accepted and absorbed, but it could not be the fault of the Letchworth architects that they did not anticipate it. They were trying to escape another kind of meaner and duller urban grimness, which atrophied the spirit by its narrowness and monotony, rather than by sharp threats and sudden alarms.

What might be carried over from Letchworth are the whiteness and tidiness, as they were in Germany from the Fagus Werke of Walter Gropius of 1911 through the war to the Bauhaus of 1925. The pristine quality remained intact; what was added after the war to the meaning of "modern" was simply a greater emphasis on economy in cost and function in structure. This had much to do with the fact that Germany and America experienced the industrial revolution later than Britain did, and also that the fighting had focused attention on the almost infinite possibilities in modern technology for good or evil. The tension, doubt, and struggle and their omnipresent reflection in architecture were to appear later under the stimulus of further depression and war. Parker and Unwin, together with Howard, honored the thought of a city in the historical sense, but they disliked the quickly improvised modern commercial and industrial city because they believed it to be an anomaly or, indeed, a monstrosity, and therefore had no inclination to redevelop, reform, or compromise with it. Any "large acceptance" of contemporary urban life was a gesture of empty bravado so far as they were concerned.

How convincing and welcome the garden city alternative was, at least to the relatively unsophisticated inhabitants of Letchworth, becomes evident if one learns a few of their reasons for moving there. A printer recalls:

> I was born in a north Midland town and served my apprenticeship
> in a mining town in lower Derbyshire [where Parker and Unwin

had also begun], the sludge country described by Hilaire Belloc. Life was hard in those parts. . . . I wanted now both the busy life of industry and the healthy life of the country, and when I heard of Letchworth and read Ebenezer Howard's *Garden Cities of Tomorrow* this seemed to offer all I needed, so in 1911, now married, with two children, I came to Letchworth, and so found happiness.[22]

Another older inhabitant, a woman, who had perhaps not heard that tension, doubt, and struggle were always supposed to be evident in a town, wrote: "Letchworth was already ten years old when we came to it from the bleak industrial North. . . . And we never ceased to be grateful to the good fairy who guided us there when we began our married life, for assuredly in one stride she landed us in Utopia."[23]

Possibly the world has changed more than Letchworth has failed, in a short half century. In any case, it seems evident that to the original settlers Letchworth meant, despite its deficient expression in some respects, a great new beginning. Some residents, on the other hand, appear to have taken the implication of a new start too literally, and Letchworth came to have a reputation for unconventionality, harboring those who did not believe in hats but did wear sandals, and including suffragettes, theosophists, vegetarians, and folk-dance enthusiasts. This fondness for novelty appears even to have had an architectural manifestation, for in the oldest settlement, built before Parker and Unwin had a grip on the situation, there was a round house, one dwelling that resembled a "dismasted ship," and some bungalows which were "abnormally long" or narrow, while others appear to have had gables almost touching the ground.[24]

These were but minor aberrations. The more profound failures were essentially temporal and sequential, rather than results of social or aesthetic conviction. In many respects these miscarriages offer the soundest indictment of garden city thought at large. A few events which were intended to assure success, never happened at all, or much later than they ought to have. From the outset Letchworth was chronically undercapitalized. At the formal opening of the estate, October 9, 1903, only £40,000 of a projected £300,000 had been subscribed, which was barely a quarter of the purchase cost of the land. For a long time it was not possible to undertake more ambitious proj-

22. W. Francis Moss, "Fairies at the Bottom of the Garden," *Town and Country Planning,* Letchworth Jubilee Issue, p. 481.

23. Trudi Fitzwater-Wray, "Joyous Memo-

ries," ibid., pp. 476–77.

24. Letchworth Urban District Council, *Letchworth, Hertfordshire,* The Official Guide (Cheltenham and London, Burrow, n.d.), p. 12.

ects for putting up houses, shops, factories, or public buildings. A dividend to the stockholders was not forthcoming until 1913, and then it amounted to only 1 per cent. In 1923, twenty years after the founding, the full amount of 5 per cent was declared for the first time. Payment of arrears on the limited dividend was begun in 1927 but not completed until 1945. One of the discouraging factors was the inability of the trustees to revise the land taxes often enough under the 99-year lease-hold system. The unearned increment was there but without any mechanism for translating it into ready cash. Howard and his associates did not know how to set up a fiscal system flexible enough to operate under the buffeting of depressions, wars, and inflation. And at the outset all the working capital was swallowed up in the development of roads and sewers, and the provision of water, gas, and electricity. What has several times been pointed out by Lewis Mumford, John Burchard, Paul Rudolph, James Marston Fitch, and others—that mechanical equipment has taken a larger and larger portion of construction money in contemporary architecture—evidently applied as well for the building of towns. Howard did not sufficiently anticipate this, although Parker and Unwin were always conscious of rising road and service costs and the subsequent reduced budget for architecture. Nevertheless, one economist reported by June of 1908 that there were 5,600 inhabitants and 1,020 houses, and that 55 shops and 14 factories had been built in Letchworth. A revaluation at the time showed that the original land over four years had appreciated, even after deducting the cost of roads and utilities, by £131,693 6s. 1d.[25]

In the end prosperity almost ruined Letchworth, much as poverty had years before. In 1956 the *Manchester Guardian* reported that its wealth had become a subject of public note. "With the passage of years the freehold properties have increased in value, and the limit on the dividend has prevented the distribution of these gains until a point was reached at which the company became an attractive prize for the take-over bidder."[26] A private bill, the Letchworth Garden City Corporation Act (1962), instituted by the local authority, appears to have saved the day and to have established Letchworth as a statutory corporation to be henceforth managed for the benefit of the community itself. The moral again is that where the planning arts can be focused to produce and sustain a superior environment, superior financial values will also be created which in time will make the improved object a magnet for the more specialized and hardheaded profit takers.

25. F. W. Rogers, "Garden City; Its Social and Economic Aspect," *Clare Market Review* (June 1908), p. 109.

26. "Vote to Increase Dividend of First Garden City," *Manchester Guardian* (April 6, 1956), p. 20.

World War I left social and physical as well as psychological scars. A Zeppelin hunted for the town but bombed an open field by mistake. A great number of Belgian refugees had been brought in under emergency conditions to work in an armaments factory (the real target of the Zeppelin) that was much larger than any industrial unit planned for, throwing the social situation further out of balance. Partly as a result of this sudden intrusion, many of the pioneers went off to build a new garden city at Welwyn in 1920. Workers' housing also consistently failed to keep pace with employment opportunities. As early as June 1906 Ralph Neville was lamenting that there were at least three hundred men working on the estate for whom no housing could be found.[27] In 1953, forty-seven years later, Frank Rowe, managing director of the K & L Steelfounders and Engineers, deriving from the original armaments plant and still the largest employer, remarked that, "All industrialists would be happier if their personnel were put to less inconvenience and cost by being able to live nearer their work."[28] A survey taken at the time revealed that 90 per cent of the executives running the hundred odd works lived within the boundaries of the town, demonstrating once more that in an environment of planned amenity, even when it has been originally conceived for the poorer citizen, the well-to-do tend to be more quickly accommodated.

Increasing authority given to local government bodies by the nation also nibbled away at the initiative of the company, not to mention the source of income which entirely disappeared when the gas and electric facilities were nationalized. Parker's conclusion was that under the circumstance all planning ought to be nationalized. He maintained in a newspaper interview of 1941 that, "divided responsibility arises from First Garden City being the land owner and the Letchworth Urban District Council being the Town and Country Planning Authority and the Hertfordshire County Council the authority for some roads, and administering the Restriction of Ribbon Development Act."[29] He regarded his town of Wythenshawe, done for the Manchester Corporation, as a proper step to correct this and said he felt that Howard would have established his garden cities on public land had it originally been possible.[30] Actually, Howard had stated that he did not care under what auspices the garden city would be begun, so long as it got built.

27. Ralph Neville, "The First Garden City," *The Garden City* (June 1906), p. 116.

28. Frank Rowe, "Appreciation by an Industrialist," *Town and Country Planning,* Letchworth Jubilee Issue, p. 484.

29. Parker, "No Alternative to National Ownership of Land for Real After War Planning," *Letchworth Citizen* (July 25, 1941).

30. Parker, "The Future of Letchworth and the Garden City Movement," *Letchworth Citizen* (March 1944).

However, he thought that private control would "have the advantage over a municipality, in that it could devote the land to any purpose, whereas the municipality would not have this flexibility."[31]

Most disillusioning of all at Letchworth is the fact that it has never attained its maximal population limit, a precept which was to become the most promising theoretical contribution for the future of urban planning as a whole. As Lewis Mumford has tellingly observed, the limit set by Howard was really something of "a shot in the dark."[32] In one place he speaks of it as being 30,000 and on his diagram it appears as 32,000 in greenbelt and town. This is still the official figure. Ralph Neville writes of 33,000 in his Fourth Annual Report of 1902. Unwin mentions "something like 35,000" in his pamphlet *Nothing Gained by Overcrowding!* There was apparently a tendency to revise the figure slightly upward on the part of the creators, depending upon their optimism, while some of the inhabitants felt it was already too large when it hovered in the vicinity of 20,000. But at least Howard had the courage to fire the first shot. Some day, not too far off, as Lewis Falk has half-humorously remarked, there will be a hurried gathering of anxious councillors to deal with the announcement that a completely innocent baby has arrived to make the population 32,000 and one![33]

31. Howard, p. 40.

32. Lewis Mumford, "A Successful Demonstration," *Town and Country Planning*, Letchworth Jubilee Issue, p. 134.

33. Lewis Falk, "Trials of an Industrialist," ibid., p. 476.

10. HAMPSTEAD GARDEN SUBURB

Authorities as diverse as Frederick Gibberd, Martin S. Briggs, Steen E. Rasmussen, Clarence Stein, and Lewis Mumford have written of Hampstead Garden Suburb near London as the best of its kind, "a masterpiece and an artistic triumph."[1]

An indication of its quality is that it never appears to be discussed with condescension or greeted with faint amusement, as Letchworth sometimes is. Yet a brief visit to it can be almost disappointing. It appears today so complacent, enjoying its own maturity, so submerged in greenery, so near the end of the ripest English domestic style before it moved over into the sedate and symmetrical neo-Georgian, that it is difficult to accept the judgment, by even the best critics, of its outstanding merit.

The difference in rating given Hampstead Suburb by experts and by those who are able to visit it only briefly is due to a single cause: it is a work of art that cannot be perceived as such except by those willing to spend some time studying it. They must also bring to the examination a general awareness of the history of planning and architecture in Britain.

Within Hampstead are distant echoes of Wren's seventeenth-century plan for London after the fire as well as Nash's early nineteenth-century promotion of an urbane naturalism at Regent's Park. In company with this enrichment from the past goes an opportunity to gauge the contemporary urban efforts of other countries. Nothing could make clearer the distinction between what was occurring on the Continent and in England than the crafts exhibits of the immediately preceding years. *The Studio* had already noted, regarding the exhibition of 1896: "It is especially good that his [Voysey's]

1. Martin S. Briggs, "The Plan and Architecture of Hampstead Garden Suburb," *Town and Country Planning* (July 1957), p. 297. See also W. A. Eden, "Hampstead Garden Suburb 1907–1957," *R.I.B.A. Journal* (Oct. 1957), p. 495. Eden, who tends to be a little dyspeptic about garden cities and suburbs, also notes that the virtues of Hampstead "reside in its details" and the "lively, gentle and affectionate spirit" shown in its buildings.

influence, which tends to simplicity and severity, should be made very prominent at a time that sees, especially in France and Germany, a tendency to be bizarre at any cost."[2] Britain had started toward simplicity and away from eclecticism before Europe emerged from the self-induced fever of the Art Nouveau, but because the puristic image was first engendered within the arts and crafts and then in architecture, its priority has gone largely unnoticed.

The contrast with what was going on in the United States is equally instructive. There too in the early 1890s began an effort to redefine the city in visual terms, from which rose Burnham's neo-Renaissance City Beautiful movement. Raymond Unwin was by now well informed about what was going on in both America and on the Continent. In reviewing an exhibit in 1910 of Daniel Burnham's plans for Chicago (1909) and Washington (1901), he concludes that they show "a grasp and breadth of treatment of the whole question quite American in its scale."[3] The greatest American planner conceived a monumental plan for his cities, while the British planner took only a fragment, in this case a suburb, and attempted to achieve a valid reform through a more careful integration of the social and economic needs. The primary concern for beauty is the major link between the two.

One of the most instructive ways in which Hampstead Garden Suburb can be interpreted is as an accomplishment of the determinative powers of three distinct individualists: Dame Henrietta Barnett, Sir Edwin Lutyens, and Sir Raymond Unwin. No matter how cumulative or broad the forces of urban resolution might appear to be toward the end of the nineteenth century, they were still being initiated by well-placed and highly articulate personalities in Britain.

Hampstead Suburb started as an effort to save a portion of the disappearing landscape around London. During the seventeenth, eighteenth, and nineteenth centuries Hampstead Heath had served as a resort from the city. Some of Constable's most subtle and moving compositions depicted the Heath (Fig. 81). The tragic genius, Leigh Hunt, had also described it well:

> A steeple issuing from a leafy rise,
> With farmy fields in front, and sloping green,
> Dear Hampstead, is thy southern face serene,
> Silently smiling on approaching eyes,
> Within, thine ever-shifting looks surprise,

2. *Studio, 9* (1896–97), 189–90.
3. Raymond Unwin, *Town Planning in Practice* (2d ed. London, Unwin, 1911), p. xiii.

Fig. 81. Harrow from Hampstead Heath, Sunset; John Constable, 1821. Constable sent his family to Hampstead for the summers and made quick sketches there which were very popular in Paris and were in many ways the forerunners of Impressionism. This scene, after a rain, shows the fleeting quality of British light, merging earth and sky. The opportunity to look out from a high place over the countryside was dear to the English heart and played a basic part in the evolution of Hampstead Garden Suburb.

> Streets, hills and dells, trees overhead now seen,
> Now down below, with smoking roofs between—
> A village, revelling in varieties.[4]

By the end of the nineteenth century London had made its way around to the northern side of the Hampstead hill. In 1896 Mrs. Barnett heard from an American while on ship to Russia that proposals for the extension of the London tube system included a station near the ancient farmstead of Wyldes, which had been the dwelling of Constable and would later be the permanent

4. As quoted in *Garden Suburbs, Town Planning and Modern Architecture*, with contributions by M. A. Baillie Scott, "Home Counties," Professor S. D. Adshead, P. W. Wilson, E. G. Culpin and Alderman Thompson (London, Unwin, 1910), p. 6.

home of Unwin.[5] She returned to engage in a campaign during the summer of 1903 to enlarge the Heath for public recreation by eighty acres. The energies of a committee, of which she was the honorable secretary and Lord Eversley the chairman, were devoted for five years to this end. During this period the possibility occurred to her of using the 240 acres remaining in the hands of Eton College after the removal of the proposed Hampstead Extension as a plot for residential development.[6] It was a timely thought. As much as a decade before, William Morris too had prophetically observed in *News from Nowhere* that, "North, again, the land runs up high and there is an agreeable and well-built town called Hampstead, which fitly ends London on that side."[7]

The value of the land was about to jump from £600 per acre to as many thousands with the advent of the underground station. Mrs. Barnett sought to take advantage of the impending inflation by invoking a traditional English solution, the house facing on the green. "This tongue of common land thrusts itself through in the 240 acres, thus giving to the Garden Suburb Trust the monopoly of the advantage which frontage on to this new and beautiful open space confers," she writes in her first article proposing the suburb in the *Contemporary Review* of February 1905.[8]

The lifework of Canon Samuel A. Barnett and his wife up to this time had lain in the slums of London's East End. They had moved into the Whitechapel district there after their marriage in 1873. Social service in the slums might appear a far cry from the salvation of pastoral beauties, except that Mrs. Barnett did not believe it was and neither did her even more famous mentor in housing and social work, Octavia Hill. Miss Hill, Canon Rawnsley, and Sir Robert Hunter (one of the original directors of the Hampstead Garden Suburb Trust and the partner of Mrs. Barnett in saving the Heath Extension) had been the three founders of the National Trust in 1895. This governmental organization, now better known for its holdings of historic country houses, began its existence in a private struggle to preserve and extend commons and open spaces in and around London. It was Miss Hill, "who first inspired the young Henrietta to devote her energies to dealing

5. Henrietta Barnett, *Canon Barnett, His Life, Work, and Friends*, 2 (2d ed. London, Murray, 1919), 312.

6. Henrietta Barnett, D.B.E., *The Story of the Growth of Hampstead Garden Suburb,* *1907–1928* (The Hampstead Garden Suburb Trust, Ltd. 1928?), pp. 5–6.

7. William Morris, *News from Nowhere* (London, Reeves and Turner, 1891), p. 75.

8. "A Garden Suburb at Hampstead," *87,* 232.

with the interrelated problems of poverty and housing, and she became 'the heroine of my life.' "[9]

This personal influence is one possible explanation of the keen attraction which the form of the Hampstead Garden Suburb held for Mrs. Barnett. Nigel Bond, the early secretary of the National Trust, reports in his notes on the history of the organization that Octavia Hill "constantly stressed the view that every effort should be made to keep open the tops of hills round London and other big towns. If that were done it would matter much less, she thought, if the lower land were developed."[10] Mrs. Barnett assumed that Hampstead Heath varied from 170 feet to 360 feet above sea level when she was working out her scheme, but her estimate seems to be low on both ends. The significant difference, however, is that Hampstead lies higher than any other metropolitan borough.

As Mrs. Barnett tells it, one day after lunch at her cottage near The Spaniard's Inn, "Lord Crewe and I walked across the fields, climbed the hedges, and toiled through stubbly grass until we reached the central hill. 'This is the highest place, and here we will have the houses for worship and for learning,' I said; and here they stand."[11] The center having been thus chosen, the western side was deliberately left open to capture the view of the spreading fields past Harrow and on to the Chiltern Hills.

It was later evident that she had not picked the highest spot after all and that Raymond Unwin and Edwin Lutyens were inclined to attribute the location and success of the Central Square to their own discrimination; but underlying the choice and spatially restrained development of the particular site was Miss Hill's aim to keep the heights open.

On the first map of the Suburb, dated February 22, 1905, and issued from the office of Parker and Unwin, "Architects, Baldock, Herts and Buxton," it is noted that "although for the sake of clearness," the contour lines are omitted, the scheme was based on an earlier map having them marked every five feet. But there are lines of another type which are more interesting: dashed angles of sight from the houses on the slopes down toward the Heath (Fig. 82). Since Mrs. Barnett's article was published in the same month that the first plan was submitted, it is again difficult to discover to whom this unique feature should be credited. However, her words in the article describe their purpose well.

9. R. L. Reiss, "Henrietta Octavia Barnett and Hampstead Garden Suburb," *Town and Country Planning* (July 1957), p. 277.

10. Mimeo., p. 3.

11. Barnett, *The Story of the Growth of Hampstead Garden Suburb*, p. 6.

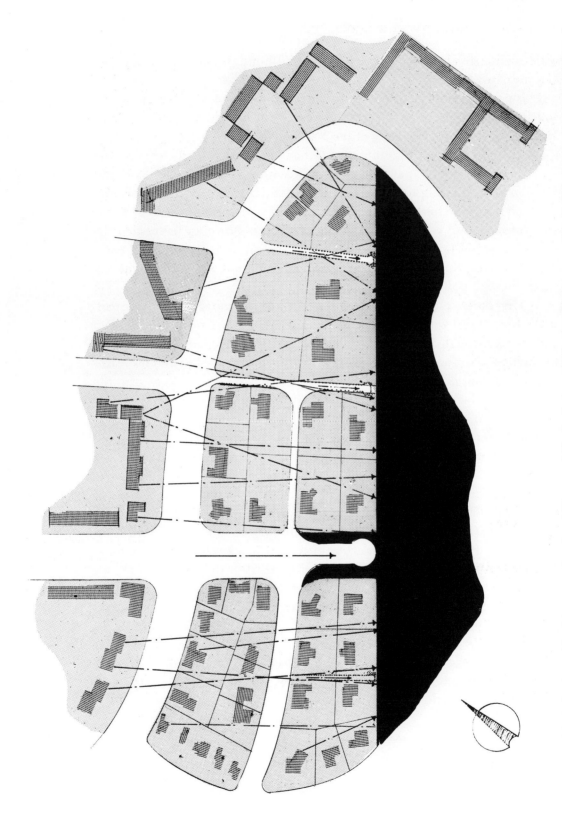

Fig. 82. Original plan for residential area on the edge of Hampstead Heath; Parker and Unwin, February 1905. The English desire to look out and down is already evident in this first plan. Sight lines were drawn by the architects themselves. Note also the care with which these lines are preserved from the larger houses for the elderly and unfortunate behind the more expensive homes in the foreground.

Fig. 83. La Grande-Jatte; Georges Seurat, 1884–86. Proximity of many people to each other and to nature appears earlier in the painting of the age than in the planning, but later it is present in both media. The nearness of the island to Paris in some respects presents the same set of conditions as the nearness of Hampstead to London. Both were traditional places for urban recreation. The tightness of composition becomes the major issue and the abstraction of nature or reality the only way to realize it.

> The houses will not be put in uniform lines, nor in close relationship, built regardless of each other, or without consideration for picturesque appearance. Each one will be surrounded with its own garden, and every road will be planted with trees, and be not less than forty feet wide. Great care will be taken that houses shall not spoil each other's outlook.[12]

She likewise wanted numerous balconies from which the elderly might enjoy nature without being obliged to venture out into it. Human proximity was beginning to be more thoughtfully studied. Hampstead dealt with the question of bringing people closer but not too close, and in the process aligned itself aesthetically with such works of art as Georges Seurat's La Grande-Jatte (Fig. 83). Each object on the site becomes more real in its presence but

12. Barnett, "A Garden Suburb at Hampstead," p. 235.

more abstract in its relations with the other objects around it in the visible environment.

The basic economic aim of the new suburb was to furnish a home for the working man for a 2d. fare from London on the tube. What was "common to all," natural beauty, would then be made "enjoyable to all" through open spaces, green gardens, and tree-planted streets.[13] Canon and Mrs. Barnett had been previously forced to seek respite from the noise and dirt of Whitechapel parish by the acquisition of their own weekend cottage overlooking the future ground for the Suburb. Now Mrs. Barnett determined to transport the inhabitants of the city out to the country with her. In her first article on the Suburb she explains her dream clearly:

> Toynbee Hall [in Whitechapel] is but an artificial protest against the massing in one locality of the poor, whose engrossment in daily labour often makes them both deaf to higher calls and dumb to their own deepest needs. When the poorer people are crowded together in the mean, gardenless streets, the neighbourhood becomes less desirable for those who, being blessed with more of this world's goods, or who, having reached the "afternoon of life" wish to live with more repose, surrounded by the indefinite influences known as amenities. Those therefore, who are able to choose seek other neighbourhoods, and thus the poor localities are deprived of the contagion of refinement which contact brings, and the richer people lose the inspiration which knowledge of strenuous lives and patient endurance ever provokes.[14]

However well grounded her theories of housing and the slum may have been—and her tutelage under Octavia Hill and her apprenticeship in Whitechapel should have made them reasonably sound—what is still more engaging is her audacity in the face of the gigantic task she set herself. Primarily she was out to reform the suburb by reintegrating all classes within it. "The classes are divided in the suburbs as definitely as in the towns," she said.[15] She felt that laws such as the Housing Act of 1890 were further promoting this isolation by confining workers' housing to special areas.[16]

Within the career of the Barnetts social reintegration represented a second thought improving on the first. It had been their habit at Whitechapel to

13. The Hampstead Garden Suburb, the proposed church, to be dedicated to St. Jude, Jan. 1909 (Parker Collection).
14. Pp. 234–35.

15. Ibid., p. 231.
16. Mrs. S. A. Barnett, "Of Town Planning," *Practicable Socialism* (London, Longmans, Green, 1915), p. 266.

invite well-to-do, cultivated, and intellectual individuals into the East End to mix with the less fortunate. Mrs. Barnett felt that the flaw in this arrangement was that diverse groups could be brought together only on infrequent and formal occasions with a long journey home waiting for the outsiders. What was required now was a more natural, day-by-day coexistence which would sooner heal the estrangement of the classes. That this purpose was to be thwarted ultimately at Hampstead by the inevitable economic pressure which pushes values up as an environment is improved does not detract from the acuteness of her vision or the nobility of her motive.

The same inflationary force operated here which had caused George Cadbury to abandon his system of freehold at Bournville in favor of rents. Both Cadbury and Lever were trustees for the debenture stockholders of Hampstead Garden Suburb. As Mrs. Barnett too modestly declared, Hampstead "was not an original idea; Mr. Cadbury and Lord Leverhulme had already erected Garden Villages around their factories, and the proposal for a Garden City at Letchworth was attracting thoughtful attention."[17] But George Cadbury's influence is most often felt in the background, as was true also of the Rowntrees at New Earswick. Cadbury's image appears in the ideal of individual gardens worked for health and profit and roads bordered with flowering trees and hedgerows with sweet briar, yew, holly, and wild rose.

Like Lever, Mrs. Barnett was attracted by the uniform open front system. "It was in America that I first saw wall-less gardens, and great was the outcry when it was proposed to adopt the idea in the Garden Suburb."[18] A few open fronts were achieved at Hampstead, but generally the matter was again settled by conservatism and compromise. "Now nearly everyone agrees that hedges are preferable to walls," she reports in graceful capitulation.

Sir Robert Hunter predicted in 1906 that in the Hampstead of the future "The eye will roam over waving trees and smiling gardens, diversified rather than marred by the gables and chimneys of the homes of those who are swiftly borne from their work by tube or tramway into pure air and agreeable surroundings."[19] Special pains were taken to assure a blend of roofing materials and cornice lines (Fig. 84), which was also in accord with the final phases of the English domestic style when there was a revival of the hand-crafting of slate and the slightly more expensive sand-finished tile. Much of this attitude originated with Morris. He had already said,

17. Barnett, *Canon Barnett, His Life, Work and Friends,* p. 313.

18. Barnett, *Story of the Growth of Hamp-* *stead Garden Suburb,* pp. 61–62.

19. Ibid., p. 18.

Fig. 84. Air view of Hampstead Garden Suburb; Parker and Unwin, 1905. In the open Central Square are the two churches, Anglican and Free. In the foreground Meadway and Heathgate cross in an offset, showing German influence. Part of the Morris philosophy was that communities should look well from above.

Moreover, the smaller & more unpretentious a building is, the more effect the roof has in producing a pleasant-looking building: so that if the roofs of many of thousands of small homes throughout the country were of beautiful materials, we should have to-day comparatively little to complain of, and especially the beautiful landscape of the countrysides in England would escape the marring which it now almost always receives from ordinary modern houses.[20]

The first principle was harmony with nature. But the unity of roofing material would offer flexibility in other directions as well. Unwin reported about Letchworth, for example,

By keeping to tile roofs, a unity of effect is produced which in no other way could be so easily or completely attained. The securing

20. William Morris, "On the External Coverings of Roofs," *Architecture, Industry and Wealth,* Collected Papers of William Morris, *II* (London, Longmans, Green, 1902), p. 161.

of that degree of unity, moreover, allows greater freedom to be given in other respects, without injury to the whole effect. In the days when towns were beautiful places, and in nearly all towns that still are pre-eminently beautiful, much of this beauty has resulted from the almost universal use of the local roofing material.[21]

The recognition of the communal appearance of roofs was one reason why the modern flat roof never became wholly acceptable in Britain, despite its early and avid promotion by Edgar Wood, an acquaintance of Unwin's from Manchester.

The innovation of narrow grass verges with trees along the streets at Letchworth for screening purposes and the introduction of nature was a source of pride for Parker and Unwin. Earlier, however, where no space at all for nature could be managed, as in the Barnett's Whitechapel slum, a picture gallery had to be built as an alternative, for beauty's sake. This gallery was proposed in 1896 and was intended to become the "National Gallery of East London."[22] The Barnetts had already opened the Hull House Art Gallery in Chicago in June 1891 for their friend Jane Addams, who freely admitted their inspiration in this direction.[23] The Whitechapel Gallery facade by C. Harrison Townsend (1896–1901) is now almost as well known to art historians as Wright's epoch-making Hull House speech of 1901, "The Art and Craft of the Machine." But why did both of these galleries arise out of social settlement activity? Because these patrons of spiritual reform of urban slums were thoroughly convinced that beauty had to be made fundamental to urban life, not tangential or incidental. Regular exhibitions of pictures were started at Whitechapel as early as 1880 and had been going on for over sixteen years when the gallery itself was proposed.[24] From the lists of loans most of the exhibits seem to have been Pre-Raphaelite. The paintings of G. F. Watts were particularly favored.

Charles Rowley believed he had given the impetus for the gallery to Canon Barnett when he launched, also in 1880, his "first exhibition of high-class varied works of Art and Craft right among the people of our dreary Ancoats," the notorious slum of industrial Manchester.[25] Rowley in turn appears to have been inspired by a lecture Morris gave to the Ancoats Brother-

21. Raymond Unwin, "Cottage Building in Garden City," *The Garden City, 1* (June 1906), 108.

22. "The Whitechapel Picture Gallery," *Studio, 10* (1897), 130.

23. Jane Addams, *Twenty Years at Hull House* (New York, New American Library, 1961), p. 257.

24. Barnett, *Canon Barnett, 2,* 173.

25. Charles Rowley, *Fifty Years of Work without Wages* (London, Hodder and Stoughton, n.d.), p. 174.

hood in which he spoke movingly of the weight of "appalling ugliness" which hung over ordinary folk and put forward what Rowley believed to be the "childlike" notion that they would rise and rid themselves of the horror of their surroundings once they could be brought to see them in their true light.[26] However childlike the notion was, it was evidently shared by Canon Barnett. He wrote in a letter of 1906 about his own gallery,

> Then we are getting ready a Country in Town Exhibition for July, and I saw Imre Kiralfy on the subject. I hope he will get pictures done of East London as it is and as it might be. If only public opinion could be made disgusted with dirt, squalor, and meanness! It is so curious that people should be vain about dress, so anxious to look nice, and be so careless about their offices, the streets which they look at, and the buildings they inhabit.[27]

The passion for fusing superficially incompatible elements within a narrow compass is certainly Victorian (reinforced concrete, after all, comes from this same age), but even more interesting is the persuasion that the experience of art and beauty can be counted on to raise the level of the total culture. One of the ways in which the attitude might be forwarded would be through the exhibition of positive examples of art in the living environment, even in a slum, so that people might divest themselves of the tendency to identify beauty only with the faraway or unattainable, the dream-like sequence of Romanticism.

Edwin Lutyens carried out just a small portion of Hampstead Garden Suburb, but that part was of the greatest import because it was the Central Square. Christopher Hussey, in his biography of the architect, mentions that Lutyens was commissioned as consulting architect to Hampstead in the autumn of 1908 and was then asked to prepare designs for the central buildings.[28] He believed this was largely on the recommendation of Alfred Lyttelton, Chairman of the Board, for whom Lutyens was remodeling Wittersham, his country house near Rye. Lutyens' son puts the date two years earlier (1906), and Martin Briggs says it was 1907. Mrs. Barnett mentions that Lutyens was appointed as architectural advisor as soon as a board was organized (March 1906). But it matters little, since it is evident that a square was already suggested in that location on the first Parker and Unwin map of

26. Ibid., p. 130.
27. Barnett, *Canon Barnett*, 2, 179.
28. Christopher Hussey, *The Life of Sir*

Edwin Lutyens (London, Country Life, 1950), p. 188.

February 1905. Besides a church and chapel (which were built in other positions), Parker and Unwin planned a public hall, library, picture gallery,
and museum (all in one building), a bandstand, and an institute and club.
Surrounding it would have been quadrangles of homes for widows or single
ladies, "working lads, hostle, & c."

Despite the continuity of thought built up during the evolution of this
square, a certain rivalry about its origins and final form occurred among the
principals. Mrs. Barnett was the dominating personality, with her large concern for the social effects of architecture. Mr. Lutyens was occupied with
the relatively uncomplicated goal of achieving a monumental effect with
his buildings at the highest point in the Suburb, and Unwin again had a
foot in each camp. Few events of this period can better expose the militancy
with which the social reformer advanced the cause of art or the fastidious-
ness, verging on distaste, with which the fashionable architect circled a public problem. The Central Square experience also offers an opportunity to
understand why the big scale of American City Beautiful planning would
be inapplicable in Britain, despite the similar aspiration toward monumentality.

As previously mentioned, Mrs. Barnett had reported that about 1905 she
and Lord Crewe visited the undeveloped site and selected "this highest
place" for "the houses for worship and for learning." It seems equally
plain that Raymond Unwin felt that he was responsible for choosing this
spot. He says in an article on the Suburb in 1911, "I further felt it to be very
important to secure some good centre to the estate, which it was intended
should be developed as a community having a certain unity of social character."[29] And indeed, if Unwin's statement at Bournville on September 9,
1901, on his imaginary garden city be consulted, he seems to have had a
central feature like this firmly in his mind four years earlier, long before he
knew of Hampstead. He described it quite lucidly,

> Let us assume then that the general plan of our Garden City has
> been arranged in conformity with the land; and that sites for our
> civil, religious, and recreative public building have been deter-
> mined, dominating the city. Wide avenues or roads must be
> planned to lead off from these sites in all directions, so that
> glimpses of the open country beyond shall be obtainable from all

29. Unwin, "Town Planning at Hampstead," *Garden Cities and Town Planning* (April 1911), p. 7.

parts of the town, and vistas leading up to the finest buildings shall greet the visitor from every direction, giving impressions of dignity to those who come, leaving with those who go a remembrance of beauty.[30]

He then quotes the historical studies of W. R. Lethaby on the ancient building laws of Constantinople, which saved the open view toward the sea: advantage should be taken of a "hillside slope or wide diverging roads to preserve for the inhabitants a clear view of the landscape beyond." It is in exactly this position and relationship that the Central Square appears at Hampstead.

Despite the mild competition for credit between Unwin and Mrs. Barnett and their undeniable talent for self-assertion when the occasion arose, they were equally capable of self-abnegation. The importance of Christian behavior to both of them probably had a restraining effect at times upon their statements and modes of action. Yet Mr. Lutyens had been asked to assume responsibility for the final appearance of the central site at Hampstead, and his talent for dramatic architectural presentation and biting satire in speech and letter were legendary. A clash was inevitable.

The socially prominent reformer took precedence even over the socially prominent artist in late nineteenth-century Britain, and Lutyens knew it but he did not like it. Hussey can speak well for the architect on this score.

> In obtaining the agreement of the Board to his designs he soon came up against some opposition from Mrs. Barnett who, great-hearted and earnest philanthropist that she was, and taking her visual ideals very much, one imagines, from William Morris and cottagey things, saw her homely village–suburb being apparently magnified into a conception beyond her aspirations. "A nice woman, Lutyens described her tartly (to Herbert Baker, July 15, 1909) "but proud of being a philistine—has no idea much beyond a window box full of geraniums, calceolarias and lobelias, over which you can see a goose on a green."

He was evidently still smarting from the defeat Mrs. Barnett had handed him during the previous April and May when, riding roughshod over her board, she had insisted that his structures be lower in appearance.

---

30. Unwin, "On the Building of Houses in the Garden City," *The Garden City Conference* *at Bournville* (London, Garden City Assn., 1901), p. 70.

Mrs. Barnett was awfully upset about it. I want a certain height of building in a certain place for general effect. Mrs. B. dead against this certain height on the ground of other houses being overshadowed. They would naturally like not to disappoint Mrs. B., the pioneer of the movement and mother of Hampstead. I feel this, but the Board refers it back to *me*. Unwin warns me it will make things difficult. Alfred Lyttelton in agreement and enthusiastic.[31]

On her part the lady understood quite well what she was doing to Lutyens, for she refers to her own attitude toward his proposals as stubborn and tiresome, and she notes that he sighs frequently in her presence. But in the end all becomes sunshine. "To me he gave time, thought, ideas, innumerable comic drawings (mainly to illustrate our respective relations of loved tyrant and loving slave) and a friendship that storms cannot shatter."[32] It is possible to sympathize with both parties in this dispute, which finally led to lowering the cornice lines of both churches, Anglican and Free, to the level of the houses around them on the square, as Mrs. Barnett wished.

Of course Lutyens did not want to fumble this opportunity to assemble a truly architectonic composition upon a hill. The presentation of the grand ensemble on a higher plane has supremely dramatic possibilities, as was well demonstrated by Eliel Saarinen in the Cranbrook settlement near Detroit, which in many aspects is a continuation of Lutyens' best thought. The views up the streets of Hampstead demonstrate now that the leaded steeple, the Free Church cupola, and the bulk of the buildings beneath on the main square might have been raised with more telling effect, particularly since the grown trees today mute their prominence (Fig. 85). It is equally evident, however, that Mrs. Barnett had some reason to impose her preference on the architect, especially when one recalls the disturbing contrast in scale between the monumental and outsized Lady Lever Gallery at Port Sunlight and the small houses along its Diamond. Furthermore, if Lutyens had been more certain of his own tenets at the moment, which was a transitional one in his style, he might not have been so bothered by the resort to "cottagey" principles and could have sympathized with the absorption of Mrs. Barnett and Unwin in obtaining a visual and domestic synthesis for the community. They were most apt to view the Suburb from above the trees in bird's-eye perspective, where it was fully effective, while he looked at it from below.

31. Hussey, p. 191.
32. Barnett, *The Story of the Growth of Hampstead Garden Suburb*, p. 47.

Fig. 85. The spire of St. Jude's from Hill Close. From some angles the Central Square and its churches do not count as much as they might, just as Edwin Lutyens predicted.

What is highly significant in motif, regardless of the relative height of ground, cornice level, or spire, is the fact that with the committee's search for domesticity went (somewhat in contrast) its desire to make the church and chapel rise symbolically over the rest of the community. Hampstead has been criticized, along with Letchworth, for having public spaces in which people did not easily congregate; but the intent was to impress them—not to entertain or offer them recreation, or provide them with a shopping center. This, of course, would place the project somewhere between 1890 and 1910 in any western country. The English character of it consists of a peculiar mixture of domestic, ecclesiastic, and civic scales and the fact that it was intended to stir up old memories of the church spire above the country village. Canon Barnett hoped that this ancient relation would be further strengthened in other places, after he saw Hampstead completed.

St. Jude-on-the-Hill, Hampstead, was named for the humbler St. Jude's, Whitechapel, which was deplored for its cheapness even by the tolerant Canon Barnett and had to be torn down in 1923. At the dedication of the replacement on May 8, 1913, Arthur Foley, Lord Bishop of London, observed that although they were indebted to Unwin and Lutyens for the beauty around them, "Everyone here who knows the history of the scheme knows that the whole thing would never have been taken up but for Mrs. Barnett who, because she has seen what I have also seen—the misery and squalor of East London—was determined that others should share in the good things of life—art, music, scenery, the green grass and the flowers."[33] Mrs. Barnett scrupulously reports that she and Canon Barnett were not present to hear this fulsome praise, but it should be noticed in the Bishop's remarks that the "good things in life" are communal, not private. Half of them are man-made and half are natural, but controlled and cultivated. They had to be striven for—especially in the environs of London. It is regrettable perhaps that Parker and Unwin's planning masterpiece should be a suburb, instead of a garden city, but it also demonstrates that the suburb was a legitimate invention of the age, after all, which was only wanting the master touch to give it true form.

Lawrence Weaver felt that both Hampstead churches exhibited a larger dignity mixed with a domestic character.[34] Hussey also observes the domestic character of the square and its homogeneity with the houses around it, of which Lutyens completed about half before the job was taken from him, ostensibly because of impracticalities of internal planning. Hussey believes that Bentley's Westminster Cathedral may have influenced the designs. He notices that Lutyens' architecture has a strong pictorial quality, with its silver-gray bricks with red dressings, white window sash, balustrades, and big roofs. It brings to mind Shaw's Bedford Park in many of its features, but Hussey is convinced that these derive rather from Lutyens' enjoyment of Randolph Caldecott's pictures of little Georgian houses in nursery classics. Caldecott was a friend of the Lutyens family and had a direct influence on Lutyens' architecture in the same manner that Gertrude Jekyll personally affected his attitudes toward the building crafts and landscaping. Lutyens' son, Robert, looks upon the Square as providing the first significant transition between the country house and town planning in his father's work, with the two churches ending his earlier style, while the Institute for communal activities and education, which links them on the eastern edge of the ensemble, belongs to his middle phase, being more uncompromising in its

33. Ibid., p. 31.
34. Lawrence Weaver, *Houses and Gardens* by *E. L. Lutyens* (New York, Scribner's, 1914), p. 284.

formal symmetry.[35] Unwin felt that the big difference between it and the square at Letchworth was the use of "places" or enclosed subsidiary spaces with secondary buildings surrounding them.

After the firm received the commission for the Suburb, Unwin became resident partner there, making his home henceforth at Wyldes, the original farmstead on the southwestern fringe of the estate. Mrs. Barnett tells how she came to engage him in her story of the Suburb.

> In September, 1904, I was called suddenly away from Whitechapel by the serious illness of one very dear to me, and stuffing a few more dull documents into the bursting bag, I tore off for the train. Amid the anxieties attending the illness, I read on and on, not even noticing who wrote what, until putting down: I said, "That's the man for my beautiful green golden scheme."[36]

There may have been more to it because, as she later remarks herself, Unwin reminded her that he had been among her husband's social service followers at Oxford. His brother, William, also appears to have been Canon Rawnsley's colleague and did much of the "dog-work" while the National Trust was being organized by him, Sir Robert Hunter, and Octavia Hill at the Crosthwaite Vicarage, Keswick.[37]

Unwin realized he was up against a difficult topographical problem from the start. "The shape of the land was very irregular," he said.[38] The primary drawback was that where the eighty-acre tongue of the Extension came down off the Heath proper, it left only a narrow lip along each side which could be profitably developed (Fig. 86). This, in effect, threw the burden of financial and visual exploitation upon the southern slope of the hill below the Central Square. Unwin underlined the circumstance when he drew the boundary between the built-up slope and the open Extension by means of the terraced "great wall" with its summerhouses (Fig. 87), exemplifying his belief that the beauty of medieval towns partially depended upon the open countryside coming up to them "clean and fresh."[39]

The diversity and variety of layout patterns within a relatively small area

35. Robert Lutyens, *Sir Edwin Lutyens, An Appreciation* (London, Country Life, 1942), p. 46.

36. Barnett, *The Story of the Growth of Hampstead Garden Suburb*, p. 7.

37. Letter to author from Mrs. William Sully Unwin, Aug. 9, 1956.

38. Unwin, "Town Planning at Hampstead," p. 6.

39. Unwin, "Building & Natural Beauty," *The Art of Building a Home* (London, Longmans, Green, 1901), p. 84.

Fig. 86. Map of Hampstead Garden Suburb.

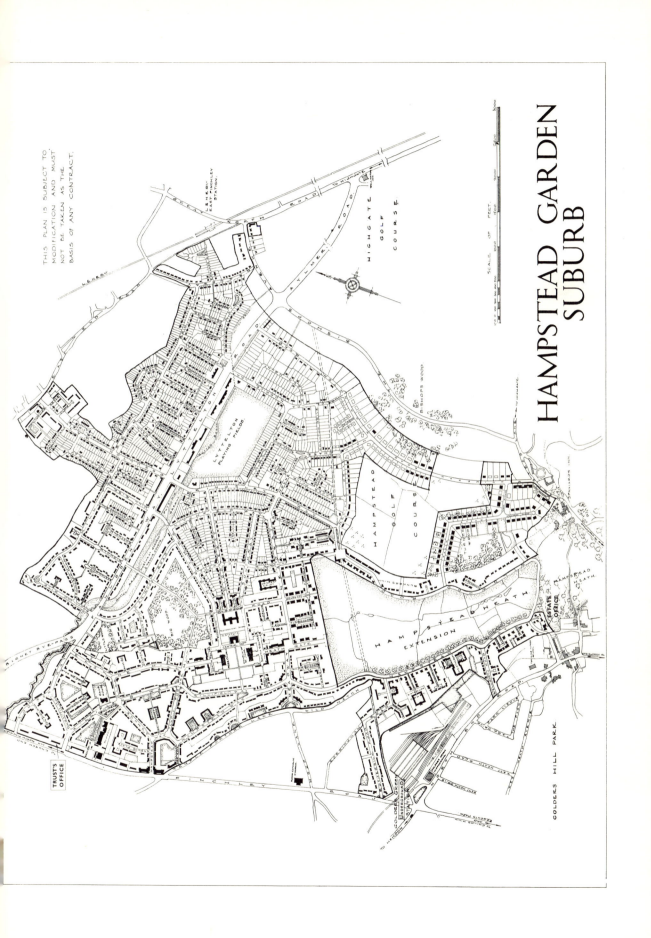

HAMPSTEAD GARDEN SUBURB

Fig. 87. Great wall on the Heath Extension, Hampstead. Unwin wanted a town that made a clean break with nature and was secure within, as towns were built in the Middle Ages. At Hampstead the automobile was somewhat the enemy without.

at Hampstead were due to one major reason and several minor ones. Basically they reflected Mrs. Barnett's policy of seeking to attract the widest range of social and economic representation. That this was more than a pious hope is evident from the prices of homes offered for sale in the early prospectus, ranging from £425 to £3,500. The middle-class villas were to be built on the western portion of the estate. On the southern end, around the Extension, would be placed the large houses of the affluent. These were expected to subsidize the ground rents of the approximately seventy acres of workers' cottages to the north.[40]

Today the biggest error in Hampstead and Letchworth is often accounted to be the lack of through roads and provision for traffic. His defenders have only claimed that Unwin could not have anticipated the awesome number of motor cars that would appear in the twentieth century.[41] Yet, contrary to what is usually assumed, Unwin did take cross-circulation into account at Hampstead. He declared: "There was no call to provide for any very important through lines of communication, and there seemed no probability of any large amount of through traffic passing over the estate, though one or two routes of secondary importance might possibly in the future develop from east to west."[42] Later this happened with the Barnett By-pass.

The road system within Hampstead was then by no means an accident or

40. Unwin, "Town Planning at Hampstead," pp. 7–8.

41. E. L. B., "The Jubilee at Letchworth,"

R.I.B.A. Journal (Sept. 1953), p. 442.

42. Unwin, "Town Planning at Hampstead," p. 7.

an afterthought. It was simply calculated from the first for the benefit of those living in the community and secondarily for those passing through. Unwin makes no apology for his negative attitude toward automotive traffic.

> The idea that a town consists of streets is to be very much avoided. Streets are not a virtue in themselves. In fact, the less area given over to streets, the more chance one has of planning a nice town. To be obsessed with the idea of planning for traffic is a mistake. One rather plans to avoid all needless traffic as far as possible.[43]

The proportions of circulation at Hampstead dwindle and descend from roads and streets to the lane and way, then to the pedestrian close and walk, and finally to mere paths. At the same time, the road was not permitted to pick up spatial momentum. Unwin set about recapturing the medieval implication of mystery, safety, and enclosure within the settlement. In an expanse covering originally only 243 acres, concern for the pedestrian has reason and weight. As Rasmussen has described it,

> Other suburbs of the day consisted of parallel roads of standard width, whether they carried through traffic or merely served as accesses. In Hampstead the road net is differentiated in order—well equipped roads for the primary traffic routes and cheap little narrow roads as private access to individual houses. It is like a tree with branches, an organic pattern channelling traffic down to the smallest leaves of the plant.[44]

The "smallest leaves" fed by the organic pattern were, of course, the cottages. It was Unwin's misfortune to attempt to reinstate the home as the focus of the community just as the automobile was beginning to devalue this concept. This was a historical mishap, but all that needs to be acknowledged for Hampstead now is that he *did* include the automobile in his calculations and that his plan was not intended to be valid for a whole city, because he was dealing primarily with a limited area where people dwelt rather than worked or shopped.

The wish to further a mood of inwardness, of serene self-contentment, in the community brought him ultimately to the court or quad. Unwin and Parker make it plain that they were consciously reviving motifs which had

43. Unwin, *Columbia University Lectures, 1936–37*, p. 46.
44. Steen Eiler Rasmussen, "A Great Planning Achievement," *Town and Country Planning* (July 1957), p. 286.

been outlawed by earlier reforms, especially the courts and yards which had been corrected by the bye-law streets. Their explanation for doing so was that all urban instruments and principles were meaningless if interpreted out of phase. Unwin wrote,

> Another bye-law which is not uncommon is that against roads having no through way, known as cul-de-sac roads. This action has, no doubt, been taken to avoid unwholesome yards; but for residential purposes, particularly since the development of the motor-car, the cul-de-sac roads, far from being undesirable, are especially to be desired for those who like quiet for their dwellings.[45]

Modern solutions could not be considered final because the problems themselves kept altering. To emphasize his point, with the help of John Burns Unwin shepherded the "Hampstead Garden Suburb Act," a private bill, through Parliament in 1906. This suspended the local building regulations. The most important provision encouraged the creation of closes and cul-de-sacs by permitting roads to be chopped into lengths of less than 500 feet and their carriageways to be reduced to 12 and 16 feet. There was evidently something in the nature of a trade involved, with the looser street net allowed by the government in return for the unusually low density of eight houses per acre over the whole plot.

Unwin felt that modern man needed to be, above all, open-minded and inventive in his approach to urban problems. One of his unique values for his own time was that he refused to be overawed by many of the "improvements" which were then taking place. It appeared to afford his partner some amusement that Unwin would cancel one well-intentioned reform by another. "It was characteristic of Unwin, that he could not rest content that existing legislation should thwart us in this, but secured the passing of The Hampstead Garden Suburb Act, under which it was accomplished."[46]

The immediate reason for the 1906 Act was undoubtedly the difficulty of building along the narrow lip of ground around the Heath Extension. Yet there were older and deeper causes behind the need to further particularize the forms. Mrs. Barnett would be the last to be satisfied even with a normal range of income levels within her suburb. She wanted the whole rainbow of human existence plainly visible. Being a Christian, she felt that a

45. Unwin, *Town Planning in Practice* (London, Unwin, 1909), p. 393.
46. Parker, "The Life and Work of Sir Raymond Unwin," *Journal of the Town Planning Institute* (July–Aug. 1940), p. 161.

place in the Suburb for the lame, the halt, and the blind had to be found. She insisted not only on an educational center and a school of art, so that "a knowledge of all that is lovely" might be spread, but also believed "in the beneficial influence on normal people of the weak, the handicapped and the young."[47] Both she, in trying to make allowance for the unfortunate or non-normal person, and Unwin, in attempting not to be stifled by the conventional house and street, ignored at their own risk some great and impersonal forces within the contemporary situation. Fortunately, they found common cause in the essential purpose and form of the charitable institutions of Hampstead. Most of them were to be built around tiny courts or greens, such as The Orchard for old people (1909) by Parker and Unwin (Fig. 88)

Fig. 88. The Orchard, Hampstead; Parker and Unwin, 1909. This was a quadrangle for older people. Parker and Unwin's scale tended to be small, the second story lower, and the gable and roof edges more picturesque than those of their contemporaries.

or Waterlow Court for working women (1911) by Baillie Scott. There was a blind people's quad intended too, but never built. As planners Unwin and Parker were also interested in the quadrangle because it reduced road costs by taking up less frontage and made the street more interesting visually. One

47. Barnett, *The Story of the Growth of the Hampstead Garden Suburb*, p. 62.

cannot entirely discount the influence in this respect of Oxford, the youthful home of Unwin, nor the ancient recollection of medieval almshouses, but much of the feeling appears to come from the memory of the colony of Edward Carpenter in Derbyshire and William Morris' speculations about long, low, quadrangular guest houses. It was the possibility that the warmth of human association could be stimulated by the quadrangular pattern that intrigued Unwin most. "Why should not cottages be grouped into quadrangles, having all the available land in a square in the centre?" he asked in 1901 in *The Art of Building a Home* (which may have been the booklet that inspired Mrs. Barnett to hire him). "Some of the space so often wasted in a useless front parlour in each cottage, could be used to form instead a Commons Room, in which a fire might always be burning in an evening, where comfort for social intercourse, for reading, or writing, could always be found."[48] All the better houses on the south slope from the Central Square down toward the Heath Extension were likewise grouped around modest greens. Unwin says again,

> So long as we are confined to the endless multiplication of carefully fenced in villas, and rows of cottages toeing the same building line, each with its little garden securely railed, reminding one of a cattle-pen, the result is bound to be monotonous and devoid of beauty. It must be our effort to counteract this tendency and to prove that greater enjoyment to each householder can be secured by grouping the buildings so that they may share the outlook over a wider strip of green or garden—in fact, that by some degree of co-operation more enjoyment of the available land can be secured than by dividing it all up into individual plots, and railing each in.[49]

This presupposes that there would be some general control and pooling of land in every development, and that has proven a hurdle not easily surmounted.

If there is one objection that may be conscientiously made against Hampstead, it is that Parker and Unwin's repertoire had, by this time, a tendency to proliferate too often and far. If Letchworth was too loose, Hampstead was in some places overly organized. One becomes aware of this possibility even in their early domestic architecture, as with their use of double inglenooks,

48. Unwin, "Building & Natural Beauty," p. 104.

49. Unwin, *Town Planning in Practice*, 2d ed., p. 353.

or when they strive overhard to demonstrate the advantages of their "twelve to the acre" motto. They were self-educated in the literal sense and partially lacked the inner restraint upon which more formally trained minds can often draw. In compensation, however, all ideas appeared to them fresh and uncommitted, and they never lacked courage to apply them. In this respect they made excellent partners for both Mrs. Barnett and Ebenezer Howard. A good instance of this open-mindedness and its employment is contained in the German influence on Hampstead.

A book by Baillie Scott and others, *Town Planning and Modern Architecture in the Hampstead Garden Suburb* (1909–10), states that the Suburb was "laid out mainly on German models."[50] Thomas Mawson, in writing about British planning and landscape in 1911, said the German style was inspired by medieval cities. Since it was an outgrowth of local needs and circumstances in Germany, he had some reservations about its being introduced wholesale into Britain. He writes,

> It is known in this country as the informal method, and may be said to correspond to the landscape gardening of Capability Brown in its avoidance of straight lines and its preference for twists and curves. Whilst this method often produces happy effects, its weakness for short irregular vistas, each terminating in its little clock turret or other device, is at times irritating.[51]

Unwin did adapt at Hampstead the German mode for massing buildings and achieving more effective street pictures. It is possible that he was becoming anxious about whether the simple English domestic style, as practiced at Letchworth, could hold its own in a more elaborate setting closer to London. The employment of Lutyens to do the monumental Central Square suggests that this attitude was prevalent among the Board of Directors, at least. Unwin reports that he did not know Camillo Sitte's *Der Städtebau* (1889), which he takes to be the classic of German planning theory, when he laid out the center of Letchworth. He did know it by the time he carried out Hampstead,[52] where he appears to have been searching for an antidote to the monotony of the English bye-law street (against which his own Hamp-

50. M. H. Baillie Scott and others, *Garden Suburbs, Town Planning and Modern Architecture* (London, Unwin, 1910), p. 15 (1st ed. summer 1909, called *Town Planning and Modern Architecture in the Hampstead Garden Suburb*).

51. Thomas Mawson, *Civic Art Studies in Town Planning, Parks, Boulevards and Open Spaces* (London, Batsford, 1911), p. 71.

52. Unwin, *Town Planning in Practice*, 2d ed., p. 225.

stead Garden Suburb Act was passed) and particularly to offset its indifference to converging perspective. He explains in his review of Hampstead what he was attempting in this reference:

> In suburban roads, where the houses stand far apart in relation to their height, straight roads are apt to be unsuccessful for want of any definition in the centre of the picture, hence it is desirable that the length of such roads should not be too great without some break. The buildings may be brought forward at certain points to partially close and define the view and to replace by a portion of building standing approximately square with the line of vision a part of the street picture which would otherwise be filled with the fronts of the buildings seen in too acute perspective to be interesting.[53]

The offsets, focal points, curves, and angles produced in the Hampstead streets as a result of these rules encourage through traffic as little as the cul-de-sac and inner green, but as visual elements they are almost uniformly satisfying. Only at the secondary center of the Suburb, where he purposely piles up shops and flats on either side of Hampstead Way as it empties into Finchley Road (Fig. 89), does it seem to be overdone in the way Mawson feared. Unwin says that he resorted to height in order to screen out some objectionable buildings and a large pub across the street, and internally to furnish a backdrop for the roads feeding into the subsidiary public green, which was supposed to have a reflecting pool in its center. He had wanted to create a hollow marketplace and a public forum there. Externally the massing of the buildings does provide a monumental entrance to the Suburb, their greatest virtue.[54] The tower of the Clubhouse (1909) on Willifield Green (Fig. 90) (destroyed by bombs in World War II), such houses by Unwin as the seventy-six artisans' flats on Addison Way, with their steep roofs, square towers, and balconies, the small place at the offset crossing of Heath Gate and Meadway, and the "great town wall," all suggest German precedents, especially from medieval Rothenburg and Nuremberg, which Parker and Unwin so greatly admired.

53. Unwin, "Town Planning at Hampstead," p. 83.

54. Mr. John Brandon-Jones has told the author, and other sources suggest, that A. J. Penty did much of Hampstead when he worked for Parker and Unwin, particularly this main entrance. W. H. G. Armytage mentions Penty in his *Heavens Below* as a man deeply interested in the applications of Christianity to labor movements (pp. 406, 435). See also obituary in the *London Times* (Jan. 23, 1937).

Fig. 89. Shops at Hampstead Garden Suburb; Parker and Unwin. This was the major example of German influence at Hampstead. In effect it was a monumental gate.

Fig. 90. Clubhouse on Willifield Green, Hampstead; Parker and Unwin, 1909. Its tower was partly influenced by the German picturesque. It was Old English in its effort to provide social interaction around a court and on a playing field or green.

As Bruno Taut put the matter in speaking generally, without reference to Unwin, "The aspects of the mediaeval German towns gave nourishment for romantic sentiments to the cool, organizing Englishman."[55] But in spite of the impression that some of Unwin's buildings done under German influence are contrived, it is clear that he was not uncritical of the German School. Unwin holds a reserved attitude toward both American and German planning:

> While, therefore, it is to be hoped that we may learn much from the scale and breadth of treatment adopted in the great town-planning schemes of America, we may also learn from the German school both a greater respect for the opportunities afforded by the undulations and other characteristics of the site and a greater appreciation of the possibility which town planning affords for the creation of beautiful architectural groups of buildings, one of the imaginative aspects of the art of town planning which is not so apparent in some American work. On the other hand, in studying German work for the sake of the careful adjustment of the plan to the site, we shall be wise to remember the natural and proper part that formality and symmetry play in architectural grouping, and, by the careful study of Classic and Renaissance planning, learn to appreciate the importance of maintaining simple, orderly, broad lines of design, characteristics which we find lacking in many German plans, where the designer seems sometimes to neglect the broader elements of his art in undue concentration on a somewhat forced picturesqueness of treatment in the minor details.[56]

The difficulty was, of course, that being English, Unwin would be instinctively receptive to the picturesque, no matter from what direction it came.

Parker and Unwin's work at Hampstead may also appear to lack the marks of inward tension and struggle—to be too clear, clean, and wholesome, as the artist Townsend remarked of Letchworth. But it is incorrect to believe that it therefore lacks depth or is in any respect trivial. Anyone accustomed to employing maps of cities in day-to-day planning may be impressed in studying Letchworth or Hampstead to discover how easily each part of the town remains in ones' memory and how these images, when put together,

55. B. Taut, "Characteristics of German Town Planning Up to Date" (Letchworth, International Garden Cities and Town Planning Assn., n.d.).

56. Unwin, *Town Planning in Practice,* 2d ed., p. xvii.

constitute a satisfying whole. The intervals of verdure, the intimate and modest scale throughout, and the effect of privacy radiate a definite feeling, a national aspiration, controlled and guided by a large measure of technical skill. It is difficult to entertain the possibility that a map can be a work of art in itself, rather than a stage on the way to one, but in the diagram for the original part of Hampstead, where the houses are as varied in size and grouping as Mrs. Barnett might have wished, the synthesis appears almost like a rich musical notation. We know Unwin collected older maps for their own interest, and he sometimes compared good planning to music.

In the elevation too there is a special character, a happy rhythm of composition, difficult to describe. Rasmussen, again, puts it very well.

> Some town planners (usually Germans) have interpreted town planning as the art of creating enclosed spaces. And others—as Le Corbusier—have reacted against this theory and maintained that we must recapture the open horizon: the town should be transferred into a green landscape with enormous trees and tall buildings dotted round here and there. I shall always remember that afternoon with Unwin in Hampstead, that day in the quiet study and on the large Heath, as a lesson in better understanding: man must have both, the enclosed wall as well as the open space. . . . We live as rhythmic beings, changing through the hours of the day. We can be active, longing for freedom and openness in the morning, and still—like the flowers that close at sunset—want the warming feeling of protection and peace in the evening and night.[57]

That the quest for open and closed spaces and viable dimensions in time was not merely a figment from Rasmussen's imagination is evident from Mrs. Barnett's original essay.

> It will be an essential condition of building that the dwellings of all classes be made attractive with their own distinctive attractions, as are the cottage and the manor house of the English village; the larger gardens of the rich helping to keep the air pure, and the sky view more liberal; the cottage gardens adding that cosy, generous element which ever follows the spade when affectionately and cunningly wielded as a man's recreation.[58]

57. S. E. Rasmussen, "A Great Planning Achievement," *Town and Country Planning* (July 1957), p. 285.

58. Barnett, "A Garden Suburb at Hampstead," p. 235.

If Hampstead is a kind of graphic music, then it is a peculiarly haunting melody, for at Vällingby and Farsta, the Swedish new towns, these spatial rhythms are still being explored. Sven Markelius writes in discussing the new town plans and architecture for Stockholm, as late as 1956,

> There can be different opinions as to which is preferable, the intimate scale and the natural contact with neighbours which is achieved in this way, or anonymity and the feeling of distance and space which can be achieved in an environment dictated by the scale of multi-storied buildings with big proportions and a large number of people.[59]

In 1909 John Burns secured passage of the first national town planning act, in partial emulation of the Hampstead Garden Suburb Act of 1906. In 1914 Raymond Unwin left private practice to become Chief Planning Inspector to the Local Government Board and later, in 1918, Chief Architect for Building and Town Planning to the Ministry of Health, which put him in a very favorable position to influence the wave of postwar housing legislation. About the same time Parker expanded the scale of his operations. In August 1915 he went to Oporto, Portugal, for four months to design a civic center, which was not completed, and from January 1917 until February 1919 he was engaged in São Paulo, Brazil, on a garden suburb and parks for the City of São Paulo Improvements Co., Ltd.[60] As the partners were coming into national and international prominence the conditions of practice were changing. The government, partly at their urging, was beginning to recognize its responsibility for better planning and housing. With World War I private philanthropy would disappear along with great private wealth. Most important from the visual side would be the creative void imposed by years of armed conflict and, after that, less confidence in the common sense and good will of men, which had been the basic faith of Morris and Howard. It is therefore with some melancholy that one observes the architects of the English domestic style carrying out their last great cooperative enterprise in the buildings of Hampstead Garden Suburb.

Unwin was the supervising architect of Hampstead until 1914. Succeeding him up to 1951 was J. C. S. Soutar, who persisted in the effort to maintain some kind of stylistic continuity. He was followed by F. J. Landor. Parker

59. Sven Markelius, "The Structure of the Town of Stockholm," trans. by D. and P. Holmgren, *Byggmästaren* (1956), A3, p. 75.

60. Mrs. Barry Parker, material available for a memoir of R. B. Parker, typescript, Parker Collection.

and Unwin's own domestic work there fell mostly between 1909 and 1911. After 1912, and especially with the building of Lutyens' Central Square, there was a gradual relinquishment of the picturesque gabled house with its prominent chimneys, roughcast walls, and casement windows in favor of the more formal brick neo-Georgian with white-sashed, double-hung windows and hipped roofs. C. Harrison Townsend and M. H. Baillie Scott (Fig. 91) both worked at Hampstead (also at Letchworth and Gidea Park). Other architects were C. Cowles Voysey, C. M. Crickmer from Letchworth, and Edgar Wood from the Manchester area. Geoffrey Lucas (Fig. 92), E. Guy Dawber, and W. Curtis Green were all men who had been active in the restudy of local styles, and some of this experience is evident in their houses at Hampstead, especially those featuring recollections of the Cotswold District, which Unwin himself considered the epitome of the authentic folk tradition in England.[61]

In contemplating the environment which these men fashioned at Hampstead, several thoughts come readily to mind. The first is that the spirit of the preindustrial folk architecture has been adequately employed to re-establish a mood of rural peace and security close to the city which, of course, was Hampstead's original function (as a resort area for London). The techniques for emulating the mellowing effects of time had become well enough understood to have general currency. Unwin believed that the beauties of the old towns largely depended upon the higher quality of individual buildings, simply constructed, and upon the weathering of surfaces and softening of lines as the timber frames sagged. The implication was that the architect was needed now, more than ever, because only he had the perception to discern these subtleties. As soon as his supervision was removed, houses were bound to degenerate into routine, unimaginative, minimal types. As Unwin writes of Hampstead, "It was the architect in almost every instance who was the first to cooperate with us; the speculative builder in many cases preferred to go elsewhere. This was also true in our experience at Letchworth."[62] When there was no longer a living tradition to guide or restrain the builder, the architect was even more necessary.

Hampstead was also another attempt to provide an answer to the issue raised long before by Disraeli. In his novel *Sibyl: or, The Two Nations*, he

61. Martin S. Briggs, "The Plan and Architecture of Hampstead Garden Suburb," pp. 294–97. Also "The Hampstead Garden Suburb and Its Architecture," *Builder* (Aug. 30, 1912), pp. 250–56; *Architectural Review* (June 1922),

pp. 225–28; and Lawrence Weaver, The "Country Life" Book of Cottages (2d ed. 1919), pp. 250–53.

62. Unwin, *Columbia Lectures*, 1936–37, p. 13.

Fig. 91. Houses facing Hampstead Way and Meadway, Hampstead; M. H. Baillie Scott. The two great houses by Baillie Scott at this spot typify the last effort to scale up to the street, begun at Port Sunlight. Grey roughcast, red tile roofs, oak beams, and brick panels reflect the authenticity of materials, first recommended in the Queen Anne style.

Fig. 92. Lucas Crescent, Hampstead; Geoffrey Lucas, pre-World War I. Lucas was one of the architects who most carefully studied old English cottage styles, particularly those of the Cotswold district, which Unwin also considered the best of the traditional.

has one of his good characters declare, "There is no community in England: there is aggregation, but aggregation under circumstances which make it rather a dissociating than a uniting principle."[63] The amelioration early proposed was social justice, followed by economic adjustment and better living conditions. Finally came the recognition of the need for a wider aesthetic and psychological range in the whole urban pattern. The conscious identification of this need came fairly late, but the problem was an early and lasting one as was the talent to settle it—the British pictorial imagination. The Hammonds bring this out well in their study of industrial England from 1832–54.

> The men and women who now lived in blind streets had lived, themselves or their fathers, beneath the open spaces of heaven. In the high moments of his history man has answered the beauty of nature with the beauty of cities, but for these exiles the dreams of mind and hand were as faint and distant as the mountains and forests whence those dreams had come. No public grace adorned their towns; religion was too often a stern and selfish fantasy; music and painting were strangers, at home among the elegant rich, but doubtful of their welcome in this raw confusion.[64]

Disraeli's indictment was that no true communal feeling had existed in England since the Middle Ages. It was the Hammonds' contention that although overseas wealth had poured into England during the nineteenth century, there was little manifestation of this on the more elevated side of human creativity. Religion, art, all aspects of urban life had degenerated before the onslaught of radical change brought on by the accumulation of wealth and efficiency.

Disraeli was no amateur in interpreting social and political signs, nor were the scholarly Hammonds. Neither was Canon Barnett, who spent so many years working in the slums of London's East Side. What he says on the subject of beauty has the authentic ring of personal experience and comes remarkably close to the notions of the Hammonds.

> Yes, the Church, familiar with the lives of inhabitants of mean streets, can speak with authority. It can tell how minds and souls are dwarfed for want of outlook, how pathetic is the longing for

63. (New York, Dolphin Books, Doubleday, 1961), pp. 82–83.
64. J. L. and Barbara Hammond, *The Age* of the Chartists *1832–54* (London, Longmans, Green, 1930), pp. 364–65.

beauty shown in the coloured print on the wall of the little dark tenement, how hard it is to make a home of a dwelling exactly like a hundred other dwellings, how often it is the dullness of the street which encourages carelessness of dirt and resort to excitement— how, in fact, it is the mean house and the mean street which prepare the way for poverty and vice.[65]

These commentators seriously believed that as physical rebuilding took place, a charting of new social and aesthetic goals would be required. The artist, contrary to popular expectation, would have a high priority on the list of socially desirable individuals. It was he who had been chosen by earlier societies for bringing color and spiritual conviction to these communal values. In Unwin's estimate this incorporating function would even be a first need:

> We have been considering almost exclusively the practical utility and the economic facility of regulating our town development on better lines than in the past; but the purpose of all this is to make of our towns dwelling places more fitting for a race of beings who do not live by bread alone, but who require also mental culture and an outlet for the expression of their spiritual aspirations. . . . When sociologists and surveyors have settled the requirements, and economists and engineers have settled the possibilities, then we, as our forefathers did, must call in the man of imagination, the artist, to clothe these requirements in some beautiful form.[66]

Canon Barnett broadly reinforces this with his observation, "The Church might help town-planning as it might help every other social reform, by charging the atmosphere of life with unselfish and sympathetic thought,"[67] precisely the generous attitude which Howard perceived would be necessary to invoke for his garden city movement. But the Church had lost the secular power it held during the Middle Ages and could no longer directly influence the urban environment. It was this double lack which caused Pugin to draw his *Contrasts* of English cities and institutions of 1840 to those of 1440, with a heavy bias toward the earlier. It has the close familiarity of chronic pain and there is a touching recognition of the enormousness of the task of overcoming the unfortunate contrast of old and new in the relationship be-

65. Canon S. A. Barnett and Mrs. S. A. Barnett, "The Church and Town Planning," in *Practicable Socialism* (London, Longmans, Green, 1915), p. 302.

66. Unwin, "The Town Extension Plan," Warburton Lectures, *13, 14* (Manchester, The University Press, 1912), pp. 60–61.

67. Barnett, *Canon Barnett, His Life, Work and Friends,* 2 (London, Murray, 1919), 321.

tween Unwin and Barnett—the artist and the churchman—both improvising but determined to be morally and perceptively responsible. The family legend is that Raymond Unwin as a youth had asked Canon Barnett whether he ought to go into the Church of England. Barnett asked in return whether Unwin was more troubled by the unhappiness of men or their wickedness. When Unwin replied that he was concerned only with their unhappiness, Canon Barnett advised him not to go into the Church. The priest and the artist were then to play closely parallel, but different roles. The association is represented in all its essentials in the career of Morris too, with his early interest in the Church; and later in the life of the Dutch artist, Van Gogh, with his unhappy venture into school teaching and the ministry, and his final resort to painting, devoted to the same spiritual quest. A similar attitude appears in Barnett's writing after he had been scolded for the frivolity of art exhibits in the Whitechapel settlement. In rebuttal he wrote in 1883,

> If to anyone the thought occurs, that art exhibitions will not save the people, I at once concur; but I submit that neither will preaching nor any other means. It is the working together of many influences—and the brush of the artist may be inspired as the tongue of the speaker—which creates the tone of mind in which the Love of God and the love of men become possible.[68]

To humanize rather than brutalize the urban population was their aim, and the artist could be an important agent, really the only hope, toward this goal. He symbolized the Victorian dream of multiple causes bringing forth multiple effects which at last could be reconciled in an outward, visible harmony to which everyone would be entitled.

How much of a success this effort was at Hampstead may be measured again through the sensitivity of the Dane, Steen Eiler Rasmussen. He explains that when he is asked to consider Hampstead as a technical achievement, he becomes instead

> "quite sentimental, almost as if I had lived there in my childhood. Here for the first time I experienced what modern town planning can achieve, and when I see other examples of urban planning I cannot help comparing them with Hampstead—often to their disadvantage. To me it is inseparably connected with the personality of Sir Raymond Unwin whose humanity I see displayed in every road and place.[69]

68. Ibid., p. 168.
69. Rasmussen, "A Great Planning Achievement," p. 283.

The highest test is that even the expert not only thinks well of the community, he feels well within it. And he discerns the artist through it.

The artist in this view is not a Bohemian, detached and in revolt against a shallow society, somewhat in the D. H. Lawrence manner, but an equally sensitive yet gentler person, a kind of chivalric hero. He alone could stimulate a renewed appreciation of an environment which had lost its universal meaning as a center of well-being for the whole population through the overexcitements of specialization. Even the concept of "artistic genius" is a symptom of this, according to W. R. Lethaby, the sage of the Arts and Crafts movement. He felt that he understood it almost too well.

> Beauty is not some strange phenomenon only to be attained by a genius in a dream . . . the faculty for design has been allowed to fall into disuse and decay under the supposition that it is a special "gift" only to be exercised by a sort of "inspiration" . . . Everyone really has the designing—the contriving and experimenting—instinct, and driven in our days out of work (sad unemployment!) it has found refuge in games. Our delight in games largely depends on the fact that we may in them freely experiment and make variations.[70]

The game was at least socially active. To wean the people from passivity, to stimulate them out of their unwholesome lethargy, was an urgent necessity from Morris' viewpoint. The artist and art should be the chief instruments for this revival, but if its true spirit could only be recognized still through games, then even they would be valuable in pointing the way in which the society ought to progress. Unwin knew this too and said so, "It is perfectly true that on these commons the squire's son and the agricultural labourer's son do play together. We are trying to keep this attitude and conception of recreation alive in England, and to extend it. In the Hampstead Garden Suburb, for example, a village green was placed opposite the clubhouse."[71] The understanding of the way to live in communal or democratic association had declined in Britain during the nineteenth century until it could be found only on the playing fields of remote villages. The positive virtues were hidden, but not dead. Someone was needed to fan the spark into a flame again.

70. *Catalogue of the Exhibition of the Red Rose Guild of Artworkers*, Foreword by W. R. Lethaby (Manchester, Oct. 1921).

71. Unwin, *Columbia Lectures*, 1936–37, p. 61.

11. WYTHENSHAWE

 The Wythenshawe Satellite City of Barry Parker (without Unwin this time) has a maturity from which any flaws in execution can hardly detract. As Parker's last and largest work (1927–41), it exhibits an assurance he could not have commanded at an earlier date. By this time he was a qualified expert, universally respected. The ease with which he refers to planning developments in Europe, Canada, the United States, and Brazil when he discusses Wythenshawe suggests an international authority.[1] When his humble start as an apprentice decorator under Armitage in nearby Altrincham is recalled, one cannot but realize how far the artist, turned architect, turned planner, has come in his career. The absence of a required formal degree or registration for practice surely had something to commend it, for it permitted Parker a professional mobility which he otherwise could never have exercised. This condition was indispensable for the ultimate realization of the Arts and Crafts philosophy and partially explains why the revolt against the registration of architects in the early 1890s was led by Norman Shaw and his pupils and was so vehement.

Wythenshawe's greatest misfortune was that it lay between two World wars and athwart a great depression—various emergency programs and expedient adjustments would interfere with its systematic realization. But its temporal position also coincided with the emergence of the kind of settlement that both Howard and Unwin had contemplated for some time, the self-contained subcity or "satellite garden town." Chronologically it fitted as nearly as could be wished between Letchworth and Harlow New Town. In a newspaper article of August 1945 at the close of World War II, Parker stated that Wythenshawe "is now the most perfect example of a garden city."[2] His positive evaluation rested on the fact that the increment on the land as a

1. Sir Ernest and Lady Simon, *The Rebuilding of Manchester* (London, Longmans, Green, 1935), p. 18.

2. "Letchworth Architect Talks to Women Housing Managers," *Letchworth Citizen* (Aug. 10, 1945).

result of its development would return to the municipality, fulfilling Howard's hope in a way that Letchworth had so far been unable to do. Associated with this in Parker's mind was the impression that Wythenshawe was a heartening way station on the road to national planning. In the same interview he is quoted as saying, "Today there is no national planning . . . There is a certain amount of sewing together of local plans, each containing an industrial area, but this does not create a national plan and it does render a proper distribution of industry and population impossible." He felt that the Manchester Corporation knew what it was about, and the national government should likewise have the power to carry out its own best intentions.

Wythenshawe did meet some early resistance from county and rural district councils, but the political and financial strength of Manchester prevailed. There were two aspects in this situation that seemed to fascinate Parker. The first was that the taxing and borrowing power of a great city ought to permit the heavier capitalization and rapid growth which had not been possible at Letchworth. As partial proof, by 1935 Wythenshawe had already outgrown Letchworth and Welwyn, in spite of its much later start.[3] The second was that these same powers would enable a logical sequence in putting a town together. Schools, particularly, could be built before the arrival of the children in the town.

It might be said from the national aspect that Wythenshawe rose out of the "Homes for Heroes" campaign and the Tudor Walters housing report of 1918, which was greatly influenced by Unwin as a government official. He mentions in his notes that the town was contemplated as early as 1919. What Manchester also apparently did was to transfer the causes of its crowded and unsavory (and highly profitable) slums to its satellite. The proprietor was different, but the crisis remained: the density would be reduced, but the number of less fortunate people needing accommodation would be relatively constant. Therefore Wythenshawe was conceived initially for 80,000 to 100,000 inhabitants, rather than the more conservative 30,000 to 35,000 of Letchworth. It was inadvertently thrust into the population class of a new town long before the new towns were built.

After World War I nearly 2,000 acres of land had been purchased by the Corporation for housing within Manchester itself, at an average price of £400.[4] Ultimately there was no land left, even on the outskirts of Manchester, except on the north where the ground was rough and the atmosphere

3. The Simons, p. 18.   4. Ibid., p. 15.

bleak and smoky. In the center of the city the density of housing units was as high as sixty per acre. By buying the ancient Tatton Estate of 2,500 acres southwest of the city in 1926 and later adding several thousand acres more, the land cost was reduced to £80 to £100 per acre, well below the £300 limit which Parker believed to be the breaking point for high-density housing. It still appears to have been £40 to £60 above the price of the land on which Letchworth was built. The site was protected by the prevailing southwest wind from the smoke of Manchester itself. Professor Patrick Abercrombie made a special report approving the site.

Besides the twelve-to-the-acre standard, there were many other limits carried over from the past that qualified the undertaking. We read in the early stages: "A special provision has been made in Wythenshawe of including, in its plan, sites suitable for all purses and all classes of society; we thus avoid the danger of creating a satellite town populated exclusively by one class, made up of those bordering on or just above the poverty line."[5] However, the aim was not realized, even after encouragement to developers to build larger houses for private sale. In the postwar *City of Manchester Plan* of 1945 the admonition still had to be repeated, "A proper distribution of income groups within the estate should be quickly obtained. In both these respects including more rapid industrialisation the development of Wythenshawe has been deficient in the past."[6] Working against this appears to have been the depression-born tendency to drop building standards for minimal housing as far as possible, and the tardiness of the city itself in installing sufficient amenities.

There are echoes out of the past in some of the architecture of the 1930s too, such as in Chamberlain House or Mitchell Gardens (Figs. 93, 94). It is easy to recognize in their flared gables, arched doors, contrasting window sizes, and white walls some of the mannerism that typified Parker's designing as far back as Earswick. His mansarded cottages, possibly influenced by German examples, were also unusual in design—long, low, and full of repose, with a savings expected from the elimination of a full second story (Fig. 95). Parker always sustained his end-of-the-century feeling for expressive content in architecture, much as Unwin preserved his ability in writing and speaking to communicate the expressive episode. Nine- and twelve-story flats have now been built on the estate.

5. Alfred P. Simon, *Manchester Made Over*, with a foreword by Barry Parker, p. 12 (London, King, n.d.).

6. R. Nicholas (Norwich and London, Jarrold, 1945), p. 156.

Fig. 93. Chamberlain House, Wythenshawe, 1931–39, single-person flats. It had white walls (in the early Parker and Unwin tradition) originally.

Fig. 94. Mitchell Gardens, Wythenshawe; terrace bungalows for old people.

Fig. 95. Mansarded cottages, Wythenshawe; Barry Parker, 1930–39.

Despite the municipal parsimony which inhibited the power of the body politic, upon which Parker pinned his hopes for Wythenshawe, the search for beauty in the environment continued. In 1929 Wythenshawe Hall, which had been presented with its 250-acre park to the city by Sir Ernest and Lady Simon, was opened as a Branch Art Gallery. Alfred Simon repeats the conclusion advanced by Unwin and others; "How different Manchester might have been had the leaders of industry, the elected representatives, and the chief officials of the municipality in the past, one and all, in addition to their other qualifications as economic, legal or scientific specialists, had that of taste trained to eye values!"[7] The persistence of some of these issues within the movement gives one the sensation of *déjà vu,* of moving again and again through the same experience. As the adherence to tradition furnishes continuity of thought, so the conservatism in the handling of materials and methods and patterns of layout sometimes proves a detriment. For instance, at Wythenshawe in 1953 a report was still being made on the possi-

7. *Wythenshawe, Plan and Reality* (Manchester, Municipal Information Bureau, 1953), pp. 105–06.

bility of open fronts, which was revolutionary half a century before, but ought by now to have led to alternative solutions, since this attempt evidently ran so counter to national custom. Still the official booklet on Wythenshawe announces that, "Open development is under experiment, which means there are no front fences and no garden gates."[8] The choice of materials after World War II was not quite so rigid, and we read in the same booklet that one type of house had a steel frame with cladding of aluminum or corrugated steel sheets. Another had a honeycomb wall of foamed slag or glacial rubble. Yet another displayed a light concrete frame covered with precast concrete slabs.[9] The relaxing attitude of labor toward new materials appears to have had something to do with these experiments.

After the second war also there was increased agitation for two other building programs. One was the proposal of ten neighborhood units, each with its own shopping center, community and health service, a church, one or two licensed premises, and a cinema.[10] The other was for a large shopping and civic center of sixty-seven acres in the southeast quadrant of the plan. There was a growing conviction that the town had achieved no logical focus and that its social atmosphere was becoming "somewhat anaemic" owing to the lack of communal facilities.[11]

There is an implication in the literature that these building programs are a favorable departure from Parker's plan and intention, but a careful examination of his proposals shows that they represent more of an alteration in emphasis than any major change in policy. He had already specified a town square, although it was to be in the southwest quadrant and a little smaller than the shopping center. His plan also has a similar number of minor shopping centers and primary schools, worked out on "open air" principles with as few main roads as possible to cross in order to get to them, following the Radburn model.[12] Parker often used the American term, "Neighborhood," in his original discussions relating to Wythenshawe. And, of course, the meaning of the term depended upon the school as its center. So the principles had not failed. What occurred instead was the frustration and forgetfulness of cumulative delay. Manchester did not obtain full control of the land until 1930. By March 1934 only 4,606 houses had been built. By 1939

8. Ibid., p. 3.
9. Ibid.
10. *Manchester and How It Is Managed* (Manchester, Municipal Information Bureau, n.d.), p. 154.
11. Nicholas, p. 145. See also Wesley Dougill, "Wythenshawe: A Modern Satellite Town," *Town Planning Review* (June 1935), p. 212.
12. Barry Parker, "Highways, Parkways and Freeways," *Town and Country Planning* (Feb. 1933), p. 42.

and the outbreak of the war only 8,145 houses were finished for a population of 39,180. Having been inspired by the first war, the town was only half finished when construction was halted by the second outbreak of hostilities.

Altogether it is Parker's vision of what the garden satellite city might be, rather than what it did become, that is most informative. His original plan included approximately 5,500 acres, of which a thousand would constitute a greenbelt for permanent agriculture and a thousand more for open green space of one kind or another within the community itself. One thinks by way of difference of the industrial cities in the North of a century before, which provided no access at all to the sun and open air and, by way of similarity, of Olmsted's Riverside of 1869–71 (about the same distance out from Chicago as Wythenshawe is from Manchester), with its strips of green and its projected parkway joining it to the city. The inspiration for the Princess Parkway at Wythenshawe (Fig. 96), the first in Britain, apparently did come from America, particularly from the parkway system of Chicago, of which Unwin was well aware, and of Westchester County, New York, with which Parker seemed best acquainted. The latter had visited Philadelphia, Chicago, and New York while attending the International Town, City and Regional Planning and Garden Cities Congress in New York City in 1925. Howard and Unwin were also there. It is likely that Parker was made additionally conscious of the New York version through Thomas Adams, who had been the first secretary of the Garden City Association, the editor of its magazine, the first manager of Letchworth, and President of the Town Planning Institute before he departed first for Canada (1919–21) and then for the United States to take charge of the regional plan for greater New York with its parkways (1922–31).[13] Sir Ernest Simon in discussing Wythenshawe also refers to the parkway as an American invention. Parker sees in the device the resolution he had looked for all his life, the closer tie between the functional and the beautiful in a community. "So again it has been proved that that which is best practically is best aesthetically, and parkways evolved to meet traffic, and other needs, meet those needs artistically."[14] The ironic result was, of course, that the parkway tended to become autodidactic, evolving its own rules and environment out of key with the rest of Wythenshawe.

The houses were 150 feet back from the parkway, and limited access from

13. Parker, "Where We Stand," Presidential Address, Town Planning Institute, Nov. 1929 (Parker Collection), pp. 8–9.

14. Parker, "Wythenshawe," lecture given before the Chartered Surveyors Institution, n.d., Parker Collection, p. 8.

Fig. 96. Princess Parkway, Wythenshawe. Although this first parkway in Britain appears to have been directly inspired by the American examples around New York and Chicago, the broad verge and rows of hedges and trees are quite British.

side streets occurred approximately every quarter mile (Fig. 97). With these two qualifications, it is interesting to notice the variations Parker worked out of them. He thought first of the parkway as an alternative to the ribbon or strip development, abolishing at one stroke the usual "shoddy houses, cheap shacks, petrol filling stations, garages, advertisement hoardings, shabby tea-rooms,.and miserable shops."[15] The parkway would offer a further advantage, he said, in keeping four lanes of traffic permanently open, whereas a more conventional in-town street usually had two of its lanes occupied with parked cars. Drawing upon his earlier economic precepts, he pointed out that the service roads running beside the main artery could easily be paid for by eliminating the more customary short-length streets of multiple access. The partners were forever robbing Peter to pay Paul, the justification in their minds being that Paul deserved it more than Peter. The willingness to tamper with or reconstruct the urban value system, especially through phys-

15. Parker, "Site Planning at New Earswick," *Town Planning Review* (Feb. 1937), p. 19.

ical arrangements, was always one of the characteristics of the garden city group.

After this, Parker went on to distill various supplementary benefits from the parkway: the areas of green would not only provide a buffer, like the earlier cul-de-sac, against "the dust, smell and noise of motors on the main roads" but also avoid the waste of many of the more formal or inaccessible open spaces. These "pedestrian parkways" would be usable for daily routines. They would follow the direction of the main streams of traffic but still

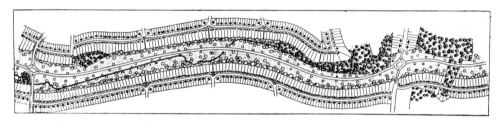

Fig. 97. Parkway with limited access as developed by Parker for Wythenshawe. The parkway looks like a giant plant stem or a backbone with its units of cells and its emphasis on circulation. Through "organic" evolution in planning, a "superform" has come into existence. The necessity of great size in modern planning has led toward this, as did the proximity factor and the greater contrast in scale. The "living" quality in organic planning is not so vital as the more complicated relation of part to part.

be protected from them (Fig. 98). They would screen the houses from cars, break down the scale of transition from moving to static objects, and boost residential values through the older English device of gaining by looking out on green.[16] They would supplement the more conventional parks but not replace them.

One of the objections to the Parker plan after World War II is that too much traffic was beginning to pass through the garden satellite city. More was to come as Princess Parkway was extended out from Manchester beyond its first stopping point at Altrincham Road. Parker had devoted so much care to Wythenshawe's internal circulation, made it so efficient, that he literally flooded his city with traffic. Manchester's record might be vulnerable in any number of ways, but the charges against it could always be minimized, for "What is one more crime when Manchester has committed so many?" The paradox of Wythenshawe was instead that of a large art object exposed in an open field, where its very prominence demanded uncompromising standards of judgment.

Parker says,

16. Parker, "Highways, Parkways and Freeways," p. 38.

Fig. 98. Path on Princess Parkway, Wythenshawe. With the amount of walking in Britain, such a path had an internal amenity value equal to or greater than the roadway itself, which was mainly for through traffic. This side benefit was exploited by Parker.

> When we come to consider the town plan for the Wythenshawe Ward I may be asked where are the ring, circumferential or orbital roads which are to be found in other town plans. Such roads are reasonably effective, as compromises, meeting the traffic requirements of existing towns, so closely built up as to preclude the possibility of introducing anything more effective.[17]

He had projected the parkway directly through Wythenshawe because he was aware of the inordinate length and, hence, cost of a ring road. And to him the ring seemed an inferior thought. He had decided by 1933 that in the interest of the orderly growth of cities, through-traffic roads should come out of the city as parkways or freeways, and the old radial streets could be left as developmental roads (Fig. 99). Extended into the greenbelt, this reasoning would allow main highroads between communities to remain as conventional arteries. Other newer roads or parkways would then be built

17. Parker, "Wythenshawe," pp. 8–9.

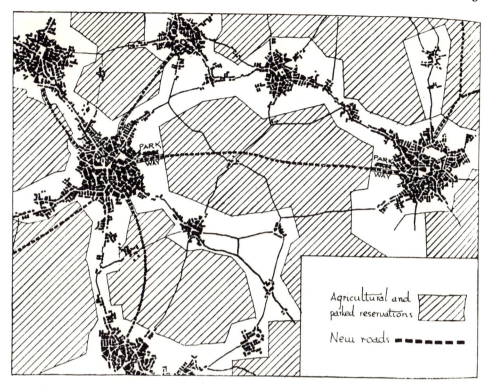

Fig. 99. Parkway in Parkland diagram; Barry Parker, 1937. This was one of Parker's last ideas for combining the greenbelt with the parkway, anticipating the high-speed, linear, landscaped freeway between cities.

parallel to them through open agricultural land. Their much wider right-of-way with limited access would allow the greenery to be more satisfactorily protected than the old rear-guard action along existing highways against creeping commercial and residential strip development. He almost arrives at a linear city like Benoit-Lévy's *Paris s'étend* concept of 1927 when he observes in passing,

> Still, just as it is natural to lay new through traffic roads between the points of the star forms which towns tend to assume, it is natural also to visualise that those who build new traffic roads will make use of the opportunities afforded by the openness of agricultural belts and to foresee settlements forming *between* "parkways" and "freeways" and separated one from another by the parkland comprised within these parkways and freeways.[18]

18. Parker, "Highways, Parkways and Freeways," p. 41.

The greenbelt in Parker's philosophy was beginning to be elongated rather than circular because he felt that was more consonant with the velocity and direction of traffic.

When it came to intersections, he introduced islands or roundabouts. The first one in Britain had appeared at Letchworth, at the end of Broadway. It is possible to trace their origin back to France, for Unwin cites Eugène Hénard's "Études sur les Transformations de Paris" for the *carrefour à giration* in his *Town Planning in Practice* (1909). The idea in actuality was too timidly handled at Wythenshawe. The radius was not wide enough for the amount of traffic to be accepted. Although Parker hoped that the roundabouts might be useful in reducing speed as well as promoting continuous flow, he realized fairly early that he had been too cautious in this regard. "It has already become clear that we have islands at Wythenshawe which are considerably smaller than they should be, but possibly not too small to function tolerably well."[19] After the second war, overpasses were to be substituted.

Parker had become wrapped up in what he often referred to as "the present motor age." In attempting to combine the hexagonal schemes of the city planner of Ottawa, Noulan Cauchon, with the Radburn Plan of Stein and Wright (1928–29), he appears to be carrying this preoccupation further into the fabric of his planning. It is known that the authors of Radburn had discussed their ideas with him in 1924, and he mentions the Radburn Plan in his report on Wythenshawe to the Corporation of Manchester in May 1928. He also says that the parkways, "bound neighbourhood units, and schools are so placed that no children cross them when going to school, nor need people cross them when going to shops," much in the Radburn vein, even though Radburn was just getting under way.[20] He was interested at the time in the decentralization of elements like churches and playgrounds for easier walking distance, and the Radburn influence fell right in with this too because it permitted the older superblock figure to be hollowed out for the purpose (Fig. 100). In substance he took his own cul-de-sac theme, put it in the Radburn version of the superblock, and then framed it with a Cauchon hexagon (Fig. 101). Cauchon had demonstrated to his satisfaction that,

> a saving of ten per cent. on the length of road per house, and there-
> fore on the cost of road per house, would be made by the adop-

19. Parker, "Wythenshawe," p. 6.
20. Parker, "Manchester's Satellite Town," typescript, n.d., Parker Collection, p. 9.

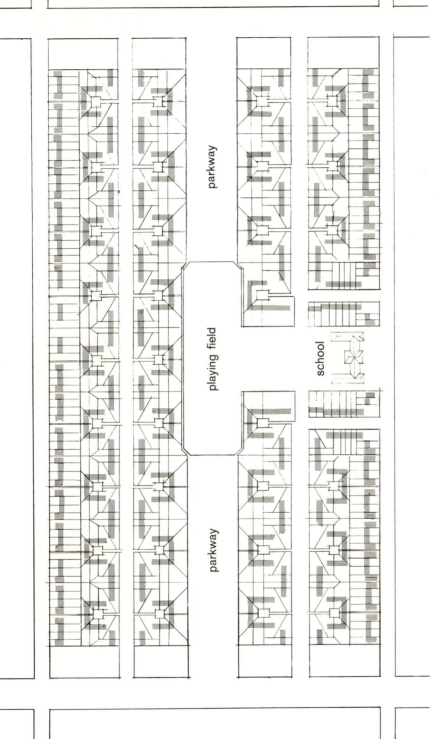

parkway

playing field

parkway

school

Fig. 100. Barry Parker's "improvement" on the Radburn Scheme, May 1928. The aim was to handle both pedestrians and automobiles more safely. This plan improvises on a theoretical plan of January 1928 by Stein and Wright. See Toward New Towns for America, Figure 16.

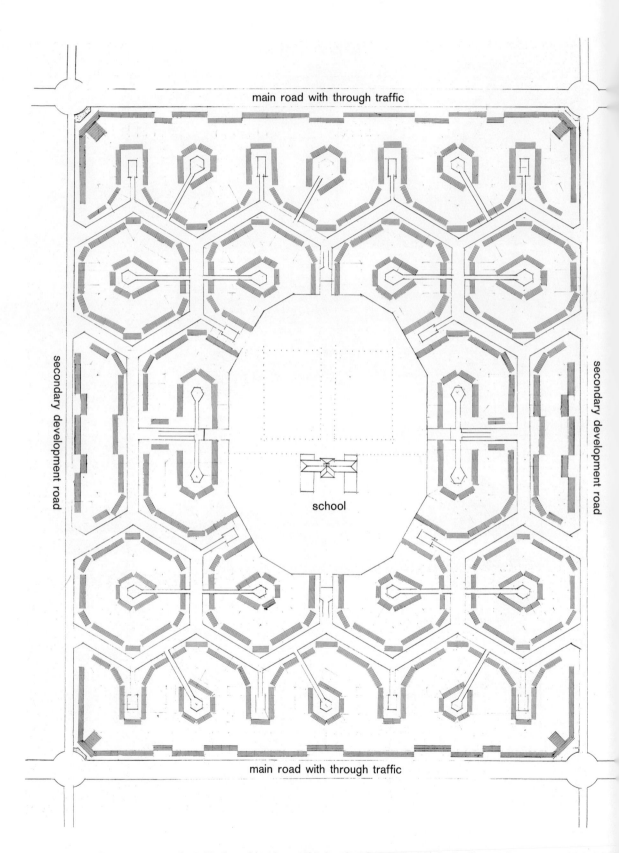

main road with through traffic

secondary development road

secondary development road

school

main road with through traffic

Fig. 101. Barry Parker's ideal combination of the Cauchon hexagon with the Radburn Scheme.

Fig. 102. *Pimpernel wallpaper; William Morris, 1876. The botanical analogy of organic growth that likened the parkway to a branch or a stem reappears when the Cauchon–Stein–Parker hexagon is compared with this Morris wallpaper. Unwin likened city design to wallpaper, in terms of the harmony desired. Parker had begun his career as a wallpaper and textile designer, as did Baillie Scott and Voysey. Under the impetus of the Crafts Movement, the microform naturally and easily became the superform.*

tion of the hexagon in substitution for the rectangle as the basis of a lay-out, and that the adoption of hexagonal planning caused there to be no right angle road junctions, and therefore only unusually safe road junctions and road junctions at which every driver could see all oncoming traffic long before he met it.[21]

On paper the Stein–Cauchon–Parker hexagon looks too farfetched to be workable. It is as pretty and botanical as a Morris wallpaper (Fig. 102). Part of this effect comes from the elements like houses and roads being clustered at Wythenshawe into larger patterns so that they become more generalized, objective, and abstract, more potentially "decorative." This could happen with any planner, however. What has to be remembered with Parker specifically is that he, like Voysey and Baillie Scott, first designed wallpapers and fabrics in the Arts and Crafts manner for a living. There is a poetic aptness in the fact that next door to Altrincham, where he began in the minor arts, he finished with his last and largest satellite town. His career extended from the microform to the superform. Neither he nor Unwin considered these two arts of composition to be totally unrelated; as is plainly evident from such articles by Unwin as "Urban Development, The Pattern and the Background." He began that essay on first principles by observing that, "to introduce the conception of large scale planning as a pattern on a background a beginning may be made by considering this relation in smaller and simpler designs in which the harmonising of use and beauty can readily be illustrated. In a wallpaper, ..."[22]

So farfetched that it looks like a wallpaper. Too farfetched to be an integral part of an actual layout of a community until one remembers the characteristic open-mindedness of the partners which carried them from art to art and idea to idea. They were as hospitable to others' thoughts as they were to other men. A scrutiny of the map around Wythenshawe Park shows a few of these hexagons (Fig. 103) in modified form actually implanted and already working.

The functionalism of postwar automotive technology and the functionalism of the environment, on which Parker and Unwin had labored for decades, seem about to meet and merge at Wythenshawe. Everything appears to have reached a fitting conclusion until one reads a final sentence by Parker. He has become so imbued with enthusiasm for the parkway that he feels:

21. Parker, "Wythenshawe," p. 9.
22. *Journal of the Town Planning Institute* (Aug. 1935). p. 254.

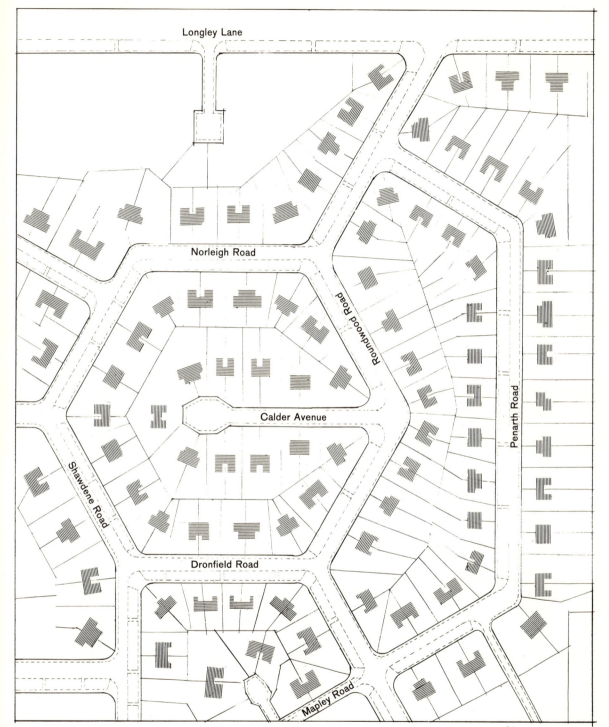

Longley Lane

Norleigh Road

Roundwood Road

Penarth Road

Calder Avenue

Shawdene Road

Dronfield Road

Mapley Road

Fig. 103. Actual settlement in Northenden District, Wythenshawe—the approximation of the Cauchon hexagon that Parker was able to place in his settlement.

SCALE 1/800

"In these roads there must be separate 'carriage-ways,' one for mechanically propelled vehicles, and another for horse-drawn vehicles, saddlehorses and bicycles, and separate tracks will perhaps be provided for trams."[23] He is obviously being influenced by American and German boulevards, perhaps even recalling Olmsted and looking forward to Corbusier's "seven ways," but this statement, made as late as 1929, had something anachronistic about it. Today the form seems correct, but the content too late. The horse-drawn vehicle has disappeared, so has the tram. The bicycle may not be far behind, especially in open country with high-speed roads. Parker and Unwin never stopped thinking, but the conditions never stopped changing either. Despite the municipal sponsorship, the flaw of Wythenshawe was essentially that of Letchworth. It took overlong to build. Theory, uninhibited and international as it now was, never quite caught up to changing technology.

23. Parker, "Where We Stand," p. 6.

12. THE ARCHITECTURE OF PARKER AND UNWIN

The artistic life of Barry Parker began at the same Manchester Royal Jubilee Exhibition from which Port Sunlight may have derived its style and atmosphere. His artistic education was initiated at the Simmons Studios in Derby in 1886. He next went to London and the South Kensington Art School for three months. In 1887 he returned north to become an articled pupil to G. Faulkner Armitage (d. 1937).[1] Armitage had drawing offices and a workshop and smithy at Stamford, Altrincham, southwest of Manchester, and long held a prominent place in the public, social, and religious life of the district. One of his more interesting activities was service on the Committee of the Manchester Art Museum, which flourished from 1877 to 1901 when it was amalgamated with the University Settlement. It devoted itself to "the better acquaintance of children and ordinary people with design and craftsmanship in the objects of everyday life." Parker did some frescoes for the Armitage firm.

At the 1887 Jubilee Exhibit Armitage was commissioned to decorate the central nave and dome of the main building. He also "showed some excellent rooms—kitchen, parlour, bedroom, designed by him for the use of the working man in which the furniture was very good and substantial."[2] A sketch of the Armitage kitchen (Fig. 104) suggests the later warmth and utility of Parker's domestic interiors, particularly in its focus on the brick fireplace, its high-back settle, and builtin cupboards. The search for an ideal cottage was already discernible in the work of Parker's master along with the ancillary problem that was destined to plague Parker and Unwin far into the future—how to arrive at a superior and tasteful effect, "at a price such as a thrifty artizan could be supposed capable of paying."[3]

1. Mrs. Barry Parker, material available for a memoir of R. B. Parker, typescript, Parker Collection.

2. Walter Tomlinson, "The Pictorial Record of the Royal Jubilee Exhibition in Manchester, 1887" (Manchester, Cornish, 1888), p. 67.

3. Ibid.

An Artizans
Model
Living Room
designed for
Mr Neville Clegg
by G. F. Armitage

Fig. 104. Artizan's Model Kitchen, Manchester Jubilee Exhibition; G. F. Armitage, 1887. Armitage was the first employer of Barry Parker. The builtin cabinets, simple furniture, and useful objects featured as ornaments follow the trend of the period and predict the bent of Parker's interior designs.

Armitage showed more interior designs at the Arts and Crafts Exhibition at Manchester in 1891 and, at the Exhibition of 1895, wallpaper and a hall, room, and gallery.[4] Walter Crane, the longtime associate of William Morris, wrote the catalogue of the 1895 show. In July 1896 Crane founded the Northern Art Workers Guild in Manchester, no doubt in emulation of the London Guild which originated in Norman Shaw's office in 1883. The aim of the new Manchester group was

> to unite within its ranks artists and craftsmen of every kind, with the one desire and purpose of breaking down the barriers that have too long separated the architect, the painter, and the sculptor from the metal-worker, pattern designer, wood-carver, and potter, to the lasting detriment of all our work. The one gospel which

4. *Studio,* 5, 128.

such a body must maintain is the essential unity of all the arts, and their true foundation in vital handicraft.[5]

The honorary members of the Guild were R. Anning Bell, Lewis F. Day, Frederic J. Shields, and Charles Rowley—the man who had, or thought he had, an influence on the Barnetts' establishment of the Whitechapel Art Gallery in a London slum, and for whom Unwin had also done volunteer work at the Ancoats Brotherhood.

By 1903 Parker and Unwin were firmly entrenched in the Northern Art Workers Guild as members of its nine-man council. Their business address at the time was "The Quadrant, Buxton," around the corner from John Carr's more famous Crescent of the last quarter of the eighteenth century. Sixteen items of architecture and furniture by Parker and Unwin were displayed in 1903, most through photographs and drawings. They ranged from a sundial to a whole hamlet, and included a full-size mock-up of an ingle-nook, one of their most representative motifs. The feature of the exhibit was their "Cottages Near A Town" display (Fig. 64). Edgar Wood, a past master of the Guild, was the other architect of repute having a place in the exhibit. Unwin spoke of him at the end of his own life as one of the earliest of "modern architects," although he noted that Wood gave up architecture for painting around 1920, when he left to live in Italy.[6]

In the display there was a hint of moral as well as aesthetic obligation. Just the year before, Unwin had written, "Every house should be designed to suit its site and aspect, and this is not less necessary when dealing with small houses built in rows, but more so."[7] Behind this declaration lie four pertinent circumstances. (1) The design exemplifies the two architects' final conception of what should be done with fringe areas of a town just as they were about to undertake the layout of an independent garden city. (2) What was presented was primarily a variation on the theme of the row house in the old bye-law street. Manchester was probably the Northern industrial city in which this type was most numerous. (3) A planning exhibit was actually present in an arts and crafts show. Planning had not been mentioned as one of the arts in the original prospectus of the Guild, and Parker and

5. *Catalogue of Works Exhibited by Members of the Northern Art Workers Guild at the City Art Gallery,* Manchester, Sept. 26–Oct. 22, 1898 (Manchester, Chorlton and Knowles, 1898).

6. Raymond Unwin, *Columbia University Lectures,* 1936–37, p. 17. See also John H. G. Archer, "An Introduction to Two Manchester Architects: Edgar Wood and James Henry Sellers," *R.I.B.A. Journal* (Dec. 1954), pp. 50–53.

7. Unwin, *Cottage Plans and Common Sense* (Buxton, 1902), p. 4.

Unwin themselves realized that this might appear incongruous; but they had an explanation ready: beauty and planning *should* be related. "In many departments of life and industry the claim of beauty or art is reasserting itself with no little success, but in no sphere of activity probably is there greater need for this influence to be felt than in that which is concerned with the laying out of building areas."[8] (4) Ruskinian social and economic thought was alluded to as a source of permanent authority. "Undoubtedly, whenever at all possible of attainment," observed Unwin in 1902, "the majority of men would accept Mr. Ruskin's ideal of a house: 'Not a compartment of a model lodging house, not the number so and so of Paradise Row but a cottage all of our own, with its little garden, its healthy air, its clean kitchen, parlour and bedrooms.' "[9]

This quotation from Ruskin appears to have had wide currency. M. H. Baillie Scott, whose ideas and buildings often approach those of Parker and Unwin, also repeats it in an article of 1897 and then continues: "if it seems to you impossible, or wildly imaginary that such a household should ever be obtained for the greater part of the English people, again believe me the obstacles which are in the way of our obtaining them are the things which it must be the main object now of all the science, true art, and true literature to overcome."[10] The general vision of the family unit as the beginning of planning was to become ineradicable in Parker and Unwin's efforts.

The major novelty in the house plan was the through living room (Fig. 105). "Living rooms with windows in both their end walls should unquestionably always be provided in every non-parlour cottage," advised Parker.[11] And it was the partners' preference that eventually every cottage should be a non-parlor cottage. They considered the parlor an extravagance, as did many earlier architects. The stairwell opened into the living room to avoid the cold and dark passage or lobby. For protection, a shallow porch was provided at the front door. An indirect result of the emphasis on the "open" plan was the concern for circulation. It was directed into a free space, reminding one curiously of the plans at the turn of the century of the Viennese architects like Wagner, Hoffman, and Olbrich, who took care of directional needs in open space with striped patterns on the checkerboard floors, indi-

8. Barry Parker and Raymond Unwin, *Cottages Near a Town*, Catalogue of Northern Art Workers' Guild, p. 43.

9. Unwin, *Cottage Plans and Common Sense*, p. 4.

10. Baillie Scott, "On the Choice of Simple Furniture," *Studio, 10* (1897), 156–57.

11. Parker, *Architecture and Home Organisation*, Foreword by Barry Parker (London, Assn. of Teachers of Domestic Subjects, 1926), p. 3.

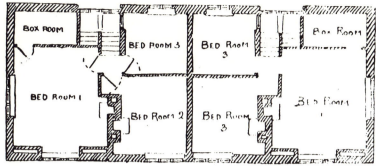

BED·ROOM PLAN

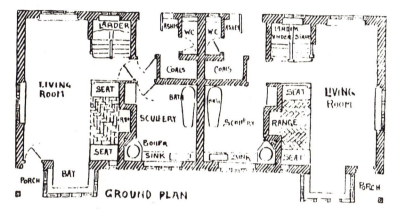

Fig. 105. Plan of a semidetached house from the pamphlet, "Cottages Near a Town," Parker and Unwin, 1903.

cating where best to walk. Light, air, and footsteps are all involved. The living room should be so arranged, the partners say, "that the main traffic lines will not cross those spaces where people are likely to sit, turning the whole room into a passage." And on the same page they add in a slightly bustling manner, "Doors should not open across, or opposite to the fire. A window should be well placed for lighting the space where people will sit round the fire, and above all things a door intervening between the fire and this window must be avoided, and of course the fewer doors opening directly into the living-room the better."[12] The moment the subject of open or flowing space is brought up it becomes necessary to recall that the British, American, and Continental versions of this must be different because of the lack of central heating in Britain. The whole secret of this kind of planning in Britain says Unwin, is to "give the best ventilation with the least discomfort."

12. Barry Parker and Raymond Unwin, *Cottages Near A Town*, p. 40.

The plan of the small semidetached cottage exhibits the Parker and Unwin stamp everywhere within it. The inglenook, the bay projection, the shallow front porch, and the tiny covered service yard at the rear identify their new brand of thought. It is the minimal architecture of economy, but it has an expansive factor in it too.

Before our eyes light is transformed from a hygienic agent, in the older housing tradition, to an activator of space for mental stimulation. The majority of the houses were oriented to the south, always an important aim for Parker especially, and the kitchen was combined with the scullery and placed at the front of the house so that the housewife might have "a sunny aspect and a pleasant outlook." Physical and mental health were to be blended in a psychosomatic relationship. "Sunlight coming from the south is more health-giving, cheering and invigorating"[13] asserts Parker. Unwin sums up the basic philosophy by proclaiming: "It is as necessary for mental and spiritual health that man should live in beautiful surroundings as it is for his bodily health that he should dwell under sanitary conditions."[14]

The trend toward associating sunshine with wholesome living, health, and beauty is everywhere in evidence toward the beginning of the twentieth century, but it has a peculiar intensity in Great Britain because of the overcast and northern latitude. Unwin reports, "Over the greater part of our country, certainly in the Midlands and the North, the importance of arranging for the few days when the sun is oppressive is small indeed compared with that of planning to suit the many days when every hour of sunshine is of the utmost value."[15]

If one compares such work as the Steiner house by Adolf Loos in Vienna (1910), or the Banning house in Los Angeles (1911) by Irving Gill, or even the phantasmal dwellings of Tony Garnier's Cité Industrielle (1901–04) in France, one can see that the Stanley Parker Cottage on Wilbury Road in Letchworth (1908) and the Aitken House on Cashco Lane (1914) (Figs. 106, 107) are stylistically similar expressions of a more innocent, pre–World War I proto-Internationalism. All that is conspicuously missing are the flat roofs, the prescripts of mechanization, and the assertive forms of Cubism. It was, no doubt, the break in succession caused by war that led Katharine Gilbert to puzzle over the persistence of the "one good word, clean" in her pioneer

13. "Letchworth Architect Talks to Women Housing Managers," *Letchworth Citizen* (Aug. 10, 1945).

14. Unwin, *Town Planning in Practice* (2d ed. London, Unwin, 1911), p. 62.

15. Unwin, "The Art of Designing Small Houses and Cottages," *The Art of Building a Home* (London, Longmans, Green, 1901), p. 113.

Fig. 106. Stanley Parker cottage, Wilbury Road, Letchworth; Parker and Unwin, 1908. For eclectic style had been substituted clean planes, volumetric emphasis, the ribbons of small windows, and an abiding sense of shelter.

Fig. 107. Aitken house, Cashco Lane, Letchworth; Parker and Unwin, 1914.

effort to straighten out the semantics of postwar Internationalism.[16] She notices the word frequently, even in the writings of the avowed opponent of
Internationalism, Frank Lloyd Wright. Twice she quotes a prophecy from
his autobiography, "A sense of cleanliness directly related to living in the
sunlight is coming." Before World War I it was the wholesome and optimistic aspects of the "purifying" ceremony that were emphasized; after the
war it was the ascetic and self-disciplinary tendencies that were uppermost.

In a speech in April 1916 Parker's views appear as a part of the contemporary revolt against eclecticism and revivalism. He deplores "harking back
to this or that period of architectural history," the dependence upon a mere
"series of revivals." Then comes the British reservation: this should not go
so far as complete iconoclasm. He is looking more for an architecture "developing from stage to stage, influenced by a living tradition, and gradually
evolving one form from another, and ever acquiring a greater mastery over
materials."[17] The last phrase recalls the long shadow of Norman Shaw.

In referring again to the Stanley Parker and the Aitken houses in Letchworth, one is reminded of Voysey's style in the former and Baillie Scott's in
the latter. And with reason. Baillie Scott did a very similar house at Letchworth (Fig. 108). Stanley Parker was the brother of Barry Parker and a furniture designer by profession. He had been a pupil of Voysey. Cowles Voysey, the son of C. F. A. Voysey, was employed for a while in Barry Parker's
architectural office. Stanley Parker had also been a friend of Ernest Gimson
and Edward Barnsley at the Bedales School in Petersfield, allying him with
the so-called Cotswold Group. Hence, it would seem that the rough-cast
simplicity and "cleanliness" of the houses were arrived at through personal
as well as philosophical channels.

Unlike Edgar Wood, their fellow architect in the Northern Art Workers
Guild, Parker and Unwin never felt the need of the flat, reinforced concrete
roof, which Wood employed as early as 1906 and regarded as an indispensable feature of modernism.[18] This does not mean, however, that they could
find absolutely no room in their discussions for the new materials. Unwin
stated in the first decade of the twentieth century that, "Provision is also
necessary for the utilisation of new materials, such as ferroconcrete, concrete blocks, and the many fireproof concrete and plaster slabs which are

16. Katharine Gilbert, "Clean and Organic:
A Study in Architectural Semantics," *Journal
of the Society of Architectural Historians, 10*
(Oct. 1951), 3–7.

17. Parker, "Horizontality and Verticality in

the Architectural Treatment of Town Planning
Schemes," *Journal of Town Planning Institute,*
2 (1916), 136.

18. Archer, p. 52.

Fig. 108. Norton Way North, 7 and 7a, Letchworth; M. H. Baillie Scott. The less expensive work which Parker, Baillie Scott, and Voysey were doing in the domestic field, just before World War I, was very close in type, character, and location.

now made."[19] But they were looking more seriously for another kind of functionalism at the time, the *functionalism of environment*. So the partners wrote in 1901: "The essence and life of design lies in finding that form for anything which will, with the maximum of convenience *and* beauty, fit it for the *particular functions* it has to perform, and adapt it to the special circumstances *in which it must be placed.*"[20]

If the roof of the Aitken house with its clipped gables, thick, handmade tiles, and flareouts, be compared with that of the Stanley Parker house, it becomes apparent that in six years the architects had moved quickly toward a more plastic and picturesque emphasis. One practical explanation for the sweep of the roof was, of course, the addition of the bicycle and tool shed at either side of the house, a convenience also installed at New Earswick to avoid the usual backyard clutter. But the deeper reason was probably that "the low house is more successful, more in harmony with the

19. Unwin, *Town Planning in Practice*, 2d ed., p. 400.

20. *The Art of Building a Home*, p. iii (italics are mine).

scenery; perhaps because it is suggestive more of man's dependence upon Nature, less of his defiance of her powers."[21] Too often, Unwin observed, the architect placed his buildings in opposition to nature and the surrounding environment, resisting the "living shell and skin of the earth," as Morris had put it. No barriers should be arbitrarily raised between architecture and nature or tradition because to do so would be to cut architecture off from the two sources of primal strength. We see these sources as one in Unwin's earliest thought.

> It is not however with suburbs only that we spoil scenery; in isolated buildings, or groups of buildings, we very often put up what is offensive to the lover of country; and it will I think be both interesting and useful to enquire a little further why the buildings which our forefathers put up mostly adorn a landscape, while our own erections so frequently spoil it."[22]

It was the self-conscious independence and exclusiveness of the century that so bothered him.

The interiors of the Parker and Unwin Letchworth houses are as frugal as the exteriors (Figs. 109, 110). The natural wood grain of the doors, cupboards, gunstock posts, and major beams is contrasted with the whitewashed bricks and the ceilings, with their exposed joists. That this treatment of an interior would have a social and ethical cast would seem likely from these two long-term followers of Ruskin and Morris. It may not be without significance either that most of Voysey's earliest clients were Quakers and that Barry Parker completed his life as a Quaker, as did his sister, Raymond Unwin's wife. "If necessary, let the rest of the walls go untouched in all the rich variety of colour and tone, of light and shade, of the naked brickwork. Let the floor go uncarpeted, and the wood unpainted, that we may have time to think, and money with which to educate our children to think also."[23] This was written by Parker and Unwin in 1901. That this ascetic attitude had a wide circulation appears from an essay of a few years earlier—the "Ideal Suburban House" by Baillie Scott. "The key-notes of the design may be said to be simplicity and homely comfort, and the doll's-house-like prettiness of the so-called Queen Anne bijou residence has been held to be as undesirable on the one hand, as the stolid ugliness of the commoner box of bricks style of suburban house on the other."[24] Unwin's comparable slo-

21. Ibid., p. 111.
22. Ibid., p. 84.

23. Ibid., p. v.
24. *Studio, 4* (1894–95), 127.

Fig. 109. Interior, Stanley Parker cottage, Letchworth; Parker and Unwin, 1908.

Fig. 110. Interior, Aitken cottage, Letchworth; Parker and Unwin, 1914. They esteemed open or flowing space with an emphasis on the textured surfaces of simple planes and materials.

gan was "art and simplicity." In his essay of that title he calls attention to the part that light must play in achieving this end. "It is not easy to create a decoration more beautiful than the play of sunlight or firelight on a white-washed wall: . . . it is refinement that teaches us to appreciate the subtle colouring of the varying light and to be content with it."[25]

The matching of cultivated pleasure with frugality is what Unwin was advocating. Without doubt, this theme came to him out of the writings and personal examples of Hinton and Carpenter, but Morris was involved too. Parker often quoted Morris' rule for furnishing a home so that nothing would obtrude that could not be considered either useful or beautiful. Especially with the studio house for Stanley Parker, where the whole living floor is one vast room, the image of Morris' ideal dwelling becomes apparent. "I would like a house like a big barn," Morris had said, "where one ate in one corner, cooked in another corner, slept in a third corner, and in the fourth received one's friends." The medieval tithe barn and manor house were never far back in his cultural memory.

Besides Emerson and Whitman, whom Unwin came to know through Carpenter, there was another American of importance, to Parker particularly —Henry David Thoreau. He was the first literary figure to attempt to return to the elemental environment. His "universal space" for the setting of this life would be "A vast, rude, substantial, primitive hall, without plaster or ceiling, with bare rafters and purlins supporting a sort of lower heaven over one's head." In reading one of Parker's essays published in 1895, the year before Unwin joined him, we discover him saying, "Thoreau, you will remember, threw away the fossil, the only ornament in his room, because it required dusting. . . . And I believe in the main that the more adapted to its use anything is the more graceful it will be in shape. The bent handle of the axe, more comfortable to hold, is also more beautiful than the straight, and in the degree the curve and form of the handle is adapted to its uses as an axe, by just so much the more beautiful it becomes." Then Parker reverts in the article to a more English and Morris-like attitude and goes on to modify this frontier functionalism.

> The charm of the farm-house kitchen, with everything in its place because of its usefulness, can of course be increased to an unlimited extent by making all the useful articles also beautiful in form and harmonious in colour. This is the line on which alone, I con-

25. Unwin, *The Art of Building a Home,* p. 59.

tend, a really beautiful room is to be got, and I would discourage
all attempts at adornment by finding places for useless things.[26]

Such evidence encourages the historian to seek a place in time for Parker
and Unwin somewhere between Horatio Greenough and the *Deutsche
Werkbund,* keeping in mind the while that both the American and the German functionalist movements were largely devoted to promoting the greater
efficiency of objects connected with extractive labor and production, first
with hand tools and later with machinery, while the English effort was
directed primarily toward achieving a better living environment and accord
with the land after the impact of factory location and urbanization had
been partially absorbed. In this latter situation the functionalism of spatial
and locational planning may be ascendant over the functionalism of technology for, says Parker, "Fitness for purpose is the prime essential of a work
of art, and town planning is the art of fitting a town to fulfill its purpose
more sensibly, more economically and more beautifully."[27]

In a lecture at Oxford in 1925 he observed: "The tea clipper improved
in line and gained in beauty as forms were evolved for it which each in its
turn enabled it to increase in speed, breast the waves better, and sail nearer
the wind, until the perfection of the 'Cutty Sark' was reached."[28] We gather
from this that he was acquainted with the progressivism of either the Englishmen Garbett and Fergusson or the Americans Greenough and Emerson.
He then says that he believes the steamboat and the motorcar to be evolving
in the same progressive direction. He apparently missed the point, as have
so many before and after, that this brand of functionalism works only so
long as there is a causal relationship between the power source and the
moving part that is still evident, as when the wind fills the straining sail and
moves the boat through the water, the chips fly from the blow of the ax
wielded by the strong-armed man, or when the wheels of the sulky become
transparent after the horse breaks into a trot. Here the quality of motion or
velocity can be fairly estimated through the elements that activate it.

But as the technical cause and effect become more involved and less visible the "democratization" of functionalism becomes less feasible. The
meaning of a design can be communicated only to those highly trained in
its interpretation, an elite of the specially educated. As Buckminster Fuller

26. Parker, "Some Principles Underlying
Domestic Architecture," *Journal of the Society
of Architects* (Sept. 1895), pp. 253–54.
27. Parker, "A Lecture on Art and Indus-

try," delivered at Balliol College, Oxford, Oct.
3, 1925 (Parker Collection), p. 4.
28. Ibid.

was to put it, "Thus in World War I industry suddenly went from the visible to the invisible base, from the track to the trackless, from the wire to the wireless, from visible structuring to invisible structuring in alloys. The big thing about World War I is that men *went off the sensorial spectrum forever* as the prime criterion of accrediting initiations."[29]

World War I intensified the magnetism of the symbol of the machine at the same time that it deepened its mystery. The factories turning out acres of war material, the first British tanks, the planes dog-fighting and bombing, the great ships traversing the Atlantic, the long strings of trucks and freight cars, even the French buses to Verdun and the thousand taxis to the Battle of the Marne, gripped the popular imagination in a way that decades of peaceful evolution could never have done. The drama of good and evil was becoming constantly more evident, but the forces behind its working promised to become increasingly obscure.

Parker and Unwin were to be as baffled by this as was everyone else. But their approach to the larger problem was initially different in that they moved back into tradition in order to find a solid base or beginning. They asked more questions about the origins of the technological revolution rather than its latest trends. And they sought to cope with the increasing complexities of social and psychological need arising out of a more complicated physical environment more than with isolated architectural objects or the rudimentary mechanical relationships of actual power and motion. After the war they did not defy the machine but tried to come to terms with it in the broader context of their earlier social thought. The adjustment of the parkway planning at Wythenshawe would be one instance of this. Parker advised the new generation in his 1925 talk at Oxford that, "The machine has come to stay, and we must accept it." He added only in mild protest that the machine-made object up to this time had not been, in his estimation, better made or more purposefully designed than many of the older, handmade items. The criterion for the future would still have to be whether the object was well adapted to its need, whether handmade or machine made.

Before the war he had been much more vehement in his opposition to the machine.

> We call the present the "Machine Age." Now the influence of machinery on art is one of the most degrading we have to contend

29. R. Buckminster Fuller, *Education Automation* (Carbondale, S. Illinois Press, 1962), p. 62.

with, for every advance made by machinery must mean a corresponding retreat on the part of art. . . . Today, if we require a beam in our building, we take every bit of natural character out of it, and bring it, by mechanical processes, to as dead and flat, as lifeless and monotonous a state as possible.[30]

The machine destroyed the grain and figure of the wood and then tried to compensate for the loss by the overapplication of cheap ornament. Again Parker and Unwin are not far from Baillie Scott, who says in a similar vein,

> Here as elsewhere we have to contend with that mechanical ideal which is the mark of almost all modern work, and which takes no account of textures and surfaces, but reduces everything to one monotonous dead level. Those who have felt the charm of an old beam with its adzed surface will be able to appreciate how all this is lost under the modern joiner's plane, and this is but one example amongst many of the degradation of modern craftsmanship in this respect.[31]

Unwin likewise observes that modern tiles gave a roof a flat and polished effect whereas "the old tiles were a little curled in burning, and had a surface rough enough to afford lodgment for moss and lichen; and so the lines were less hard, and the newness of surface and colour soon mellowed into all sorts of lovely shades."[32]

The industrial revolution had raised more questions than it solved, so far as Parker and Unwin were concerned. They would set its great potential aside, at least temporarily, until a few of the more basic social and aesthetic dislocations, such as the breakdown of the family, the decline of human relationships, and the absence of beauty, could be corrected. They did not wholly approve of the slick impersonality of the machine nor of its threat of dominance over the other creative acts of man. Parker still adhered to Ruskin and Morris' basic tenet in his Oxford Lecture of 1925. "If the producer of a thing has taken no pleasure in creating it the user cannot take pleasure in using it."[33] The joy of creation would have to be visible in the finished article or it would have no vitality for the beholder.

This central purpose as applied to cities appears many times in the writ-

---

30. *The Art of Building a Home*, p. 30.
31. Baillie Scott, "The Fireplace of the Suburban House," *Studio, 6* (1895–96), 104–05.

32. Unwin, *The Art of Building a Home*, p. 87.

33. Parker, "A Lecture on Art in Industry," p. 9.

ings of the partners, especially those of Unwin. He observed that, "there are in our great cities square miles laid out under stringent bye-laws—the most dreary, depressing, and hopelessly ugly areas upon the face of the earth. They have lacked one thing, the touch of Civic Art, that margin which would have constituted the well doing."[34] He also shrewdly recognized another circumstance which each new generation seems to have to uncover for itself and hail as a new planning discovery: that slums already possess an inner life and vitality of their own, "There is a certain picturesqueness and excitement about the slum life near the busy centre of the town, and it is essential to offer some more wholesome counter attraction if we are to draw the people into healthier districts."[35] He does not believe that the social unity of the slum, although valuable, necessitates its artificial maintenance. What is required instead is the achievement of the same inner security and communal warmth that the slum afforded, in a new and better settlement.

> It is that which is provided over and above the bare house and street which really counts. It is just that little margin of imaginative treatment which transforms our work from the building of clean stables for animals into the building of homes for human beings, which is of value; for it is just this which appeals to and influences the inner heart of man.[36]

It was the provision of the supraminimal which was so important. Parker and Unwin could easily annoy any dedicated and practical municipal servant with vaporings about the inner heart of man. But as Unwin suggested in his anticipation of this response, it was not his idea but Aristotle's. The Greek had described the city over a thousand years before as "a place where men live a common life for a noble end."[37]

How misleading this may all become when our contemporary authors and planners insist upon operating without historical knowledge but with a high degree of cultural awareness, under the illusion that modernism as they know it has no history, is perhaps best demonstrated in the popular writings of individuals like Jane Jacobs or Nathan Glazer in the United States. They consider the garden city attitudes at the root of most of the failures in modern planning. Yet within their attacks they clearly repeat

---

34. Unwin, "The Improvement of Towns," paper read at the Conference of the National Union of Women Workers of Great Britain and Ireland, Nov. 8, 1904, p. 2.

35. Ibid., p. 8.
36. Ibid.
37. Ibid., p. 1.

many of Unwin's basic contentions, completely without recognition. In a very characteristic article, Glazer writes,

> No plan has ever come within hailing distance of recreating what are in some respects the best and richest parts of our cities— Greenwich Village in New York, North Beach in San Francisco. Such areas seem to require a mixture of lower-class residential area, preferably Italian, as a base—with its stores, coffee shops, churches, and the like—offering cheap living for poor young people, combined with expensive apartments or town houses, combined with art stores, used furniture and antique stores, night clubs, restaurants, all kinds of shops."[38]

If one can eliminate the faint aroma of espresso and discount the resentment of American blanket zoning, he has a message about the picturesque slum almost identical with that of Unwin himself of half a century before. But, asserts Glazer, the garden city thinkers were never concerned with such vital urban realities because the garden city "dream" was "an essentially small-town vision concerned with small town values." From its inception it "was thus suburban planning, not city planning." Unwin, of course, would deny it. He disliked suburbs too.

What to do about the present city? "Perhaps one answer," says Mr. Glazer, "lies in attempting models of much larger cities than have ever been planned, plans maintaining the variety, density, and richness of a city, yet limited by green belts: cities of a half-million people, rather than 50 thousand." He is apparently unaware that the optimal population of the garden city had been steadily rising since Robert Owen's proposal of a few hundred in the early nineteenth century to the 20 to 100 thousand of the newest new towns in Britain and Sweden. Unwin had plainly stated that a planned community had no need to stay within Howard's limit of 30,000 as long as its functional and human integrity could be maintained. It *was* open-ended. Vällingby almost exactly fulfills Glazer's requirements of "an urban variety of residential quarters, cultural amenities, and economic opportunities" in such new cities (Fig. 111), because the society behind it put a wholehearted effort into it—as Howard had advocated—no more no less. Finally Mr. Glazer notices, as a modern social scientist, that there has been a "catastrophic decline in taste that has accompanied the industrial revolution.

38. Nathan Glazer, "Why City Planning Is Obsolete," *Architectural Forum* (July, 1958), pp. 96–89.

Fig. 111. Shopping Center, Vällingby, near Stockholm, 1949–59. The ideal of the good family life, stimulated by a variety of surroundings, was the goal of the garden city movement, carried on in many respects in the Swedish, Finnish, and British new towns.

This is the most difficult thing to talk about . . . What can be done about the fact that buildings, neighborhoods, squares, and streets lack beauty, variety and exhilaration?" So what can be done about this most difficult thing to talk about which Unwin and Morris, Ruskin and Pugin, talked about all their lives? Glazer says, "One very small thing can be done, and is done increasingly, is for people to become aware of the minor virtues in design that turn up almost continually in old buildings, old neighborhoods, old streets and they need not be very old to compare favorably with much contemporary design." In other words, Glazer wants us not only to look at the urban picture with a fresh and "unprejudiced" eye but also to be sure to preserve some of the good old elements from the past, precisely the kind of dual creative traditionalism which Parker and Unwin advocated. Thus it is almost the complete set of Arts and Crafts attitudes toward urbanism which Glazer expounds as he denounces their earliest outcome in the garden city as due to the worst sort of fuzzy thinking.

Parker and Unwin admonished without partiality those who built cottages and those who lived in them. As early as 1895 Parker had complained that too much social ambition in a fluid society caused the cramming of too many rooms into the smaller houses. "Everyone is seeking to get a step further up the social ladder. The result is a demand for houses which look as though they belonged to the next social grade above that of the people who are to live in them."[39] Unwin uttered the same complaint, adding that this "middle class" ambition was at the bottom of the unfortunate tendency to cut the cottage up into a series of minute compartments. Baillie Scott described it as a shoe that pinched everywhere. "The whole interior is cramped and the family spend their time at home wedged between a table and a modern grate, and every inch of ground is disputed by useless furniture and 'ornaments' which do not ornament."[40] He recommended that these irrelevant divisions be broken down and the central portion of the house organized "to form an interior which conveys the impression that it is indeed the house."[41] This had been done in the open plan for Parker and Unwin's "Cottages Near a Town" project of 1903.

The tenants aimed too high. The landlords stooped too low. When it came to the cottage-building crisis at Letchworth, where the argument was advanced that dwellings should be built rapidly and cheaply to fit the work-

39. Parker, "Some Principles Underlying Domestic Architecture," p. 252.

40. Baillie Scott, "The House As It Is and Might Be," *Garden Suburbs, Town Planning,* *and Modern Architecture* (London, Unwin, 1910), p. 84.

41. Ibid., p. 85.

man's purse and attract more building capital, Unwin cried out for a little overall understanding and patience, "if Garden City stands for anything, surely it stands for this:—a decent home and garden for every family that comes there. That is the irreducible minimum. Let that go and we fail utterly. And if we succeed utterly, what then? A beautiful home in a beautiful garden in a beautiful city for all!"[42] The happy medium apparently had a tendency to make all parties unhappy. Could town building ever become an art in a society where subtlety and nuance were not so far viable?

If the E. R. Woodhead house near Chesterfield of 1903 be compared with a semidetached house on Rotherwick Road, Hampstead, of 1908–10 (Figs. 112, 113), it will be seen that Parker and Unwin's architectural work outside Letchworth also had a certain inner consistency. The Hampstead Garden Suburb dwelling, which was one of their minimal types, exhibits a hipped roof, arched door lintels, string courses, quoins, and a slight swelling of the two corner bays. Unwin had written in his "Cottage Plans and Common Sense" of 1901 that "windows facing the street are much less depressing if slightly bayed to invite a peep up and down as well as across."[43] He never missed an opportunity to relate one element to another in a setting. Other features and the date suggest that Lutyens' Georgian houses going up around the Central Square at Hampstead were influencing the Rotherwick Road house, since there is a definite change from the picturesque folk architecture which is more typical of Parker and Unwin's previous work at Hampstead. Nevertheless, there is a solidity and robustness about the house that could come from no other hand and which also appears in the Woodhead house.

The latter was the best of their early private dwellings in the North. In this instance the meticulous fitting of the hipped roof, the tall and very prominent bay projections with their irregular window patterns, the ribbons of leaded casements, and the corner buttresses, which Unwin claimed were both functional and necessary to lend a visual effect of stability, make it evident that it was partially inspired by Voysey's house, Broadleys, on Lake Windermere (1898–99). The latter was built by the Briggs family which drew its wealth from the coal of the Derbyshire–Yorkshire region. The Briggs also commissioned Voysey to do the model housing and an inn for the Whitwood Colliery at Normanton near Leeds in 1905 (Fig. 68). The touch of the partners can be recognized in the rough-dressed local stone, the lack

42. Unwin, "Cottage Building in Garden City," *The Garden City,* 5 (June 1906), 111.
43. P. 12.

Fig. 112. E. R. Woodhead house, Ashgate Road, near Chesterfield; Parker and Unwin, 1903.

Fig. 113. Semidetached house, Rotherwick Road, Hampstead Garden Suburb; Parker and Unwin, 1908–10.

of moldings, the orientation of the principal rooms toward the south, and
by the fact that all the furniture, gaslight fittings, metalwork, and decoration were done to their designs.[44] It was during this period and shortly before that Unwin was said to be designing his family's blankets, curtains, and clothes of Ruskin flannel, hand-woven at the Laxey Mills on the Isle of Man. He was also placing thick rush matting on his floors and using horn-handled knives, wooden door latches, and wrought-iron hinges.

The interior of the Woodhead home, Homestead, was as conscious an expression of the partners' spatial and functional approach as might be imagined. Much of the furniture is built in (Fig. 114). Parker argued that

Fig. 114. Interior, E. R. Woodhead house; Parker and Unwin, 1903. The inglenook adjoins the two-story living room. Much of the furniture is built in to capture a sense of permanence.

"most things to look right and happy in their places must be designed *for* their places." Furniture should be conceived by the architect to afford an effect of "unity, completeness, comfort, and repose." The partners disliked

44. Mervyn Macartney, "House for Mr. E. R. Woodhead," *Recent English Domestic Architecture* (Westminster, Architectural Review, 1909), p. 161. See also, Katharine Bruce Glasier, "The Passing of Sir Raymond Unwin," *Labour's Northern Voice* (Aug. 1940), p. 2. The Unwins at that time lived at the lodge in the Beeches at Chapel-en-le-Frith.

the transitory nature of the contemporary scene as well as its distracting complexity. Furniture should not have, said Parker, "a look of being on the alert and ready to move on at a moment's notice."[45] The architect should never fear to repeat himself in a single room. He believed it helped to establish a mood of familiarity and protection within the enclosure. So here he repeats a fireplace, an inglenook, and cabinet rows. They never hesitated to repeat a motif or a phrase if they felt it might have some persuasive effect.

The spatial dynamic of the two-story living room with the low inglenook off it, making up a portion of its total space, was one of Unwin's favorite mental pictures of the past. "Just as in the middle ages the great hall was in the centre of the house, all the other chambers clustering round and being subordinate to it; so in the modern middle class house a good living room is the first essential, and all the other rooms should be considered in relation to it."[46] In another source he explained that the ancient origin of the inglenook about the fireplace lay in an effort to protect the residents from cross draughts and especially to allow the aged and feeble to keep warm in the great hall. He also thought it was a useful location for a girl to receive a suitor in a modicum of comfort and privacy. He mentions the visual pleasure from the fire casting its glow over the inglenook and reminds the reader that his forefathers liked the contrast of the hall—dark, wide, and lofty— with the cosy, sheltered, low recess. Each aspect of the relationship, the play of light, the reference to medieval precedent, the comfort of young and old, is typical of the catholicity of their attention. The architectural opening and closing of the spaces equates with the alternation of adventure and security, "the field and cave instinct" of their town planning, with the much smaller and more intimate quadrangles and cul-de-sacs contrasting with the big commons, woods, and heaths which always held a place on their maps (no matter how pressed they were for land), with the light flickering through the trees and bushes to give visual delight everywhere.

By the time of Whirriestone near Rochdale (1906–07), there is a complete integration and balance of large and smaller spaces throughout the house (Fig. 115). As the American magazine *House Beautiful* put it in considering this and other Parker and Unwin houses, they so arranged their rooms "that one gets the impression of really inhabiting the whole building, not one room at a time."[47] Only the kitchen remains permanently apart in this house. Whirriestone represents simultaneously a whole and a sequence of spaces.

45. Parker, "Some Principles Underlying Domestic Architecture," p. 250.

46. Unwin, *The Art of Building a Home*, p. 66.

47. Sept. 1911, pp. 119–20.

Fig. 115. Interior, Whirriestone, near Rochdale; Parker and Unwin, 1906–07.

As Parker had observed long before, "there is a great charm in a room broken up in plan, when that slight feeling of mystery is given to it which arises when you cannot see the whole room from any point in which you are likely to sit; when there is always something round the corner."[48]

The space flows more readily than six years earlier at the Homestead, and the planes are more pronounced. The vertical wooden members are slender, and the ceiling beams and joists are clearly exposed, also giving more emphasis to the horizontal. Japanese prints were a great influence on Parker at this stage. From these derive the feeling for panels and the stick-like character of the furniture. There is also something of Voysey's influence, witnessing his talk of the importance of light, two-storied halls, ceilings serving as reflectors, and long low beams contributing "towards the effect of spaciousness and respose."[49]

Affinity to Baillie Scott is not entirely absent either. He writes at about the same time, "Thinking, then, of the house as mainly consisting of this one good-sized apartment, the other smaller rooms may well be made as re-

48. Parker, "Some Principles Underlying Domestic Architecture," p. 243.

49. C. F. A. Voysey, "Remarks on Domestic Entrance Halls," *Studio, 21* (1900–01), 242.

cesses or appendages to it, and so, in seeming to share in its central spaciousness, lose something of that sensation of a cribbed and cabined refinement
which belongs to the isolated rectangular box."[50]

There has been a sustained conviction in America that the rebellion
against the "box" in architecture was a one-man insurrection on the part of
Frank Lloyd Wright. So it is probably fruitless to point out that M. H.
Baillie Scott appears to have had the same prejudice. Nor is it perhaps politic
to mention that in 1895 he was advocating the insertion of small heraldic
or floral designs of rich coloring in squares or diamonds of clear glass in casement windows so as to "have a brilliant jewellike effect,"[51] and that Frank
Lloyd Wright later called his colored insets of glass in leaded panes his "jew-
els." Nor need we draw further attention to the similarity of their interest
in Japanese prints, two-story living rooms, low ceilings, and open but complex interior space. We can but put Voysey and Baillie Scott in one place,
Parker and Unwin in another not far off, and Frank Lloyd Wright in another, still not too far off, and remind ourselves that in spite of the fact that
these men took considerable pride in their independence and individualism,
still the Bohemian pose of the swirling cape, the long hair, and the flowing
tie had its international typology.

The particular message of Parker and Unwin's architecture seems to be
that British planning as we know it arose as much out of William Morris'
Arts and Crafts as out of any independent thought about cities alone. The
houses of Parker and Unwin are a visible link between the crafts of Parker
and Unwin and the towns they created. It is evident that this was at least
one instance in the annals of twentieth-century art when specialization sur-
vived despite its own confining methods and ends, in such a way that one
activity reinforced rather than debilitated the other.

Their writings show too that the definition of "functionalism" originally
had a much broader base than architecture or planning alone. Its meaning
was not to be contained alone in the more efficient or complicated use of a
new material, such as concrete, steel, or glass; or in a given building type,
such as a factory or office structure. In the vocabulary of the early planner
it referred to the adjustment of a particular element to all the other objects
surrounding it in the same environment, whether it was a solid like a tree,
house, or school; a void like an inglenook; or an outdoor feature like a
street, quadrangle, or green. No material, object, or space could ignore the

50. Baillie Scott, "The House As It Is and Might Be," p. 84.

51. Baillie Scott, "The Decoration of the Suburban House," *Studio*, 5 (1895), 20.

presence of adjoining materials, objects, or spaces. For this reason function-alism in the environmental reference involved a manifest relation with time and nature, as well as with solids and voids, because its chief outcome was cumulative and apt to be all-embracing.

What the modern age needed more than a greater pride was a new creative humility, thought Parker and Unwin. A careful, honest, better-informed examination of the current environment and of the past was one of the best ways to instill it. This in turn was supposed to lead toward a communal humanism and thus restore to the artist his rightful place in the society as the individual who, through intuition, could stabilize mental and emotional pressures within the society. This side of man's nature had been sadly neg-lected and undernourished throughout the nineteenth century, they felt.

Unwin had copied down in his personal notes another quotation from Ruskin: "Architecture is the art which so disposes and adorns the edifices raised by man, for whatsoever uses, that the sight of them may contribute to his mental health, power and pleasure."[52] Unwin's planning career in es-sence conveyed Ruskin's outlook into the twentieth century and extended the awareness of the connection between the inside and outside of buildings in his pursuit of the Ruskinian social ideal of architecture as an environ-mental conditioner toward mental health.

52. "Ethics and International Relations," Unwin R.I.B.A. papers.

A glance at the effect of the garden city image outside England shakes one's faith in the interchangeability of modern forms and also in their ability to achieve parthenogenesis. Local conditions and attitudes seem to shape the major result everywhere. The cul-de-sac principle as the British cultivated it is thus of little value in Scandinavia and Finland because the desire for privacy is not so great there, the hold of antique land patterns is not so intense, and there is more snow than in Britain. The shining water, the heavy stands of timber, the craggy hills and valleys of situations like Vällingby near Stockholm (1949–59) or Tapiola Garden City outside Helsinki (1956–62) demand a completely different treatment than the gentle hills of Britain.

This differentiation extends far back. The most fervent of foreign admirers noticed it early. The German H. E. Berlepsch-Valendas, writing of the movement in 1911, observed that already in the 1840s in London, "Auch im Massenmiethause wurde immer auf volle Abgeschlossenheit der Einzelwohnung gesehen."[1] And, of course, even in Hampstead Garden Suburb this curious need for privacy in proximity was highly developed and duly noticed by the equally observant Dane, Steen Eiler Rasmussen.

Yet somehow the garden city message was disseminated. Other countries were also compelled to adjust to the industrial revolution, although later and on a smaller scale. In the 1870s the steel town of Sandviken, north of Stockholm, would be one manifestation known to garden city commentators, as would be M. Godin's early Familistery in Guise in the 1850s, or the Cités Ouvrières at Mulhouse. Moreover, the admiration for the Arts and Crafts movement and its accompanying domestic architecture carried with it a receptivity to whatever theory of planning might come out of England.

1. ("Even in large flatblocks complete privacy for individual dwelling units could be observed.") H. E. Berlepsch-Valendas, *Die Gartenstadt-Bewegung in England* (Munich and Berlin, Oldenbourg, 1911), p. 53.

This attitude is especially evident in the writings of Hermann Muthesius, the German cultural attaché in London from 1896 until 1903, who founded the Deutsche Werkbund in the Morris vein in 1907, intended "to ennoble industrial work, to bring about cooperation between art and industry and the work of the artisans by means of instruction, of propaganda, and of common action." The same can be said of Alexander Koch, who published both in London and Darmstadt. The Grand Duke of Hesse-Darmstadt asked Baillie Scott to do some interior decorating for him in 1898; and Koch, from Darmstadt, commissioned Baillie Scott and Charles Rennie Mackintosh to do a house to be published in *Meister der Innenkunst* in 1901. In Koch's *Architecture: An Annual Architectural Review,* published from 1888 through the 1890's in London, Paris, and Berlin there is a similar search for the best and newest of the works of people like George and Peto, Lutyens' early employers; Owen, the major architect of Port Sunlight; Wood, Harrison Townsend, Shaw, Voysey, Baillie Scott, Dawber, Walton, and Parker and Unwin, along with others from abroad like Cuypers and Berlage from Holland, Wallot from Belgium, Wagner from Austria, and John Calvin Stevens from the United States.

From the 1890s on the architectural world shrank rapidly, particularly through publications. It was now really possible in architecture, planning, or the crafts to have a prominent local master suddenly assume an international stature. That this situation was quite evident in planning was made clear in an interview Barry Parker gave to a local newspaper not long before his death. He mentioned the pilgrimage to Letchworth and Hampstead of Clarence Stein and Henry Wright in 1924 before Radburn, New Jersey, was planned. He also reported that, "Dr. Lilienberg, the Stockholm city planner, came here and talked it over with me and I went to Stockholm to have further discussions with him,"[2] before the replanning of that city. From this exchange in part came the garden suburbs of Äppelviken, Alsten, and Enskede, and the "garden cities" of Bromma and Brännkyrka, developed from 1908 until the early 1930s, when they gave way to the denser three-story, narrow flat blocks (lamellas) and ultimately to high-rise towers.

Parker also speaks of his role in helping to train Alwyn Lloyd, the leading Welsh planner, Albert Thompson, active in South Africa, and Masoud, who played a large part in Egyptian town planning. He refers to Ernst May of Germany (who worked with Unwin in 1910–11), although not by name,

2. "Letchworth's Example to the World, Influence on Other Countries," *Letchworth Citizen* (March 5, 1943).

perhaps because a war was then going on. May later told a touching story of how the Unwins guaranteed money for his personal needs and the education of his children when he was caught in Kenya and interned in South Africa at the outset of World War II.[3] Owing to Parker's friendship with "John Nolen, the 'father' of American Town Planning, Naulon Cauchon, the City Planner of Ottawa, and Kepler the Director of Housing at Amsterdam, the principles on which Letchworth is founded were well known to these men and influenced their work in their own countries."

He also mentions in passing that M. Georges Benoit-Lévy, the secretary of the French Garden Cities Association founded in 1904, had dwelt in Letchworth for some while, but he does not allude to the Belgian architect Eggerickx, who lived in Coventry during 1914–15 and laid out the garden suburb of Logis Floreal near Brussels in 1924–27.

Through the quiet haze over everything just before World War I, somehow the Damplassen of Ulleval near Oslo (1918) (Fig. 116) appears to re-

Fig. 116. *Damplassen of Ullevål, near Oslo; Oscar Hoff and Harald Hals, 1918. This suburb and Kingsport, Tennessee, were the most important derivatives from Hampstead Garden Suburb just before and after World War I.*

semble the distant religious and civic center of Kingsport, Tennessee (1919–20) by John Nolen. Each was semi-Georgian in architecture, formal and

3. Ernst May, "Unwin as Planner for Social Welfare," *Town and Country Planning* (Nov. 1963), p. 428.

symmetrical in presentation, and exploited the fan layout of exit streets to connect with the rest of the town.

At this moment Unwin also wrote of Nolen and Arthur Comey as two of the most enterprising planners in the United States.[4] Unwin had visited Kingsport. Nolen discusses the garden city influence and shows a map of Letchworth at the beginning of his *New Towns for Old*. He is eager to achieve better site planning, and his way of going about it, with careful attention to ground slopes and contours, recalls the English approach. He was looking toward new towns of thirty to fifty thousand which would result from the decentralization of industry—mentioning specifically the moves of the Ford, General Electric, and Westinghouse companies in this direction. He believed that some of the residential sections in his towns "compare favorably with some of the celebrated model communities in England."[5]

Most notable among Nolen's works were Kingsport, enlarged to provide new markets for a railroad; his emergency war housing on the edge of Wilmington, Delaware, called Union Park Gardens; and the model suburb of Mariemont near Cincinnati which followed the war. They have a certain intrinsic American quality about them too, with an amplitude of scale and a devotion to entrance gates, parks and playgrounds, and green Olmstedian strips. But, "In its conception," Nolen avers, "Mariemont follows in general the example set in the creation of Letchworth and other garden cities in England."[6]

A recognition of garden city idioms had prevailed over most of the world, but with the onset of the first war they were interpreted through a crisis which meant more to Americans with their penchant for sudden alarms than it did to the British. As Professor Roy Lubove and others have indicated, Charles Whitaker, editor of the *Journal of the American Institute of Architects,* sent Frederick L. Ackerman to England in 1917 to investigate the war housing of which Unwin was in charge. Ackerman had discovered that the British considered the home essential to the war effort in that it ensured stable workers (thus following the older model village attitudes of Lever and Cadbury), and that over the longer period the house was merely one component of a successful total community. So the house and public and recreational buildings ought to be considered together and had to be

4. Raymond Unwin, "American Architecture and Town Planning," *R.I.B.A. Journal* (Nov. 12, 1921), p. 78. See also John Hancock, "John Nolen," *Journal of the American Institute of Planners* (Nov. 1960), pp. 307–08. This author believes Nolen came under the influence of the garden city about 1911.

5. John Nolen, *New Towns for Old* (Boston, Marshall Jones, 1927), p. 59.

6. Ibid., p. 121.

accepted as total and permanent entities in order to achieve the proper benefit, even in the war crisis. Thousands of dwelling units were to be built by
the United States Shipping Board's Emergency Fleet Corporation and the
Department of Labor's United States Housing Corporation, and they were
unusually good, partly because of the British experience. But with the end of
the war these houses were sold.

Another crisis, that of boom or bust, presented itself in the 1920s. Unwin,
like Lewis Mumford, was particularly occupied by the rapid construction
of skyscrapers in New York and Chicago (Figs. 117, 118) and what this implied for other urban factors such as traffic and transport.[7] Unwin began to
interest himself in the density problems of the American metropolis and
what they might mean for the future of the two countries.

The greatest difference between American and European conditions during these years was the sudden return of prosperity in the United States. This
produced, except in the more serious minds, an optimism and extroversion
which became characteristic of the decade up to 1929. Most typical of the
genera produced was the country club, with homes surrounding the greens
and fairways. One of the best suburbs of the period was the Country Club
District of Kansas City, developed by J. C. Nichols and visited several times
by Unwin. It was also fitting that the motifs of Sunnyside and Radburn by
Stein and Wright were concentrated around inner greens and lawns, well
protected from the automobile traffic which the new prosperity was prolif-
erating in and out of the city. In this decade and nation the country club
and the superblock had much in common.

But the bigger issue of the 1920s in America was the external green—the
regional plan. Benton MacKaye and Lewis Mumford were most active in
fostering this new concept. Mumford was then under the influence of the
French regional geographers like Charles Brun, the American George
Perkins Marsh, and Patrick Geddes' biosociological regionalism.[8] He and his
associates would not champion the garden city as a distinct entity but only
as it would take its place in a regional network. He said, "The point is that
the garden-city is useful only as a concrete objective in a complete scheme of
regional cities," in an article commenting on Frederic Osborn's conclusions
about why further headway was not being made with the garden city theory

7. See Unwin, "Higher Building in Relation
to Town Planning," *R.I.B.A. Journal* (Jan. 12,
1924), pp. 125–40. Reprinted in the *Journal of
the A.I.A.* (March 1924), pp. 124–31. Unwin,
"Architecture and Broad Planning," *Journal of*
the *A.I.A.* (June 1925), pp. 195–98.

8. Roy Lubove, *Community Planning in the
1920's: The Contribution of the Regional Planning Association of America* (University of
Pittsburgh Press, 1963), pp. 83–91.

Fig. 117. Standard Oil building, New York, from an etching by Joseph Pennell, 1924. This was used as one of the illustrations for Unwin's article on "Higher Building in Relation to Town Planning" in January 1924. The urban buildup of the 1920s in the United States was of great interest to him, as it was to Lewis Mumford and his colleagues.

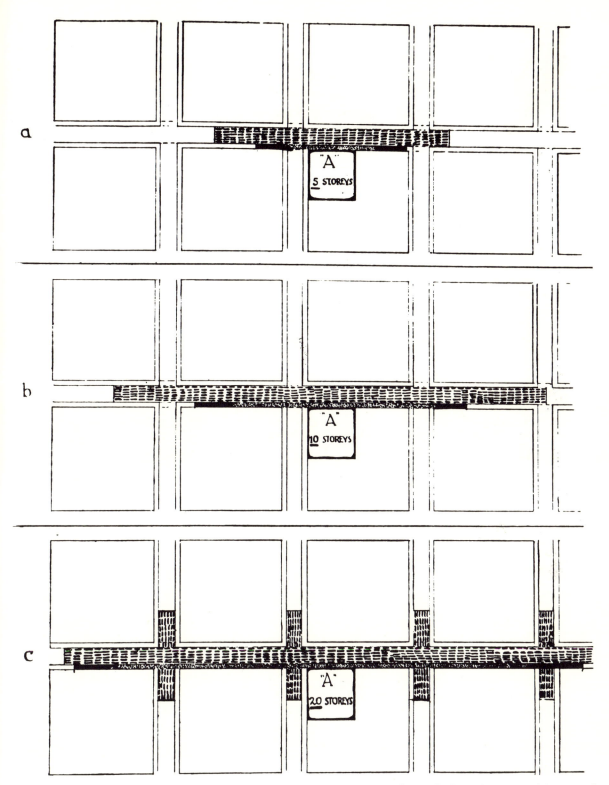

Fig. 118. Unwin's diagram of how single skyscrapers of 5, 10, and 20 stories would flood the streets with cars and pedestrians as work let out; 1924.

in England—of which Welwyn was the only postwar example. "Saltaire, Pullman, Port Sunlight, Letchworth are drops in the bucket"; Mumford asserted, "the aim of a garden-city movement must be to change the shape of the bucket itself; that is to say, the frame of our civilization."[9] The norm would have to evolve into the supernorm, with the whole enterprise reaching out far beyond the possibility of a satellite city like Welwyn, Wythenshawe, or even the much later new towns. The scale and dimension of thought enlarged greatly during the 1920s, but it is doubtful whether the superform of regionalism would ever have been attained if it had not been for the designation in Unwin's time of the superman, the image of a European or British leader entitled to think in terms of hundreds of square miles.

Mumford's highly influential attitude is also reflected in the unusual contrast he makes between the "Regional Plan of New York and Its Environs" (1922–31) by Thomas Adams, which was financed by the Russell Sage Foundation, and that of 1925–26 for the New York State Commission of Housing and Regional Planning by Henry Wright (Fig. 119), helpfully endorsed by

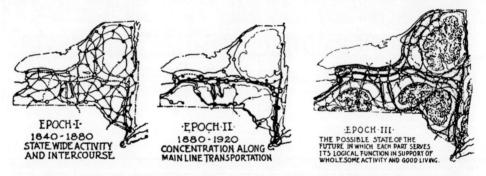

·EPOCH·I·
1840-1880
STATE WIDE ACTIVITY
AND INTERCOURSE

·EPOCH·II·
1880-1920
CONCENTRATION ALONG &
MAIN LINE TRANSPORTATION

·EPOCH·III·
THE POSSIBLE STATE OF THE
FUTURE IN WHICH EACH PART SERVES
ITS LOGICAL FUNCTION IN SUPPORT OF
WHOLESOME ACTIVITY AND GOOD LIVING.

Fig. 119. New York State Regional Plan; Henry Wright. In Epoch III a new mobility and specialization would set in, fostered by good roads and electric power lines. The green spots are the reforested catchment areas. The superform (in this case regionalism) was everywhere proposed in the 1920s.

his partner Clarence Stein. Adams' plan included only the area within a fifty-mile radius of New York City, while Wright's covered the whole state. Mumford made his reservations obvious when he addressed the national American Institute of Architects in New York in 1925 and revealed that the two plans had been on display side by side at the International Town, City, and Regional Planning and Garden Cities Congress in the same city shortly before. He said,

9. Lewis Mumford, "The Fate of the Garden Cities," *Journal of the A.I.A.* (Feb. 1927), p. 38.

These plans stood symbolically at opposite poles: one [Adams'] as-
sumes that technical ability can improve living conditions while
our existing economic and social habits continue; the other
[Wright's] holds that technical ability can achieve little that is fundamentally worth the effort until we reshape our institutions in
such a way as to subordinate financial and property values to those
of human welfare.[10]

Wright's chief aim had been to demonstrate that good roads and electric
power could revitalize the smaller towns and factories of the state, parallel-
ing the similar interest of Nolen in industrial decentralization. This would
relieve the concentration of wealth, intellect, and culture in the one great
city of New York. Besides a more even distribution of wealth, intellect, and
culture and the broader spread of commerce and industry, Mumford was
urging a more satisfactory administrative unit than either the state or the
city had so far proven to be. This was the political region. It might truly be
said that the garden city and the regional scheme held in common the wish
to offer a legitimate alternative to big-city existence through a synthesis of
administrative and physical elements. All admitted the attractions of the
great city but deplored its lack of discipline. Mumford did not sympathize
with Adams' viewpoint, despite the latter's early and close association with
the garden city, because his New York plan appeared to be based on the
maintenance of artificial values and the status quo: "an attempt to promote
better living conditions by costly plans for more traffic, higher buildings,
increasing land-values, more intensive congestion."[11] The boom psychology,
which began about 1922 with the recovery of the building trades, worried
Mumford as much as it did Unwin.

Henry Wright's proposal, seconded by Stein and Mumford, derived also
from the informal discussions of the Regional Planning Association of America. This was formed in 1923 and lasted approximately a decade. Lewis
Mumford has noted in his extremely useful introduction to Clarence Stein's
Toward New Towns for America that its charter members were F. L. Ackerman (the man who went to Britain for Whitaker in 1917), Frederick Bigger, A. M. Bing, John Bright, Stuart Chase, R. D. Kohn, Benton MacKaye,
Lewis Mumford, C. S. Stein, C. H. Whitaker, and Henry Wright. "In time,
a handful of others joined the association, including Edith Elmer Wood,

10. Lewis Mumford, "Realities vs. Dreams," *Journal of the A.I.A.* (June 1925), p. 198.
11. Ibid.

Tracy Augur, and Catherine Bauer."[12] Charles Whitaker organized the association, although he later left it.

Speaking that same evening with Mumford in New York before the American Institute of Architects were Whitaker, Frederick Bigger, and Raymond Unwin. The latter had come over to the International Town Planning Congress with Ebenezer Howard and Barry Parker. Patrick Geddes had attended the first meeting of the Regional Planning Association of America in May 1923 at the Hudson Guild Farm in Netcong, New Jersey, but Unwin was to have the more sustained influence in formulating its thought on site planning and economic matters.

Nothing appears to have been more stimulating to Unwin than actual group experience and action. Perhaps that is one subconscious reason why he returned so often to America during the twenties and thirties. Stein and Wright consulted with Ebenezer Howard and Parker and Unwin in 1924 when they went abroad to look at British and European planning. Stein had been appointed the previous year by Governor Alfred E. Smith as chairman of the New York State Commission of Housing and Regional Planning. He wanted to be more conversant with the "constructive action" of the British as contrasted to the "legal don'ts" of American housing legislation. In 1925 Stein and Bing invited to their Hudson Guild Farm about twenty-five of the distinguished foreign visitors to the New York planning congress, along with a corresponding number of Americans. Benton MacKaye was at the time anxious to revive the square dances and Appalachian folk ballads, and when the local farm people arrived to show the distinguished visitors the old country dances, Unwin took off his coat and joined them.[13]

During August 1934, while he was part of a select commission traveling about the United States for the National Association of Housing Officials under a Rockefeller grant, his younger colleagues used to cancel Unwin's after-dinner speaking engagements, trying to spare him, only to learn that he was re-engaging himself in order not to disappoint a local audience.[14] The report of this trip, "A Housing Program for the United States," largely pre-

12. (University Press of Liverpool, 1951), p. 16.

13. Letter from Clarence Stein to Carl Feiss, Sept. 27, 1963.

14. Carl Feiss, "Unwin's American Journeys," Town and Country Planning, Part II, (Dec. 1963), p. 471. Other members of the select commission were Ernst Kahn of Frankfort-am-Main, Alice M. Samuel of the Bebington Urban District Council, and the British Society of Women Housing Estate Managers, Ernest Bohn, and Henry Wright. They visited fourteen major cities in two months. See also C. Feiss, "Letchworth and the U.S.A." Town and Country Planning (Sept. 1953), pp. 415–19, and C. Feiss, "America's Debt to Sir Raymond Unwin," Journal of the Town Planning Institute (Nov. 1963), p. 301.

pared by Unwin with the assistance of the executive director, Coleman Woodbury, was adopted at a meeting of housing officials in Baltimore in October 1934. Twenty-five thousand copies of a summary were published in November, in time to have an influence on the first slum clearance and housing legislation of the New Deal in 1935.[15] Both President Coolidge and President Franklin D. Roosevelt had spoken to Unwin about his planning experience and views.

It seems clear that Unwin had come to the United States in the fall of 1922 to consult for the Russell Sage Foundation on the projected New York Regional Plan, although Carl Feiss says Unwin's first postwar trip must have been in 1923 when he joined with Hugh MacRae, Thomas Adams, John Nolen, Elwood Mead, and Gifford Pinchot in the formation of the abortive Farm City Corporation of America.[16] This was for the promulgation of model farm colonies of a type already established by MacRae in North Carolina. This episode, too, was later to play a part in the resettlement program of the New Deal, especially through the homestead colony of Penderlea in North Carolina, laid out by John Nolen; but the closest derivatives of the garden city theories were probably the greenbelt towns made possible by the Emergency Relief Appropriations Act and the National Industrial Recovery Act of 1935. Under the direction of brain-truster Rexford Guy Tugwell, who believed in many of Ebenezer Howard's basic dicta and knew Unwin, the Suburban Resettlement Division was set up to carry them out. In the larger context Greenbelt, Maryland; Greenhills, Ohio (near Cincinnati), and Greendale, Wisconsin (near Milwaukee), were the result of the earlier exchange between Stein and Wright and Parker and Unwin, with the additional seasoning of Mumford's writing. Of the garden city examples they probably most closely resembled Wythenshawe as satellite bodies to larger cities.

When he was seventy-six years old Unwin set out in the midst of winter on "MacKaye's March" up the flooded Connecticut Valley to debate the possibility of a Connecticut TVA and the virtues of upstream dams and reforestation against downstream dikes and dams. Also on the trip besides Benton MacKaye, were Clarence Stein, Louis Wetmore, and Carl Feiss. In

15. See especially "Appendix II, Developments in Housing Policy, November 1934–September 1935," *A Housing Program for the United States*. Public Administration Service No. 48, Chicago, 1935.

16. John M. Glenn et al., *Russell Sage Foundation 1907–1946*, II (New York, Russell Sage Foundation, 1947) p. 441. Feiss, Part I, Nov. 1963, p. 424. Mr. Feiss cites Paul K. Conkin, *Tomorrow a New World: The New Deal Community Program* (Ithaca, N.Y., Cornell University Press, 1959) as a valuable source.

the chilly December weather everyone caught fierce colds except Sir Raymond, who ascribed his immunity to strong tea, with lots of cream and sugar.[17]

Toward the end Unwin seemed to be more attracted to and more needed by Americans than by his own countrymen, and particularly by American students. Henry Wright had begun a division of planning and housing at Columbia University in 1935 with funds from the Carnegie Foundation.[18] In the spring of 1936 he employed as his assistant Carl Feiss, fresh from the Massachusetts Institute of Technology where he had studied with Thomas Adams and his son Frederick. During the next summer Wright died and the division was left without a director. Clarence Stein, Henry Churchill, and Ralph Walker advised the university to persuade Sir Raymond to fill the place. This was made less difficult by the recent marriage of Unwin's daughter to Curtice Hitchcock of New York, and he agreed to come to New York for four of the nine academic months, beginning in the fall of 1936. The arrangement lasted until his death in 1940.

It is interesting that in the same year of 1936 Dean Joseph Hudnut, who had left Columbia, was in Europe interviewing Dr. Walter Gropius for a similar post at Harvard University. If Sir Raymond had been younger then and had spent the entire academic year at Columbia, instead of less than half of it, one wonders whether he would have had an all-prevailing and long-lasting influence on American planning education similar to that of Gropius on architectural training. What is most striking during the latter half of the depression decade of the 1930s is the hunger for seasoned and philosophical minds in the schools, the invitation to deeper thought and longer and harder experience, in contrast, to the preference, especially in the East, for the earlier comfortable success in practice as a teaching pre-requisite. Although Unwin was beyond his three score and ten when he came to Columbia, he contributed a great deal to its energy. We hear from Carl Feiss again that, "Stein, Henry Churchill, Albert Mayer, Lewis Mumford, Ascher and many others would come into our little office and sit on the drafting tables and talk with the students. It was a fine and stimulating time and I doubt if ever at any other time students anywhere have had the opportunity of meeting so brilliant and capable a galaxy of people interested in planning and housing."[19] The 1920s had developed the talent, and the 1930s provided the opportunities. Creativity in planning was in the air, but another shattering war was about to cause many to forget again.

17. Ibid., p. 427 (this must have been 1939 rather than 1938).

18. Ibid., Part II, p. 473.

19. Ibid., Part I, p. 426.

The most notable model villages in France and Germany were at Noisiel and Essen. In 1874 Gustave Menier began to build semidetached brick cottages with tiled roofs for the employees of his chocolate works, not far out of Paris. He was the same manufacturer who had commissioned the mill over the Marne there by Jules Saulnier in 1871, with its diamond-patterned frame of iron and in-fill of colored bricks and terra-cotta, characteristic of the decade. It may be historically significant that Menier was taking a step forward in sociology, technology, and art combined, as it was when Titus Salt employed William Fairbairn as his consulting engineer for the factory at Saltaire and the promoters of Riverside used William Jenny, the builder of the first Chicago skyscraper. Menier's colony had its own public square with shops, a concert hall, a library, and a restaurant for workers. Each pair of dwellings faced a side garden rather than the street and was staggered so that the house on one side of the street was opposite a garden on the other.

The fourteen Krupp Colonies were built in Essen. They were begun between 1859 and 1862, after Alfred Krupp had gained recognition for exhibiting a solid-cast ingot of steel weighing two tons at the Crystal Palace in London. There was also a premonition of the Seven Weeks War of 1866 and the Franco-Prussian War of 1870–71. Because of the abrupt expansion of the Krupp works, the colonies were at first little more than corrugated iron barracks. From this crude beginning followed a series of improvements leading up to the Baumhof in 1890, with its first picturesque, two-story, detached houses and larger gardens; Alfredshof in 1894; Altenhof for the aged; and the Margaretenhöhe in 1906, sometimes called the German Bournville. Parker and Unwin were well acquainted with this German progression. Moreover, in 1896 Theodor Fritsch had published a pamphlet, *Die Stadt der Zukunft,* which contained a number of theories and schemes similar to those of Howard's *Tomorrow* (1898). The coming end of the century was forcing an intellectual stock-taking.

There was also a German Garden City Association founded under the leadership of two cousins, Hans Kampffmeyer and Adolf Otto. Kampffmeyer of Frankfort was a great admirer of Unwin and published a monthly magazine on the garden city; he also organized trips to England in 1904 and 1908. Unwin says in his first 1909 preface to *Town Planning in Practice,* "I am particularly indebted to Dr. Stübben and to the editor and publisher of 'Der

Städtebau,' also to Herr Berlepsch-Valendas, and to the officials of many German towns, who have given me the greatest assistance at different times, and have always been willing to help an Englishman to understand their town-planning methods and to profit by their experience." He felt that their care and perseverance were remarkable and that their interest in the subject had begun with the publication of Camillo Sitte's book, which initiated the theory later held by Eliel Saarinen that the Middle Ages possessed informal principles of urban composition which called for further exploration.

But Culpin observed that even by 1913 there was only one authentic garden suburb in Germany—Ratshof, outside Königsberg.[20] And World War I put an end to further cooperation between the two countries. We hear of other settlements like Wandsbeck near Hamburg; Stockfeld near Strassburg, a municipal effort; a project for Krefeld; Hellerau, near Dresden, the largest of them all and a place where each architect was assigned a section; suburbs like Schlactensee and Falkenberg near Berlin; and another outside Nuremberg which was supposed to resemble Hampstead. But in general the lending institutions were not set up to assist the building of single houses, and the Prussian landowners had even less desire than their British counterparts to see fertile fields covered with homes. Custom dictated broad avenues and huge flats, especially in the imperial city of Berlin. According to German architects like Berlepsch-Valendas, the garden city movement on the Continent was regarded more as an agrarian reform than a reaction against urbanism or industrialization.[21]

In the Netherlands the response to theory appears to have been even less pronounced, perhaps because of the excellent housing and work of native planners like Berlage and de Klerk in Amsterdam, and the great economy in land use made necessary by its scarcity. Only the Rotterdam garden village of Vreewijk, the garden villages of Amsterdam, and the unsuccessful movement between 1925 and 1930 to establish a true garden city in the vicinity of Amsterdam seem worthy of mention.

In Denmark only the small settlement of terrace houses near Copenhagen (Bakkehusene) of the 1920s and the similar row houses of Open Air City (Friluftstaden) in nearby Malmö, Sweden (1943–46), by E. S. Persson appear to be influenced by British ideas.

Spain produced an individual whose stature is comparable to Ebenezer Howard's, and an alternative to the garden city which was often to be compared with it in the literature. As early as 1882 Arturo Soria y Mata—in-

20. Ewart G. Culpin, *The Garden City Movement Up-to-Date* (London, Garden Cities and Town Planning Assn., 1913), p. 61.
21. Berlepsch-Valendas, Foreword.

ventor, politician, traction executive, and author—first proposed his Ciudad Lineal. By the summer of 1894 his pilot project was actually underway as a kind of necklace around Madrid. These events occurred well over a decade before Howard and Unwin's exposition of the theory and construction of Letchworth. It was greatly affected, as was the garden city, by the land theories of the American Henry George. But like Howard's dream it suffered from war and crises, especially those brought on by undercapitalization.

As Professor Collins has shown in his thorough study, "Linear Planning Throughout the World,"[22] the nature of Soria's effort to promote the idea, and the subsequent foundation of societies and a magazine, made it inevitable that the English and the Spanish concepts should be compared. He tells us that there was even a specialist to devote his time to contrasting the merits of garden and linear cities, Hilarión González del Castillo. At the congresses of the International Housing and Town Planning Association the Ciudad Lineal was sometimes spoken of as a "Spanish type of Garden City." Both movements shared the apparently inexhaustible energies of Georges Benoit-Lévy, who eventually transfused his Association des Cités-Jardins de France with a linear vitality, naming it then the Association Internationale des Cités-Jardins-Linéaires.

The original Spanish settlement extended along two sides of a trolley and freight line, with trees and fields beyond, taking advantage of the dispersion that rapid transit invites, yet keeping all residences within easy walking of the chief artery. "Buildings would be of modest height, separated from each other by masses of vegetation and from the street by a compulsory five-meter strip of greenery."[23] A feature that dates the plan to the later nineteenth century is the placement of the best houses on the main street, along the trolley line, instead of on the side streets.

The most important distinctions of the linear city from the garden city are that the commuter to the city can find his acknowledged and legitimate place in it, that it contemplates no limit of population, that it is almost infinitely expansible, "from Cadiz to St. Petersburg, from Peking to Brussels," and that it plays up contemporary methods of transport. The fact that during this era the street was developing into the boulevard, which would become the parkway and ultimately the freeway, also lent the form a distinct pertinence.

Although the merits of the two types of layout were debated at length,

22. George R. Collins, *Journal of the Society of Architectural Historians* (Oct. 1959), pp. 74–93.

23. George R. Collins, "The Ciudad Lineal of Madrid," *Journal of the Society of Architectural Historians* (May 1959), p. 39.

any conclusive assessment appears to depend upon the final needs of the settlement. Prof. Collins reports that Soria himself observed that the success or failure of his experiment would depend upon the temperament and desires of the Spanish people and this might well be said of the British experiment too. The essential difference is not so much between the abstract concept of the linear and concentric forms as between the dissimilar social outlooks of the two nations. The garden city ideogram is directed inward, and W. A. Eden's objection that Buckingham's, Howard's, and Unwin's schemes were hollow at the core is only further proof of it. The lines of organization move in rather than along, and the exclusive and self-contained quality of its disposition are attempts to improve its privacy and to offer opportunity for cross reference and contact within the "village" compound. Although the obvious similarity between the two model cities is, of course, the desire to return the urban population again to a direct acquaintance with nature, the differences between them are perhaps greater, and their worth depends not so much upon their ultimate workability as upon their suitability to a particular mode, or pattern, of group thought. Planning ought to reconcile new and conflicting factors in the immediate environment, and upon this dynamic process would seem to depend its permanent accomplishment.

14. THE NEW TOWNS

It is disconcerting for the planning novice, especially one who returns to Britain after an absence, to encounter the sudden gusts of feeling which the new towns generate. Their very newness might seem to protect them from the storms of opinion, at least until a few of the more basic assumptions can be settled. Yet the incontrovertible fact is that literary and philosophical debate about such issues as housing and planning has gone on for decades, with much of it for high stakes. What Professor Lloyd Rodwin wrote about garden cities and the metropolis, just as the war ended and Stevenage was about to be gotten under way: "Urban patterns will be as much a product of the past as the future. Thinking, however imaginative, must reflect continuities, not mutations, if it is to find practicable expression,"[1] might be applicable all over the world, but would be especially pertinent when addressed to Britons.

Around the metropolis and new town alike gathered the need for demonstration of a more efficient existence. Thus Unwin was always disturbed by gray areas and vacant lots in the great cities, because they appeared so wasteful, and those who opposed new towns were likewise opposed to their low residential density. The parts must be tightly joined and their spatial allegiance conspicuous, regardless of whether there was as yet any consensus as to what the ultimate, broad social purpose of a modern community (garden city, new town, or metropolis) was supposed to be. At this stage of discussion, the purposes of the garden city and new town are much easier to define than those of the great metropolis, because it has nearly always been more feasible to set and answer specific questions through them—they were actual experiments. The metropolis continues to swell and grow but remains reluctant to reveal its inner raison d'être.

1. Lloyd Rodwin, "Garden Cities and the Metropolis," *Journal of Land and Public Utilities Economics* (Aug. 1945), p. 281.

The other general advantage which the new town holds in open British debate is the connection with a tradition of personal dynamism. The work of Victorian reformers still bears considerable weight. London in the south and Manchester in the north have legions of cultural heroes with whom the past can be associated, but no single contemporary figure identifies as closely with their physical fabric as Howard with Letchworth, Mrs. Barnett with Hampstead, Cadbury with Bournville, Lever with Port Sunlight, and Titus Salt with Saltaire. The role of Christopher Wren in London is most often described by regrets that his plan was never executed after the fire of 1666, which should have occasioned a new magnificence. After the blitz of World War II much was promised for the rebuilding of London and the other major cities, but little achieved, with the possible exception of the Coventry town center. On the other hand, from the same disaster emanated fifteen new towns, not wholly satisfactory in all their parts, but nevertheless forms that could be readily understood as large, creative, contemporary efforts.

Even outside Britain, wherever there is interest in garden city thought, the identification of the individual with the project has been paramount.[2] The characters of Parker, Unwin, and Howard are of more immediate import than the utility of garden city techniques or theories. Ernst May speaks for the rest when he declares that it was his sojourn with Sir Raymond that laid "the foundation on which the whole of my work is based."[3] Clarence Stein writes of Unwin and Howard: "It was the inspiration of two great human beings who loved their fellow men and who had so much to give that counted most."[4] The great metropolis cannot often be identified with the warm and humane figure of one man, or a pair of men. What has always counted heavily in the British context is the willingness of almost all leaders to carry these personal lessons over from generation to generation.

Lloyd Rodwin also puts his finger on the precedence of the individual before any program when he explains in his essay on the new towns that the endurance of the effort was largely due to the peculiar coordination of Howard's nature, his inventiveness and practicality, and "a mesmeric quality capable of infusing his book and his personal appeals with the indefinable contagious vitality which excites men's imaginations and attracts their

2. See Barry Parker, "Letchworth's Example to the World, Influence on Other Countries," *Letchworth Citizen* (March 5, 1943). Carl Feiss, "Letchworth and the U.S.A.," *Town and Country Planning* (Sept. 1953), pp. 415–19. Raymond Unwin, "American Architecture and Town Planning," *Journal of the R.I.B.A.* (Nov. 12, 1921), p. 78.

3. Letter to the author June 5, 1956. May worked with Unwin about 1910.

4. Feiss, p. 419.

allegiance."[5] When Unwin moved into government service in 1914 he was likewise placed in a position from which he could influence through his magnetism postwar legislation, administrative directives, and parliamentary investigations for a long time to come. Howard's good will was known to many, and his courage and persistence helped to keep the principles going through the interwar years up to his death in 1928. At the same moment Parker was preparing for the new town by his work on the garden satellite of Wythenshawe. Parker and Unwin had imbibed deeply from the springs of Ruskin's and Morris' aesthetic standards in the seventies and eighties and had this taste further refined by the universal yearning for civic beauty of the 1890s. Howard, by contrast, was no artist and had no inner need to busy himself with the construction of either buildings or cities as three-dimensional enclaves. He could devote himself mainly to outlining new social and financial possibilities and expanding public sympathy, and he was followed in this by the unusually able and energetic Frederic Osborn, again an administrator at Welwyn and a propagandist by temperament, rather than an artist or architect. Diversity of talent and its uses was a crucial factor in what was achieved.

In 1899 Howard had characteristically founded the Garden City Association to discuss his own book, *To-morrow: A Peaceful Path to Real Reform* (1898), and to prepare a scheme whereby a first garden city might come into existence. This turned into the Town and Country Planning Association in 1907, to be finally directed by Osborn, who for sixteen years would also be the manager of Welwyn Garden City, founded in 1919–20. The organization provided a running commentary on the garden city venture through lectures, inexpensive literature, conferences, and its journal, *Garden Cities and Town Planning*, begun in 1904 as *The Garden City*.

It was these agencies, fomented by these men, which were to keep alive the garden city attitudes between the wars. In 1918 Osborn and his friends published a book asking for a hundred new towns after the war.[6] This was to be refurbished and republished in 1940. In the earlier crisis he and his colleagues had used the terms "garden city" and "new town" interchangeably. A major purpose of the new towns was to furnish employment after the war and reduce the accumulated housing shortage, then estimated by Osborn as over one million units. Grants for housing and factories (in sec-

5. Rodwin, *The British New Towns Policy* (Cambridge, Harvard University Press, 1956), p. 22.

6. New Townsmen, *New Towns After the War* (London, Dent, 1918).

tional or divisible form) were to come from the national treasury, with the whole enterprise turned over to local authorities when sufficiently developed.

The National Garden Cities Committee had already been formed to urge the building of new towns, together with the further development of existing small towns, when in 1919 another group, the New Town Council (fifty-two members, mostly Quakers), was similarly organized to found a co-operative city under the leadership of Dr. Ralph Crowley, Chief Medical Officer of the Ministry of Education and the Ministry of Health. It is revealing, in terms of the nineteenth-century past, that the Council describes one of its goals as "recolonizing our own country."[7] It recommended that, "in the heart of the New Town will be the School, and much of the Civic Endeavor and ideal will gather around it." As Osborn pointed out after the second war, much of the neighborhood unit concept had been included in Howard's original prospectus.[8] The New Town Council favored a population of ten to twenty thousand, learning from the slow progress of Letchworth, rather than the thirty thousand recommended by Howard. The more optimistic National Garden Cities Committee believed that the maximum population might be comfortably pushed up to fifty thousand, closer to the early limits of the later new towns.

The Depression brought another surge of such proposals. Although A. Trystan Edwards disagreed with many of the architectural tenets of the garden cities and particularly their lack of concentrated layout, their too great interest in relating to nature, and their disregard of formal Beaux-Arts principles of urban composition which would give the "dignity and power" he felt necessary for this scale of planning, he advanced his recommendation for a hundred new towns through an association of that title in 1932. He used his old military serial number from the First War, J–47485, to denote his authorship. He conceived the purpose of the new towns "as the last and greatest of our war memorials."[9] They would provide employment in the aftermath of a depression rather than a demobilization. There were to be seventy-six towns in England, fifteen in Scotland, and nine in Wales, none to be closer to London than twenty-five miles. Fifty thousand inhabitants

7. W. R. Hughes, *New Town: A Proposal in Agricultural, Industrial, Educational, Civic and Social Reconstruction* (London, Dent, 1919), p. 12.

8. F. J. Osborn, "The Garden City Movement," *Landscape Architecture* (Jan. 1946), p. 46.

9. J–47485, *100 New Towns for Britain: Solve the Slum Problem, Give Creative Employment, Save the Countryside, Make an A-1 Population* (London, Gresham Press, 1934), p. 3. Cf. *London Times* (Feb. 24, 1934) and Edward's "Model Town Designed for Traffic," *Town Planning Review, 14* (May 1930), 31–41.

in each seemed to him again the correct figure. New governmental currency would be issued to pay for the construction.

With decent lapses intervening, such proposals kept coming up, sparkling with novelty and invention, but it is valuable to keep in mind Professor Rodwin's admonition of 1945 that it is wise to look before in order to thoroughly understand what is about to happen after. As far back as the first half of the nineteenth century there was a substantial indication of the advent of the new towns. In 1843, a good six years before James Silk Buckingham recommended his "new Town" of Victoria, that extraordinarily foresighted commentator on the first phases of the industrial revolution, T. J. Maslen, had written,

> It may startle some political economists to talk of commencing the building of *new cities* in England. I say new cities, planned as cities from their first foundation, and not mere small towns or villages, or emigrant settlements. A time will arrive when something of this sort must be done in England. . . . England cannot escape from the alternative of new city building.[10]

And this time did arrive, a whole century later, in the midst of the distraction of wars and worldwide depression. It proved to be as disturbing still in some quarters. From this extended perspective we are more inclined to comprehend the new town movement as a reaction from the industrial population pressure, and overurbanization, both of which began in the North, than as an elementary problem of metropolitan overspill in the South, as it has been more lately interpreted.

Maslen's writing is also useful for recalling that the whole apparatus of open planning and greenery in the garden cities was not the last flutter of maudlin romantic sentiment, as it is sometimes labeled, but grew out of the direct confrontation of art and industry. It reflected the urgent and literal need of the early industrial towns for breathing and recreational space within reasonable walking distance. Maslen in 1843 was infuriated that the animals of the menageries in the northern towns were fed better and more regularly than many of the human inhabitants. He urged the closing of the Leeds Zoo and Botanical Garden for that reason and to "give the people a taste for and the knowledge how, to *cultivate and enjoy gardens of their own.*"[11] He looked unfavorably on zoos and public gardens because they

---

10. T. J. Maslen, *Suggestions for the Improvement of Our Towns and Houses* (London, Smith, Elder, 1843), pp. 244–45.
11. Ibid., p. 110.

failed to contribute a genuinely active and participating experience, close to home and family; they merely provided too convenient a distraction, like the pubs, where it was customary in Leeds to give the workmen their pay. He also recommended in 1843 for the new towns in Australia that,

> All the entrances to every town should be through a park, that is to say, a belt of park about half a mile in width, should entirely surround every town . . . This would greatly contribute to the health and pleasure of the inhabitants; it would render the surrounding prospects beautiful, and give a magnificent appearance to a town, from whatever quarter viewed.[12]

Further, Maslen endorsed the circumferential parkway first suggested, as he acknowledged, at Hull in Yorkshire: "The only avenue of trees necessary for equestrians and carriages, should be round the outer circumferential boundary of the park, and of course extending entirely round the park and town."[13] He had probably been inspired to some degree by John Arthur Roebuck and the Philosophic Radicals in their demands for public greenbelts and in 1833 by the Report of the Select Committee to Consider Public Walks and Places of Exercise. Maslen's other great aspiration for a rational Britain resembled that of Thomas Jefferson for the United States. He wanted to introduce a decimal system of money, weights, measures, and time!

Maslen was a typical English utopian, insofar as he was an amateur with several daring, if somewhat premature, schemes. This species, when combined with the Victorian reformer and artist, could prove formidable indeed. Britain never lacked such individuals. In his essay of 1918, which called for a hundred new towns, Osborn referred to John Bellers, a Quaker, as the first of these utopians, although he at other times nominated Sir Thomas More for the honor. Bellers had proposed a community based on a joint stock issue in his 1696 publication, *Proposals for Raising a College of Industry of all Useful Trades and Husbandry*. Robert Owen reprinted the Bellers pamphlet in 1818.[14] The Quaker lived long before the need for open green space became acute. He visualized a collegiate system of housing therefore, a modified version of which Robert Owen had also used as an illustration in his "Villages of Unity and Mutual Co-operation" in the open

12. Ibid., p. 194.
13. Ibid.
14. W. H. G. Armytage, *Heavens Below: Utopian Experiments in England, 1560–1960* (London, Routledge and Kegan Paul, 1961), pp. 30, 81. Osborn thus speaks of Bellers in *New Towns After the War* (London, Dent, 1918), p. 36.

country (for 800 to 1,200 inhabitants). This sketch was included in his report to the Poor Law Committee of the House of Commons in 1817. The medieval college (or hospital, or almshouse) reappeared in Morris' description of communal quadrangular dwellings[15] in the countryside in *News from Nowhere* (1891), from whence it appears to have evolved into Unwin's preferred dwelling type at Hampstead Garden Suburb.

Raymond Unwin was no longer available for much home or town design during the interwar period. In 1909 he had published his classic *Town Planning in Practice* in response to the first housing and town planning statute, partially inspired by his own Hampstead Act of 1906, which had also been guided through Parliament by John Burns. It was to implement this 1909 act that Unwin was asked into government service in 1914, first as Chief Town Planning Inspector to the Local Government Board, and then in 1916 as Director of Housing for the Ministry of Munitions, when he laid out the war housing at Gretna Green, Mancol Village, and Queensferry. In 1918 he became Chief Architect, and later Chief Technical Officer, for Building and Town Planning to the Ministry of Health. In 1921 the Ministry issued the reports of the Unhealthy Areas Committee, which officially recommended the establishment of garden cities through state aid. From 1929 to 1933 he worked as Technical Adviser on the Report of the Greater London Regional Planning Committee, which affected the Greater London Plan of 1943–45, drawn up by Sir Patrick Abercrombie and J. B. Forshaw under the extreme stress of the second war. It also followed Abercrombie's work for the Barlow Commission of 1937–40, appointed by Neville Chamberlain to deal with the redistribution of the industrial population. The Greater London Plan recommended new towns within sixty miles of London to which industry and people from overcrowded London boroughs could repair. In August 1946 (after the Uthwatt and Scott reports of 1941–42) the New Towns Act itself finally came into being. Shortly before, in May 1946 with World War II hardly over, the first new town, Stevenage, was under way.

The heritage of the past was perennially useful, even in projecting an absolutely new town after the total shock of war. By September 1945 it had become imperative to have a master plan for Stevenage (Fig. 120) and there was no legislation with which to accomplish it. Hence it was begun under the

15. (London: Reeves and Turner, 1891), pp. 81, 180, 215. For quadrangular medieval hospital and almshouse plans see Walter H. God-frey, *The English Almshouse* (London, Faber and Faber, 1955).

Fig. 120. Standard housing, Broom Barns, Stevenage.

venerable Section 35 of the Town and Country Planning Act of 1932 which had legal, but no financial, provisions for the founding of garden cities.

It is possible to explain some of the attitudes toward new towns as the result of a series of historical blackouts such as may have been limiting the young social planner of Stevenage just after the war, who told a BBC audience that, "The policy of aiming at a 'balanced and self-contained community' for a town is quite new and the methods of attaining it are still untried."[16] Such untutored observations (although wearying for the informed) cheerily sustained the popular illusion (also pushed by the avant-garde magazines) that there was nothing so new as a new town.

To begin to comprehend the new town under this postwar regimen it is probably best to set aside temporarily the contentions of the agriculturalist that the new towns absorb precious food-growing land (when there is barely half enough in Britain); or the demographer's plaint that the towns can sup-

16. Charles Madge, "The Social Pattern of a New Town," *Listener* (Feb. 17, 1949), p. 267. For an excellent review and analysis of the density problem in the new towns see Peter Will-mott, "Housing Density and Town Design in a New Town: A Pilot Study at Stevenage," *Town Planning Review* (July 1962), pp. 115–27.

ply only a fraction of the new housing units needed (which opens up the old and painful subject of whether it would not be better to encourage emigration, to which Maslen and Wakefield addressed themselves a century before); or the geographer's viewpoint (in some ways affirmed by Letchworth's tardy growth), that they cannot flourish because they are not "natural" towns, existing in particular spots for specific geographic reasons; or even the sociologist's conclusion that there are too many children for the schools, that the neighborhood units do not really work, that there are not enough aunties and mums about, that white-collar and professional men are too scarce, and that community facilities for social gatherings are altogether too meager. To all this would have to be added the vital question whether enough industry could be attracted to provide full and varied employment for men and women and the coming generations.

The reason for artificially narrowing the debate over new town shortcomings at this point is that one should again recall that the Arts and Crafts Movement, as it nourished garden city thought, demanded a reformation of the man-made environment in the fullest artistic sense. As Pugin, Ruskin, Morris, and Parker and Unwin (and even Howard with his claim that it was the "attractions" that mattered) phrased the problem, the dislocations and distortions which the industrial revolution had brought with it were the residual challenge to the artist turned reformer. Without a substantial adjustment in this sphere there could be no assurance that the advent of the machine and cheapness of production would be of permanent benefit. This would mean only half a reform, as Morris had observed. It might be good for some people in some parts of the society, but it was not favorable to the outward health of the organic body of the society as a whole. The ultimate test of progress would have to depend instead upon the visible proof of a functional community because, for the modern, seeing was believing. The new town also therefore must be "functional" in the broadest and most convincing sense and on the highest level as well as in the supply of public utilities, traffic circulation, room sizes, schools, churches, health and social centers, financing systems, marketing facilities, and industrial opportunities.

The need to depend upon and embody the invisible, especially on the part of the democratically liberated but emotionally and intellectually handicapped, was only grooved deeper by the industrial revolution than it had been in the Middle Ages, for feeling and intuition seem always to have to surround and contain the accumulated knowledge of a culture, no matter how basically factual or objectively scientific. In the Middle Ages this need

had been met by the presence of beauty almost everywhere, quickly accessible to the humblest inhabitants of a town. A higher standard of living
would similarly require a higher standard of living art in the environment,
for the city equipped only with material and manipulative systems was not
enough. It merely stimulated greater social hungers without providing adequate responses or satisfactions. Barry Parker reviewed the condition in his
very simple and direct way:

> The meanest things of life are most easily expressed. We can give
> our financial position with clearness in figures. We can express
> the composition of a gas with absolute accuracy in a formula . . .
> We can even state the properties of a triangle with some definite-
> ness. But beyond this we cannot go without calling Art to our aid;
> and the higher we attempt to soar the more dependent upon her
> we become.[17]

The critical question in reference to new towns as they relate back to the
garden cities and before has to be then—are they, or can they be, function-
ing works of art? Even within this area of reference a stupendous range of
opinion is encountered. With ratiocination this appears to have come mostly
from a migration of meaning over a period of time.

It is usual for the objections to the new towns to take exception to the old-
fashioned architecture of the garden cities. As Parker and Unwin withdrew
from private practice and as the British school of domestic architecture went
into eclipse after World War I, the actual quality of the houses in the garden
cities did indeed drop, and an imbalance was set up among architecture,
planning, and nature. This was helped along, as at Earswick and Wythenshawe, by the more rigid minimal requirements of housing subsidies and
the general stringency of an economy righting itself after a war. As idealism
was inflated by strife and suffering, so was the actual economy. Loftier ideals
were left with correspondingly smaller national resources with which to satisfy them. As the public expectation from the "Homes for Heroes" movement
rose, the budget to support it was cut. Moreover, at Welwyn Garden City
the Georgian style became much more academic. We know that Parker and
Unwin disapproved of the revival of historic styles. The opponents of the
garden city nevertheless point to the conservatism of the neo-Georgian architecture at Welwyn as convincing evidence that the principle had outlasted
its time, while Osborn in particular hails that town, with justification, as a

17. Barry Parker and Raymond Unwin, *The Art of Building a Home* (London, Longmans,
Green, 1901), p. 25.

step beyond Letchworth because its architecture was better controlled and its layout more ordered and compact.

Everyone is really right. The differing viewpoints pass like majestic ships in the night, each resolutely bent on its own course. After the war, opinions and information on architecture and planning tended to diverge further and further from the renewed compatibility that had been earlier expected.

In addition to the formal stiffness which the architectural critics detected at Welwyn, they disliked even more the stylistic and spatial passivity they thought they uncovered at Letchworth. They mistook the spirit of humility at Letchworth for naiveté. All through the 1920s and 1930s the more progressive architects of Britain felt, again with reason, that they were not keeping up with the Continent. In the 1930s especially they wanted assurance, propping up, from their surroundings, in a political and financial world gone shaky, much as the German and French moderns had in the 1920s. The English Victorians, unfortunately, had possessed self-assurance in great abundance and hence had not provided any built-in, self-renewing principles for the society as a whole, beyond expecting that brilliant individual reformers would turn up from generation to generation. It left the society fairly strong in terms of initiative, but hampered it badly in the face of possible indictment of nominally accepted systems and conventions. For example, in a prolonged critique of the garden city attitudes as they were assumed to be usually employed, really the first big barrage against the general theorem and practice rather than the individuals who had first conceived it, Thomas Sharp wrote in 1932.

> Little dwellings crouching separately under trees on either side of a great space—how can they look other than mean and contemptible? They are unworthy of us. We want something to reflect our achievement, our great over-topping of Nature; something that is a worthy symbol of civilization, "of society, of broad expanding sympathies, of science, art and culture" . . . Town-country, garden-city will never give it. Only sheer, triumphant, unadulterated urbanity will.[18]

Sharp considers buildings and their disposition as indices of social weakness or strength and also advances the opinion, more often repeated as the past grows dimmer, that outdoor space in the garden cities was ineptly handled

18. Thomas Sharp, *Town and Countryside: Some Aspects of Urban and Rural Development* (London, Humphrey Milford, 1932), p. 163. For the garden city review of the book, see "A Challenge to Garden Cities," *Town and Country Planning* (Feb. 1933), pp. 62–63.

and that this life-giving element in the town (which loomed larger as enclosed spatial effects came to be the criterion of great architecture in the theory of the 1930s) had been callously allowed to bleed out into the landscape between the buildings. In the older market towns which he illustrated, space had been held in close check by small-scaled, cohesive, but irregularly shaped squares, closes, and greens. In the next decade this impression would be reinforced by G. M. Kallmann and others with their rediscovery of "precinctual" compositions in London, supported by the "cellular" motifs of Corbusier's and Hilbersheimer's urban projects. Kallmann's article on the subject was revealingly entitled (from the point of view of functionalism as understood in that decade) "Structural Trends in City Planning."[19]

Once this conviction was set in motion, another and even more popular legend was easily tied to it—that the suburbs were derived from the garden city and included all its faults, well magnified. Yet it was clearly stated by Unwin in 1901, thirty years before Sharp made his case and two years before Unwin himself undertook the first garden city:

> No weak compound of town and country, composed of wandering suburban roads, lined with semi-detached villas, set each in a scrap of garden, will ever deserve the name of Garden City. Acres of such suburbs are only one degree less dreary than miles of cottage rows; they cover an extravagant amount of land while missing most of the advantages which a generous use of land can give.[20]

What these critics had entirely forgotten was that the land policy of Unwin and his predecessors moved steadily away from the inviolability of the single lot and ownership whenever other communal values were at stake.

Sharp brandishes the cudgel and attacks with a rush. If we want a more urbane performance, backed by a better acquaintance with contemporary architectural theory, we can turn to the writings of J. M. Richards. The sequence of his intellectual concerns make him a typical author for this period. There can be little doubt that the intricate planning and the wider use of flats in the newest new town of Cumbernauld (Figs. 121–123), begun in 1959 by L. Hugh Wilson and others, and the project for Hook by the London County Council, or Roehampton near London (begun in 1953, also by the Council), have been influenced by his skillful essays.

19. *Architectural Review* (Nov. 1946), pp. 125–28.

20. Raymond Unwin, "On the Building of Houses in the Garden City," *The Garden City Conference at Bournville* (London, The Garden City Assn., 1901), p. 70.

The first in this vein appears to be "The Failure of the New Towns" in the *Architectural Review* of July 1953, which was backed in the same number by Gordon Cullen's "Prairie Planning in the New Towns." Quite significantly, Richards uses the title, "garden-suburb sentimentalists," in his charge against the perpetrators of the new town "failure." He too regards the issue as primarily one of architecture rather than town planning. He reports that the "town-minded modern architects failed to win a clear cut victory over the garden suburb sentimentalists, in spite of all the practical arguments, like the transport difficulties and the waste of agricultural land that accompany decentralization, in their favour."[21]

The use of the term sentimentalists donates the clue to Richards' commitment, since it follows that he regards the garden cities chiefly as holdovers from late Victorian humors. This attitude may also explain another shift in focus. He and his contemporaries had been conditioned by the inferior state of British architecture during the 1920s and 30s to resist prettiness. There is no gainsaying that Welwyn Garden City of the 1920s was intended to be pretty. So he concludes:

> The new Towns constitute, collectively, the biggest building enterprise of the post-war era; yet, looking at them, one might almost imagine oneself back, not only in the era before the war but in that of the nineteen-twenties, when the little red-roofed villa scattered over mile upon mile of countryside was the only kind of housing thought of.[22]

Sir John Summerson, with his deftness in penetrating such subjects, observes (1955) in "Ten Years of British Architecture," that between the wars the mainstream of modern architecture had bypassed Britain, the only variants allowed being those from the half-moderns, from what he terms the "Swedish charm school," and from the more conservative Dutch group, as represented by Dudok.[23] In an era that called for greater innovation, toughness, and backbone—a New Brutalism if carried far enough—all that could be obtained was confectionery: Welwyn was a frosted town and the suburbs were underdisciplined, hence garden cities before and new towns after would be undesirable because they appealed too cleverly and insidiously to the emotional sweet tooth of the English people.

The great international document from the end of the 30s was, of course,

21. P. 32 (cf. Wyndham Thomas, "The Ten-Year Experiment: New Towns: Success or Failure?" London *Sunday Times* [June 25, 1961], for a rebuttal).

22. P. 31.

23. John Summerson, "Introduction," *Ten Years of British Architecture, 1945-55* (London, Arts Council, 1956), pp. 8, 10.

Fig. 121. Cumbernauld near Glasgow; L. Hugh Wilson and others, 1959–. Cumbernauld reflects the latest thought about the new town, particularly in regard to its more dense, intricate, and linear housing pattern. From the air the similarity to Saltaire is notable. Saltaire is the model village most approved by recent critics.

Fig. 122. Single-story bungalows, Cumbernauld. The old row theme at Cumbernauld is used as a kind of scenic telescope to perform the ancient British act of looking out over a landscape from a relatively low vantage point. The means may appear to be new and different, but the relation to the landscape is that of the garden city, and goes as far back as the People's Park by Paxton, and farther.

Fig. 123. Kildrum 5, Adventure Playground, Cumbernauld. There was objection to the first new town of Stevenage because the houses appeared too routine, thin, and sweet (Figure 120). A major problem was that postwar ideological expectations had become inflated along with the currency. There was bound to be underachievement. At the newer Cumbernauld the houses have more body and evocative force, despite their really greater eclecticism, deriving from Swedish and Scottish house types. The postwar euphoria wore off—children would have to learn to play in a more difficult, hard, and three-dimensional world like this Adventure Playground.

Sigfried Giedion's *Space, Time and Architecture,* first delivered as a series of Charles Eliot Norton Lectures at Harvard. This proposed that spatial definition was the major ingredient in the successful development of an authentic modern architecture. It also put forth the thesis that Britain had moved into the modern age first with its early nineteenth-century iron bridges and factories, that America had advanced next with its steel-framed Chicago skyscrapers of the 1880s and 90s, and then it had become Germany's turn in the 1920s with its still newer factories by Behrens, Mendelsohn, Gropius, and others, and the Bauhaus School, rigorously and economically pursuing art by relating it logically, at last, to technology and mass production. Le Corbusier was the French counterpart of Gropius and equally important because he applied a similar logic to urban planning and high-rise dwellings. A little earlier Nikolaus Pevsner, Richards' fellow editor at the *Architectural Review,* had pointed his remarkable scholarship in the same general direction in *Pioneers of the Modern Movement,* appropriately subtitled for the British, *From William Morris to Walter Gropius.* To Richards it was not so much a matter of whether architectural leadership had passed from England to the Continent about 1900, as Pevsner believed, as of embarrassment that Britain, which had begun by setting the pace, had by now fallen so far behind. The contents of his *Introduction to Modern Architecture* (1940) and his other important book, *The Functional Tradition in Early Industrial Buildings in Britain,* show him seriously concerned with the twentieth-century problem of relative national position on an international stage. And in the background, of course, he had to keep the realization that Morris, Shaw and Voysey (unlike Unwin) had declined to have anything to do with professional organizations, academic training, or governmental guidance of the architect; yet after World Wars I and II the country was abruptly faced with housing needs which had to be handled on just those unpalatable terms if they were to be met at all.

There appears to have been a lasting conviction among Richards' generation that the legitimate historical line in modern architecture had been posited by a series of large, open-framed, glass-enclosed, modular buildings, whose prototype lay in the early British textile mills. Thus the Crystal Palace of 1851 would be an ideogram of a factory for the exhibition of factory-made products. The greenhouses which preceded it were figurative factories for flowers. The British built them long—the Americans built them tall. The Bauhaus had been a design factory complete with curtain walls. The Hertfordshire schools would be elementary brain factories. Therefore, the absence of large, positive, factory-like forms and skyscrapers in the new towns disturbed the iconological equilibrium. Yet the piece that would not fit was that the house had been the international unit of architectural exchange from the 1860s up to World War I and Britain had also shown the way with it. Schools had then been scaled down to look like houses, shops had looked like houses, churches had been reduced to look like houses (as at Hampstead with Lutyens), even factories looked like houses when consciously designed (as at Letchworth).

Now the current had reversed and the new town authorities would not play fair and acknowledge it, according to Richards. What he does not see, or fails to find room for, in his outline of the "Failure of the New Towns," is the fact that the garden city–new town movement had been intended to be as functionalistic in its own wide-ranging communal way as the British factories had been for their more precise and particular requirements. And the historic balance of need in this environmental functionalism had been, first, the desire for green, open space to refresh the eyes and mind and offer physical recreation within a convenient walking distance: and second, the requirement of an adequate and decent home, because it stood for all the family, which nourished the sound individual for the benefit of the whole society, securing him against the destructive forces of the factory system. So, reiterates Unwin at the end of his life,

> All through the history of English housing the cottage has been tied up with human life, human desires, needs, habits as well as man's mere physical necessities . . . In the early industrial age, standards in family life and in housing deteriorated rather than progressed. What we are trying to do in England is to get back to the cottage and garden type of housing . . . Such housing allows for the growth of individuality and imagination which are so vital to cooperation.[24]

The difference in representational status almost seems to repeat the ancient question: Where did the industrial revolution actually begin, and where should it all end—in the small cottage industry or in the big factory system? Unwin would designate the first, Richards the second, as a fitting precedent in fostering more efficient patterns for civilization without eroding its humane content.

24. Unwin, *Columbia University Lectures*, 1936–37, p. 6.

The dichotomy has a traceable origin, even if its solution is not readily apparent. In 1833, before many authorities believe the industrial revolution had even begun to manifest itself fully, P. Gaskell in writing of changes wrought by manufacturing on social conditions, had already concluded:

> This disruption of all the ties of home, is one of the most fatal consequences of the factory system. The social relations which should distinguish the members of the same family are destroyed. The domestic virtues—man's natural instincts, and the affections of the heart, are deadened and lost. . . . The more delicate shades of character [disappear and into their place fall selfishness and avarice, reducing the working people in the end] to a heartless assemblage of separate and conflicting individuals, each striving for their "own hand," uninfluenced, unmodified by the more gentle, the more noble, and the more humanized cares, aspirations and feelings, which could alone render them estimable as fathers, mothers, brothers and sisters.[25]

The age of the Vast Delinquency was about to begin. There was to be less time now for the dignities of age, sex, or familial obligation.

Richards was the first writer to rediscover Saltaire. As early as 1936 he was calling it in a special article in the *Architectural Review*,

> not a garden city, but a compact community of entirely urban character . . . It is the prototype not of Welwyn or Wythenshawe but of the modern residential unit that we are now coming to appreciate as the only one capable of preserving for our continued use the distinctive advantages of the town and countryside. Its neat rows of terrace houses are not broken up by garden plots, and thereby gain both compactness and architectural unity.[26]

There is no need to probe further for the reasons he approved of Saltaire. It is the single instance among the model villages where factory and home were drawn up by the same hands and employ the same style throughout, and where there is little hollowing for green spaces. Lockwood and Mawson had previously used the Renaissance style in the redevelopment of Bradford. It was therefore an urbane as well as an industrial style, and it acknowledged

25. P. Gaskell, *The Manufacturing Population of England* (London, Baldwin and Cradock, 1833), pp. 94–96.

26. J. M. Richards, "Sir Titus Salt or The Lord of Saltaire," *Architectural Review* (Nov. 1936), pp. 216–17.

the virtues of high density and geometric order. The later entrepreneurs of
the North like Cadbury, Rowntree, and Lever had attempted instead to
romantically revert, to split off and remove the cottage from the factory in
appearance and hide it in greenery, while bringing them closer together in
location. Possibly this is what Richards and his coterie meant when they
spoke of the new towns as representing a "cult of isolation." To attempt
to escape from the power or prestige of industrialization or urbanism was,
in their view, a form of aesthetic cowardice.

Richards wrote a whole book in the giddy euphoria of the first year after
the second war, *The Castles on the Ground,* about the suburb as a type, calling it an "*Ad hoc* world, created rather than evolved," and distinguished
"for its scenic effects, which outweigh strictly architectural considerations,"
the lair of the amateur gardener. It was a curious and rather English reversal of the original contention, for here the offense was that the garden city
had formalized and professionalized the qualities of amateur romance and
rhetoric, the quaint make-believe and harmless eccentricity of the genuinely
picturesque suburb. Yet despite his long-standing opposition and exception
to the garden city and new town, Richards' intuitions led him finally to an
acceptance close to that of the earlier British searchers for a better environment. His rediscovery of Saltaire is one instance of this. In "The Failure of
the New Towns" he similarly writes:

> It should hardly be necessary to emphasize that a town is, by defi-
> nition, a built-up area, whose role is to provide for a particular
> mode of living. It is a sociable place, for people who want to live
> close together, and expresses itself as such through the compactness
> of its layout, through the sense of enclosure experienced within
> it and through being composed of streets.[27]

Hardly a better or more British description could be given of the Hampstead
Garden Suburb by Henrietta Barnett herself. What Richards sought in
1953, Mrs. Barnett and her compeers, along with Unwin and Lutyens, had
been looking for about 1900. The British longing for communality is forever bringing forth new quests after it, and long disputes over it.

The real case against the administrative leaders between the wars and
after is that they gradually left as open and optional the absolute requirement for art and amenity in the everyday environment. The government

27. P. 31.

abetted this attitude with a constant bureaucratic nagging about costs in every phase of building and layout. Richards rightly points this out as a flaw in the new town program. Yet it was a cardinal belief with Parker and Unwin that the arts must be steadily and adequately cultivated in a consistent direction or the knack of them would be lost again. This was the lesson that came to Unwin from Lethaby as well as Morris. Lethaby thought of creativity as a matter of comparable degree and accumulating tradition, rather than of the rebirth of individual genius in each generation.

Under the pressure of the accumulated housing shortage many of the other communal elements such as cinemas, dance halls, larger shops, health and social centers, and churches were left out entirely, particularly during the credit squeeze of 1948–49, when even house sizes for subsidy were shrunk substantially. There was a reversion to the minimal standard which had so plagued Parker and Unwin at New Earswick and Letchworth and had deprived Unwin of his fondest dream of a beautiful dwelling in a beautiful garden in a beautiful town for all. The Town Development Act of 1952, whereby existing small towns could be expanded, seems a similar result of a policy of "make-do" under less favorable financial conditions and a cooling of the idealistic ardor of the 1940s.

Unwin felt this emphasis on economy in construction was symptomatic of the modern age and said, long before either war, "It is one of the curses of our time that this idea of cheapness becomes attached first to one subject and then to another, and acquires an artificial and altogether misleading meaning."[28] When one goes about looking for a worthwhile architectural accent at the top of a rise or a turn in the road in a new town, consequently, he is more than likely to be met by something shoddy or temporizing as a focal point, which hardly deserves the modest assistance of the carefully graded land contour or the adventurous implication of spatial movement. This never happens at Hampstead. Moreover, the subtleties of texture, line, and color that the garden city architects had begun to accumulate, such as the use of suitable materials for early and adequate weathering, or the gentle curve or sag of a wall plane or roofline, were completely forgotten. The new concrete, glass, and metals were felt to be so durable and self-sufficient that no concern should be expended on these earlier problems. Efficient as well as abstract use of space, outside and in, became the major point of reference, and the solids tended less and less to be really seen. In

28. "Cheap Cottage Exhibition," typescript in the R.I.B.A. Unwin Collection.

the shopping centers of the new towns a kind of flat, pretty paste-up, or collage effect prevailed (Fig. 124), in emulation of modern painting, complete with its two-dimensional inference of three-dimensional volumes in space. The government preference for the cheapest building types, the contemporary architect's persuasion that bareness and austerity and the free manipulation of picturesque materials represent modernism, and the inhabitants' supposedly returning desire to be discreet and anonymous (not at all Victo-

Fig. 124. Market Square, Town Centre, Harlow. To the left and right can be noticed the collage-like impression from the use of different materials, which resulted from the first wave of postwar gaiety and renewed self-assurance. In the middle there is a more serious breakdown in scale and proportion and the disturbance caused by varying roof lines. These impulsive effects were unfortunately aggravated by postwar cheapness of construction.

rian individualists), probably contributed to the mundane expression too often encountered along the new town roads. The eclecticism of planning survives in the best new towns, but the mix of architecture is apt to be pinched and overdiluted, a fatal hesitancy under eclectic conditions.

These were lid-like restraints imposed by officialdom. Pushing up from below was the eternal ambition of the working class (which Parker and Unwin and Bernard Shaw in his plays had noted long ago) to attain the broad middle-class plateau of respectability. This presented everyone, especially foreign visitors, with the expectation of seeing a radical, new, different, and comprehensive planning experiment, only to face the disconcerting realization upon arrival at the site that it was full of middle-class proprieties. No doubt it was this paradox that irritated the London intellectuals and caused them to foster (somewhat overenthusiastically it appears) the identification of new towns and garden cities with middle-class suburbs. They seem to equate middle-class aims with mediocrity, a compulsion to play it safe, and perhaps worst of all, an insensate willingness to dominate national taste as well as legislation by sheer weight of numbers. Sir John Summerson helps greatly here, as before, when he writes, in discussing the new towns,

> The feeling was for eclecticism and loose pictorial values, and in some quarters it went further than that; it was argued that architecture as a public service implied architecture which captivated, which was middlebrow and instantly acceptable by everybody except members of the MARS group [the British offshoot of the Internationalist CIAM, which was most active on a linear plan for London between 1938 and 1942]. The word "humanistic" temporarily acquired a meaning almost equivalent to "cosy."[29]

The "people" and their representatives then wanted no unseemly architectural demonstrations in the streets while they went about building the New Jerusalem. In this posture, of course, they noticeably differed from the politicians, industrialists, and influential citizens of countries like Brazil, France, Italy, Germany, Sweden, Finland, and India, where new planning was apt to draw a large measure of its prestige from its execution with even newer and more extraordinary architecture. The city of Brasilia in Brazil would be one instance of this, but the archetype would be Le Corbusier's *Habitation* in Marseilles, where what was essentially a small French village was lifted off the earth and incorporated in a single brilliant building. This slablike novelty, this vertical thunderclap, in general concept goes back to the early nineteenth-century and the Fourieristic *phalanstère* in France.

Whether this architecture vis-à-vis planning problem would have been alleviated if talents like those of Gropius, Breuer, Mendelsohn, Moholy Nagy, Chermayeff, and Tunnard had remained in Britain during the troubled 1930s, instead of moving on to the United States and its universities, is certainly open to conjecture. As soon as the second war was over, the younger English architects turned their attention outward again to the

29. Summerson, p. 13.

Continent and the accomplishments of Le Corbusier. In the new town connection they looked up the latest efforts of the Swedes, who before the war had learned a great deal from British planning layouts. This renewed search overseas for models of excellence found its first conspicuous architectural embodiment in the ten-story point block at Harlow New Town in 1951 by Frederick Gibberd (Fig. 125).

Fig. 125. Ten-story point block, The Lawn, Mark Hall North, Harlow; Frederick Gibberd, 1951. The first "high rise" in Britain, by contrasting so clearly with the tiny houses around it, brought on a discussion of the assertion of postwar confidence over cost and utility. Its value seems to be chiefly symbolic, although there is also the old problem of scaling up of important buildings and heights to the whole town.

One instinctively asks why, when flats cost approximately twice as much to build as houses in England (the reverse of Sweden)[30] and there was no indigenous habit of tall dwellings or centralized heating, the importation of the point block was ever thought necessary. Yet exotic though it was, there are some eminently logical reasons for its construction if one also considers the architectural urge to catch up, which is reflected in the writing of men like Richards, the active discussion about the need to preserve open agricultural land which the war made so obvious, and the call to emphasize modern architecture so that it could provide a suitable and visible analogue to modern planning and furnish visual concentration points to hold the larger new towns together. In addition, the arduous adjustments to modern in-

30. In 1960 Wyndham Thomas asserted this comparative cost to be 40s. per square foot for a house, 74s. for an eight-story flat, and 83s. for a twelve-story flat. "Letters to the Editor," London *Sunday Times* (July 24, 1960), p. 12.

dustrialism and technology had come a little earlier and rested a little more heavily on the English. When this experience was combined with victory over the threat of extermination in an all-out war, the emergence of a prominent architectural symbol from the earth, even if it could later be demonstrated by "functional" and "economic" analysis to have been only an adapted and somewhat expensive pseudo-symbol, was foreordained.

It appears to have been Corbusier's visit to Stockholm in 1933 that welded together the two major influences on the dwelling types of the later English new towns. From his visit arose in South Stockholm the long, narrow, three-story strip dwellings, followed by the tall point blocks. The three-story lamella slabs of South Stockholm must have had a direct effect upon the later three-story maisonettes of the new English towns. But even the Swedes who, incidentally, did openly acknowledge the need for amenity (and through their ability to keep out of war could provide it), were not completely uncritical about high-rise dwellings, regardless of their relative cheapness in Sweden as contrasted to Britain. As late as 1956 Sven Markelius, the architect–planner of Stockholm, was calmly observing,

> There can be different opinions as to which is preferable, the intimate scale and the natural contact with the neighbours which is achieved in this way with low houses in small groupings, or anonymity and the feeling of distance and space which can be achieved in an environment dictated by the scale of multi-storey buildings with big proportions and a large number of people. There is reason to believe that the first of these environment types —in particular, for practical reasons—better meets the wishes and needs of families with children.[31]

Despite the considerable investment of symbolic intent in the first high-rise building of the new towns, the greater meaning still seems to be reserved for the treatment of the land itself. When Frederick Gibberd describes how his new town of Harlow was first conceived, he speaks with the maturity of a very long sequence behind him: "If the landscape is learnt and felt and the building groups designed into it, the landscape pattern itself will form a structural framework which will fuse together the built-up areas of the town."[32] He sounds as if he were dealing with the skeleton of a large steel

31. Sven Markelius, "The Structure of the Town of Stockholm," *Byggmästaren* (1956), A3, p. 75.

32. Frederick Gibberd, "Landscaping the New Town," *Architectural Review* (March 1948), p. 85. For an excellent summary of how the Englishman has looked at his landscape over several centuries see David Lowenthal and Hugh C. Prince, "The English Landscape" and "English Landscape Taste" in *Geographical Review* (July 1964 and April 1965).

building, out of the mechanistic habit of the 30s and 40s, but his instinct
for the land is undeniably in tradition (Fig. 126).

Markelius believed that wholesome family life has as much claim on
planning as sophisticated building arrangements and telling silhouettes,
and we must return to the vital unit of the family if we hope to obtain a
better understanding of the origins and deeper motivations of the new town

*Fig. 126. Harlow, view along First Avenue toward Stow Shopping Centre. The open, overall net
of Letchworth has disappeared under the pressure of through roads, but the planning to gentle
drops and rises of the land remains. The single or semidetached house is still invoked as an ideal.
The tendency to reduce and offset streets and houses goes back to Hampstead.*

movement. We may indirectly comprehend some of its durability through
the sculpture, *Family Group,* by Henry Moore (Fig. 127), which was located
within view of the first point block at Harlow (Fig. 128). This type of figurative association chiefly engaged the sculptor between 1944 and 1949, just
when the idealization of a new town life was being formulated.

Moore was, like Unwin, a person from the dark and rainy dales of the
North where the industrial revolution had begun and where gloom and

Fig. 127. Family Group, Harlow; Henry Moore, dedicated 1956. It represents a type with which Moore was occupied in the immediate postwar era. There is another such family group by Moore at Stevenage.

Fig. 128. Family Group by Moore in the Landscape Wedge at Mark Hall North, Harlow New Town. The first point block in Britain (Fig. 125) is visible in the distance. Both statue and building are acclamations of survival after a great war.

vacuity could be nearly as often experienced in the open and hilly landscape as in the dirty and congested towns. From this setting may have come the dual concern with loneliness and the frictions of tight physical proximity and how the artist ought to cope with both. Sir Herbert Read, in discussing the entirety of Moore's sculpture, has offered a vantage point from which to begin to understand this family group and possibly the whole new town. He has noticed that,

> We normally associate monumental sculpture with crowded cities, but if we watch the people passing *King Charles* in Trafalgar Square, or *Gattemalata* in Padua, how few glance up to the familiar figures. A great work of art, however, only yields its essence to an act of contemplation—of recognition in a park or garden: but attention is best induced when it stands dramatically isolated in a landscape.[33]

33. Sir Herbert Read, *Henry Moore: Sculptures and Drawings Since 1948*, 2 (London, Lund, Humphries, 1955), xii.

So, for a moment at least, we might be inclined to understand the new town better as a static, isolated, British work of art externally viewed in open countryside than as an enclosed and live social-science laboratory, as it has been more often and lately investigated.

This superior sculpture, as well as the similar group at Stevenage, is not, however, of remote political or military heroes or of the abstract virtues such as Justice, Wisdom, or Peace. The statue stands free and the town remains unencumbered as a solid in space, but they are both closely aligned with the ordinary and usual in British existence, made more precious by the near loss of them during the war. Yet the figures have the features abstracted, suppressed, and fused as if to convey more poignantly the familial interdependence. Anonymity does not equate with loneliness here. There is an extraordinary effort on the part of the sculptor to locate and hold the thread between the ordinary and the profound, the abstract and the real, nature and man, and the transitory and the lasting. The classicized ideal of Family, like the classicized idea of House for Unwin, at once becomes all-important to the individual on one side and to the society on the other.

This pull among various meanings may have been ascendant in the artist's mind just then because these family groups followed on Moore's government-commissioned drawings of windrows of humanity huddled underground in the London tubes during the war, hoping against hope for mere survival from bombing (Fig. 129).

The essential change is from weary numbness into the realm of feeling, from artificial darkness up into natural light, from individual loneliness into expansive association, and from twentieth-century destructivity into procreation again. Unwin had long before also crystallized its ramifications in terms of a professional approach:

> If you become really interested in the house you cannot stop there; you will be led to think of its surroundings, or the laying-out of sites, provision for recreation and the enjoyment of life, preservation of the natural amenities or the creation of new ones. You will thence find yourself involved in wider and wider interests until all the questions of town planning and city building are brought within the sphere of your attention.[34]

34. Raymond Unwin, "The Architect and His City," address to the Convention of the American Institute of Architects, April 1925, printed in the *R.I.B.A. Journal* (Feb. 10, 1926), p. 4.

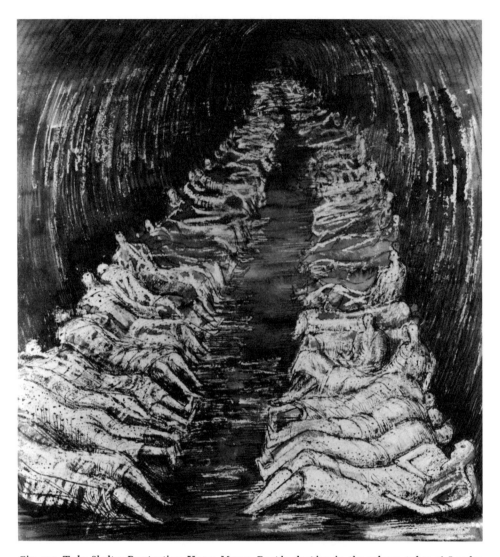

Fig. 129. *Tube Shelter Perspective; Henry Moore. People sleeping in the subway tubes of London during World War II recall the flickering illuminations of London life of seventy years before by Gustave Doré (Fig. 23). The repetition of anonymous human forms in a tubelike space and the simultaneous threat and fascination of urbanism and the machine in human hands furnish the drama in both series.*

This type of controlled explosion of psychological and aesthetic awareness, in Parker and Unwin's view, led to worthwhile answers to many questions. It might ascertain more easily and often who we are and exactly what our role is to be as individuals and families within a highly intricate culture (Fig. 130) rather than condemning us forever to repeat the first question of the industrial and agricultural revolutions, "How am I, what is my particular physical and material condition right now?" It might eventually also relieve the impersonality and awful neutrality of the great metropolis so that crowding and feverish activity could be turned into associational pleasure (or "cosiness" as Summerson phrased it for Everyman).

But the ability to solve pressing social problems may not yield enough in time unless some cumulative experience or overview is readily available too. The British had been searching for a suitable environment for over a century before they arrived at the new town. By means of extrapolation in time, as well as among spaces, solids, and ambience, they may have rediscovered that together the arts, like the sciences, can have a continuous and pervasive effect on culture as it evolves. Or as Barry Parker once observed, following the precedent of Morris and Ruskin, "The kinship between all the various branches is so very close, that instead of speaking of them as different arts, it would really be more accurate to describe them as only different media for expression of the same truth."[35] The arts could synthesize, the arts could code or symbolize, the arts could order and dignify; and the modern scientific demand that ultimately visible evidence be made available for every postulate caused the visual arts to hold great promise as an antithesis, the English urban reformers thought.

Yet they also found (almost incidentally) from their study of the Middle Ages that the arts could likewise be the vehicles of communal temperance and mercy, as well as apparent rationality and rising pride. And who will ask after the Second World War, and while contemplating Moore's *Family Group* in Harlow New Town whether the language of moderation, reassurance, and reconciliation in art can not still be communally useful (or functional) so long as memory is allowed to exist?

35. Parker, *The Art of Building a Home*, p.21.

Fig. 130. King and Queen, Shawhead, Scotland; Henry Moore, 1952–53. The British citizen would know that loneliness and anonymity in a given situation were the common experience of the modern world, even for kings and queens.

INDEX